VOICES FROM THE PAST

Volume Two

TRUTHFORLIFE®

THE BIBLE-TEACHING MINISTRY OF **ALISTAIR BEGG**

The mission of Truth For Life is to teach the Bible with clarity and relevance so that unbelievers will be converted, believers will be established, and local churches will be strengthened.

Daily Program

Each day, Truth For Life distributes the Bible teaching of Alistair Begg across the U.S. and in several locations outside of the U.S. through 1,700 radio outlets. To find a radio station near you, visit **truthforlife.org/stationfinder**.

Free Teaching

The daily program, and Truth For Life's entire teaching archive of over 2,000 Bible-teaching messages, can be accessed for free online and through Truth For Life's full-feature mobile app. Download the free mobile app at **truthforlife.org/app** and listen free online at **truthforlife.org**.

At-Cost Resources

Books and full-length teaching from Alistair Begg on CD, DVD, and USB are available for purchase at cost, with no markup. Visit **truthforlife.org/store**.

Where to Begin?

If you're new to Truth For Life and would like to know where to begin listening and learning, find starting point suggestions at **truthforlife.org/firststep**. For a full list of ways to connect with Truth For Life, visit **truthforlife.org/subscribe**.

Contact Truth For Life

P.O. Box 398000 Cleveland, Ohio 44139

phone 1 (888) 588-7884 **email** letters@truthforlife.org

/truthforlife @truthforlife **truthforlife.org**

VOICES FROM THE PAST

Volume Two

PURITAN DEVOTIONAL READINGS

Edited by
Richard Rushing

THE BANNER OF TRUTH TRUST

THE BANNER OF TRUTH TRUST

Head Office
3 Murrayfield Road
Edinburgh
EH12 6EL
UK

North America Office
PO Box 621
Carlisle
PA 17013
USA

banneroftruth.org

First published 2016
Reprinted 2019 (special)

*

ISBN
Print (clothbound): 978 1 84871 727 5
Print (paperback): 978 1 84871 945 3
Epub: 978 1 84871 728 2
Kindle: 978 1 84871 729 9

*

Typeset in 10.5/13.5 Adobe Caslon Pro
at The Banner of Truth Trust, Edinburgh

Printed in the USA by
Versa Press Inc.,
East Peoria, IL.

DEDICATION

Enjoy life with the woman whom you love all the days of your fleeting life which He has given to you under the sun; for this is your reward in life and in your toil in which you have labored under the sun.

—Ecclesiastes 9:9 (NASB)

I would like to dedicate this
volume to my lovely wife Dianne,

and, in the happy providence of God,
to the family he has given us:

Our children:
Rebekah & Harrison Farr
David & Steffany Rushing

My sisters and their husbands:
Peggi & Bob Ammon
Julia & Steve Armitage

My grandchildren and joy:
Sean, Caleb, Noah, Faith, Lila

PREFACE

I believe that David Wells was right when he said, 'The fundamental problem in the evangelical world today is that God rests too inconsequentially upon the church. His truth is too distant, his grace is too ordinary, his judgment is too benign, his gospel is too easy, and his Christ is too common.' [1]

The Puritans didn't have that problem—they served a big God! If the doctrines we preach are true, God is worthy of our deepest worship, trust, and obedience. He is worthy of our unconditional devotion! In reading these selections, if you find yourself with a desire to be more holy, to trust more, to pray more, to worship more, then you have received a touch of the puritan 'fire'. They were men who understood what it meant to suffer for Christ's sake, and the Spirit of power is still using them through their writings and the example of their lives.

In reviewing the manuscript I noticed that I could now recognize periods of life I was passing through in the selection of certain portions, though unaware at the time of writing. It is my prayer that in your reading, the One who orders all things well, will so direct the selections to be of help at the needed hour.

I am thankful for the vision of the Banner of Truth Trust for making the precious volumes, from which many of these selections are taken, available to our generation. If the Lord waits his coming, another generation will arise that will greatly need the message of the Puritans!

The devotions are generally composed of extracts which spanned multiple pages in the original works, and have been condensed into single readings. I have sought to be faithful to the intent of the author, and I hope if you go to the original source material and

[1] David F. Wells, *God in the Wasteland* (Grand Rapids: Eerdmans, 1994), p. 30.

read the entire section that has been condensed, you will find these devotions true to the author's intent. In some places the devotions may seem abrupt in their flow of thought, due to the abridgement of multiple pages down to one. I do hope these meditations will open the door for many to seek the treasures contained in the Puritans.

Richard Rushing
Martinez
California
2016

Because you are but a young man, beware of temptations and snares; and above all, be careful to keep yourself in the use of means; resort to good company; and howbeit you be nicknamed a Puritan, and mocked, yet care not for that, but rejoice and be glad, that they who are scorned and scoffed by this godless and vain world, and nicknamed Puritans, would admit you to their society; for I must tell you, when I am at this point as you see me, I get no comfort to my soul by any second means under heaven but from those who are nicknamed Puritans. They are the men that can give a word of comfort to a wearied soul in due season, and that I have found by experience since I did lie down here.[1]

[1] 'The Last and Heavenly Speeches, and Glorious Departure, of John, Viscount Kenmure', in *Scottish Puritans—Select Biographies,* Vol. 1 (Edinburgh: Banner of Truth, 2008), p. 400.

Do not be anxious about anything, but in everything by prayer and supplication with thanksgiving let your requests be made known to God.

Philippians 4:6

Is it our duty to give thanks in everything? What about our afflictions, are we to give thanks for these? Yes, there is something even in them for which we may and ought to be thankful! Not for the afflictions in themselves for they are not joyous, but grievous. But if they are for righteousness' sake, then they are blessed dispensations and occasions of joy for us. Yea, when we are under chastisements for our miscarriages, yet even then we may be thankful that our afflictions are not as much as we deserve. When it is but a rod, it might have been a scorpion! When it lies on us only a while, it might have oppressed us all our days and made our whole life a sorrow and affliction. Then consider our sufferings compared to Christ's, or to the sufferings of others (*Heb.* 11). We may be in troubles, but we are not in hell! The Lord has taken this or that from you, Oh, but has he taken his lovingkindness from you? Has he divorced you from Christ? Has he cut you off from hopes of glory? Has he extinguished his grace in you, or taken his Holy Spirit from you, or shut you out from the covenant of grace, or separated you from his love? No! (*Rom.* 8). When we find ourselves under the power of a temptation, we may yet give thanks that it did not prevail. Or, if we do fall into sin, we can yet be thankful that we are not left in it! It is a great cause for our sorrow and deep humiliation, but because he does not leave us to sin more or cast us off, this is a matter of great thankfulness. He might have proceeded much more severely and easily satisfied his just displeasure in destroying us. But he overrules this desperate evil and works a cure of this deadly poison. Thus you see how we may give thanks in everything!

David Clarkson, *Works*, 11:172-175

But Christ is all, and in all.

Colossians 3:11

Christ is the perfect Saviour. From the first to last, in all the parts of salvation, Christ is the Alpha and Omega, the beginning and end, the author and finisher of all. In having an interest in him, we have enough for the supply of all wants, the prevention of all dangers, and the procuring of all good! He is a full fountain from whom flow all the blessings that concern either our present comfort or future happiness. Yea, in him dwells all the fullness of the Godhead bodily, and we are complete in him (cf. *Col.* 2:3, 9-10). The Greeks considered it an excellent speech to give their hearers 'an ocean of matter in a drop of words'. So here, the apostle gives us gold by the pound in this small word 'all'. Certainly Christ is the medicine suited for all diseases, and the remedy for all distempers. He is 'all' in making expiation for sin—'Behold, the Lamb of God, who takes away the sin of the world!' (*John* 1:29). Christ is our all to free us from the dangers and oppositions of Satan since he spoiled and triumphed over him (*Col.* 2:15). Also, Christ frees us from the dangers of the threats, allurements, discouragements, promises, smiles, and frowns of the world—'Take heart, I have overcome the world' (*John* 16:33). He has overcome it for us, and in some measure in us! Christ fills the souls of believers with all the good which may enable them to be happy—with the sweetness of spiritual enjoyments. He gives us something of heaven here on earth! His grace creates a suitableness and harmony between our souls and heavenly mercies to make us capable of tasting the sweetness of them. 'I came that they may have life and have it abundantly' (*John* 10:10). Like the healing Christ wrought in the days of his flesh, he ministers grace upon the souls of those whom he prepares for heaven! (*Eph.* 5:8; 2:5, 10).

WILLIAM WHITAKER, *Puritan Sermons 1659-1689*, 1:500-508

For to me to live is Christ, and to die is gain.

Philippians 1:21

Christ is able to fill every condition with comfort. The best of conditions is not good without him, or the worst, bad with him. The only true comfort of life consists in living communion with God. It is his presence that fills heaven with its glory, and it is his presence that fills every condition with all of its sweetness. The way to heaven is no smooth or easy way (*Acts* 14:22). Our victory is not from any inherent strength, but supplies of grace from Christ, for without Christ we can do nothing (*John* 15:5). In Christ we are able to do and bear whatever God would have—'I can do all things through him who strengthens me' (*Phil.* 4:13). Elkanah said to Hannah, 'Am I not more to you than ten sons?' (*1 Sam.* 1:8). In the same way, is not Christ better to you than all? The cistern may well be dispensed with by him who lives by the fountain, or the candle by him who enjoys the sun. This explains why the fatherless have a father, the poor are rich, those who have nothing possess all things, and the sorrowing are joyful! It is our interest in Christ! In Christ we have all. If the Father was willing to give us Christ (*Rom.* 8:32), then this removes all grounds of questioning his bounty in anything else. If God has given you his Son, it is more than if he had given you a whole world! Be settled in the belief of this great truth, that all things in the world are nothing without Christ. Man, in the midst of worldly riches, is poor without Christ. Labour to see through Scripture that all the excellences of this world are but a balloon filled with air. But Christ is the everlasting fountain of all good that can never run dry. He is a never failing spring of blessings. We must engage our souls in an earnest pursuit after Christ: or, in the Psalmist's words: My soul clings to you (cf. *Psa.* 63:8).

William Whitaker, *Puritan Sermons 1659–1689*, 1:508-514

Though the fig tree shall not blossom, nor fruit be on the vines ... I will take joy in the God of my salvation.

Habakkuk 3:17-18

The ark and Dagon cannot stand together in the same room; if the ark stands, Dagon falls (*1 Sam*. 4:4). 'Can two walk together, except they are agreed?' (*Amos* 3:3, KJV). Christ and our corruptions have no agreement. They cannot dwell together under the same roof. Take care to renounce fellowship with all things that hinder our communion with him. He will have no rivals, no competitors, and not a part of our heart, but all! There can be no terms to gain an interest in him. He requires self-denial and full resignation of ourselves. Count all things best that give you desire to wait upon God, and account those the worst which estrange you from Christ. Resolve this great question: is Christ all to you? It is a question of such importance that all your comfort depends upon it, yea, all your hopes. Is the same mind in you that was in him? (*Phil*. 2:5). Are you holy, humble, and as self-denying as Christ? Have old things passed away? (*2 Cor*. 5:17). Causes are best known by their effects, trees by their fruits, fountains by their streams, and so our interest in Christ is known by our conformity to him! Are you prizing him above all your affections? Can you account all as nothing in comparison to him? So Moses, to the treasures in Egypt (*Heb*. 11:26). If Christ is of low importance in our affections, it is an argument we have no part in him. The affections are the truest pulse of the soul, the most genuine and natural symptom of its frame and temper. Is Christ uppermost in your heart? Do you find your contentment, satisfaction and all in him? Do you desire his glory beyond your private advantages (*Phil*. 1:20)? If so, it is an evidence that Christ is all to you. And how well provided for are they who have him as their portion!

William Whitaker, *Puritan Sermons 1659-1689*, 1:514-516

He began to say to his disciples first, 'Beware of the leaven of the Pharisees, which is hypocrisy.'

Luke 12:1

Hypocrisy is a dangerous leaven. It feigns virtue and piety to be seen of men. It is a subtle evil, and a secret poison. The devil watches night and day in readiness to plant the seeds of a false heart to engender this spurious offspring. There is a great danger in it. The hope of glory and heaven will perish with it, and pay its reward of everlasting horror and eternal despair. Its sign is a great love for the world, for there can be no serving God and mammon. Hypocrites hear the powerful word of God but show no change or alteration. They are still where they were ten or twenty years before! Consider your motive. Do you desire his glory and to please him? Or, are you an empty vine only bringing forth fruit for yourself? Is there any corrupt lust or ungodly way you hug close to your bosom? Do you plead for it and consider it harmless and tolerable? What shall we do to acquit ourselves from this leaven of hypocrisy, and be saved from the wrath it exposes us to? Be much and daily in the renewing of faith and repentance. Rise and return as soon as you are convinced of sin. If repentance followed hard after sin, this would break you from sin. Then, cherish and strengthen the graces that oppose it, as love to God, humility, self-denial, heavenly-mindedness and much communion with God. As God urges and presses you in his word, so press him as much in your prayers. Spread out his own hand-writing before him. Say—'Lord, why not apply these promises to me? I hunger, I need, I thirst, I wait; here is your own hand-writing! I am resolved to wait upon you. I cast my soul upon you!' O beloved, if there would be such a heart in us with such wrestlings, a soul of such prayers and tears should not perish, and can escape the leaven of hypocrisy.

ANDREW BROMHALL, *Puritan Sermons 1659-1689*, 1:535-553

For the eyes of the Lord run to and fro throughout the whole earth, to give strong support to those whose heart is blameless towards him.

2 Chronicles 16:9

'Run' denotes diligence and care, an industrious inspection into all things. There is a providence exercised by God in the world, and that for the good of his people. As God made all things for himself, so he orders the ends of all things for his glory. Nothing is acted in the world without God's knowledge and the arm of his omnipotence to guide them. Not the most retired corner, the darkest cell, the deepest cavern, the most secret wickedness, but the eye of the Lord beholds it (*Prov.* 15:3). He hears the words, sees the actions, knows the thoughts, registers the gracious discourses, bottles up the penitent tears, and considers all the ways of men; not a whispered oath, not an atheistical thought, and not a disorderly word, but he knows and marks it. Nothing is acted in the world without the will of God. His will either commands or permits it (*Eph.* 1:11). Nothing can subsist without God's care and power. Like a skilful pilot, he sits at the helm and steers the world in what course it should sail. In the least moment, if God should withhold the influence of his providence, we would melt into nothing. God's providence is universal. It is over all his creatures, the highest and lowest. God's providence was in a special manner fixed upon Jesus Christ (*Acts* 2:23). Angels and men are included. The life of the least animal and the smallest plant is formed and preserved by God. God sheltered Jacob from Laban's fury, and brought Haman out of favour and set Mordecai in his place. The devil cannot arrest Job, nor touch a lamb of his flock or a hair of his head without a commission from God! God's special providence is over all his people!

Stephen Charnock, *Works*, 1:6-14

Far be it from you to do such a thing, to put the righteous to death with the wicked ... Shall not the Judge of all the earth do what is just?

Genesis 18:25

Question: If there is a providence, why is it so bad with good men as if they were enemies of God, and so well with the wicked, as if affectionate friends? Does not virtue languish in obscurity while wickedness struts about the world? Why is virtue oppressed by injustice, and why are notorious vices are triumphing in prosperity? It would make men believe the world was governed by a blind governor, rather than by a wise, good, and just one, when we see things in such disorder. Answer: This consideration has strengthened the minds of many against God's providence and has been a stumbling block to many: 'Why does the way of the wicked prosper?' (*Jer.* 12:1); 'Why do you idly look at traitors and remain silent when the wicked swallows up the man more righteous than he?' (*Hab.* 1:13). Is it not high presumption for ignorance to judge God's proceedings? In the course of providence, such things are done that men could not imagine could be done without injustice, yet, when the whole connection of their end is unravelled, they appear highly beautiful, and discover a glorious wisdom and righteousness. It will be proven to be so at last, in God's dealing with all his members. We are incompetent judges of the righteousness and wisdom of God. We would need infinite wisdom to understand all of God's actions. We judge according to sense and self, which are inferior to the rules by which God works. A false judgment is easily made when the counsel of men's hearts, or the particular laws of God's actions, are not known. He may see some inward corruption in good men to be demolished by afflictions, or some useful design or service he may employ through wicked men. It is certain, God righteously orders his providences.

STEPHEN CHARNOCK, *Works*, 1:30-31

Strive for peace with everyone, and for the holiness without which no one will see the Lord.

Hebrews 12:14

What is this holiness? (1.) *The imputed holiness of Christ.* By his active obedience he perfectly fulfilled the commands of the law, and by his passive obedience, his voluntary sufferings, he fully satisfied the penalties and curses of the law. This holiness of Christ is ours by imputation! It is reckoned unto believing sinners. Certainly, without this mediatory holiness we cannot stand before God. (2.) *Inherent, internal holiness.* This is God's supernatural infusing of holy principles, divine qualities, or supernatural graces into the soul by the Holy Spirit. This is the new nature that God created in righteousness and true holiness. These gracious habits of holiness are the candles of the Lord, set up in us to walk by. A holy heart is always attended with a holy life, and without this, there is no hope or possibility of ever seeing the Lord. The more these spiritual habits are acted and exercised, the more they are increased and strengthened. Holy habits are golden talents that must be employed and improved! (3.) *Relational holiness.* We have been separated from common use and set apart for the worship and service of God! God will have no communion with any that are not separated from the sinful practices and unholy courses of the world. He will own none, delight in none, acknowledge none, and receive none for his sons and daughters but such as are separated from all evil vices and unholy courses. God will be only theirs that are really his, and he will be altogether theirs that are wholly his! God will resign himself up to them who resign themselves up to him; he will give up himself to them that have given up their names and their hearts to him. He that does not dedicate himself really to God, wholly to God, only to God, and always to God on earth shall never come to a vision of God in heaven (*2 Cor.* 6:17-18)!

THOMAS BROOKS, *Works*, IV:37-47

Then I said, 'Behold, I have come to do your will, O God, as it is written of me in the scroll of the book.'

Hebrews 10:7

There is no way to be higher than others, happier than others, more noble and honourable than others, than by dedicating ourselves to God. He that dedicates himself to God, dedicates all; he that does not dedicate himself, dedicates nothing at all! What Aeschines once said to Socrates—'Others give you gold, silver, jewels, but I give you myself'—that, must Christians say to their God, 'Ah, Lord! There are some that give you their lips, but I give you my heart; others give you good words or good expressions, but I give you the best of my affections; others give you a few cold prayers, but I give you my whole soul; and had I as many hearts in my body as I have hairs on my head, I would give them all to you: for you are worthy—you only are worthy!' The king of Israel once said to the king of Syria, 'I am yours, and all that I have' (*1 Kings* 20:4). So must a Christian say to Christ. A Christian must cry out, 'Lord, I have two mites, a soul and body, and I give them all to you!' There is no better present than to present yourself to God. There is no present more honourable or acceptable to God than this giving up ourselves to God. In the tabernacle, the oil, shew-bread, first fruits, incense, altars, vestments, the priests and Levites, the Sabbath day, and all other festival days were separated from all others for the worship and service of God. The people of Israel are frequently called a sanctified and holy people because they were dedicated to the Lord. We must be separated from the corruptions and pollutions of the world, and we must dedicate ourselves to God—'I appeal to you therefore, brothers, by the mercies of God, to present your bodies as a living sacrifice, holy and acceptable to God, which is your spiritual worship' (*Rom.* 12:1).

THOMAS BROOKS, *Works*, IV:43-45

O you who hear prayer, to you shall all flesh come.
Psalm 65:2

We see by God's titles and attributes that he is strongly engaged to hear prayer. Faith may conclude that he will hear, for he cannot be false to his engagement. He never rejects any prayer that deserves the name, no matter how weak or unworthy the petitioner is: 'For the same Lord is Lord of all, bestowing his riches on all who call on him' (*Rom*. 10:12); 'For you, O Lord, are good and forgiving, abounding in steadfast love to all who call upon you' (*Psa*. 86:5); 'He rewards those who seek him' (*Heb*. 11:6). As sure as God is the true God, so sure is it that none who sought him diligently departed from him without a reward. And if all, why not me? You may as well doubt that he is God as doubt that he will hear prayer! Also, we may consider that he is both able and willing to hear because of his power and goodness. These are strong supports of faith! It is gross atheism to doubt God's power. He is able to do all things. Omnipotency has no bounds but his will (*Psa*. 135:6). He is able to answer *abundantly* (*Eph*. 3:20). He can do more than we ask! He is able to answer *easily* (*Matt*. 8:8). All that the united strength of men and angels can do, he can do as easily as moving a finger with a word. How easily he can do all that you need to ask! He can do it *safely*. When God acts, there is no loss or damage to himself, nor does it diminish the infinite store he is in himself. Whatever he gives, he never has less. All that you can desire is not so much to God as a drop is to the whole ocean. And he is willing! Faith seldom questions God's power, but it doubts whether he is willing. But he *IS* as willing as he is able! His goodness is infinite, and so nothing less than his omnipotence. He is as willing to hear, as you are to pray; as willing to grant, as you are to ask; and as willing for you to have, as you desire to have it!

DAVID CLARKSON, *Works*, 1:202-203

Before they call I will answer; while they are yet speaking I will hear.

Isaiah 65:24

God's willingness to answer our prayers is seen—(1.) *In his secret will.* He was willing, resolved, and determined to hear, before you were willing to ask. He decreed it from eternity; he was willing before you had a will, a being. Nay, he was not only willing before, but he was the cause why you are willing! You must not think that your prayers move God to be willing; his will is the same forever, and not subject to the least motion or alteration. Prayers are a sign that God is willing, rather than the cause for his willingness. He is not made willing because we pray, but because he is willing, he stirs up our hearts to pray. He is first desirous to do us good, and then makes us desire it and pray for it that we may have them in his own way. (2.) *His revealed will.* The Lord has commanded such a course of prayer that we might get audience without fail, and if punctually followed, prayer can never return without the answer desired. But the best of men are more or less negligent in observing this instruction, therefore he is more willing our prayers should be heard than we ourselves! If God is so willing to hear, why should we not believe that he *will* hear? What strong encouragement is this to pray in faith! There is as much reason to believe that God will hear, as there is to believe that you are willing to be heard. (3.) *Christ's intercession.* This is a great encouragement to faith (*Heb.* 4:14-16). You may have confident freedom to speak all of your mind and heart, and speak it with the assurance of prevailing (*Heb.* 10:19, 22). Having such a high priest whose office is to intercede, gives us boldness, full assurance and access—'In whom we have boldness and access with confidence through our faith in him' (*Eph.* 3:12). This affords many things to strengthen our faith and make us confident in our access to God through prayer.

DAVID CLARKSON, *Works*, 1:203-204

For Christ has entered … into heaven itself, now to appear in the presence of God on our behalf.

Hebrews 9:24

Christ entered heaven for this very purpose. How confidently you might pray if you are assured that the one who not only has the greatest power, but all power in heaven and earth, is appearing for you! Can you doubt that your petitions will prevail when Christ owns you and stands up on your behalf? He presents us fully acquitted from guilt, adorned with his righteousness, and united to himself. If we are rejected, he must be rejected! He offers our prayers, and the Father receives our petitions from his hand. He sanctifies our prayers, and separates whatever is offensive from them (*Philem.* 18-19). He stands up as our advocate to prevent the prejudice that sin might bring to our prayers. He not only petitions, but pleads. Is there any room for faith to doubt here? Will not the Lord accept that which is rendered acceptable by Christ? Can he be displeased with that which through Christ is pleasing to him? Christ's intercession leaves no exception. Christ mingles his own prayers and intercession with our requests. He joins with us, and, as it were, petitions that our petitions may be received! He adds the virtue of his own merit to our prayers, and this as incense, sweetens and makes them acceptable, a sweet-smelling savour. While the people prayed outside, the priest offered the incense inside (*Luke* 1:8-10) to sweeten them and make them ascend as a delightful smell before God. If the Lord denies us, he must deny Christ too! We are as assured to be heard as Christ himself, and the Father always hears him (*John* 11:42). There is no surer ground of confidence in the world than Christ's prayer for us. If Christ is praying for us, this is a strong confirmation for our faith that leaves no room for doubting the success of our prayers.

David Clarkson, *Works*, 1:204-206

You make known to me the path of life;
in your presence there is fullness of joy;
at your right hand are pleasures for evermore.
Psalm 16:11

A fool prefers toys and trifles before the things of greatest worth. The wicked prefer their lusts before the Lord. They prefer this world before the pleasures that are at God's right hand. The world is full of such fools. Ah, friends! What folly to spend your time, strength and lives in getting the great things of this world, and neglecting that one necessary thing, the salvation of the soul! Though many have an opportunity, they have no heart to take advantage of it for the sake of eternity. By neglect, they cut the throat of their own souls. This worm will lie gnawing at them to all eternity that they have let slip the opportunities of grace and have trifled away the seasons of mercy. There is a great truth in what the Rabbi long ago said, 'Every man has his hour, and he who slips past his season may never meet with the like again.' Fools are all for the present, their bodies and their bellies, and they take no care to make provision for their immortal souls. Now, do you think that God, who has all wisdom, glory, dignity, riches, treasures, pleasures, comforts, delights, and joys in himself will have everlasting fellowship with fools or have his royal palace filled with fools? Surely no. He will at last shut the door of glory against them (*Matt.* 25:10-13). The trifles of this world God often gives to the worst and basest of men, but the kingdom of heaven he only gives to his bosom friends. Except a man is born again he cannot see the kingdom of God. The whole frame of the old man must be dissolved and a new frame erected. The kingdom of God is a divine kingdom and there is no possession of it without a divine nature. A new head without a new heart, or a new lip without a new life will never bring a man to this kingdom of light!

Thomas Brooks, *Works*, iv:55-62, 47-48

Who is like you, O LORD, among the gods? Who is like you, majestic in holiness, awesome in glorious deeds, doing wonders?

Exodus 15:11

How shall we know whether we have real holiness or not? (1.) A person of real holiness is much affected and taken up with the holiness of God. The more holy any are, the more deeply they cherish God's holiness. (2.) True holiness is diffused all through the soul. True sanctification reaches the soul, body, and spirit. It is a divine leaven that diffuses itself through the whole man. The holiness of Christ spread over *all* of Christ: his person, nature, heart, language and life. In every holy person there are many divine miracles: a dead man living, a deaf man hearing, a lame man walking, a heart of stone turned into a heart of flesh, and a life of wickedness turned into a life of holiness. (3.) Persons of real holiness set the highest price and the greatest value upon those that are holy. A man of holiness prefers a holy Job before a wicked Ahab on the throne. This blind, mad world rates and values men according to their worldly interest, greatness, glory and grandeur more than their holiness. (4.) He that is truly holy will be stretching himself out after higher degrees of holiness. The beauties of holiness so inflame him that he desires more and more. He prays that his spark may be turned into a flame, and his drop into a sea, and his mite into a rich treasury. He prays, 'Lord, I desire to be more holy that I may sin less against you and enjoy you more!' (5.) True holiness knows a holy hatred against all ungodliness. A holy man knows that all sin strikes at the holiness of God, the glory of God, the nature of God, the being of God, and so his heart rises against all. He looks upon every sin as a dishonour to God, an enemy to Christ, a wound to the Spirit, and a reproach to the gospel, so his heart is against every sin!

THOMAS BROOKS, *Works*, IV:103-109

I hold back my feet from every evil way, in order to keep your word.

Psalm 119:101

One flaw spoils the diamond; one treason makes a traitor; one turn sends a man out of the way; one leak sinks the ship; one wound strikes Goliath dead; and one Delilah betrays Samson. So many men, by favouring one sin, lose God, heaven and their souls forever. Sin favoured, ever ends in tragedy. A holy heart abhors *all* sin because it pollutes his soul and strikes against God's holiness. The heart of a holy man rises against *secret sins*. He rises against wickedness in the dark, against folly in a corner, and against sin in a closet. When Joseph was tempted to be secretly wicked, his heart rose against it. A holy man also rises against the *least sins*. I know there is no little sin, because there is no little hell and no little God to sin against. But some sins may be said to be little compared to the more gross and odious sins. A holy man rises against the least! Little sins, if not prevented, will bring on greater. A holy heart knows indulging in the least sin is sufficient grounds for any man to question his integrity towards God. A holy heart also knows that the least sin cost Christ his dearest blood! A holy heart also rises against his *bosom sins* that either his constitution, habit, or present inclination most dispose him to. Holy hearts rise against their darling sins. Oh, how my soul now rises against them! How I detest and abhor them. Surely I will never have more to do with them. But unholy hearts are very favourable to bosom sins; they say to them as Lot of Zoar, 'Is it not a little one?' Bosom sins have at least a seeming sweetness in them. An unholy heart will not easily let them go. But a holy heart rises most against the Delilah in his bosom. So you see how a holy heart hates and disdains all sins. Real holiness will never mix or mingle itself with any sin, it will never incorporate with any corruption.

THOMAS BROOKS, *Works*, IV:110-118

Then he will say to those on his left, 'Depart from me, you cursed, into the eternal fire prepared for the devil and his angels.'

Matthew 25:41

'*Depart from me*'—The last words that Christ will ever speak in this world will be the most tormenting, damning, stinging and wounding. Many say there is no hell and multitudes think hell is false and fabulous. They will not believe that there is a hell until they come to feel themselves in hell and find everlasting flames of fire and brimstone about them. This terrible sentence breathes out terror, horror and woe. You have delighted yourselves in cursing, and now you shall be cursed forever, in your bodies and in your souls. '*Everlasting fire*'—You shall go into everlasting fire that will never consume you. Eternity of extremity is the hell of hell. The fire in hell once kindled will never be quenched. Ah! How sad, how dreadful would it be to experience what it is to lie in unquenchable fire, not for a day, a month, or a year, or a hundred, or a thousand years, but for ever and ever! 'If it were', says one, 'but for a thousand years, I could bear it, but seeing it is for eternity, this amazes and frightens me!' To lie in everlasting torment goes beyond all the bounds of desperation. To roar forever in a troubled heart; to rage forever for madness of soul; to weep, and grieve, and gnash the teeth forever for vexation of spirit, is a misery beyond all expression. One has written with gold letters on their chimney—*Isaiah* 33:14—'*Who among us can dwell with everlasting burnings?*' The fear of Nebuchadnezzar's fiery furnace made men to do anything to avoid it (*Dan.* 3:8). Shall not the fear of eternal flames, of everlasting burnings cause men to bewail their sins, to hate all their bittersweets, and to lay hold on everlasting strength, that it may go well with them forever? 'O Lord, deliver me at the great day from that soul-killing word, depart!'

THOMAS BROOKS, *Works*, IV:74-77

Where shall I go from your Spirit?
Or where shall I flee from your presence?
If I ascend to heaven, you are there!
If I make my bed in Sheol, you are there!
Psalm 139:7-8

These words declare the glorious attribute of God's omnipresence set forth in most elegant and lofty terms. There is no place I can go, or even imagine to go, but that his presence will be with me! God is intimately and essentially in all parts and places of the world. By the world I mean all that is created by the power of God: the heavens, the earth, the sea, and all things visible and invisible. He is present with all creatures at the same time, preserving and upholding them in their beings and operations. He exists everywhere undivided in his being. He is not part here and part there. He exists infinitely even beyond our world. His nature is infinite, and therefore cannot be bounded. God can create another world greater than this, even in that imaginary space, which we can conceive beyond this world; certainly, God is now existent there. God was infinitely existent before the creation of our world since he is eternal, and the world but temporal. Before creation a few thousand years ago, there was nothing but God, and God existed eternally in himself. Therefore, though beyond this world there is nothing, yet God is there actually existing in that same imaginary space beyond this world as he existed in an imaginary space before our world was created. If God is thus infinitely present everywhere, then what an encouragement is this in prayer! God's essential presence is with you wherever you are. He can understand the secret motions of your heart. If you but whisper your prayer, God will hear it. What is whispered on earth rings and echoes in the courts of heaven! Your voice that cannot be heard beyond your closet fills all heaven with its sound. Just think, God is present in the room with you!

Ezekiel Hopkins, *Works*, III:389-404

Now faith is the assurance of things hoped for, the conviction of things not seen.

Hebrews 11:1

Do we have faith that can believe things unseen? Hope built upon outward probability is carnal hope. Faith carried out to things not seen is a faith to live by. Though Christ is now behind the veil in heaven, can you yet love and enjoy him and converse with him in heaven as if you did see him? 'Though you have not seen him, you love him. Though you do not now see him, you believe in him and rejoice with joy that is inexpressible and filled with glory' (*1 Pet.* 1:8). Though you have never seen him, can you depend upon the merit of his death and trust your prayers are effective on his account? 'In whom we have boldness and access with confidence through our faith in him' (*Eph.* 3:12). Do you pray as seeing him at God's right hand in heaven pleading your cause and negotiating with God for you? Is the awe of the Day of Judgment upon your heart? Do you live as one that will give an account for every word? Alas! Most men are not moved with these things till the curse of God seizes upon them! Have you a sight of the judgment to come like John (*Rev.* 20:12)? He saw it by vision and the light of prophecy, but the light of faith differs little from the light of prophecy. Though unseen, faith gives you evidence of it. Do you long for that day? Does it awaken your diligence? Does it make you serious in the whole course of your life since you have seen that day by faith? Do you comfort yourself in the midst of sorrows with the unseen glory of another world? Do you faint in your duty or bear up with courage and faithfulness as becomes Christians? 'Though our outer self is wasting away, our inner self is being renewed day by day' (*2 Cor.* 4:16). This is evidence that we are looking to things unseen when we do not faint because of our sight of the invisible world.

THOMAS MANTON, *By Faith*, pp. 41-43

He did not weaken in faith when he considered his own body, which was as good as dead.

Romans 4:19

How does your heart work on God's promises in difficult cases? When we judge by sense, reason, and outward probabilities we are driven to our wits' end. But faith lives above sense, and will be a support and strength to your soul. In such cases, reason and faith are in competition. How do the workings of your spirit incline you—to reason, or to faith? Faith can trust God's word in the midst of difficulties when sense sees nothing but hazards and sorrows. Faith holds to the promise against all hazards and rests on God whatever we may feel to the contrary. Hope that hangs on the creature, when the creature fails, they fail. When bread and outward supplies are gone, they are lost and undone, but the children of God have built upon a promise. When God tests them with troubles, they are able to depend upon the Lord. A believer can say yes to a promise, when all the world says no. Promises say yes to our hopes and amen to our desires! Under great difficulties, promises hold their note! If you desire a thing according to the will of God,—'*Amen*', says the promise, 'so it shall be!' May I hope for such a mercy or comfort?—'*Yes*', says the promise. You ask of creatures, 'By all appearances may I look for good?' 'No', one answers, but the promise says 'yes'. Believers are content with the promises, yea, though all the world says 'no way'. Christians, for your comfort you only need the affirmation of the promise! Can you with certainty depend upon the promises and with a calm expectation wait for the blessing in the midst of all pressures whatsoever? Carnal men limit God. But faith enables Christians to commit their souls and affairs to God (*1 Pet.* 4:19). He is faithful and mindful of them. He has the power to help them, and this quiets and calms their souls under all providences.

Thomas Manton, *By Faith*, pp. 43-44

Do not love the world or the things in the world.

1 John 2:15

Examine the affection of your soul as to things present and things to come, and to the temporal and eternal. A carnal man exhibits his esteem for the sweetness of outward comforts, and has no taste for the things that are to come. Carnal pleasures set themselves into his heart with a great deal of satisfaction, and he is moved and affected with them. They tickle him with a great deal of delight, and he has no taste for communion with God. For him, carnal riches are the only true substance, and the spiritual and heavenly things are mere imaginations. Scripture teaches quite otherwise. It speaks of outward things as a fancy, and spiritual things as true substance. What do you esteem, the world or heaven, things present or things promised? What is your heart most taken with? We toil for matters of the world: we rise up early, go to bed late, eat the bread of sorrow and all for a little wealth. We think nothing of the hardest labours to accomplish our worldly delights. Then consider prayer, reading, meditation, and worship: how difficult are these? How soon we cry out, what a weariness is this? A little time in duty is spent with a great deal of murmuring. Does this not speak of unbelief? 'So is the one who lays up treasure for himself and is not rich towards God' (*Luke* 12:21). There is a wide and noticeable difference between things temporal and eternal, and so there should be in our pursuit after them. If a prince promised you a temporal inheritance, oh how you would rest content with such a conveyance. But God in covenant has made a formal compact to us in the great blessings of the gospel, and yet how little are our hearts satisfied with it. O how we are full of doubtings! If I had such great promises from an able and faithful man, would I not be more cheerful and bear up upon these hopes? But I have these promises from God, and he cannot lie!

THOMAS MANTON, *By Faith*, pp. 45-47

The apostles said to the Lord, 'Increase our faith!'

Luke 17:5

Directions to get and increase our faith: (1.) Beg the Holy Spirit of God for illumination to show you the truth of the word, and the good things offered in it. Paul so prays for the Ephesians (*Eph.* 1:16-20). You may have literal knowledge from men, but that is weak and washy, like a golden dream of rubies; but saving knowledge is only from the Spirit. (2.) Employ your reason, serious consideration, and discourse. The devil throws the golden ball of honour, pleasure, and profit in our way to divert us from heavenly things. If the intention of the mind is diverted, the impressions of religion are weak and faint. It is like eggs that get chilled when a bird leaves her nest. Lack of attention is as great an enemy to faith as ignorance. The scattering and vanity of the thoughts makes our assent but weak and trembling (*Deut.* 32:29). Men fail to have a deep apprehension of the beauty of holiness and the excellency of Christ, because they do not exercise their thoughts more upon these things. By consideration, truths are kept near the heart and in the plain view of the understanding. (3.) Labour to get a heart purged from carnal affections. Where there is more purity, there will be more clarity; 'Blessed are the pure in heart, for they shall see God' (*Matt.* 5:8). Sin weakens our faith! We will always stagger and waver in uncertain doubtfulness concerning supernatural verities while we indulge our lusts. Sin blinds our eyes (*2 Cor.* 4:3-4). We need to keep our eyes clear that we may discern things unseen and the comforts and blessedness of another world. By sin, you grieve the Spirit who would help you in believing (*Eph.* 4:30). Men sin away their faith, wound their consciences, and put out the light that should guide them. Therefore get your hearts purged from sin. As faith makes a way for holiness, so does holiness make a way for faith.

Thomas Manton, *By Faith*, p. 50

One thing have I asked of the LORD, that will I seek after ... to gaze upon the beauty of the LORD.
Psalm 27:4

David describes the Lord in all the beauty and excellency he can. In darkness, he is 'my light'; in danger, he is 'my salvation'; in weakness, he is 'my strength'; in all my afflictions, he is the 'strength of my life';—'though an army encamp against me, my heart shall not fear' (*Psa.* 27:3). David was not courageous in himself, but his faith broke out like fire out of the smoke. He that sees God's greatness and power by faith sees all things below as nothing. 'If God is for us who can be against us?' (*Rom.* 8:31). Alas, this poor life of ours is a life of necessities. How many things are needful for our bodies? How many for our souls? But there was only one thing for holy David. God will have his whole heart! He will not have his heart divided. The soul, when it is focused upon many things, can do nothing well. The soul cannot be strong unless it minds one thing, and subordinates all things to this one thing. Though David desired many things, this one was necessary. Grace subordinates all things so the best has the pre-eminence. This shows the vanity of every worldly man that makes his by-work his main work. The first work of grace is to set the soul in order to subdue base affections, and set the soul in tune and order; to set the right price on things and to rank them as he should. What is *your* desire? What is the bent of *your* soul? The bent and sway of the soul shows what a man is. David used all means to enjoy communion with God sweetly. Those that pretend they have good desires, yet live scandalously and negligently, alas, this is a sluggard's desire. David's 'one thing' was above all other things whatsoever! If we find these holy desires, Oh! Let us take comfort, for God will fulfil the desires of them that fear him (*Psa.* 37:4). Holy desires are the birth of God's Holy Spirit and there is not one of them that shall be lost!

RICHARD SIBBES, *Works*, III:213-222

For the Son of Man came to seek and to save the lost.

Luke 19:10

Be sure you deeply apprehend the gracious nature of Jesus Christ. How could he have manifested more willingness to save or more tender compassion to the souls of men than he has manifested? That the Godhead should condescend to assume our nature is a thing so wonderful, even to astonishment, that it requires faith to comprehend it. How tenderly did Christ deal with all sorts of sinners! He professed that he came into the world not to condemn, but to save. He wept over unbelieving people who rejected him. When the disciples desired to call down fire from heaven, he reproved them. Yea, he prayed for his crucifiers and cared for the others suffering crucifixion. To those that followed him, his tenderness was unspeakable. Consider him as he washed the disciples' feet, or bidding Thomas to put his finger into his side, and saying, 'Do not disbelieve, but believe.' Alas! That the Lord Jesus should come from heaven to earth, from glory into human flesh, and pass through a life of misery to a cross, and from the cross to the grave, to manifest openly to the world the abundance of his love, and the tenderness of his heart to sinners. It is most certain that God is love, infinite in mercy, and has no pleasure in the death of sinners. Get high thoughts of the gracious and lovely nature of God! In Christ, God has come down into our nature, so that infinite goodness and mercy became incarnate. The man Christ Jesus is able to save to the uttermost all that come to God by him. Here we see the will of God putting forth itself for our help in the most astonishing way that could be imagined. It is more than mere gracious inclination. Christ has undertaken the task to seek and to save that which was lost! He is bringing home straying souls to God, making peace between God and man.

RICHARD BAXTER, *Practical Works*, 11:891-892

Blessed are those who hunger and thirst for righteousness, for they shall be satisfied.

Matthew 5:6

Make it your great business to be more holy every day. It is desire that opens the heart, and the stronger the desire is, the wider it is opened. The soul is wide open when it pants and breathes after God. Too often, we come to devotion like the Egyptian dog that laps a little as she runs by the side of the Nile, but does not stay to drink. Christ invites us to eat and drink abundantly. Be much in meditation if you desire the effect of your devotions to linger. The heart takes fire while the mind is musing. The sparks that fall from heaven upon your heart during preaching or praying will die unless you blow on them with meditation. Repeated acts beget a habit and will stay by you. The action of a Christian is expressed by 'striving', and 'wrestling'. We must put forth all of our strength so we will not be worsted. Our way to heaven is uphill, but the natural bent of our hearts is downwards. When our hearts are effectually touched, there is no keeping them in a lively frame without striving and struggling! Look up to God to continue this lively frame. Pray in faith. Seek him, and depend on him. He will be found by those who seek him (*Matt.* 7:7). Faith is the main strength of prayer, and the great supports of faith are these: *he is able*, and *willing*! That which one is both able and willing to do, shall be done! Pray then, with believing, because whatsoever you ask according to his will, believing, it shall be done (*Matt.* 21:22). Do not meddle with the world more than needs be. Carry yourself in worldly employments as among cheats and thieves. They have the art to pick your hearts silly! Nothing quenches divine influence more than this puddle. The cares and delights of the world can choke the word (*Matt.* 13:22). When your hearts are warmed in holy duties, be cautious how you venture into the world!

David Clarkson, *Puritan Sermons 1659–1689*, 1:553–563

I discipline my body and keep it under control, lest after preaching to others I myself should be disqualified.

1 Corinthians 9:27

When your heart is kindled by the word of God or prayer, how quickly it is blown out by attention to the world! It requires as much care to keep it burning, as a candle carried through the open air on a rainy, blustering night. But the further you are above the world, the longer you may retain any spiritual impressions. The closer your minds, hearts and conversations are toward this boisterous world, the less will anything that is heavenly and spiritual abide with you. When your souls are set in motion towards Christ and heaven, you must beware of worldliness if you would like to hold on in a continued course. You must keep yourself as free as you can from earthly encumbrances and entanglements. 'Let us also lay aside every weight, and sin which clings so closely, and let us run with endurance the race that is set before us' (*Heb.* 12:1). Let us persevere and hold out in that gracious and heavenly course which the gospel has put us on. In order to do this we must remove this one great impediment—'The sin which so easily besets us.' That sin is worldliness. No sin has more bountiful pleas and pretences to excuse, vindicate, and justify itself. No sin has more fig leaves to cover its nakedness, and to shroud it from discovery and conviction, than worldliness. This must be shaken off. It is the great defacer of heavenly impressions, and the chief interrupter of holy motions. If you desire to hold on to the influence of preaching, prayer, and the word that is in you, you must beware of the world, and beware of worldliness! Also, take heed of any unruly, lawful affections or inclinations. These also will hinder you in holy duties, and so limit the time spent on them. They will hurry your souls away from holy duties, and struggle to break you from their influence!

DAVID CLARKSON, *Puritan Sermons 1659-1689*, 1:563-564

It is the LORD our God who brought us and our fathers up from the land of Egypt, out of the house of slavery.

Joshua 24:17

Israel was under great tyranny in Egypt. God's children may sometimes be under sore afflictions, but God will, in due time, bring them out. Affliction tests sincerity. Hypocrites may embrace the true religion in prosperity, and court this queen while she has a jewel on her ear, but a true Christian will keep close to God in a time of suffering. To love God in heaven is no wonder, but to love him when he chastises us discovers sincerity. Affliction purges our corruptions of sloth, luxury, pride, and love of the world. It is not to consume, but to refine. What *if* we have more affliction, if by this means we have less sin! Affliction increases the graces of the Spirit. Grace thrives most in the iron furnace. Grace in the saints is often as fire hidden in the embers; affliction is the bellows to blow it up into flame. The Lord makes the house of bondage a friend to grace. God hews and polishes us by affliction that we might be fit for heaven. Though sheep have the ear-mark of election, they may have their wool fleeced off. Was not Jeremiah in the dungeon, and Paul a night and day in the deep? Oh what a merciful providence it is that though God bruises his people, yet, while he is bruising them, he is doing them good. Affliction enriches the soul and yields the sweet fruits of righteousness. We are apt to look upon the iron furnace as a frightful thing, but affliction comes from a wise God who prescribes whatever befalls us. Affliction has its light side as well as dark. God can sweeten our afflictions and sweeten our wormwood. If afflictions come, let us labour to conduct ourselves wisely that we may adorn our suffering and endure with patience. Satan labours to take advantage of us to faint and murmur. He blows the coals of passion and discontent, and then warms himself at the fire.

THOMAS WATSON, *The Ten Commandments*, pp. 29-33

Having been predestined according to the purpose of him who works all things according to the counsel of his will.

Ephesians 1:11

God embraces in his providence the lowest worm as well as the highest angel. It extends to all the actions and motions of creation. The hearts of kings are in his hand; he can work them into whatever shape he pleases! The fire did not singe the three children and Daniel's ravenous lions were muzzled. The sun stood still in the valley of Ajalon, and the waves stood up in a heap for Israel. What is casual to us is ordained by God. Things that appear random or loose acts of the creature are directed by God to a higher end than we can presently imagine. The disposing of the lot cast into the lap is from the Lord (*Prov.* 16:33). A soldier shoots an arrow at random, and God guides it to be the executioner of Ahab for his sin (*1 Kings* 22:34). Providence is the great clock keeping time and order, not only hourly, but instantly, to his own honour. By the bitterness of Joseph's brothers, God preserved Israel from famine. Pharaoh's hardness brought his own destruction and God's glory. Pilate yielded to the people and executed what God had before ordained. God's providence and ways are mysterious. Dark providences are often the groundwork for some excellent work he is about to discover to the world. He lets Sarah's womb be dead and then he brings out the root of a numerous progeny. He makes Jacob a cripple and then a prince to prevail with God. He gave him a wound and then a blessing. His ends are of a higher strain than the aims of men. Joseph's imprisonment is in order for his father's relief. He is wronged as a step to his advancement. He moves from being a captive to a favourite. All of God's providences are but his touch of the strings of this great instrument of the world. And all his works are excellent because they are the fruit of his wonderful counsel and unsearchable wisdom!

Stephen Charnock, *Works*, 1:15-20

You shall love the Lord your God with all your heart and with all your soul and with all your mind.

Matthew 22:37

Love to God must penetrate and possess our whole nature and all the powers of it. The mind must think of God, the will must delight in God, in short, our whole being must be employed to please him. We must love nothing more than God, nothing equal with God, and we must love God above all. We must be willing to lose all, yea, life itself rather than do anything contrary to the love of God. Love desires to enjoy perpetual union with the thing loved. Every faculty of the soul is engaged, the mind is musing and plotting how to please God, and enjoy him, the will does not turn from this object, the affections are passionate in their eager motion towards God, and the conscience is busy keeping watch. Our love to God should be like or exceed Jacob's love for Benjamin (*Gen.* 42:38). He would rather starve than part with Benjamin. Then when hunger forced the separation, Judah offered himself to take Benjamin's place since Jacob's life was bound up in the lad's life (*Gen.* 44:30). The soul that loves God is not able to bear the thoughts of parting with him. His life is bound up in enjoying his presence. We are to so love God, that nothing contrary to the love of God shall be entertained in our hearts. Our love to God speaks of interest and union. Love for an earthly object is earthly love; if sensual, it is a brutish love; if it be man, it is a human love; and if God, it is a divine love. The object of our love transforms us into a thing more noble or more vile. We debase ourselves in loving anything but God there is nothing else worthy of our love. Whatsoever we love, we give it a kind of dominion over us. Therefore, we must so love God as if there were nothing else in the world to bestow our love upon. Alas, outward things may be gone tomorrow, but God, once yours, will be yours forever!

SAMUEL ANNESLEY, *Puritan Sermons 1659-1689*, 1:573-581

He drew me up from the pit of destruction,
out of the miry bog, and set my feet upon a rock,
making my steps secure.
Psalm 40:2

In due time, God delivers his children out of troubles. A tree, which in the winter seems dead, revives in the spring. The sun emerges after the storm. Affliction may leap on us as the viper did on Paul, but at last it shall be shaken off. The wicked drink a sea of wrath, but the godly only drink a cup of affliction. Sometimes, God delivers suddenly. The shadow of death is turned into the light of the morning. The day Joseph was freed from prison he was made the chief ruler in the kingdom. Sometimes God delivers strangely. The whale that swallowed Jonah was the means to bring him safely to land. God brought Paul to shore by a contrary wind, and upon the broken pieces of the ship. God delivers in the greatest extremity. When there is but a hair's breadth between the godly and death, God ushers in deliverance. When the ship was almost covered with waves, Christ awoke and rebuked the wind. When Isaac was upon the altar and the knife about to be put to his throat, the angel came. When Peter began to sink, Christ took him by the hand. When the people of God are in the greatest danger, the morning star of deliverance appears. When our patient is ready to faint, the cordial is given. When affliction has done its work, he delivers his people. When the sharp frost of affliction has brought forth the spring flowers of grace, the cross is sanctified and God brings us out of the house of bondage. His deliverance makes way for his glory. By raising his people he glorifies his own attributes: his power, truth and goodness triumph. God loves to help when things seem past hope. He creates deliverance. He brought Isaac out of a dead womb, and Messiah out of a virgin's. Oh! How his power shines forth when he overcomes seeming impossibilities, and works a cure when things look desperate!

THOMAS WATSON, *The Ten Commandments*, pp. 34-35

I love the LORD, because he has heard my voice and my pleas for mercy.

Psalm 116:1

Let none despond in trouble. When God sees a fit season, he will put forth his arm to save, and he can do it with ease! He that turns the tides can turn the times. He that raised Lazarus when he was dead can raise you when you are sick. So, do not despond, believe in God's power. Faith sets God to work to deliver you! God delivers the godly in love. This then makes our hearts boil over in love for him. The wicked only increase their corruptions and grow worse, as the metal when taken out of the fire grows harder. Deliverance calls for praise, so be much in praise. Gratitude should follow a favour. The deepest springs yield the sweetest water, and hearts deeply sensible of God's deliverances yield the sweetest praises. To have a thankful heart is a greater blessing than the deliverance itself. Only one leper turned back in thankfulness (*Luke* 17:15). Have you been brought out of the house of bondage, sickness, or any death-threatening danger? Do not forget to be thankful. That you may be the more thankful, observe every emphasis and circumstance in your deliverance. These circumstances being well weighed heighten a deliverance, and should heighten our thankfulness. The cutting of a stone may be of more value than the stone itself. So, the circumstances of a deliverance may be greater than the deliverance itself. Praise God with humble hearts and acknowledge how unworthy you were for the deliverance. Praise God constantly. Some are thankful while the memory of the deliverance is fresh, then leave off. Don't become weary of sending a thank offering. The motion of our praise must be like the motion of our pulse; it beats as long as life lasts. 'I will praise the LORD as long as I live; I will sing praises to my God while I have my being' (*Psa.* 146:2).

THOMAS WATSON, *The Ten Commandments*, pp. 36-38

But when you pray, go into your room and shut the door and pray to your Father who is in secret.

Matthew 6:6

God is pleased by promise to make himself a debtor to secret prayer. When you have shut your closet and are alone with God, you have the key to open the chambers of paradise and enter the presence of divine love. Here, the door of your heart is shut out from all vain and worldly objects and you may mount up to walk among angels and stand by the throne of God. Here, the soul, like Moses, is in the backside of the desert, and talks with the angel of the covenant in the fiery bush. Here, Isaac is in the field meditating and praying to the God of his father Abraham. Here, Elijah is under the juniper tree hearkening to the still small voice of God. Here, Christ delights to hear your voice, for the melody of it is sweet! When a broken heart or wounded spirit pours out repentant tears like streams from the rock smitten by the rod of Moses, these are most beautiful prospects to the eyes of heaven. Draw sighs from the furrows of your heart; let your prayer become a hidden mystery of divine secrets. Those with a sincere heart busy themselves with heart-work. They seek to mortify sin, quicken grace, and to observe and resist temptations. The more a saint converses with his own heart, the more he understands his spiritual needs and feels his spiritual joys. He labours to walk before God, as always being in his sight, but especially when he approaches the throne of mercy. God is delighted with invisible prayers, and he takes most pleasure in the secret glances of a holy heart. When a holy soul is close to God in secret, what contentment does he have! He has bolted out the world and retired to a place that no one knows. He is free from disturbances and distractions in the secret presence of God, in the hidden place of the Most High, and in the shadow of the Almighty. O how safe, O how comfortable!

SAMUEL LEE, *Puritan Sermons 1659–1689*, II:165–169

You shall be my people, and I will be your God.

Jeremiah 30:22

God framed man to have communion and fellowship with himself. This fellowship is where happiness consists. God's love for man established the covenant of grace in the seed of the woman, Christ the Messiah, to restore mankind from the most miserable plight and misery into which Adam cast the world by his sin. It is a most sweet sign of God's great love that he would stoop so low as to make a covenant with us, to be our God and to be all in all to us! Consider such a covenant—the Creator with the creature; the immortal God and mortal man; the glorious God, and dust and ashes; the holy God and sinful man; the great King of heaven and earth, and rebels and traitors. For him to condescend so low as to make a covenant with us, to enter into terms of agreement with us, is a wondrous sign of his gracious mercy and love. This covenant is only by Jesus Christ, and to those who believe in him. We enter into a relationship greater than the world can offer, and are freed from the cursed estate we are in by nature. God delivers us from all ill, spiritually and eternally. God is able to save us against all our enemies whatsoever: our weakness, the devil, and all of our own corruptions or oppositions whatsoever. Consider the wisdom of heaven that says so much in '*I will be your God.*' His wisdom is yours and watches over you to find out ways to do you good. His power is yours to keep you from danger, and to defend and rescue you from all enemies. His providence is yours to turn all things to your good. His mercy is yours to forgive your sins. His love is yours to bestow all necessary comforts. There is no phrase in Scripture that has so much in so little as '*I will be your God.*' If we could but unfold and lay open this excellent promise. All other promises in the covenant of grace are members of this. It is a wonderful and comprehensive promise, '*I will be your God.*'

Richard Sibbes, *Works*, vi:3-8

Whom have I in heaven but you? And there is nothing on earth that I desire besides you.

Psalm 73:25

God graciously in the blessed seed, the Messiah, Christ Jesus, takes upon him to be a God to all those that are in covenant with him. He is all-sufficient to bring us to happiness in this world and in the world to come; to be our portion, and to be our all in all! When our conscience can tell us that we make God our treasure and portion above all earthly things, then we make him *our* God. A Christian singles out God above all things in the world for his happiness: 'Lord, you are mine! Whatsoever wealth is mine, or riches mine, or friends mine—I stand not upon this, but that you are mine.' A rich man may run to his wealth and make flesh his arm, or he may run to friends to help him in all causes, but a true Christian that has God for his God, singles out God for his portion and runs to him in all extremities. It is a sign we have made God our God, when we prize him and value him above all the world. What we do most for—that is our god. If we do most for pleasures, they become our god. If we do most for riches, that is our god. Whatever we value the highest, that is our god. How do we truly walk before God when there is such a great difference in our secret actions, and those before the eyes of men? Do we labour more to approve our carriage before men, than we make conscience of our spirits before God? This may shame us. Even the best in covenant with God have reason to mourn over this. Is there a difference in how you carry yourself before men in outward things in the world, than before God? A Christian that truly has God to be *his* God knows that wherever he is, he is under the eyes of heaven. If he is troubled by the most secret corruptions, he always sets himself in the presence of God, and he is full of reverence, full of fear, even in the enjoying of his Christian liberties.

Richard Sibbes, *Works*, vi:8-10

When they had finished breakfast, Jesus said to Simon Peter, 'Simon, son of John, do you love me more than these?'

John 21:15

If God is *your* God, you have grace given you to love him above all things. He loved us, and we love him back. The wicked cannot love God. They trifle with his name by oaths and blasphemy. They scorn God, and wish there were no God. They are God's enemy and God is their enemy. But if God is our God, he has set his love upon us, and we cannot but love him back. That which we make our god we cannot tolerate to be touched. If a man makes lust his god, if that is touched, he is all in a chafe. Experience shows—if that which a man loves is touched, he is immediately all on fire. Here the best Christians have cause to be abased. If God is their love, how can they bear to hear him disgraced and his name abused without being greatly moved and set on fire? Where there is no zeal, there is no love. Certainly when we can hear God's children misused, religion endangered, and profession scoffed at, and yet not be affected, nor take God's cause to heart, this is a great fault in our love. If we make God our God, we joy in him above all things in the world. He is our boast all day long. We count it our chief glory that we are his, and that he is ours. Whatsoever our estates might be, we glory in God, and not in ourselves. A Christian, when he would have joy and glory, goes to God, for he is his joy. It is a great shame for a Christian to delight and comfort in the earthly more than in God. Jonah, a good man, was distraught when his gourd was taken away. Many who should joy in God above all things, act as if there were no God in heaven when their outward comforts are taken from them. They act as if there were no providence to rule the world and as if they had no Father in covenant with them. We must rely and depend upon him above all things! Whatever we trust in most, that is our god!

Richard Sibbes, *Works*, vi:10-11

Trust in the Lord with all your heart, and do not lean on your own understanding.

Proverbs 3:5

If God is *our* God, we will trust in him. If we would examine ourselves, the best of us all, it would bring us on our knees, and make our faces confounded to consider what a deal of atheism there is in our heart that needs to be subdued. If an honest man were to say to us 'I will take it upon myself to provide for you, to defend you, to protect you, to stand by you against all adversaries'—we believe and hope that he will do it. But do we so to God? Alas, no! So far, I mean, as we are not subdued to God. A Christian, indeed, in some measure is enabled to make God his trust and confidence, but there remains an abundance of atheism even in the best of us. Why do we not trust him and depend upon him for all things? Why do we not trust him for protection and deliverance from all ill, especially spiritual ills: from sin, Satan, hell, and wrath? It is a sign that God is our God when we trust in him above all the world, and trust other things only from him and for him. We also may know that we make God *our* God by our obedience, especially by the obedience of the inward man. He aligns his thoughts and desires before God, and does not suffer anything to rise in his heart unchecked and uncontrolled. He is content to control his lusts so they do not rage, and desires God's Spirit to be his leader. God must be supreme. He especially shows it by performing inward worship to him, walking before him perfectly and sincerely. Others must be loved and feared, but God chiefly. We should love nothing in the world, fear nothing, trust nothing, or joy in nothing before God! Whatsoever we give the supremacy of the inward man to; whatsoever we love most, whatsoever we trust most, whatsoever we fear most, delight in most, and obey most—*that* is our god!

Richard Sibbes, *Works*, VI:11–13

The grace of the Lord Jesus Christ and the love of God and the fellowship of the Holy Spirit be with you all.

2 Corinthians 13:14

Saints may have a distinct communion with the Father, and the Son, and the Holy Spirit, individually (*Eph.* 2:18). When I consider anything in which we distinctly hold communion with any one person, I do not exclude the other persons from communion with the soul in that very same thing. There is a concurrence of the whole deity in the dispensations and acts in the work of our salvation. Nor do I intend to limit communion with God merely under these divisions. God's ways are exceedingly broad and unlimited. Also, I do not seek to prejudice the holy fellowship we have with the whole Deity in our walking before him in covenant obedience. There is no grace whereby our souls go forth unto God, no act of divine worship yielded unto him, no duty or obedience performed, but they are distinctly directed unto the Father, Son, and Holy Spirit. But the saint's particular communion with the Father is in his free, undeserved, and *eternal love.* This, the Father fixes upon the saints, and to this we should immediately make returns to him. This is the great discovery of the gospel. 'God is love' (*1 John* 4:8-9). The Father is full of love for us as manifest in the work of the gospel! The particular and distinct communion which we have with his Son, Jesus Christ our Lord, is as *mediator*. Christ submitted himself to become a man to redeem us (*Gal.* 4:4-5). There is all manner of spiritual refreshments for the souls of the saints in the Lord Jesus. Our particular communion with the Holy Spirit consists in his mission to be our *comforter*. He is the Spirit of consolation to believers. In a word, in all the concerns of this life, and in our whole expectation of another, we stand in need of the consolations of the Holy Spirit! The Holy Spirit gives us peace in Christ.

John Owen, *Works*, 11:17-19, 40-41, 222, 261

I do not say to you that I will ask the Father on your behalf; for the Father himself loves you.

John 16:26-27

There is love in the person of the Father peculiarly held out to the saints in which he will and does hold communion with them. This is received by faith. It is true, there is not an *immediate* acting of faith upon the Father, but through the Son (*John* 14:6). But when by and through Christ we have access unto the Father, we then behold his glory also, and see his love that he peculiarly bears unto us, and thus faith acts on this. The Father is a fountain of eternal love. Would believers exercise themselves in this, they would find it a matter of no small spiritual improvement in their walking with God. Many dark and disturbing thoughts are apt to arise in this thing. Few can carry up their hearts and minds to this height by faith. Few rest their souls in the love of the Father. They live below it, in the troublesome region of hopes and fears, storms and clouds. But all here is serene and quiet. This is the will of the Father, that he may always be eyed as kind, tender, and loving. The Father is the great fountain of all gracious communications and fruits of love. In his love is the only rest for the soul. In his love we find a design, a purpose of love, a good pleasure towards us from eternity, a delight, a contentment, a good will in Christ, and all causes of anger and estrangement taken away. The soul thus, by faith through Christ, and by him, is brought into the bosom of the Father, into a comfortable persuasion and spiritual perception and sense of his love, and thus reposes and rests itself. God loves, that he may be beloved. He says, 'My son, give me your heart, your affections, your love. You shall love me with all your heart' (cf. *Luke* 10:27). When the soul sees God, in his dispensation of love, to be infinitely lovely and loving, he will rest in this and delight in him and have communion with him in love.

John Owen, *Works*, 11:22-24

And the Word became flesh and dwelt among us, and we have seen his glory, glory as of the only Son from the Father, full of grace and truth.

John 1:14

There is a distinct communion that we have with the Son, in the grace he bestows upon us as our mediator. We have all manner of spiritual refreshments in him. He was appointed by the Father to the great work of bringing home all his elect unto his bosom. In this respect he is exceedingly excellent and desirable, far above all comparison with the most choice created good, or any endearment imaginable. He is suitable to all the desires of the souls of men. Whether it is life or light, power or joy, all is wrapped up in him. He is able to save with tenderness and power to carry on the work to the uttermost. He becomes altogether lovely, and in this the saints have distinct fellowship with him. Yea, he is a fit object for your choicest affections! It is the gladness of the heart of Christ, the joy of his soul, to take poor sinners into this relation with himself. He rejoiced in the thoughts of it from eternity, and always expresses the greatest willingness to undergo the hard task required to do it. Because of his love, he gave himself for the church, despising the shame, and enduring the cross, that he might enjoy his bride; that he might be for her, and she for him. Christ gives himself to the soul with all his excellencies, righteousness, preciousness, and graces to be our Saviour. Considering a view of all that is in this world, nothing compares to him. We should prefer him above all pretenders to our affections. Peace, natural relations, wisdom, learning, righteousness, duties are all loss compared with Christ! If all of the world set themselves to drink of the free grace, mercy and pardon of Christ, there is enough for millions of worlds, for he is an infinite, bottomless fountain. He is the beloved of our souls, holy, harmless, undefiled, full of grace and truth.

John Owen, *Works*, 11:40-66

Having loved his own who were in the world, he loved them to the end.

John 13:1

The fountain of the grace and mercy of Christ is infinite. Show me the sinner that can spread his iniquities to the dimensions (if I may say so) of this grace. Here is mercy enough for the greatest, the oldest, and the most stubborn transgressor! His love is eternal, free, and unchangeable. Whom he loves, he loves unto the end! His love is such as never had a beginning, and shall never have an end. He is the Beloved of our souls, holy, harmless, and undefiled, full of grace and truth. His fullness is sufficient for every need of grace, and full to provide the certainty of uninterrupted communion with God. It is full to suit him to all the occasions and necessities of the souls of men. He is full for a perfect victory in trials and over all temptations. He was able to bear whatever was due us. There was room in his breast to receive the points of all the swords that were sharpened by the Law against us. There was strength enough in his shoulders to bear the burden of that curse that was due to us. He was so willing to undertake the work of our redemption. Hence, he became an endless, bottomless fountain of grace to all them that believe. Upon the payment of the great price of his blood, and the full acquittal of debt on the satisfaction he made, all grace, whatever, becomes in a moral sense—his, and he bestows it on, or works it in, the hearts of his own by the Holy Spirit, according to his infinite wisdom as he sees it needful. How glorious is he to the soul on this consideration! It is most excellent to us and suits us in our needful condition,—it is that which gives bread to the hungry, water to the thirsty, and mercy to the perishing. All our reliefs are thus in our Beloved. Here is the *life* of our souls, the *joy* of our hearts, our *relief* against sin, and *deliverance* from the wrath to come!

JOHN OWEN, *Works*, 11:62-69

And do not grieve the Holy Spirit of God, by whom you were sealed for the day of redemption.

Ephesians 4:30

By his own great love and infinite condescension, the Holy Spirit proceeds from the Father to be our comforter. He knew we would grieve him, provoke him, quench him, defile his dwelling place, and yet he came to be our comforter. Lack of due consideration of this great love weakens all the principles of our obedience. We are perverse and unthankful; grieving, vexing, and provoking him; yet in his love and tenderness he continues to do us good. Let us by faith consider this love of the Holy Spirit. It is the foundation and source of all the communion we have with him in this life. The Holy Spirit in his infinite love and kindness towards me has condescended to be my comforter; he does it willingly, freely, and powerfully. Oh how he has refreshed my soul in the multitude of my perplexities. Can I live one day without his consolations? Shall I grieve him by negligence, sin, and folly? The Holy Spirit is the immediate author of all supplies, assistances, and relief that we have by grace. When we consider him who is so loving, kind and tender to us, and all his acts leading to our comfort, and on that account, are careful and watchful to improve them as coming from him, we have communion with him. As we observe every gracious act of the blessed Spirit towards our soul, and by faith consider it coming to us from his good will, this encourages us to improve upon every motion, treat with reverence his presence with us, take due regard of his holiness, and desire to fellowship with him. Thus we worship distinctly the Holy Spirit as we do the Son and the Father. The acts and effects of the Holy Spirit as our comforter ought to stir us up and provoke us to love, worship, and entreat him. Though this is directed to him as God, it is no less directed to the other persons as well.

John Owen, *Works*, 11:263-270

It is to your advantage that I go away, for if I do not go away, the Helper will not come to you.

John 16:7

Let the saints learn to act in faith distinctly on the Holy Spirit, and in all things believe him and yield obedience to him. Let us worship him, serve him, wait for him, pray to him and praise him in faith. In his operations and effects he is the peculiar object of our worship. He ought to be honoured and never sinned against. Few consider him as the Comforter, and rejoice in him as they ought! Every time he comforts us, our faith ought to resolve—'this is from the Holy Spirit; he is the Comforter, the God of all consolation.' There is no joy, peace, hope, nor comfort, but that he is working, giving, and bestowing it in his love. He was sent by the Father and the Son for this very end and purpose. By this means I have become a partaker of joy; it is *in* the Holy Spirit, *he* is the Comforter. What price, now, shall I set upon his love! How shall I value the mercy that I have received? Such is applicable to every particular effect of the Holy Spirit towards us; in this way we have communion and fellowship with him. The soul considers his presence, ponders his love, his condescension, goodness, and kindness, and is filled with reverence for him, takes care not to grieve him, and labours to preserve his temple, his habitation, pure and holy. In our communion with him we return praise, thanks, honour, glory, and blessing to him on the account of the mercies and privileges that we receive from him, which are many. When we feel our hearts warmed with joy, supported in peace, established in our obedience, let us ascribe to him the praise that is due unto him, bless his name, and rejoice in him! Considering his free engagement in this work, his coming forth from the Father for this purpose, his mission from the Son, his love and kindness—pour out your soul in thankful praises to him.

JOHN OWEN, *Works*, 11:270-271

In love he predestined us for adoption as sons through Jesus Christ, according to the purpose of his will.

Ephesians 1:4-5

The Father, our Father in Christ, is revealed to us as love, and so in this love we may have fellowship with him. This love is so full, so complete and absolute in every way, that it will not allow him to complain of anything in them whom he loves, but he is silent on this account. He rests in love; that is, he will not remove it. It shall make its abode upon the soul where it is once fixed, forever! It is a love of complacency (the fact or state of being pleased with a thing or person, tranquil satisfaction), or delight. He rejoices with singing, (*Zeph.* 3:17), as one that is fully satisfied in that object he has fixed his love on. So, the saints may, nay do, see an infinite ocean of love unto them in the bosom of the Father. It is a love of bounty, such a love that carries him out to do good things to us, great things for us. He loves us, and sends his Son to die for us; he loves us and blesses us with all spiritual blessings. It is a love like that of the heavens to the earth, when, being full of rain, they pour forth showers to make it fruitful; it is like a fountain, always flowing. It descends upon us in bounty and fruitfulness; and our love ascends unto him in duty and thankfulness. Because of his love we are able to—*rest*, *delight*, *reverence*, and *obey* him. By these we hold communion with the Father in his love. His love goes before ours (*1 John* 4:10). The father loves his child when the child does not yet know him, much less love him! He loved us while we were yet sinners (*Rom.* 5:8). Not only when we had done no good, but when we were in our blood, he loved us. It appeared when we were foolish and disobedient! It did not appear because we are better than others, but because he in himself is infinitely good. Never would the creature turn his affections toward God but the heart of God was first set upon him!

John Owen, *Works*, 11:24-29

Before the mountains were brought forth … from everlasting to everlasting you are God.

Psalm 90:2

The love of God is like himself—constant, not capable of augmentation or diminishing. It is like the sun, always the same in its light, though a cloud may sometimes interpose. On whom the Father fixes his love, he loves unto the end. His love is immutable; it does not grow in eternity, and is not diminished at any time. It is an eternal love; it had no beginning, and shall have no end. However, the fruits of love sometimes appear to be various. Who among the saints does not find it so?—What life, what light, what strength we have sometimes! Then again, as God is pleased to let out or restrain the fruit of his love—how dead, how dark, how weak! All the graces of the Spirit in us, all the sanctified enjoyments whatsoever, are fruits of his love. How variously these are dispensed, how differently at sundry seasons to the same persons, experience will abundantly testify. As God manifests a sense of his love to us it seems various and changeable; sometimes more, sometimes less; now he shines, then he hides his face, as it may be for our profit. Our Father will not always chide, lest we be cast down; he does not always smile, lest we become full and neglect him: but yet, still his love in itself *is* the same. When for a little moment he hides his face, yet he gathers us with everlasting kindness. Does God love his people in their sinning? Yes, his people—not their sinning. He does not alter his love towards them, or the purpose of his will, but the dispensations of his grace. He rebukes, chastens, and hides his face from them, but woe, woe would it be to us should he change his love or take away his kindness from us! Those things that seem to be demonstrations of the change of his affections, proceed also from love as much as those which seem the most genuine issues of love!

John Owen, *Works*, 11:29-31

I have loved you with an everlasting love; therefore I have continued my faithfulness to you.

Jeremiah 31:3

How few are experimentally acquainted with the privilege of holding immediate communion in the Father's love! With what anxious, doubtful thoughts they look upon him! What fears and what questionings there are of his good will and kindness! Without this insight in his love, souls lose his company. They fix their thoughts only on his terrible majesty, severity, greatness, and so their spirits are not endeared to him. If you could but consider his everlasting tenderness and compassion, you could not bear one hour's absence from him. Let, then, this be the saints' first notion of the Father—as one full of eternal, free love towards them. Let their hearts and thoughts be filled with it and break through all discouragements that lie in the way. His love is from eternity and has laid in his own bosom a design for our happiness. A sense of it cannot but prostrate our souls to the lowest abasement of humble reverence and make us rejoice before him with trembling. He loves us because he will; there was and is nothing in us for which we should be beloved. His love is unchangeable: though we change every day, yet his love does not. It is a distinguishing love: he does not love all the world so. Why should he fix his love on us and pass by millions? Let the soul frequently eye the love of the Father with these considerations. Eye this love by faith. His love is not ours in the sweetness of it until we receive it by faith. Let your mind know it, and assent that it is so; let your will embrace it in its being so; and let all your affections be filled with it. Set your heart to it, and let your heart be bound with the cords of this love! It is exceeding acceptable to our Father that we should thus hold communion with him in his love—that he may be received as one full of love, tenderness and kindness towards us!

John Owen, *Works*, 11:32-34

But the serpent said to the woman, 'You will not surely die. For God knows that when you eat of it your eyes will be opened, and you will be like God, knowing good and evil.'

Genesis 3:4-5

Flesh and blood is apt to have very hard thoughts of God—to think that he is always angry, yea, one that cannot be pleased, and that anything is more desirable than coming to his presence. Who can dwell with devouring fire? Who among us shall dwell with everlasting burnings? There is nothing more grievous to the Lord, nor consistent with the design of Satan, than for the soul to think such thoughts as these. Satan claps his hands (if I may so say) when he can take up the soul with such thoughts of God. Satan has all he desires! This was his design from the beginning. He led our first parents into hard thoughts of God: 'Has God said so? Has he threatened you with death? He knows full well it would be better for you.' With this assault he overthrew all mankind at once, and now he readily uses this same weapon. It is exceeding grievous to the Spirit of God to be so slandered in the hearts of those whom he dearly loves. The Lord takes nothing worse at the hands of his children than such hard thoughts of him, knowing full well what bitter fruit this is likely to bear. It alienates the heart and draws one back. It causes one to turn his back in unbelief in our walk with God. How unwilling is a child to come into the presence of an angry father! Reaching out to the Father as he holds out love to the soul gives him the honour he desires. It is folly to doubt God's love. He is good, gracious, tender, kind, and loving to his children. Doubting this comes from Satan's deceit. Assure yourself there is nothing more acceptable unto the Father, than for us to keep up our hearts unto him as the eternal fountain of all the rich grace which flows out to sinners in the blood of Jesus! Endear your souls unto God, delight in him, and make your abode with him!

John Owen, *Works*, 11:34-35

Blessed be the God and Father of our Lord Jesus Christ, who … chose us in him before the foundation of the world.

Ephesians 1:3-4

Before God made the world, he chose some persons of his own free grace to become his children to be made holy and happy. From the beginning, his Son Jesus Christ was appointed to be the medium of exercising all this grace. This work of God in the heart of man is attributed in Scripture, not to any foreseen merit in man, but to the free grace of God toward his people. Works and merit are inconsistent with an election of grace. The choice to salvation is before the foundation of the world or from eternity. We are blessed in Christ Jesus, who is chosen by the Father to be the glorious head of this holy and happy number of mankind. This sacred transaction between the Father and the Son before the foundation of the world is called the covenant of redemption. A glorious covenant! With sacred and divine engagements which are fulfilled on both sides with perfect honour and faithfulness! What an effectual security is derived in this, for the salvation of all that believe in Christ! What an assurance is hereby given, that none of his chosen ones should perish! Let us take comfort in it, rejoice in it, live upon it, and walk worthy of so divine a privilege. See that you keep ever clear and bright by holy watchfulness, that you may have a strong defence in every hour of temptation: 'Shall I who am chosen out of the world to be holy, mingle myself with sinful men and indulge iniquity? Shall I who am adopted into God's family, live like one of the children of Satan?' This is also a sweet refuge for us in every outward distress: 'Shall I, who am chosen and prepared of God for everlasting happiness, faint and be overwhelmed under a present sorrow?' Let us walk in this daily practice, in this joy of the Holy Spirit, and wait for a rich and abundant entrance into the kingdom and glory of our Lord and Saviour Jesus Christ.

Isaac Watts, *Works*, 1:509-517

Does it seem good to you to oppress, to despise the work of your hands and favour the designs of the wicked?

Job 10:3

God is wise, just and sovereign of the world. The earth is his, and all its fullness. May he not do what he will with his own? If we question his providence, we question his wisdom. Is it fit for us who know nothing, to say to infinite wisdom—'what are you doing?' His wisdom will best direct him to the best time to relieve the miseries of his people, or judge the wicked. We only see the present dispensations, but do not know God's unseen motives! All do not have the same office, but are ordered for the good of the whole. What harmony could there be if all the voices and sounds were exactly the same in a concert? Unequal dispensations do not argue for carelessness. A father may give one child a brighter coat than he gives another, yet he cares tenderly over all. According to the employment he puts his children upon, it may require a greater expense for one, and yet he loves one as well as another, and makes provision for all. Though God places some in a higher condition, he takes care of all. Every man has a share according to God's pleasure. Upon due consideration, the inequality will not appear so great. If the needs of one and the enjoyment of another were weighed in the balance, the scales might not appear so uneven. We see a man's wealth, but do you see his cares? A running sore may lie under a purple robe. Health is bestowed upon a labourer, while one that wallows in abundance has torturing diseases that embitter his pleasures. If some lack worldly ornaments, they may have more wisdom than those that enjoy them! If some are stripped of wealth and power, yea, they also are stripped of other encumbrances that go with them. It isn't desirable to be a great prince attended with the many cares in his empire. He made a true estimate of greatness that said he would not stoop to take up a crown if it lay at his feet.

Stephen Charnock, *Works*, 1:31-33

He has delivered us from the domain of darkness and transferred us to the kingdom of his beloved Son.

Colossians 1:13

Sin enslaves the soul. O how a man wears himself out in the service of sin—it wastes his body, breaks his sleep, and distracts his mind. Sin says to one, defraud; to another, be unchaste; to another, take revenge; to another, make a false vow. But sinners are content to be under the command of sin; they are willing to be slaves; they love their chains; they wear their sins, not as fetters, but as ornaments; they rejoice in iniquity. What freedom has a sinner to his own confusion, when he can do nothing but what sin will have him do? He is enslaved in the house of bondage. Satan is a tyrant over the souls of men. He fills their heads with error and their hearts with malice. He rules men's minds and blinds them with ignorance. He rules their wills, and captures their hearts to obey him. Every man by nature is in the house of bondage; he grinds in the devil's mill and is at his command. How could those swine but run, when the devil entered into them? When the devil entered into Judas, and bade him betray Christ, he would do it, though he hanged himself. It is a sad and dismal case to be in the house of bondage under the power and tyranny of Satan. He hurries men on to perdition! But God takes his elect out of the house of bondage, beats off the chains and fetters of sin, and brings them into the glorious liberty of the children of God. The saints are made spiritual kings to rule and conquer their corruptions. It is a matter of the highest praise and thanksgiving to be taken out of the bondage of enslaving lusts and made kings to reign in glory forever! Jesus Christ redeems captives, he ransoms sinners by price, and rescues them by force as David took a lamb out of the mouth of the roaring lion. Oh, what a mercy it is to be brought out of the house of bondage to be made subjects of the Prince of Peace!

Thomas Watson, *The Ten Commandments*, pp. 39-41

And if anyone's name was not found written in the book of life, he was thrown into the lake of fire.

Revelation 20:15

The wicked will be turned into hell. If any should ask where this house of bondage is, I wish he may never know experimentally. 'Let us not so much', says Chrysostom, 'labour to know where hell is, as how to escape it.' O the dreadfulness of the place. Could you but hear the groans and shrieks of the damned for one hour, it would confirm you in the truth that hell is a house of bondage and the height of misery. Besides the punishment of loss, which is the exclusion from the glorified sight of God, there will be the punishment of sense. There will be the worm of conscience. There will be the lake of fire. This house of hell is haunted with devils. Such as go to hell must not only be forced to behold the devil, but must be shut up with this lion in his den. The torments of hell abide forever. Time cannot finish it, and tears cannot quench it. The wicked are salamanders who live always in the fire of hell and are not consumed. After they have lain millions of years in hell, their punishment is as far from ending as it was at the beginning. If all the earth and sea were sand, and every thousandth year a bird should come and take away one grain, it would be a long time before that vast heap would be removed; yet if after all that time the damned might come out of hell, there would be some hope, but this word FOREVER breaks the heart. Oh, then such as are delivered from hell have infinite cause to admire and bless God. How the vessels of mercy should run over with thankfulness! How shall I know I am delivered from hell? There is no condemnation to them that are in Christ Jesus (*Rom.* 8:1). If you are in Christ, he has put the garment of his righteousness over you. Repentance and trust in the blood of Christ will quench the fire of hell so that it shall never kindle upon you!

Thomas Watson, *The Ten Commandments*, pp. 41-43

That you ... may ... comprehend with all the saints what is the breadth and length and height and depth, and to know the love of Christ that surpasses knowledge.

Ephesians 3:17-19

Breadth, length, height, and depth carry in them an inexpressible something, and *that* something far outshines all things that can be found in this world! Paul was endeavouring to bring his hearers into truth beyond what could be fully uttered. Truths are often delivered to us like wheat in full ears, to the end that we should rub them out before we eat them and take comfort in them. These words show us the infinite and unsearchable greatness of God. He is beyond all lengths, depths, and heights, and that in all of his attributes. He is an eternal and everlasting being, and that beyond all measure. His greatness and judgments are unsearchable, and he is infinite in wisdom. O, the depth of the riches of his wisdom and knowledge. If I speak of strength, lo, he is strong; yea 'the thunder of his power who can understand?' There is none holy as the Lord, and his mercy is from everlasting to everlasting upon them that fear him. If the greatness of the Father of our Lord Jesus Christ is rightly considered, it will support the spirits of those of his people who are frightened with the greatness of their adversaries. Pharaoh was great, but God is greater: greater in power, wisdom and in every other way for his people. What God is in himself and in his power is all for the use and profit of believers. This God is *our* God! There is the comfort! He who fills heaven and earth is *yours*, yea—the heaven of heavens cannot contain him. The God whose works are wonderful and whose ways are past finding out is *yours*! Consider therefore the greatness that is laid up for you; he will take part with you and always come in for your help against them that contend with you. This is my support, my relief, and my comfort in all my tribulations.

JOHN BUNYAN, *Works*, II:2-3

Jesus told his disciples, 'If anyone would come after me, let him deny himself and take up his cross and follow me.'

Matthew 16:24

Impediments to our love for God: (1.) *Self-love*—When men honour themselves with self-applause, this is an error of prime importance. Flee from it or you can never be spiritually healthy. (2.) *Love of the world*—This is so great an obstruction that John taught that the love of the Father is missing in such a one. James 4:4 charges him as an enemy of God! (3.) *Spiritual sloth and carelessness of spirit*—Spiritual sloth does more mischief than scandalous relapses. I grant that grosser falls may be worse for others, bringing reproach, but as for themselves a slothful temper has far more serious consequences. Ordinarily, a great fall will bring great repentance, and one will walk more humbly and watchfully, but spiritual sloth runs through the whole course of our life, marring every duty, strengthening every sin, and weakening every grace. It does more hurt than all the devils in hell. Shake this off and you will be more than conquerors over all other difficulties. (4.) *The love of any sin whatsoever*—The love of God and sin do not mix. Sin strikes at the being of God. How could Delilah pretend to love Samson while entertaining his enemy? How can you pretend to love God while you hide sin in your hearts? Don't just pretend to love God; he abhors your hypocrisy. Let me deal plainly with you: you are shameful strangers to your own heart if you do not know your darling sins. You are traitors to your own soul and wilful rebels against God in the least indulgence. (5.) *Inordinate love of lawful things*—In some respect this is our greatest danger. It is not easy to discern what is lawful and the first step into what is sinful. The best of the world is not an end in itself, but conducts us to our chief end. This is our sin—the replacing of the end with the means, when we enjoy our delights, but do not love God!

Samuel Annesley, *Puritan Sermons 1659-1689*, 1:586-589

Keep yourselves in the love of God, waiting for the mercy of our Lord Jesus Christ that leads to eternal life.

Jude 21

To the degree we see the love of God we are able to delight in his love. If the heart is once taken up with the eminency of the Father's love, it cannot but be overpowered, conquered, and endeared unto him. Exercise your thoughts upon this very thing: the eternal, free, fruitful love of the Father, and see if your hearts do not desire to delight in him more. Believers will find it as thriving a course as ever they set upon in their lives. Sit down a little while at the fountain, and you will quickly have a further discovery of the sweetness of the stream. We have all the cause in the world to love him. It is an honour to stand in the presence of princes, though only as servants. But what honour then have all the saints to stand with boldness in the presence of the Father, and there, to enjoy his bosom love! What a blessing did the queen of Sheba pronounce on the servants of Solomon who stood before him and heard his wisdom! How much more blessed, then, are they who stand continually before the God of Solomon, hearing his wisdom, and enjoying his love! While others have their fellowship with Satan and their own lusts, making provision for them and receiving perishing refreshments from them, we have this sweet communion with the Father. Moreover, what a safe and sweet retreat is here for the saints in all the scorns, reproaches, and scandals that they must undergo in the world. If I have hatred in the world, I may go where I am sure of love. Though all others are hard to me, my Father is tender and full of compassion. I will go to him and satisfy myself in him. On earth, I am frowned on and rejected, but I have honour and love with him. His kindness is better than life itself. There is in my Father's love everything desirable, and there is the full sweetness of all mercies forever.

JOHN OWEN, *Works*, 11:35-38

For great is your steadfast love toward me; you have delivered my soul from the depths of Sheol.

Psalm 86:13

Christians sometimes have their sinking fits. And though the depths of calamity into which the godly may fall may be as deep as hell, yet this is our great comfort—the mercy of God lies even deeper! 'For I am sure that neither death nor life, nor angels nor rulers, nor things present nor things to come, nor powers, nor height nor depth, nor anything else in all creation, will be able to separate us from the love of God in Christ Jesus our Lord' (*Rom.* 8:38-39). However, this is hard to grasp for those who are sinking and smartingly feel all of God's waves and billows rolling over them. But whether they see it or not, God's blessing lies ready to pounce like a lion upon the sinking soul. God's everlasting arms are undergirding you in your deepest extremities. His arms are strong and long, and can reach to the bottom beyond all misery and distress that Christians are subject to in this life. Indeed, mercy seems to be asleep when we are sinking, but it will awake in time for our help! God will arise at the fittest season to help and deliver his sinking people. This is worthy of consideration for all sinking souls who feel themselves descending into the pit. Some may come and tell you that you have no ground to stand on and you are in a bottomless pit with no foundation. But consider that underneath you, even at the bottom, there lies a blessing. In this deep in which you are descending, lies a delivering mercy crouching to catch you and save you from sinking forever. This will be a relief and help to encourage your hope for good. This is a stay and relief for sinking ones to be lifted up: 'He drew me up from the pit of destruction, out of the miry bog, and set my feet upon a rock, making my steps secure. He put a new song in my mouth, a song of praise to our God' (*Psa.* 40:2-3).

JOHN BUNYAN, *Works*, II:6-7

Oh, that I knew where I might find him, that I might come even to his seat! I would lay my case before him and fill my mouth with arguments.

Job 23:3-4

A child of God often receives such influences and comfort from the throne of grace, that he is led on sweetly in his path of daily duty by the guiding providences of God and the secret directions of the Holy Spirit. He finds pleasure in his morning addresses to the mercy seat and returns to the throne in the evening with joy in his heart and praise upon his tongue. If God withdraws from him, he feels the divine absence, and his heart meditates grief and complaints. When at the same time he is pressed with other burdens too, he breathes after God with a sacred impatience, 'Oh, that I knew where I might find him!' When God appears to us as an infinite ocean—the all-sufficient, almighty, and sovereign Creator—the soul, in due exercise of grace, shrinks into nothing before him. O with what deep humility and self-abasement does the creature cast himself down at the foot of God when he comes near to the seat of his majesty! 'Behold,' said Abraham, 'I have undertaken to speak to the Lord, I who am but dust and ashes' (*Gen.* 18:27). The language of a saint who draws near to the throne of God's majesty says—'Before I saw his sovereignty, I was prone to be stubborn and quarrel with God because of the difficult duties he imposed upon me and the difficult dispensations I was made to pass through. But now, I can quarrel no more with any duty or difficulty, I submit to all his will. Whatever he will have me to be—that I am! Whatsoever he bids me do—that I do! It is only fit that he should be my sovereign. I give myself afresh to him, and forever, that he may dispose of me according to his own will and for his own glory. It is only fit that he should be the ultimate end of all that I can be, and all that I can do, for he is my sovereign.'

ISAAC WATTS, *Works*, 1:52-53

And because you are sons, God has sent the Spirit of his Son into our hearts, crying, 'Abba! Father!'

Galatians 4:6

Whoever has God for his God also has the Spirit of prayer and supplication to run to God—especially in extremity. All God's children have the Spirit of adoption to cry, 'Abba, Father!' God's children can pray at all times. What miserable creatures are all who do not have God. Ahab had power and strength, but he did not have God. Saul had a kingdom and Herod eloquence, but not God. Judas was an apostle, but did not have God. What became of all these? They had strength, honour, and friends, but not God! What a miserable end. When wealth, friends, and health forsake them, terrors lay hold of them and the wrath of God rests upon them! But consider the comfort of the Christian. When he finds God, he finds everlasting favour. His love is everlasting and the graces of the Spirit are an everlasting spring in Christ. Grace never runs dry! The world will fail us; friends will fail us; comforts will fail us; life will fail us ere long, but the everlasting covenant will never fail. If I lose friends, I cannot lose God. If he is mine, he is mine forever. Whatever God takes away, he never takes away himself. He can immediately convey the comfort I have lost from others. If all of the world were taken away, I yet have all in him. This is a point of wonderful comfort. He that does not have God to trust in when he is unfaithfully dealt with in the world—what a wretched man is he! Man is but a man; a friend today may be an enemy tomorrow. But God is our God forever, and we may comfort ourselves in him through all the unfaithful dealings of men that come to us. A Christian in all the breaches of this world has this comfort—that he has a sure God to trust in. This was David's comfort. When he was beset with calamities and miseries, and the people were ready to stone him, he trusted in the Lord his God! (*1 Sam*. 30:6).

Richard Sibbes, *Works*, vi:13-21

'Oh that you would bless me ... and that your hand might be with me' ... And God granted what he asked.

1 Chronicles 4:10

If we can but comprehend the depth of Christ's love, we are more able to explain God's providences and see how God is working through them. There are two kinds: seemingly good, and seemingly bad. As Jacob blessed Joseph's sons by crossing his hands, God may lay the blessing where we would not! There are providences that smile upon the flesh, such as health, wealth, plenty, ease, and friends, but the blessing is not in them. There are also providences that take away from us, such as sickness, losses, crosses, persecutions and afflictions, and usually in these we cry out in pain when they come upon us. But God is crossing his hands for the blessing of his people in these, and sanctifies affliction. Rachel called Benjamin the son of her sorrow, but Jacob gave him a better name. Jabez, being brought forth in pain, was more honourable than his brethren. He that has skill to judge the mysteries of providence draws near to understanding the depth of God's love. Some suck honey out of that before which others tremble for fear it should poison them. Consider a man, never well, never prospering, often under afflictions, disappointments and sorrows, and if he is a Christian he is one of the best of men. I know that sufferings are not excellent in themselves, nor are they to be desired for any profit that they can yield, but God uses them as a teacher to make known the riches of his goodness that are seldom known by other means unto the sons of men. Thus, affliction yields the peaceable fruits of righteousness unto those who are exercised by them. The depth of God's love is revealed in every providence, in every change, in every turn of the wheel that passes by us in the world. There may be some that are alive that are able to say—'the days of affliction have been the best for me, for by them he caused his light to shine!'

John Bunyan, *Works*, II:11-12

Who has measured the waters in the hollow of his hand and marked off the heavens with a span?

Isaiah 40:12

If we could comprehend the depth of Christ's love, we would never be afraid of anything we shall meet with, or that will assault us in this world! To comprehend is to know a thing fully. Paul desires that we would understand and know the love of Christ with the very best of the saints—a love which passes knowledge. There are degrees of knowledge—some know more, and some less—but the apostle prays that we might see, know, and understand as much as the best under heaven (*Eph.* 3:19). To God, the heavens are but a span. He gathers the wind in his fist. He measures the waters in the hollow of his hand. He weighs the mountains on a scale. All the nations before him are as nothing, and vanity. We are said to live and move in him, and he is beyond finding out about. The great God, the creator of all things, takes part with them that fear him, and that engage themselves to walk in his ways. They may boldly say, 'The Lord is my helper; I will not fear; what can man do to me?' (*Heb.* 13:6). Would it not be amazing if you should see a man surrounded by chariots, horses, and weapons for his defence, and yet afraid of a sparrow or a grasshopper! Why, our God sits upon the circle of the earth, and all the inhabitants of it are as grasshoppers. This is the God of all who are lovers of Jesus Christ! We should not fear man. To fear man is to forget God! Why, let us fear God, and diligently keep his way. If while doing this, God allows us to be delivered into the hands of them that hate us, let us laugh, be fearless, and without care, standing up for Christ before the workers of iniquity. We may fully conclude that both we, and our enemies, are in the hand of him that loves his people, and that God will certainly render a reward to the wicked after he has sufficiently tried us by their means.

JOHN BUNYAN, *Works*, 11:12-13

Believe in the Lord Jesus, and you will be saved, you and your household.

Acts 16:31

It is not the sight of a man's arm stretched out to a man in the water that will save him from drowning, but the taking hold of it. Faith must lay its whole weight and expectation of mercy on Christ. However, many are bold enough to think they can lean on God's arm for pardon and salvation, but never consider that the promise which presents Christ as a Saviour also presents him at the same time to be chosen as Lord and Prince! Such were the rebellious Israelites (*Isa.* 48:1-2). They were more bold than welcome, and God rejected their confidence and loathed their sauciness. Though a prince would not disdain to let a poor wounded man, faint and bleeding, and unable to walk alone, upon a humble request, allow him to make use of his arm rather than he should perish in the streets; yet he would, with indignation, reject the same motion from a filthy drunkard that is besmeared with his own vomit, if he should desire to lean on him because he could not go it alone. I am sure also that a poor humble soul that lies bleeding for his sins at the very mouth of hell in his own thoughts—is to God welcome when he comes with encouragement of the promise to lean on Christ. Yet the unrepentant profane wretch that strengthens himself to come to Christ shall be kicked away with infinite disdain and abhorrency by a holy God for abusing his promise. When a poor sinner has found a promise, and observes the terms with a heart willing to embrace them, he is able to put forth an act of faith upon the credit of the naked promise. The promise of God is the pilgrim's staff with which we set forth to heaven like Jacob on his way to Padanaram. He left only with the staff of promise. The word of promise was all he had to show, and he counted that enough to set his faith to work!

William Gurnall, *The Christian in Complete Armour*, II:6-7

By faith Abraham obeyed when he was called to go out to a place that he was to receive as an inheritance.

Hebrews 11:8

True faith is obedient from the heart, and from there it diffuses itself to the outward man until it spreads over the whole man in a sincere endeavour. Abraham is famous for his obedience. No command was too difficult for him. He was an obedient servant that only needed to hear his master knock, and he left all and ran immediately to know his master's will and pleasure. Faith was the spring that set Abraham's obedience going (*Heb.* 11:8). Faith desires to please God. It is an idle faith that has hands but does not work, or feet but does not walk in the statutes of God. No sooner had Christ cured the woman of her fever, but it is said, 'she rose and began to serve him' (*Matt.* 8:15). The believing soul stands up and ministers unto Christ in gratitude and obedience. Faith is not lazy—it does not incline the soul to sleep but to work. It sends the creature not to bed to snort away his time in ease and sloth, but into the field. When the Sun of Righteousness arises, and it is day in the soul, then the creature rises and goes forth to his labour. The first words that break out of faith's lips are those of Paul: 'Lord, what will you have me to do?' Therefore, take your foul fingers off the promise, and pretend no more you have faith if you do not freely stoop to place your neck in the yoke of obedience. You are children of Belial. The devil himself may as soon pass for a believer as a disobedient soul! Do you pretend to have knowledge? The devil is a greater scholar than you in Scripture! Do you believe the Scripture to be true? Does he not more strongly? Do you tremble? He much more! Obedience is the test of true faith. Disobedience is what makes Satan the devil, and disobedience will make you like him also. True, choice, and excellent faith in the promises of God also works obedience to the commands of God!

William Gurnall, *The Christian in Complete Armour*, 11:32-33

You who were once slaves of sin have become obedient from the heart to the standard of teaching to which you were committed.

Romans 6:17

False faith begins from without, and there ends. All the seeming good works of a counterfeit believer are like the beautiful colours of a picture. They do not come from a principle of life from within, but the painter's pencil from without. Obedience from the heart is an expression of love. We give our hearts to them we give our love to. Indeed, faith brings the heart into subjection and obedience to God. Does your soul value God's commands? Do you value them as a chain of gold about your neck and esteem yourselves favourites of the King of heaven? Do you consider sin as your prison and your obedience as your liberty? Or do you look upon them as iron chains about your legs, and think yourselves prisoners because you are tied to them? God gives true faith a large heart for duty. The only grievous thing to a loving soul is to be hindered in his obedience. Faith breaks one's love for the world and his being in it because it encumbers him in his work, and many times keeps him from it. O how it grieves a faithful servant that is lame or sick, since he can do his master so little service. The loving soul bemoans itself that it should put God to so much cost and be so unprofitable under it. Is this your attitude? Blessed are you of the Lord! You are crowned with the jewels of faith and love. The crown jewels of all the princes of the world are but dust, compared to the value of faith and love. They are yours, and with them, God and all that he has and is, is yours! But if his commandments are grievous, as they are to every carnal heart, and you count yourself at ease when you can escape duty to commit sin, this shows what spirit you are of. O it speaks you to have no love for God or true faith. You are a lame horse indeed without any spirit or vigour!

William Gurnall, *The Christian in Complete Armour*, II:33-35

For the desires of the flesh are against the Spirit, and the desires of the Spirit are against the flesh.

Galatians 5:17

Indwelling sin remains in a person after their conversion. It is a powerful and effectual indwelling principle constantly working towards evil. Though in salvation its rule is broken, its strength weakened, its root mortified, yet it is still a law of great force. The unregenerate live by this law. Believers are not wholly subject to injury from it, since grace has the sovereignty in their souls. The believer does not trade in sin. Believers have a habitual bent and inclination of the will toward the morally and spiritually good, notwithstanding the power of indwelling sin to the contrary. Here lies the beginning of the whole course of our obedience; we should be thoroughly acquainted with this battle if we intend to walk with God and to glorify him in this world. If we do not labour to be spiritually wise, how can we steer our course aright? Indeed, few labour to grow wise in this matter and study themselves as they ought. Few are acquainted with the evils of their own hearts. But what diligence and watchfulness is required for Christian living! There is a constant enemy in everyone's own heart. We may well bewail the woeful sloth and negligence that is in most. They live and walk as though they intended to go to heaven hoodwinked and asleep, as though they had no enemy to deal with. Awake, therefore, all of you in whose hearts is anything of the ways of God! Your enemy is not only upon you, as on Samson of old, but is in you! If you would not dishonour God and his gospel; if you would not scandalize the saints and ways of God; if you would not wound your consciences and endanger your souls; if you would not grieve the Holy Spirit; if you would keep your garments undefiled, and escape the woeful temptations and pollutions in which we live, awake to the consideration of this cursed enemy!

JOHN OWEN, *Works*, VI:155-163

The heart is deceitful above all things, and desperately sick; who can understand it?
Jeremiah 17:9

Indwelling sin is described as a law because of its power. It has lost its complete dominion in believers, but even in them, it is still a law. This law of sin offers rewards and punishments. The pleasures of sin are its rewards, and most men lose their souls to obtain them! The sorry reward of sin keeps the world in obedience to its commands, and experience shows its power and influence on the minds of men. This tyrant maintains a rebellion against God all our days. Sometimes it has more strength, and consequently more success, and sometimes it has less, but it is always in rebellion while we live. It is like an enemy in war, whose strength and power lies not only in numbers, but also in the unconquerable fort that it possesses. The more men exert and put forth the fruits of their lust, the more they are enraged and increased —sin feeds upon itself and swallows up its own poison, and grows by it. The more men sin, the more are they inclined to sin. This law of sin is deceitful. Do not think you can satisfy a lust so you do not need to sin any more. Every sin increases the principle, and fortifies the habit of sinning. It is an evil treasure that increases by doing evil. Never let us reckon that our work in contending against sin is at an end (*Col.* 3:5). It is necessary to watch to the end of the race! Always be watching while you live in this world! It is true—great ground is obtained when the work is vigorously and constantly carried on. Sin is greatly weakened, and the soul presses forward to perfection, but the work must be endless. If we give over, we shall quickly see this enemy exerting itself with new strength and vigour. Grace is increased by its exercise too! The more men exercise their graces in duties of obedience, the more it is strengthened and increased. He who dies fighting in this warfare dies assuredly a conqueror.

JOHN OWEN, *Works*, VI:163-175

Abstain from the passions of the flesh, which wage war against your soul.

1 Peter 2:11

The general nature of indwelling sin is that it is always at enmity with us. There can be no terms of peace. It must be abolished and destroyed, every part and parcel of it. Every drop of poison is poison, and will kill; and every spark of fire is fire, and will burn. We can admit no terms of peace or compromise. It is in vain to have any expectation of rest from lust, except by its death. Some, in the troubling of their corruptions, seek for quietness by labouring to satisfy them. This is to douse a fire with oil. Casting wood into the fire will not satisfy it, but increase it: so it is with seeking to satisfy sin by sinning, it only inflames and increases it. You cannot bargain with fire to take only so much of your house; you have no way but to quench it. It is so with indwelling sin. Sin opposes duty, and tempts us to unbelief, because of its enmity toward God. Every act of sin is a fruit of being weary of God. The great means to prevent the fruits and effects of this enmity is to constantly keep the soul in a universally holy frame. As we are directed to 'watch unto prayer' (*1 Pet.* 4:7, KJV), so watch in every duty. Whatever good we have to do, and we find evil present with us, we must prevent it from parleying with the soul. We must prevent its insinuating poison into the mind and affections. Be sure you are not worn out by its persistence, nor driven from your hold by its importunity. Do not faint by its opposition. It is so dangerous when the soul gives over in part or in whole, either by being wearied in the battle of sin against holy duties or wearied of communion with God. Labour to possess a mind of the beauty and excellence of spiritual things—obedience, and communion with God—so that they may be presented lovely and desirable to the soul; and this cursed enmity of sin will thus be weakened.

JOHN OWEN, *Works*, VI:176-188

Set your minds on things that are above,
not on things that are on earth.
Colossians 3:2

Indwelling sin is like a river. If the springs and fountains of a river are dried up in some good measure at their source, the river may be controlled and restrained. While the springs and fountains are open, you may restrain it for a while, but it will increase, rise higher, and rage, at one time or another, until it breaks down all your convictions and resolutions, or makes itself an underground passage by some secret lust. It seeks to erupt with unexpected and surprising imaginations. When any temptation is proposed unto a man, immediately, he not only has to deal with the temptation proposed, but now also with his own heart about it! There are certain duties, which, in their own nature and by God's appointment, have a peculiar influence upon the weakening and subduing the whole law of sin in its very principles and greatest strengths. Unto these the mind of a believer should principally attend in the course of his life. From these the deceitfulness of sin endeavours principally to draw the mind away. I shall consider only two, which seem to me to be of this nature—namely, I believe that by God's special designation these have a special tendency towards the ruin of the law of sin. Now, these duties are—first, prayer, especially private prayer; and, secondly, meditation. By meditation I mean the meditating upon the word and our own hearts, so they may be brought to a more exact conformity with each other. It is our pondering of the truth as it is in Jesus that makes it possible for it to be realized in our own hearts. This is the same intent as prayer, which is to bring our souls into a frame in all things in keeping with the mind and will of God. These duties are the life-blood in our veins.

JOHN OWEN, *Works*, VI:191-226

I have stored up your word in my heart, that I might not sin against you.

Psalm 119:11

Sin, by its deceit, endeavours to draw off the mind from a holy frame of walking with God in that in which the soul can be preserved—namely, prayer and meditation. Because many are at a great loss in this duty of meditation, and since it has so great an effect for controlling the workings of the law of sin, I shall present three directions for a right performance of this great duty, and they are these: (1.) Meditate about God with God; that is, undertake thoughts and meditations about God, his excellencies, his glory, his majesty, his love, his goodness, and let it be done by way of speaking unto God, with a deep humiliation and abasement of our souls before him. This will fix the mind to give glory unto God in a due manner, and affect the soul until it is brought unto a holy admiration of God and such a delight in him that is acceptable unto him. My meaning is, that it be done by way of prayer and praise—speaking unto God. (2.) Meditate on the word as you read it, consider the sense in the particular passages, looking to God for help, guidance, and direction, in the discovery of his mind and will in it, and then labour to have your heart affected with it. (3.) If you come short of this in evenness and consistency in thought, let it be made up in frequency. Some are discouraged because their minds do not regularly supply them with thoughts to carry on their meditations through the weakness or imperfection of their inventions. Let this be supplied by frequent returns of the mind unto the subject proposed and new insight will still be supplied unto it. These duties promote a special opposition to the very being and life of indwelling sin, or rather, faith in them does so. They are perpetually designing its utter ruin.

John Owen, *Works*, VI:224-225

Practise these things, immerse yourself in them, so that all may see your progress.

1 Timothy 4:15

Through prayer and meditation there is wrought upon the heart a deep, full sense of the vileness of sin, that it may be loathed and cast away as a filthy thing. Since prayer and meditation is the way blessed of God to obtain strength and power against sin, the deceitfulness of sin endeavours to draw away the mind from a due attention to these and like duties. Consider three: (1.) Sin takes advantage of the weariness of the flesh. There is an aversion, in the law of sin, unto all immediate communion with God. It seeks to make it wearisome and burdensome to flesh. (2.) The deceitfulness of sin also reasons concerning the urgent occasions of life. 'Should we,' it says in the heart, 'attend strictly to these duties, and neglect our principal responsibilities in the world?' Business does require particular duties in their due place and time, but it is certain that God gives us enough time for all that he requires of us of any kind in this world. Duties don't need to jostle with one another. If we take more upon ourselves than we have time to perform well, this God does not call us to do. Through the deceitfulness of sin the souls of men are beguiled by this! By gradual degrees they are at length driven from this important duty! (3.) Sin by deceit feeds the soul with promises of being more diligent in this duty when the occasion will permit it. By this means, it brings the soul to say to its convictions of duty, as Felix did to Paul, 'Go thy way for this time; when I have a convenient season, I will call for you.' And often by this means the present season and time, which alone is ours, is lost irrecoverably. Thus, the deceit of sin endeavours to draw off the mind from its due attendance unto this duty of prayer and meditation, which aims so directly and immediately at sin's ruin.

John Owen, *Works*, VI:225-231

He saved us, not because of works done by us in righteousness, but according to his own mercy.

Titus 3:5

Mercy is an innate propensity in God to do good to distressed sinners. In showing mercy, God's glory fully appears! When Moses said to God, 'show me your glory', God showed him his mercy (*Exod.* 33:18-19). His mercy is his glory. He is the 'Father of mercies' (*2 Cor.* 1:3). His mercy is free and spontaneous. Nothing can deserve mercy or force it. We may force God to punish us, but not to love us, for he loves us freely. Every link in the golden chain of salvation is wrought with free grace. Election is free. Do not say 'I am unworthy', for mercy is free. If God should only show mercy to such as deserve it, he would show mercy to no one! God's mercy is powerful, and can soften a heart of stone! His mercy works sweetly, yet irresistibly; it allures, yet conquers. His mercy subdues the pride and enmity of the heart, and beats off those chains of sin in which the soul is held captive. His mercy is superabundant, and he stores up treasures of mercy. The vial of God's wrath drips only, but the fountain of his mercy overflows. Its depth reaches to low sinners and up above the clouds. Every time we draw our breath, we drink in mercy. His mercy abides, it is from everlasting to everlasting (*Psa.* 103:17). God's anger to his children lasts but a while, but his mercy forever. We are all living monuments of his mercy. The cornerstone of his mercy is our salvation. Here it is displayed in all of its glorious colours. God perfectly refines us from all the dregs of corruption. Saving mercy is his crowning mercy. Not only are we freed from hell, we are enthroned in a kingdom. What rich mercy will it be when we fully possess him and see his smiling face! What rich mercy will it be to lay in his bosom! This will fill us with 'joy unspeakable and full of glory' (*1 Pet.* 1:8). I will be satisfied when I awake in his likeness (*Psa.* 17:15).

Thomas Watson, *The Ten Commandments*, pp. 68-72

Who is a God like you, pardoning iniquity and passing over transgression? ... because he delights in steadfast love.

Micah 7:18

What an encouragement we have to serve God who shows mercy to thousands. Who would not be willing to serve a prince given to mercy and clemency? Judgment is God's strange work (*Isa.* 28:21). The disciples, who did not wonder at any other miracles, did wonder when the fig tree was cursed and withered. It was not in Jesus' manner to put forth acts of severity. God is said to delight in mercy. Justice is God's left hand: mercy is his right. He uses his right hand most since he is more prone to mercy than to justice. He is slow to anger, and ready to forgive. This may encourage us to serve him. What argument will prevail if mercy does not? If God were all justice, it might frighten us from him, but mercy is a magnet to draw us to him. Hope in God's mercy! 'For you, O Lord, are good and forgiving, abounding in steadfast love to all who call upon you' (*Psa.* 86:5). 'But I have been a great sinner, and surely there is no mercy for me!'—Not if you are resolved to go on in your sin, but, if you will break off your sins, the golden sceptre of mercy shall be held forth to you! 'Let the wicked forsake his way, and the unrighteous man his thoughts; let him return to the Lord, that he may have compassion on him, and to our God, for he will abundantly pardon' (*Isa.* 55:7). Christ's blood is a fountain opened for sin and uncleanness. Mercy more overflows in God than sin in us. His mercy can drown great sins as the sea covers great rocks. Some of the Jews who had their hands imbrued in Christ's blood were saved by that blood. God loves to magnify his goodness, to display the trophies of free grace, and to set up mercy in spite of sin. Therefore, hope in his mercy. Labour to know that God's special mercy is for you. Put a high value and estimate upon it. This is the diamond ring that outshines all other comforts!

Thomas Watson, *The Ten Commandments*, pp. 72-73

When I am afraid, I put my trust in you.

Psalm 56:3

It cannot be said of any man that he is made without fear. Even the most courageous are not without some fear. When the church is in the storm of persecution, and almost covered with the waves, the stoutest passengers in the storm may suffer from this boisterous passion as the storm rages without, and all for the lack of thoroughly believing, or not seasonably remembering that the Lord High Admiral of all the ocean, and Commander of all the winds, is on board the ship, to steer and preserve her in the storm. The Lord of hosts governs all creatures and their actions. All the armies of heaven and earth are at his beck and command. We can rely upon his care and love if we look to him in the day of trouble. We can trust him in danger, as a child trusts in the care and protection of his father—O what peace and rest! Who would be afraid to pass through the midst of armed troops when you know that the General of the army is your own father? If we sanctify the Lord of hosts as our heavenly Father, he will be a sanctuary to us in times of danger. He will surely protect, defend, and provide for us in the worst of times and cases. We can follow him as a cloud by day and a flame of fire by night! His glory will be our defence and place of refuge. Let the winds roar, the rains beat, the lightning flash—yet you are in safety. The best of men are too apt to be overcome with fear in times of imminent distress and danger. But we do not duly consider God's almighty power, his vigilant care, unspotted faithfulness, and his engaged covenant for his people! This lies at the root of fear. If we but once thoroughly understood what power there is in God's hand to defend us, what tenderness in his heart to comfort us, and what faithfulness to all his promises given over to us, O how quiet and calm would our hearts be! Our courage would quickly be up, and our fears down.

John Flavel, *Works*, iii:242–258

Be strong and courageous. Do not fear or be in dread of them, for it is the LORD your God who goes with you. He will not leave you or forsake you.

Deuteronomy 31:6

The spring and cause of fear is unbelief in the security of divine promises. The spice of this distrust is found in the best of men. The disciples themselves found a storm inside when the weather outside began to threaten them. Their fears inside were more boisterous than the winds and needed more calming than the sea. The less their faith, the greater their fear. If a man can but rely upon God in a promise, so far as he is enabled to believe, so far he will reckon himself well secured. When Sennacherib was ready to invade Israel with a mighty host, it put them into a fright. In this distress, God assured them by the mouth of his prophet to rest in his power, and with a composed, quiet and calm temper of mind to take his promise as their security. This is your salvation and strength. This is more effectual to your preservation than all the armies and garrisons in the world. One act of faith shall do you better service than Pharaoh and all his forces. Fear sometimes puts men into such a hurry, and their thoughts into such disorder, that, for the present, there is hardly any comfort from their graces and reason. Under an extraordinary fear, both grace and reason are like the wheels of a frozen watch with no motion at all. It is rare to find a man with that largeness and constancy of heart and mind in a day of fear like Jehoshaphat—'Then Jehoshaphat was afraid and set his face to seek the LORD' (*2 Chron.* 20:3). He set his heart to prayer at the terrible alarm. If believers only thoroughly understood how dear they are to God, what value they are in his eyes, and how well they are secured by his faithful promises and gracious presence, they would not tremble at every noise and appearance of danger. 'Fear not, Abram, I am your shield' (*Gen.* 15:1).

JOHN FLAVEL, *Works*, III:248-259

Deliver me from all my transgressions … Hear my prayer, O Lord, and give ear to my cry.

Psalm 39:8, 12

To prevail in secret prayer, do not rush suddenly into the awful presence of God, but make suitable preparation. Set your heart to meditate on the attributes of God or his special promises. Meditation sparks prayer into a flame. Engage your heart to a holy frame of mind. Let the soul think upon nothing but what it is to pray for. Humble yourselves in the confession of sin—our filthy garments must be taken away when we appear before the Lord. First, 'Deliver me from all my transgressions'; then, 'Hear my prayer, O Lord' (*Psa.* 39:8, 12). A forgiven soul is a healed soul, and is able to cry strongly before God. Sin is a thick cloud that hides the face of God, so our prayers cannot enter. We must blush with Ezra (9:6) with the flushings of conscience if we expect any smiles of mercy. The blood of our sacrifices must sprinkle the horns of the golden altar before we receive an answer of peace from the golden mercy-seat. When our persons are pardoned, our suits are accepted, and our petitions crowned with the olive branch of peace! Plead with God in prayer—'Restore us, O God; let your face shine, that we may be saved! O Lord God of hosts, how long will you be angry with your people's prayers?' (*Psa.* 80:3-4). Note how Abraham, Jacob, Moses, Joshua, David, and Daniel urged arguments with God. They appealed to his mercy and his faithfulness in times past. They pleaded concerning his honour as God and his people's shame if they are not heard. We find many like pleadings in Scripture. The poor distressed woman of Canaan became 'an acute philosopher' with Christ, said Chrysostom, as she pleaded mercy from him. O, it is a blessed thing to attain this heavenly philosophy of prayer, and argue blessings out of the hand of God by holy force!

Samuel Lee, *Puritan Sermons 1659-1689*, 11:169-171

He strove with the angel and prevailed; he wept and sought his favour.

Hosea 12:4

A crying prayer pierces the depths of heaven. The Lord heard and answered the prayers and tears of Hezekiah. The tears of saints are like songs joined to the instruments of prayer; they make heavenly melody in the ears of God! Perseverance and diligence in prayer also prevails with God. Not just tedious vain repetitions, but that we should be frequent and faithful in prayer. Our Lord bids us to pray always (*Luke* 18:1), and the apostle Paul bids us to pray without ceasing (*1 Thess.* 5:17). When the soul perseveres in prayer, it is a sign of persevering faith. When we put forth our utmost strength in prayer, and will, as it were, receive no 'Nay' from heaven, our prayer is like the continual blowing of the silver trumpets over the sacrifices 'for a memorial' before the Lord (*Num.* 10:10, KJV); or like the watchmen on the walls of Jerusalem, who 'never hold their peace day or night', and are commanded 'not to keep silent, nor to give him rest' (*Isa.* 62:6-7). Such payers are, as it were, a holy assault to the throne of grace. May I say it reverently? Christ delights in such a troublesome person! When friendship would not give bread at midnight, his friend gave it for importunity (*Luke* 11:8). Cold petitioners must have cool answers. If the matter of prayer is right, and the promises of God fervently urged, you are likely to prevail like princely Israel—he held the Angel by the collar (to speak with reverence), and would not let him go until he had blessed him. It was a hot work most of the night! In some cases of extremity, we must hold out in prayer! God graciously determines that warm, affectionate prayers are forerunners of a decreed mercy! These ardent affections are kindled by divine grace when the mercies promised are about to fall on us. Prayer is the chain that draws souls up to God and the mercies of God down to us!

Samuel Lee, *Puritan Sermons 1659-1689*, II:171-174

If we ask anything according to his will he hears us.

1 John 5:14

Submission to the all-wise and holy will of God is the great benefit of a saint's communion with the Holy Spirit. When we pray for temporal mercies, we need to form our prayers in submission, guided by his counsel, and prostrate at his feet. It is well said, 'Let all your desires turn upon the hinge of the divine good pleasure. That man shall have his own will who resolves to make God's will his.' God will certainly bestow that which is for the good of his people (*Psa.* 34:17; 84:11; *Matt.* 7:11). One great point of our mortification lies in this—to have our wills melted into God's. This is a great token of spiritual growth, when we are not only content, but joyful to see our wills crossed, that his may be done. Let our prayer be sincere when we pray—'Thy will be done!' When our wills are sacrificed in the flames of holy prayer, we many times receive choicer things than we asked for expressly. It was a good saying: 'God many times grants not what we desire in the present prayer, that he may bestow what we would rather have.' He may answer our prayer more graciously than we petitioned! The Holy Spirit secretly corrects our wills and prayers according to his! (*Rom.* 8:26). Even when we pray from great anxieties and pinching troubles, and our very nature groans and cries out for relief, there are sweeter mercies than the present return of our prayers: sustaining grace and a growing holiness, a longing for heaven and weaning from the passing pleasures of earth, and insight into God's timing for deliverance. What truly holy person would lose seeing the light of God's countenance in the midst of his earthly shadows? Nay, in many cases, open denials prove the best answers, and God's not hearing us is the most signal audience! At the foot of every prayer subscribe, 'Thy will be done', and you shall enjoy preventing mercies, to change all for the best!

Samuel Lee, *Puritan Sermons 1659–1689*, II:174–176

You have received the Spirit of adoption as sons, by whom we cry, 'Abba! Father!'

Romans 8:15

Does God know your face in his presence-chamber? Do you often converse in your closet to meet him in secret with delight? Can you come as a child to a father, though knowing your own vileness in comparison with his divine love? He is full of compassion as a heavenly Father, the Father of fathers! O what generations of mercies flow from this paternity! We have access to him through the Son by the Holy Spirit. The Father sends his Spirit into our hearts, and then through the Son we cry—'Abba Father'. His love was first wrought in us: he chose us in Christ (*Eph.* 1:4-5). Do you have this access to God by the Spirit? Bosom-communion flows from bosom-affection. If your souls are truly in love with God, he will graciously say to your petitions, 'Be it done unto you according to your love!' A godly man prays in the season the Father may be found, when his heart and ears are inclined to bow down to us. There are special seasons when we draw near to him that he draws near to us. There are times of grace when he knocks at the door of your heart by his Spirit. His motions upon the heart are like the doves sent with a message around their neck. It is said of Bernard—'He knew when the Holy Spirit was present with him by the motion of his heart.' When God reveals himself to the heart, he opens the ears of his children for a gracious message. When God bids us 'seek his face', the soul must answer—One thing have I desired, that will I seek after' (*Psa.* 27:4, 8). First, holy desires warm the heart, and then the soul is set on seeking. These desires are like messengers sent from heaven to bring us into his presence. When the soul is melted by the word, or softened by afflictions, or feels some holy groans and sighs excited by the Spirit, that is a warm time for prayer! 'Abba Father!'

Samuel Lee, *Puritan Sermons 1659-1689*, II:176-178

And he said to them, 'Why are you afraid, O you of little faith?' Then he rose and rebuked the winds and the sea, and there was a great calm.

Matthew 8:26

In times of danger our heart is so prone to sinking fears. The sin of unbelief is the real cause for most distracting and afflictive fears. If men would dig to the root of their fears, they would certainly find unbelief there. The less faith, the more fear. All the skill in the world can never cure us of the disease of fear, until God cures us of our unbelief. This sin in God's own people is the cause and fountain of their fears. It is the office of faith to effect the soul with the invisible things of the world to come. This encourages us to face the fears and dangers of the present world (*Heb.* 11:27). If faith is weakened in the soul, and if invisibles seem uncertain, and visibles the only realities, no wonder we are so scared and frightened when these visible and sensible comforts are endangered. A man is afraid to stand his ground if he is not thoroughly persuaded the ground he stands on is firm. No wonder that men tremble when it seems they feel the ground shake and reel under them! But the divine promises give us a refuge from our fears. They fortify a Christian in evil times through their dependence upon God for protection (*Psa.* 143:9). The cutting off of this retreat through unbelief deprives the soul of comfort and support and fills the heart with anxiety and fear. Noah was not frightened by the flood when he was lifted above the mountains. Having foreseen it by faith, he made provision for it (*Heb.* 11:7). Unbelief places our dearest interests in our own hands, and so fills the heart with distracting fears. But believers have committed their souls and all that is precious and valuable to them into the hands of God by faith, and putting them into such safe hands, they enjoy quietness and peace!

JOHN FLAVEL, *Works*, III:259-266

Help us, O Lord our God, for we rely on you … O Lord, you are our God; let not man prevail against you.

2 Chronicles 14:11

Be sure in coming to secret prayer that you keep your conscience tender and clean from secret sins. Would you be so bold as to come before the God of heaven while you are maintaining some secret lust in your heart? Dare you bring a Delilah with you into this sacred closet? Can you prove yourself to be in the covenant? What you can prove you may plead, and have it successfully issued. Be very particular in secret prayer as to sins, wants, and mercies. Hide none of your transgressions, open all your needs. David pressed his wants before God like an earnest but holy beggar. We may speak our minds fully. Pray for the Spirit that you may pray in and by the Spirit. All successful prayer is from the breathing of the Spirit as he inspires and directs the heart. Also, apply special promises to special cases in prayer. Search the Bible and look for a promise, and then open it before the Lord. The special ground for an answer to prayer lies in the performance of a promise. But sometimes the soul depends for an answer by virtue of the covenant in general—'I will be thy God!' God's faithfulness is the soul's security! Encourage a waiting frame in prayer—'I waited patiently for the Lord; he inclined to me and heard my cry' (*Psa.* 40:1). Our eyes must wait upon the Lord until he has mercy upon us, more than they that watch for the morning! Persist in prayer and wait for his salvation—'My God will hear me; I will hope; I will expect and trust; I will live upon his promises and look for his answer of peace!' When you have been at prayer, mark your ship how it makes the port, and what rich goods are laden back again from heaven. I will attend and watch how my prayer flies towards the bosom of God, and what messages return from heaven.

Samuel Lee, *Puritan Sermons 1659-1689*, II:178-183

For those who love God all things work together for good, for those who are called according to his purpose.

Romans 8:28

You may find your fears raised and provoked by the mixed administration of divine providence in this world. We read in Scripture, that it is the same for all—the righteous and the wicked (*Eccles.* 9:2). The sword makes no difference where God has made so great a difference by grace. The wicked devour the man that is more righteous than himself (*Hab.* 1:13). Our observations in Scripture are confirmed by the accounts of former ages when precious servants of Christ fell prey to their cruel adversaries notwithstanding the holiness of their lives. The men that committed these outrages upon our brethren still rage, and the malice has not abated in the least degree. Enmity against God's people will run as long as there are wicked men. Many times God has let loose these lions on his people. And we are conscious how far short we come in holiness and spiritual excellency of those excellent persons who have suffered these things. We have no ground to expect more favour from providence than they found. Revolving thoughts like these, and like considerations, mixed with our own unbelief can create a world of fears, even in good men. Seek to do the following to heighten our Christian courage: (1.) Resign *all* to God. (2.) Set your faith on the promise that assures us that God will sanctify all of our troubles (*Rom.* 8:28). (3.) Consider that God's presence is with us in all of our troubles (*Psa.* 91:15). (4.) He moderates our troubles to the measure and degree they are bearable (*Isa.* 27:8). (5.) We will know a safe and comfortable deliverance from them at last (*Rev.* 7:17). With these considerations we may recover our hearts out of the hands of our fears again, and return them to a quiet and sweet satisfaction in the wise and holy pleasure of our God.

John Flavel, *Works*, III:266-268

Whatever is lovely, whatever is commendable, if there is any excellence, if there is anything worthy of praise, think about these things.

Philippians 4:8

To cure sinful thoughts, part one: (1.) *Get accustomed to serious meditation every morning.* Getting fresh air from heaven in our souls will engender a purer spirit and nobler thoughts. A morning seasoning will secure us all day long. Throughout the day, after we have dispatched other thoughts that are necessary to attend to our daily activities, our morning theme of meditation will return as our chief companion for the day. (2.) *Avoid entangling yourselves with the world.* This clay will clog our minds, and dirty happiness will engender but dirty thoughts. Mists and fogs near the earth do not reach near the heavens. If we were free from earthly affections, these contrary vapours could not so easily disturb our minds. If the world once settles in our hearts, we shall never fail to have these senseless thoughts torment us. (3.) *Avoid idleness.* Idleness kindles many unprofitable imaginations in the soul that would be sufficiently diverted if the active mind were kept intent upon some stated work. Empty minds are the fittest subjects for extravagant fooleries. (4.) *Awe your hearts with the thoughts of God's omniscience.* Imagine the last trumpet and the judgment seat of Christ. Consider his omniscience calling out singly all the secrets of your heart. Does not this consideration alone allay the heat of all other imaginations? If a foolish thought breaks in, consider—what if God, who knows this, should presently call me to judgment for this sinful glance? Is it fit for God's glory or our own interest that he should find such a nasty dunghill and swarms of Egyptian lice and frogs creeping up and down in our chambers? If our heart is possessed by the truth of his omniscience, we would be ashamed to think what we shall be ashamed to own at the last day!

Stephen Charnock, *Works*, v:308-311

We destroy arguments and every lofty opinion raised against the knowledge of God, and take every thought captive to obey Christ.

2 Corinthians 10:5

To cure sinful thoughts, part two: (5.) *Keep a constant watch over your hearts.* We need grace to stand as a sentinel over our thoughts. Our minds are like idle schoolboys that are unruly if the master's back is turned. There are particular seasons when we must double our guard, such as opportunities that may set some inward corruption aflame. Opportunity may ambush unguarded thoughts or affections. (6.) *Examine your thoughts.* Consider what thoughts are lingering in your heart. Inquire what business they have there, and what their design is. Bring every thought to the test of the word of God. Ask yourself why you entertain such company. (7.) *Put a check on thoughts at their first appearance.* If a thought has the reasonable mark of sin, do not even give it the honour of examination. If leprosy appears on one's forehead, thrust it out! Quench it instantly as you would a spark in a heap of straw. We do not debate whether we should shake a viper off our hands. If a thought is plainly sinful, any treaty we make with it is a measure of disobedience! If it does not savour of the things of God, do not listen to its reasonings. Do not excuse it because it is little. Small vapours grow into great clouds. If entertained, it may force our judgment, drag our will, and make all of our affections a bedlam. The devil can immediately imprint his suggestions on our imagination. We are not even aware of the army he has to back up any sinful thought, if once the gate is set open to him. Let us crush the brat immediately, and fling the head over the wall to discourage further attack. Let us be ashamed to cherish in our thoughts what we would be ashamed to have break out in our words or actions. Therefore, as soon as you perceive a thought as base, spit it out with hatred.

Stephen Charnock, *Works*, v:311-313

Submit yourselves therefore to God. Resist the devil, and he will flee from you.

James 4:7

To cure sinful thoughts, part three: (8.) *Use corrupt thoughts as motivation.* Poison may be made medicinal. Let the thoughts of old sins stir up your anger. Feel the shivering in your spirit and the boiling of your blood at the very thought of the bitter potion you have formerly taken. Strike some sparks from those past hellish thoughts, to kindle your love for God. Renew your repentance, raise your thankfulness, or quicken your obedience. Use it as an occasion for deeper reverence of his majesty. Open the flood-gates of your godly sorrow, and groan about your original sin. Let your heart praise him who delivered you. Endeavour to be more zealous in your duty. Let Satan's fiery darts inflame your love rather than your lust. The skilful pilot will make use of the violence of the wind and the raging of the sea to further him in his voyage. This is to beat the devil with his own weapons. (9.) *Continue your resistance.* Do not lay down your weapons until your sinful thoughts wholly shrink from you. If you suffer them to gather strength, they may end in madness. If they resume their arms, we must continue our shield. Resistance makes the devil flee. If we entertain them they become bolder. We must not leave the battlefield until they cease their importunity. Do not allow them to increase their courage by your own cowardice. (10.) *Join supplication with your opposition.* Watch and pray! Our own weakness should make us pray that we may be powerfully assisted. Be as frequent in soliciting God as wicked thoughts are in soliciting you. As they knock at your door for entrance, knock at heaven for assistance. Take this for your comfort: as the devil takes their part, so Christ will take yours at his Father's throne.

Stephen Charnock, *Works*, v:313-314

How precious to me are your thoughts, O God! How vast is the sum of them!

Psalm 139:17

To cure sinful thoughts, part four: (11.) *Welcome and entertain holy thoughts.* Good thoughts may spring naturally from the grace in our hearts, or be peculiarly breathed in by the Holy Spirit. There are ordinary bubblings of grace in a renewed mind as there are of sins in an unregenerate heart. As it is our happiness and duty to stifle evil thoughts, so it is our misery as well as our sin to extinguish heavenly. Strange fire should be presently quenched, but that which descends from heaven upon the altar of a holy soul must be kept alive by quickening meditation. When a holy thought lights suddenly upon you, receive it as a messenger from heaven. You do not know but you may entertain an angel, yea, something greater than an angel, even the Holy Spirit. Open all the powers of your soul to receive the breath of this Spirit when he blows upon you. It is evident by its holiness, sweetness, and spirituality. The more such sprouts are planted and nourished in us, the less room will stinking weeds have to root themselves and disperse their influence. As for your own good thoughts, feed them and keep them alive and brood upon them. (12.) *Encourage holy thoughts to their natural end.* Don't just give holy thoughts a bare reception, but consider what results are properly encouraged by them: as the search of some truth or the performance of some duty. The gleams of holy thoughts that suddenly shoot into us have some lesson sealed up in them to be opened and learned! Be quick in any duty that the Spirit suggests. His injections are like water poured into a pump to prime it. Do not lie at anchor when a fresh gale would fill your sails, but lay hold of the present opportunity. The breathings of the Spirit, if not entertained with suitable affections, may be lost forever!

Stephen Charnock, *Works*, v:314-316

Search me, O God, and know my heart!
Try me and know my thoughts!

Psalm 139:23

To cure sinful thoughts, part five: (13.) *Add new holy thoughts to your reservoir of morning meditations.* Throughout the day, when holy thoughts arrive, they are like little brooks rising from several springs that will meet in the channel created by your morning meditations, and grow to a more useful river. It is like the constable who, in a time of necessary business for the king, will gather others to join him to better accomplish the desire of the king. Many of these thoughts will strengthen your morning meditations. If your holy thoughts are an extraordinary injection along another theme, go ahead and follow it, and let your thoughts run where they will lead you. A theme of the Spirit's setting is better than one of our own choosing. (14.) *Record the choicest thoughts.* We may have an occasion later to look back upon them as grounds of comfort in some hour of temptation or some sudden emergency. They lie by us as money in our pocket. We should preserve the whisperings of what the Spirit has taught us. If we forget them it will discourage the Spirit from sending any more, and then our hearts will be empty! And we know who is ready to clap in his hellish swarms and legions of wicked thoughts. (15.) *Turn your choicest thoughts into prayer.* As God turns his thoughts of us into promises, so let us turn our thoughts of him into prayers. As he darts these beams upon us, let us reflect them back to him in thankfulness for the gift, and for their continuance and increase! When the Spirit renews in our minds a gospel truth, let us turn it into a present plea and remind God in prayer of his own promises. We do not need to doubt that some rich fruit of application will come at such a season, since, without question, the impressions the Spirit stamps upon us are according to God's will (*Rom.* 8:27).

Stephen Charnock, *Works*, v:316-317

But for me it is good to be near God;
I have made the Lord God my refuge,
that I may tell of all your works.

Psalm 73:28

Fellowship with God in prayer is the life and pleasure of a pious soul: without it we are not Christians, and he that practises it most is the best follower of Christ. It is a balm that eases the most raging pains of the mind. Here the wounded conscience comes to find pardon and peace. This is the cordial that revives our nature when the spirit is broken with sorrows and is almost fainting to death. Drawing near to the almighty physician brings healing and refreshment. The mercy seat is our surest and sweetest refuge in every hour of distress and darkness. This is our daily support and relief while we are passing through a world of temptation and hardships on our way to the promised land. Yet human nature has sunk down and fallen so from God, that even his own children neglect to converse with him if their soul is not set upon a careful watch. But let it be remembered, as we neglect this divine entertainment for the vanities and amusements of the world, or the businesses and burdens of life, so much we lose the glory and joy of our faith, and deprive our souls of the comfort that God invites us to receive. After Job was surrounded by sorrow, and his friends censured him as a vile hypocrite and great sinner, where else could he run to but his heavenly Father and tell him of all his sufferings? From the practice of this holy man we have sufficient warrant to draw near to God in prayer and plead for help! We can spread all our concerns before his eyes, and plead with him for relief. This is such a privilege. At such a season, the holy soul will enjoy an adoring sense of the majesty of God, a becoming fear of his terrors, and a sweet taste of his love! It teaches us of the divine hatred for every sin and desire to resist every temptation, and it brings a heavenly temper diffusing itself through the whole soul.

Isaac Watts, *Works*, 1:62-63

Casting all your anxieties on him, because he cares for you.

1 Peter 5:7

When a saint draws near to God, he has all the fullness of his heart breaking out into holy language. He pours out his whole soul before his God and his Father! All the infinite affairs of life, body and spirit, this life, and the one to come, all things in heaven and earth, created or uncreated, may at one time or other be included in our conversation with God. A good man in devout prayer can spread his hopes and his joys before the Lord as well as his sorrows, fears, and distresses. Here at the mercy seat we may confess how great our sins are, and pray for pardoning grace. As we draw near we can tell him how malicious and full of rage our enemies are, and how the world strikes at our senses, ears, eyes, and outward faculties to draw us away from God our best friend. We may lay before him the rage of Satan that is ready to throw in some foolish suggestion to divert us. I would also beg the presence of my God to assist me, and become a conqueror through him that has loved me as I look forward to my last great enemy—death. I can share my perplexity of mind, and that I realize how few hours I devote in my communion with him. I would tell him of my temporal troubles and spread before him all the sorrows and vexations of life that unhinge my soul from its centre and throw me off my guard. I would not go away without a word for my family and friends that are far from God, and put in a word of petition for them that are careless. I would weep for my children, brothers or sisters, that they might be brought near to God. Why do we delight to tell him all of our circumstances and sorrows?—Because he is our best friend, and it soothes the soul to unburden our cares in the bosom of a friend. This is the noblest and highest friendship. Amazing grace of God to man! Rejoice in this, and delight in all opportunity to employ and improve it.

Isaac Watts, *Works*, 1:63-66

Call upon me in the day of trouble; I will deliver you, and you shall glorify me.

Psalm 50:15

Why does a saint delight to draw near to God? It is the way to maintain the strength of piety, and to keep all the springs of divine love ever open and flowing in his heart! Therefore, he makes many visits to the mercy seat. Every troublesome occurrence in life is an opportunity to betake himself to his knees. It improves every sorrow when you increase your acquaintance with heaven. I may commit my sorrows to God, since he is my best friend. I may cast my burdens upon him, and leave them there in peace. You may pour out your soul there in perfect confidence that he will never publish it to the world! Our guilt and the inward workings of iniquity we may spread before him. He is our best friend and dearest relative! We may leave our case with our God as secure as though we had communicated it to no one. He knows all beforehand, but it eases our souls, and gives us sweet satisfaction in having such a friend to speak to. We may trust his faithfulness and love as we spread our case before him. Shall not the judge of the whole earth do right? In his faithfulness he will fulfil all his promises; in his love he will take compassion on those who are afflicted and tend to those who are miserable. It is no trouble to God that we so often repeat our requests. He delights to hear often from his people, and to have them ask continually at his door for mercy. There are troubles that creatures cannot help, and our hope is only from him, and in a more immediate way. Whatsoever our distress—the violence of temporal afflictions, the power of indwelling sin, or the torments of past guilt or an anxious and troubled conscience—God is able and willing to give relief. 'I did not say to the offspring of Jacob, "Seek me in vain." I the Lord speak the truth; I declare what is right' (*Isa.* 45:19).

Isaac Watts, *Works*, 1:66-68

O LORD, you hear the desire of the afflicted; you will strengthen their heart; you will incline your ear.
Psalm 10:17

He who orders all the circumstances of our lives is acquainted with all of our sorrows, and has not neglected us or forgotten our distress. All things are open before his eyes! The Shepherd of Israel cannot slumber. He would have us to plead and argue with him that we sense our great need and depend entirely on his mercy. He invites us to humble conference with himself. Come now, and let us reason together, says Isaiah. Often in Holy Scripture God represents himself as moved and influenced by the prayers and pleadings of his afflicted saints. He has ordained beforehand that the day when he prepares our hearts to pray shall be the day when his ear shall hear the desire of the humble, and shall become the season of our deliverance. There is not a circumstance but we may draw some argument from it to plead for mercy. There is not one attribute of the divine nature, but we may use it with holy skill to plead for grace. There is not one relation in which God stands to his people, or one promise of his covenant, but it may at some time or other afford us an argument in prayer. But the strongest and sweetest argument that a Christian knows is the name and mediation of Jesus Christ our Lord. It is for the sake of Christ, who has purchased all the blessings of the covenant, that a saint hopes to receive them, and for the sake of Christ he pleads that God would bestow them! It is a very melancholy thing to be at a distance from God when we cannot tell him all our wants and sorrows at the mercy seat! The soul is grieved and never rests till this distance is removed. How happy to draw near to God daily and hourly when he takes us by the hand and leads us into his secret place, and have the ear of God so near. I feel such a sweet freedom of soul in his presence; he is my everlasting friend!

ISAAC WATTS, *Works*, 1:68-71

Watch and pray that you may not enter into temptation. The spirit indeed is willing, but the flesh is weak.

Matthew 26:41

He that walks along the brim of a deep river or the brow of a steep hill needs to be wide awake! The Christian's path is so narrow and the danger so great that it calls for a steady eye to keep watch. A Christian's duty brings him near the enemy's quarters, who soon takes the alarm, and comes out to oppose, so we must always keep a watch on our hearts. Keeping watch frustrates the designs of Satan upon you. If it is worth keeping watch to secure your house from a thief, how much more the heart from a rifling by the devil! It is a precious price to pay for sleep if your throat gets cut for it! Failure to watch one night may keep you awake many more upon a more uncomfortable occasion. Is it not better to watch with care to avoid mischief? You know how sadly David was bruised by a fall in his spiritual slumber. Watchfulness invites the dear Saviour in to sweet communication and discourse about the things of your Father's kingdom. The enjoyment of this heavenly entertainment does not covet the ease of sleepy Christians. If you love your soul, would you not enjoy David's songs more than his sleeping in the night? Who would not rather have Christ's comforting presence as a waking soul than his absence as a sleepy one? It is the watchful soul that Christ delights to be with and opens his heart to. We do not visit our friends when they are asleep in bed; and when we are with them as they grow sleepy, we think it is time to leave them to their pillow, and so verily Christ does so too. Christ will give his choice favours to the souls that are awake. We must watch constantly. The devil tempts when we cease to watch. When the staff is thrown away the wolf appears. Labour in holy care! Oh, don't lie down like some lazy traveller by the wayside to sleep. Save your resting time till you are home from all danger!

William Gurnall, *The Christian in Complete Armour*, 1:286-289

For you have died, and your life is hidden with Christ in God.

Colossians 3:3

The hidden life of the Christian is his spiritual life in which he is devoted to God, and lives to the purposes of heaven and eternity. This life is hidden from the world, and its progress is secret. While the world is following after idols and vanity, the Christian is in his retired chamber and breathes after his God and Redeemer, where he can express his warmest affections in the pursuit of his almighty and best-loved friend. While the world is fretting under present disappointments, the Christian rejoices in secret in the hope of the glory of God. His meat and drink is to do the will of his Father who is in heaven. The motives that awaken a Christian to maintain this spiritual life (things eternal and invisible) are hidden from the eyes of the world. The Christian counts the joys or sorrows of this world as things of little importance. He lives for everlasting acceptance before the throne. He depends on the grace and strength of Christ to encounter the boldest temptations, the most difficult duties, or to sustain him in the heaviest strokes of a painful providence. Don't be content with mere externals and outward forms of the Christian life. We must daily seek conversation with God in our daily secret exercises as we retire with him. Do you spend time quietly about the affairs of eternity? Do you have seasons allotted for prayer, meditation, and reading in secret? Do you fail to spend time alone with God in a whole day? Surely this can never be the life of a Christian! Remember that the hypocrite can imitate zeal or devotion in public. True Christians are known by the exercises of the hidden life in secret transactions between God and the soul. True religion is in the heart and spirit, and not in outward forms. Here the Christian receives his praise from God and not man!

Isaac Watts, *Works*, 1:95-100

Praying at all times in the Spirit, with all prayer and supplication. To that end keep alert with all perseverance, making supplication for all the saints.

Ephesians 6:18

Men of this world wonder what a Christian can have to say to God in so many hours of prayer, and what a strange business he can employ himself in! The carnal mind has no idea to explain it. The saint, on the other hand, considers the spare moments he can find between necessary earthly duties far too little to enjoy those secret pleasures. The children of God pray to their heavenly Father in secret, and they feel unknown refreshment and delight in it; and they are well assured, that their 'Father who sees in secret will reward' them openly (*Matt.* 6:6). The world sees nothing of our inward labour and strife against the flesh and thinks it strange that we do not run into the same excess of dissipation (*1 Pet.* 4:4). They know nothing of our sacred contest for the prize of glory, or our earnest enquiries after an absent God and hidden Saviour. They know nothing of the holy joys and retired pleasures of a Christian. The Christian lives in sight of the world of invisibles! There is no envy of the riches in the world—they have a God whom they worship in secret. If they find themselves exalted by providence to high stations in the world, they are not puffed up, nor swell in the heart, but labour to keep their divine life vigorous. All their advancements on earth are low, despicable things in comparison to their highest hopes and their promised crown in heaven. They can meet threatening dangers, diseases and deaths without those terrors that overwhelm the carnal sinner. They can sustain losses by the providence of God with a humble resignation of spirit, and serenity and peace. The secret life of a Christian grows much in the closet, and without a secret retreat it cannot grow. Abandon the secret chamber, and the spiritual life will decay!

Isaac Watts, *Works*, 1:101-103

We know that if the tent that is our earthly home is destroyed, we have a building from God … eternal in the heavens.

2 Corinthians 5:1

How little is death dreaded by a believer, since it will bring the soul to the full possession of its hidden life in heaven! It is a dark valley that divides between this world and the next, but it is all a region of light and blessedness beyond it. We are now on the border of the eternal world, and we know but little of that invisible country. Approaching death opens the gates to us, and begins to give our holy curiosity some secret satisfaction, and yet how we shrink backward when that glorious unknown city is opening upon us! We are often ready to beg and pray that the gates might be closed again: 'O! For a little more time, a little longer continuance in this lower visible world!' This is the language of the fearful. But it is better to have our Christian courage brought up to a divine height, and to say, 'Open ye everlasting gates, and be lifted up ye everlasting doors, that we may enter into the place where the King of Glory is'. (cf. *Psa.* 24:9, KJV). There shall we see God and rejoice in his overflowing love. We shall see him face to face, and not through the glass darkly. What supreme glory shall our life display. This is life eternal indeed, and joy unspeakable. How gloriously shall the perfections and honours, both of body and mind unfold themselves. Is this the crown I fought for on earth at so feeble a rate? And was this the prize for which I ran so slow and lazily? O shameful indifference! O undeserved prize and crown! Had I imagined how bright the blessing was which lay hidden in the promise, surely I would have ventured through many deaths to secure the possession of it. O guilty negligence! And criminal unbelief! But your sovereign mercy has pardoned both and made me possessor of this fair inheritance. Behold I bow at your feet forever, and adore your riches of overflowing grace.

Isaac Watts, *Works*, 1:105-107

But, as it is written, 'What no eye has seen, nor ear heard, nor the heart of man imagined, what God has prepared for those who love him.'

1 Corinthians 2:9

God's mercy is for those that love him. Love is a holy enlargement of the soul that delights after God. It is the first and great commandment. We must love God not only for the good that flows from him, but for the good which is in him. True love is not mercenary; he who is deeply in love with God does not need to be hired with reward, but can love God for the beauty of his holiness. Though it is not unlawful to look for benefits, we must not love God for his benefits only. This is not love of God, but self-love. Our love must be with all the heart. We know we truly love God when we desire his presence and enjoy him in the word and prayer. Also, he who loves God does not love sin. Every sin loved strikes at the being of God! How can he say he loves God who loves sin? This is God's enemy! He who loves God is not much in love with anything else. He that loves God uses the world but chooses God. The world is his pension, but God is his portion. He who loves God cannot live without him; he is our chief good! He who loves God will go to any length to know him; 'My soul followeth hard after thee' (*Psa.* 63:8, KJV). He who is in love with God never rests till he has a part in him. He prefers him before estate and life. If we love him, we can't but be fearful of dishonouring him. Let us be lovers of God, and inflame our love to him. Consider all the benefits he bestows on us. We cannot but love him! Eye has not seen all God has prepared for them that love him! Labour to know him in all his excellencies, holiness, wisdom, love and truth. If we knew him more, our hearts would be fired with love to him. Meditate much on God and his word. Beg that your love might burn on the altar of your heart—he will not deny you such a request!

Thomas Watson, *The Ten Commandments*, pp. 74-79

Greater love has no one than this, that someone lay down his life for his friends.

John 15:13

Christ is a person of no less quality than very God, and the very same nature as the Father! That such a person—so great, so high, so glorious—should have love for us, passes all knowledge. It is common for equals to love, and for superiors to be beloved, but for the King of princes to love man, this is amazing! Christ is called the king of glory, the Lord of glory, the brightness of the glory of his Father, the head over all things, the prince of life, the creator of all things, the upholder of all things, the disposer of all things, and the only beloved of the Father. Those whom he loves are called transgressors, sinners, enemies, dust and ashes, fleas, worms, shadows, vapours, vile, filthy, unclean, ungodly fools and madmen. Is it not to be wondered at that he set his heart upon us? Our love is weak, unorderly, and it fails and miscarries. But the love of Christ is essential to his being, for God is love. Christ is love *naturally*. He may as well cease to be, as to cease to love! His love does not ebb and flow or come short, as our love. There is no uncertainty in his love. His love acts by and from itself. It was shown when he laid down his life for us, and the love of Christ appears wonderful in such a death that he died! It is strange, according to the custom of the world, that he was moved to die for us. He laid down his life for his enemies. They railed on him, degraded him, and called him a devil. They said he was mad, a deceiver, a blasphemer, and a rebel. A disciple sold him, one denied him, and they all forsook him. They beat him with fists, spat on him, mocked him, crowned him with thorns, scourged him and hung him on a tree. Yet all this could not take his heart off the work of our redemption. To die he came, and die he did for our sins, that we might live through him! Oh what infinite love!

John Bunyan, *Works*, 11:15-19

If you love me, you will keep my commandments.

John 14:15

The son that loves his father will obey him. Obedience pleases God. To obey is better than sacrifice! Our obedience springs from our faith, and seeks to keep all his commandments. Though we cannot fulfil all perfectly, we may keep them substantially: (1.) When we include every command as a part of our conscience, and though we come short in every duty, we dare not neglect any. (2.) When it is our desire to keep every commandment, for what we lack in strength we make up in will. (3.) When we grieve that we cannot do better, weep when we fail, and prefer bills of complaint against ourselves for our failings. (4.) When we endeavour to obey every commandment by pressing toward the mark (*Phil.* 3:14). (5.) When we fall short, we look to Christ's blood to sprinkle our imperfect obedience. We need to obey God willingly, not like the devils who came out of the man at Christ's command against their will. Good duties must not be pressed or beaten out of us as the waters came from the rock, when Moses smote it with his rod. They must drop freely as a sweet-smelling savour to God. Our willingness is more esteemed than our service. When we fall short, God sees us in Christ who fulfilled all righteousness. God's commands are sweetened with joy and peace. If a man carries a bag of heavy money, the delight takes away the burden. Nothing is commanded that is not for our good. If a friend said, 'Come, I will supply you with money', would you think it troublesome to visit that friend often? We obey for our good! Our obedience must be as the fire of the altar, which never went out. We have our being from God, and is it not just that we should obey him? All our provisions are from his hand; should we not give him our allegiance? O how many mercies we have to allure us to obey! Even the wind and the sea obey him; shall not we?

Thomas Watson, *The Ten Commandments*, pp. 79-84

There is therefore now no condemnation for those who are in Christ Jesus.

Romans 8:1

Our justification in the sight of God is made up of two parts—(1.) The forgiveness of our offences committed against the Lord. We are acquitted from guilt, and freed from condemnation. As soon as any man sins, he is guilty, and is bound over to the wrath and curse of God. Sin deserves no less than everlasting condemnation. When the Lord forgives a man, he discharges that obligation of wrath. God stands in between sin and the curse. When the law says, 'Ah, you are a sinner! You have transgressed, omitted duties, committed all manner of sins, abused offers of mercy, neglected means and slighted offers', God steps in and says, 'I must and do pronounce you to be guilty, and as I am a just and righteous God, I cannot but judge you to die eternally. But such are the riches of my mercy, that I will freely justify you through the righteousness of my Son. I will forgive your sin and relieve you of wrath, and curse, and condemnation.' The justified person may triumphantly say, 'Who is to condemn?' (*Rom.* 8:34). I can now read over the most dreadful passages of the law without being terrified or alarmed, for the curse is removed and my sins are pardoned. It is just as if I have never sinned! (2.) The second part of justification is that God sees the sinner's person as perfectly righteous in his sight! He pronounces him such, and deals with him as such, and brings him under the shadow of divine favour. God beholds his people in the face of his Son, and sees nothing amiss in them. He sees the sinner without spot or wrinkle. Christ makes us comely through his beauty. The Father honours us, delights in us, is well pleased with us, extends his love and favour to us, esteems us, and gives us free access to himself, in Christ. We are covered and hid under the precious robe of Christ's righteousness!

Thomas Brooks, *Works*, v:218-220

Christ redeemed us from the curse of the law by becoming a curse for us.

Galatians 3:13

There are four things that God cannot do: (1.) he cannot lie, (2.) he cannot die, (3.) he cannot deny himself, and (4.) he cannot behold iniquity with approbation and delight. Such is the holiness of God's nature that he cannot behold sin, and he cannot but punish sin wherever he finds it. God is infinitely, immutably, and unyieldingly just *and* incomprehensibly gracious! In justification, God acts as a God of justice as well as a God of compassion. God is infinite in all his attributes; he is infinite in his justice as well as in his mercy, and these two cannot interfere. Justice cannot entrench upon mercy, nor may mercy encroach upon justice—the glory of both must be maintained. By the breach of the law, the justice of God is wronged, and though mercy desires to pardon, justice requires satisfaction and calls for vengeance on sinners. Every transgression requires a just recompense (*Heb.* 2:2), and God will not in any case absolve the guilty (*Exod.* 34:7). The hands of mercy are tied so she cannot work! Satisfaction cannot be made to an infinite majesty except by an equal person and price, therefore the Son of God must become a curse for us, taking our nature and pouring out his soul to death. By this means justice and mercy are reconciled and kiss each other, and mercy is set at liberty and has free course to save poor sinners. God will have his justice satisfied to the full, and therefore Christ must bear all the punishment due to our sins or else God cannot set us free and go against his own just will. The Saviour's sufferings were necessary, but he died freely and voluntarily. God who is justice itself is fully satisfied, and Christ's sacrifice is fully agreeable to his holy nature, and most suitable to his high and sovereign ends: man's salvation and his own glory!

Thomas Brooks, *Works*, V:221-222

For the wages of sin is death, but the free gift of God is eternal life in Christ Jesus our Lord.

Romans 6:23

The sinner deserves to die for his sins. Since God is a just and righteous God, sin cannot absolutely escape unpunished. God must deny himself to be unjust, but this he can never do. Sin is of an infinite guilt, and has an infinite evil nature in it. Therefore no person in heaven or on earth can procure the pardon of it or make satisfaction for it but the Lord Jesus, who is the God-man; who has infinite dignity. No prayers, no cries, no tears, no humblings, no repentings, no resolution and no reformations can stop the course of justice and procure the guilty sinner's pardon. It is Christ alone that can dissolve all obligations to punishment, and break all bonds and chains of guilt, and hand a pardon to us through his own blood. We are set free by the blood of Christ. The truth of God requires it. As God is just, he is also true, and must make good the threatenings that have gone out of his mouth: 'In the day that you eat of it you shall surely die' (*Gen.* 2:17). God cannot break his word. O sirs, there is no standing before a God that is a consuming fire, a just judge, and a holy God, unless we have one that is mighty to undertake for us and satisfy divine justice; one mighty to pacify divine wrath, bear divine threatenings, and mighty to forgive sin! The Father is just in forgiving our sins (*1 John* 1:9) in Christ. The sentence of death against sinners who are denounced by the law was inflicted by God upon Christ! This satisfaction was most agreeable to divine wisdom. Since the fall of Adam, the only way sinners can appear in comfort before the justice of God is in the obedience and suffering of Jesus Christ, in the righteousness of our mediator. No other way can the justice of God be satisfied and our sins pardoned, but in Christ our righteousness! Jehovah-Tsidkenu, the Lord our righteousness!

Thomas Brooks, *Works*, v:222-225

Blessed are those whose lawless deeds are forgiven, and whose sins are covered.

Romans 4:7

Through the imputation of Christ's righteousness believers are righteous in the sight of God—full and complete as if they fulfilled the law themselves. Christ fulfilled the law for us both actively and passively. He not only performed what the law required, but suffered the penalty that the law inflicted. No one can have fellowship with God until he is clothed with his righteousness. The Lord is as true and faithful with his threatenings as his promises. As Adam's transgression is imputed to all his posterity, who are liable to eternal death, so Christ's obedience is imputed to the members of his body. Oh, what wonderful wisdom, grace, and love is here manifested! When we were not able to satisfy the penalty of the law, Christ became both redemption and righteousness for us! This imputed righteousness is the righteousness required by the law perfectly performed to the utmost iota. It fully satisfies the Father's judicial anger and fury. Christ's righteousness is so perfect, so full, so exact, so complete, so as to fully satisfy the justice of God, that the divine justice cries out—'I have enough, and I require no more.' The believing sinner may rejoice and triumph in God's justice as well as his mercy. If there is no accusation against the Lord Jesus there can be none against the believer. The second Adam is able to save to the uttermost all that come to God through him (*Heb.* 7:25). Christ bestows a better righteousness than Adam lost. The sinner receives a safer, higher, more honourable and durable estate than that from which Adam fell. All the attributes of God acquiesce in the righteousness of Christ, so that a believer may look upon the holiness and justice of God and rejoice and lie down in peace. It cancels every bond and presents us perfect in the sight of God!

Thomas Brooks, *Works*, v:225-227

The Lord will rescue me from every evil deed and bring me safely into his heavenly kingdom.

2 Timothy 4:18

The imputed righteousness of Christ will answer all of the fears, doubts, and objections of your soul. How shall I look up to God? —In the righteousness of Christ. How shall I have communion with a holy God?—In the righteousness of Christ. How shall I find acceptance with God?—In the righteousness of Christ. How shall I die?—In the righteousness of Christ. How shall I stand before the judgment seat?—In the righteousness of Christ. The only sure way under all the temptations, fears, conflicts, doubts, and disputes, is by faith to remember Christ and the sufferings of Christ your mediator and surety. O Christ, I am your sin, but you are my righteousness; I am your curse, but you are my blessing; I am your death, but you are my life; I am the wrath of God to you, but you are the love of God to me; I am your hell, but you are my heaven. His righteousness answers all objections, though there may be a million of them made against the good estate of a believer. This is a precious truth, worth more than a world, that all our sins are pardoned. In Christ, justice and mercy kiss each other, yea justice says, 'I am pleased.' We own a kingdom that will not shake, one eternal in the heavens. We have a certificate of guarantee for all the happiness and blessedness in the world to come. The righteousness of Christ is your life, your joy, your comfort, your crown, your confidence, your heaven, and your all. In righteousness you may safely and comfortably live, and happily and quietly die. Ah, that believers would dwell much upon this truth. The righteousness of Christ cannot be lost; it is from everlasting to everlasting. When once this white raiment is put upon a believer, it can never fall off. Interest in his righteousness guarantees all the glory of the heavenly kingdom!

Thomas Brooks, *Works*, v:238-240

Jesus answered him, 'Truly, truly, I say to you, unless one is born again he cannot see the kingdom of God.'

John 3:3

It is impossible for men to convert themselves by their own strength and industry, or by exercising their natural abilities and principles of the soul. What is gained after this manner of gradual acquisition, and not instantaneously begotten by God, is entirely of a different nature. All that men can do by their own strength and industry is to gradually improve the qualities they already have by nature, and therefore it is impossible by this only to bring to pass anything that is not already present in the nature of the soul. The new birth requires an immediate infusion or operation of the divine being upon the soul. Grace is an immediate work of God's almighty power! It is like the change made on Lazarus when Christ called him from the grave. At the call of Christ, there was immediate life! Conversion is frequently described in Scripture as a 'calling'. The call is done at once, and not gradually. Christ, through his great power, must only speak the powerful word, and it is done, and the sinner immediately comes! The miracles of Christ were types of conversion, because of their instantaneous accomplishment. With a spoken word, the sea was calm. Knowledge and conviction may be gradual, but conversion—in which a person is brought out of a state of total corruption and depravity into a state of grace—happens in a moment, as the opening of the eyes of the blind. He is now in a new state entirely different in nature and kind from before! It is the creation of an instant. God speaks, and it is done; he commands, and it stands fast! The natural man is destitute of any sense of the things of the Spirit. He has no knowledge of spiritual things, and no fellowship with Christ. But Christ calls and the sinner immediately comes. The first moment sinners have any life is the moment Christ calls!

Jonathan Edwards, *Selections from Unpublished Writings*, pp. 19-29

He who loves me will be loved by my Father, and I will love him and manifest myself to him.

John 14:21

The saving grace that lives as a principle in the hearts of the saints, that distinguishes them from unconverted men, is their love for God. Love is the very essence of Christianity and proves the sincerity of our faith. Without it, the greatest and most glittering show in religion is nothing. Love is the essential soul of all grace. It is so essential that all religion without it is vain and hypocritical. There can be no true honour or praise without it. The fear of God, without love, is like the fear the devils have. Outward obedience, the forms of religion, and outward devotion, without love, is a practical lie. There is not a devil in hell that would not perform outward rites that many a man has performed with no love for God, and a great deal more in like circumstances if they would hope to gain by it. From fear of torment, the devil seemed to be religious when he fell down before Jesus (*Luke* 8:28). Here is external worship: The devil is religious—he prays; he takes a humble posture—he falls down and lies prostrate; he prays earnestly—with a loud voice; he uses humble expressions—I beseech you; he uses adoring expressions—Jesus, Son of the God Most High. Nothing was lacking here, but love! If a child was respectful to his father from fear alone, or hopes of a larger inheritance, but not from the heart, would that be acceptable to the father? Love for God is the enjoyment of the loveliness and sweetness of his divine nature as one's chief good. When once the soul is brought to relish the excellency of the divine nature, it will naturally incline to God in every way. It will seek to be with him and enjoy him. It will be glad that he is happy. It will desire his glory, and desire to do his will in all things. To once taste the loveliness of God makes one long more for it.

Jonathan Edwards, *Selections from Unpublished Writings*, pp. 30-38

Be watchful, stand firm in the faith, act like men, be strong.

1 Corinthians 16:13

The Christian life requires holy courage. As we become soldiers of Christ and resolve to live in earnest, we must reckon upon opposition and prepare to endure hardness in the practice of our duties. Not only do we meet with difficulties from a degenerate and sinful world, many other trials attend the Christian life. Sorrows and sufferings belong to human nature in this fallen and unhappy state: 'Man is born to trouble as the sparks fly upward' (*Job* 5:7). Earth is a stage of conflict, a scene of probation where each of us must act our parts under the eye and notice of God, our supreme governor and final rewarder. He expects that we should put on a sacred hardiness of soul, armed with power and courage, that we may endure to the end. There is both active and passive courage. Active courage is that tenor of soul that attempts and ventures upon any bold act of duty that may endanger your present state. It is a steadiness and bravery of mind that is undaunted at opposition or threatening dangers. Passive valour is that constancy of soul that enables us to bear sufferings without repinings or outward tokens of sinking or despondency. Behold Jesus, the Son of God, as he suffered shameful indignities as the powers of darkness fell upon him with fury. He endured such hostility of sinners against himself lest you faint in your minds (*Heb.* 12:1-3). Or behold a Paul in the midst of a violent multitude of unbelieving Jews. We too are soldiers of the cross marching under the banner of the Redeemer to fight all the armies of darkness. Consider the promises of the divine presence and help for us as God encourages and chides his people into courage. Then finally consider the large and never-fading crown of glory that awaits the conqueror at the end of the conflict (*Rev.* 2:10).

Isaac Watts, *Works*, 1:325-338

If God is for us, who can be against us?

Romans 8:31

Fear is an excellent provision of God to guard us from many dangers when fixed on a proper object and proper degree. When God is the object of our fear, we are able to maintain a holy awe of his majesty, and it awakens a constant desire in us to please him. But when fear ruffles the spirit, throws the soul into unrest, and turns us from a steady course of duty, it becomes a sinful and forbidden passion. For some, fear is a constant tyrant over them. This ought to stir them up as far as possible to shake off this bondage that robs them of comfort. May the Spirit help the following methods to be happily successful: (1.) Keep your faith awake and living. Remember you are under the special eye and protection of your God and Saviour! Brighten your faith and hope daily by a frequent examination of your hearts, and walking before God. Commit your souls into the hands of Jesus and his Spirit for pardoning and renewing grace. A living faith gives divine courage. Faith is a noble shield to ward off fear, and our helmet is the hope of salvation. (2.) Take heed of defiling your souls with sensuality. Guilt will create fear and fill the soul with a perplexing tumult of thoughts. (3.) Consider the covenant of grace as a blessed treasury. Here is an armour of defence found for every assault and danger! Get a large acquaintance with the promises of the gospel, that in every special time of need you may have a suitable word of refuge and support. In special seasons of trial keep your mind fixed upon some single promise that is most suited to the present danger or suffering, and to the present taste and relish of your soul. Fixing and living on a particular word of grace for the whole day will let it abide on your heart and whisper to your soul with divine sweetness in the dark and solitary watches of the night. In a fresh assault, fly to the word you have chosen for your refuge and meditation.

Isaac Watts, *Works*, 1:338-340

The name of the Lord is a strong tower;
the righteous man runs into it and is safe.
Proverbs 18:10

Combating sinful fear, Part 2. (4.) Pursue the spirit of prayer, and moral strength and courage will descend upon you! Address the throne of God with earnestness and faith, and cry to the God of your salvation without ceasing. He gives renewed strength for the battle, courage in the midst of terrors, and he can preserve and secure us in the most extreme peril. He may repel the most imminent danger, and rebukes the spirit of fear to gain moral courage. While at the mercy seat, keep an eye on Christ Jesus—your mediator, advocate and the captain of your salvation. He is engaged to see you brought safely home to heaven. Many a feeble Christian, in coming to the mercy seat with overwhelming fears, has risen from his knees with a heavenly calmness and composure! The army of fears has vanished, and he has gone out to face the most formidable of his adversaries with divine resolution and courage. (5.) Wean yourself more from the flesh and the delights belonging to this mortal life. Learn to put off a little of that sinful tenderness for self which we brought into the world with us. One of the first lessons in the school of Christ is self-denial (*Matt.* 16:24). We must subdue this self-love and softness if we would be good soldiers of Jesus Christ and gain a spirit of sacred courage and resolution. We must be dead to the things of the flesh and sense if we would gain a victory over the complaints and groanings of nature. (6.) Endeavour to keep yourselves always employed in some proper work, that your fears may be diverted. If our thoughts and hands are idle and empty, we lie open to the invasion of our fears from every side. The imagination at leisure can sit and brood over its own terrors. Lack of occupation exposes the mind to frightful images that fancy can furnish.

Isaac Watts, *Works*, 1:341-342

Therefore we will not fear though the earth gives way, though the mountains be moved into the heart of the sea.

Psalm 46:2

Combating sinful fear, Part 3. (7.) Keep your eye on the hand of God in all the affairs of men. View his powerful and over-ruling providence in all things, including your most troubling fears. Learn to see God in all things, and behold him as your God, and the distressing fears within you will have little influence to awaken the passions of your soul. Do thunder and lightning frighten you? In whose hand is the thunder? Who directs its flashes and every sweeping blast of wind or fire to its appointed place? Do political upheavals awaken your fears? Rejoice and stand firm amidst the tumult and shaking of the nations (*Psa.* 46). Perhaps personal dangers threaten your good name, estate, flesh, or your life. The presence of God is a universal spring of comfort and courage, and a wide spreading shield against every mischief. Does slander, poverty, or sickness frighten you? Remember that diseases are servants of our Lord Jesus, and he can bid pains and anguish of body go or come as he pleases. None will tarry with you beyond his appointed moment. He is a wise physician and he will deal tenderly with you. Are you afraid of persecuting enemies? These are but instruments to execute his divine purposes, and are chained under the sovereign dominion of Christ. They cannot move or act beyond his permission! We are all immortal till our work is done! (8.) Recollect your own experiences of the goodness of God in carrying you through former seasons of danger and sorrow. Remember how high the tempest of your fears has sometimes risen, and how God has sunk them at once into silence. Remember how extreme your danger has been, but the eye of God has found a path of safety for you! He has led you as one blind by the way you didn't know, and has made darkness light before you, and the crooked straight!

Isaac Watts, *Works*, 1:342-344

Fear not, you worm Jacob ... I am the one who helps you, declares the Lord; your Redeemer is the Holy One of Israel.

Isaiah 41:14

Combating sinful fear, Part 4. (9.) Consider the divine commands to put aside fear. Remember that exercising faith and showing courage are duties as well as blessings! 'Fear not' is often repeated because God knows very well how prone our feeble natures are to become frightened at every appearance of danger (*Matt.* 10:28). The Lord of Hosts alone is the proper object of our supreme fear. He will overrule and abolish all other fears. The fear of the Lord is an effectual cure for sinful fear. Christ chided his disciples when they were afraid in the storm. For a Christian to give himself up to the wild tyranny of his fears is contrary to the very spirit and design of the gospel (*2 Tim.* 1:7). Remember that you are the sons and daughters of God. It is below your dignity to yield to this slavery. Your Father himself reproves, and your Redeemer forbids it. (10.) Consider the many advantages that arise from a courageous spirit in the midst of dangers: It establishes your feet on a solid rock in the midst of storms; it motivates you to practise every duty; it prevents many of the mischiefs you fear; it will preserve the soul in serenity and calmness under painful events of providence; it will make sorrows lighter, and the heaviest afflictions become more tolerable. If we give in to fear, it throws the whole frame of our nature into tumult and confusion. Fear is a dreadful bondage of the soul, and holds the man in chains. It feels the smart of those very evils that frighten us at a distance that may never come near to us. When afraid, the very sufferings which are prevented by the mercy of God we must endure in our thoughts. We must feel the pain of them by indulgence in excessive fear. But always remember, Jesus can support me in the heaviest distresses. He can bear me on the wings of faith and hope, high above all the turmoils of life.

Isaac Watts, *Works*, 1:344-348

I have been crucified with Christ. It is no longer I who live, but Christ who lives in me.

Galatians 2:20

True faith is full of self-denial. Faith keeps us low. Paul didn't want us to be mistaken—'It is Christ that lives in me, I don't live in my own power. It is Christ that keeps house. I mortify my corruptions and vanquish my temptations, but I am a debtor to Christ for the strength.' Blessed Paul acknowledges that God is the sole founder and benefactor of all the good he has and does; 'I laboured more abundantly than they all, yet not I, but the grace of God which was in me.' Jacob said, 'these are the children which God has graciously given me.' All is *ex dono Dei*—from the gift of God. How hesitant are the saints to write about themselves concerning good works or abilities! 'Are you able,' said the king to Daniel, 'to make known unto me the dream which I have seen?' Now mark, Daniel does not speak as the astrologers; he was careful to stand clear from any stealing of God's glory, and therefore he answered—'There is a God in heaven that reveals secrets.' The secret was revealed from God to Daniel. The faith that enabled him to beg the mercy of God also enabled him to deny himself and give the entire glory of it to God himself. As rivers empty their streams again into the bosom of the sea from which it was received, so men of faith give the praise of what they do unto God who enables them. Faith is not like Nebuchadnezzar, who looked no higher than himself in building his great Babylon—'Is this not Babylon that I have built by my power and for the honour of my majesty?' But faith teaches us to blot out our own name, and write God's name for all that is accomplished! When the servants brought in their accounting, mark, it was not—'I have gained', but 'Your pound has gained!' He that did the very least said—'what I have kept.' The least doers are the greatest boasters! (*Luke* 19:16-20).

William Gurnall, *The Christian in Complete Armour*, ii:35-36

And he told them a parable to the effect that they ought always to pray and not lose heart.

Luke 18:1

Faith cannot but pray as a baby that comes crying into the world. Faith assists the soul in prayer with wrestling grace. Faith takes hold of God and will not easily take a denial. It fires up the affections, and sets them at work. Faith uses arguments and helps the soul to wield and use them, both valiantly and victoriously, upon the Almighty. Faith teaches us to press God with them, humbly, yet boldly. Faith melts promises into arguments as a soldier melts lead into bullets, and then helps the Christian to send them with force to heaven in fervent prayer. Faith also enables the soul to persevere in the work. False faith may show some mettle for a while, but will give up at length. The hypocrite will not pray always, he will break at last. He prays himself weary of praying. Something or other will in time make him quarrel with that duty which he never inwardly liked. The sincere believer has in him that which makes it impossible to quit. Prayer is the very breath of faith. It is true that the believer, through negligence, may find it more difficult at times, but the Christian's needs, sins, and temptations continue to return upon him, and he cannot but continue also to pray for them. Faith supports the soul to expect a gracious answer. It fills the soul with expectation. This expectation quiets the soul while it waits for its return. Sometimes faith comes from prayer in triumph, and before the answer is received it cries—'victory'. At other times disquieting thoughts continue to burden the soul after praying, but faith yet keeps the head above the waves as they abate little by little like a falling tide. Faith is not overwhelmed though fears are not yet all drained away. The ship that rides at anchor is safe—though it may be a little tossed to and fro while the anchor keeps its hold.

William Gurnall, *The Christian in Complete Armour,* 11:36-40

By faith Sarah herself received power to conceive … since she considered him faithful who had promised.

Hebrews 11:11

The more a Christian can rely on the bare word alone in a promise, the stronger his faith. If you trust a man's word alone without a surety when you lend him money, this shows a greater confidence in the man. When we trust God for his bare promises, we trust him on his own credit, and this is faith indeed. He that walks without a staff is stronger than he that needs one to lean on. The promise is the ground that faith rests on. Sense and reason are crutches that a weak faith leans on. Can you bear up when the crutches of sense and present feeling are not at hand? Perhaps you sense God's love and favour upon you, and the sun is shining in the window of your heart. You feel at this moment that you will always trust God and never listen to your unbelieving thoughts again. But how do you find it when those sensible demonstrations are withdrawn, and some frowning providence comes? Do you presently doubt the promise in your thoughts, not knowing whether you can venture to cast anchor on it or not? Because you have lost the sense of his love, does the eye of faith fail you also in trusting his mercy and truth in the promise? If so, the eye of your faith is yet weak, since it needs the spectacles of sense to support it. Christian, bless God for the experiences of sensible tastes of his love, but these are not proof of a strong faith. Learn to lean more on the promise, and less on sensible expressions of God's love, whether present feeling or past experiences. You may improve these, just don't lean on them. A strong man may make good use of a cane now and then to defend himself when set upon by a thief or dog in his way, and so a Christian may make good use of his experiences in some temptations, though he does not lay the weight of his faith upon them, but on the bare promises of God.

William Gurnall, *The Christian in Complete Armour*, II:60-61

In hope he believed against hope, that he should become the father of many nations.

Romans 4:18

Can you bear up in faith upon a promise when the crutch of reason breaks under you? Does your faith fall to the ground with it? A strong faith indeed can trample upon the improbabilities and impossibilities that reason casts upon the performance of a promise by God. Faith gives credit to the truth of God notwithstanding. Noah fell hard to work on the ark, giving credence to the threats and promises of God. It never troubled his mind to justify the matter to his reason, or question that these strange things could come to pass! Abraham's faith was strong when reason could have questioned the fulfilment of a son in his old age—'He did not weaken in faith when he considered his own body' (*Rom.* 4:19). Skilful swimmers are not afraid to go in deep water, though young learners must stay next to the shore to touch the bottom. Strong faith does not fear when God carries them beyond the depth of reason; 'We do not know what to do,' said good Jehoshaphat, 'but our eyes are on you' (*2 Chron.* 20:12). It was as if he said, 'we are in a sea of troubles, beyond our own help, and we have no idea how we can get out of this problem; but our eyes are on you. We do not dare give up our case as desperate so long as there is strength in your arm, tenderness in your heart, and truth in your promise!' However, weak faith looks for some footing for reason to stand on. It is taken up with how to reconcile the promise with the understanding. When Jesus said, 'you give them something to eat', his disciples asked him, 'Shall we go and buy two hundred denarii worth of bread?' As if Christ's bare word could not spare that cost and trouble! 'How shall I know this?' said Zacharias to the angel, 'For I am an old man' (*Luke* 1:18). Alas! his faith was not strong enough to digest, at present, this strange news!

William Gurnall, *The Christian in Complete Armour*, II:61

Preach the word … For the time is coming when people will not endure sound teaching … and will turn away from listening to the truth.

2 Timothy 4:2-4

If it is in your power, live under a faithful, searching, serious, powerful minister, and diligently attend his public teaching and private counsel. Though God can work without means, it is his ordinary way to work by means, and we should not neglect duty upon a presumptuous expectation of a miraculous or extraordinary work. Alas, how apt are the best to cool if they are not kept warm by a powerful ministry! We are apt to lose the hatred of sin, the tenderness of conscience, fervency in prayer, and the delights and power of heavenly meditations. How apt is faith to stagger if it is not powerfully undergirded. How hardly will we keep the heat of love, the confidence of hope, the resolution of obedience, without the help of a powerful ministry. Can any that are not blind or proud imagine that they are so holy and good that they are above the necessity of such assistance? Alas, we are under languishing weakness and need to be fed by the best, or we shall soon decay. The minister must have the savour of the Spirit in him to be fit to make us spiritual, and the savour of faith and love to kindle faith and love in us, and speak with feeling to make us feel! Christians are, like infants, unable to help themselves, and need the continual help of others. God will have no men to be self-sufficient; we all have need of one another. God uses us to be his messengers and instruments of conveying his mercies to each other! Our souls must receive their part of mercy as well as our bodies nourishment. Young Christians who are weak and inexperienced above all others should be desirous of help from an able, faithful guide. Let the judgment of your pastor or judicious friend about the state of your souls be much regarded by you, though it is not infallible.

Richard Baxter, *Practical Works*, 1:44-46

But I say to you, Love your enemies and pray for those who persecute you.

Matthew 5:44

Take heed, lest any persecution or wrong from others provokes you to unwarranted passion, or deprives you of the love, meekness and innocence of a Christian. Don't think that such treatment is strange; suffering which makes your reason go down and your passions up is ordinary treatment for the godly. It is by overwhelming reason with passion and discontent that some wise men go mad, for passion is a short, imperfect madness. You will think in your passion that you do well when you do ill, and you will not perceive the force of reason when it is never so plain and full against you. Remember, the great motive that caused the devil to persecute you is not to hurt your bodies, but to tempt your souls to impatience and sin. If it can be said of you like Job, 'in all of this Job did not sin', you have won the victory and are more than conquerors (*Rom.* 8:37-39). It is not a strange thing that the wicked should hate the godly, and the world should hate them that are 'chosen out of the world'. Why should this seem strange? This is the common lot for the faithful, and knowing this will better help us be prepared for it. Imitate your Lord, who 'when he was reviled, reviled not again; when he suffered, he threatened not, but committed all to him that judges righteously'. An angry zeal against those that cross and hurt us is so easily kindled and hardly suppressed. We are too ready to call fire down from heaven upon the enemies of the gospel. But Christ said, 'love your enemies, and bless them that curse you.' Take heed of giving way to secret wishes of hurt to your adversaries, or to reproachful words against them. Take heed of hurting yourself by passion or sin because others hurt you by slanders or persecutions. Keep in the way of your duty, and leave your names and lives to God!

Richard Baxter, *Practical Works*, 1:48

You shall not take the name of the Lord your God in vain, for the Lord will not hold him guiltless who takes his name in vain.

Exodus 20:7

The tongue is an unruly member. All the parts and organs of the body are defiled with sin, as every branch of wormwood is bitter, but the tongue is full of deadly poison (*James* 3:8). There is no one member of the body that breaks forth more in God's dishonour than the tongue. Great care must be taken that the name of God is not profaned by us, or taken in vain. We take God's name in vain—(1.) When we speak irreverently of his name, or use it in idle discourse. He is not to be spoken of but with a holy awe upon our hearts. To bring his name in at every turn when we are not thinking of him, or to say, 'O God!'—is to take his name in vain. How many are guilty here! Though they have God in their mouths, they have the devil in their hearts. (2.) We take God's name in vain when we confess his name but in our works deny him. When men's lives and tongues are contrary to one another they make use of God's name to abuse him, or to worship him with lips but not the heart. Hypocrites seem to honour God, but do not love him. Their eyes are lifted up to heaven, but their hearts are rooted in the earth. (3.) When you make trifling oaths in God's name. Many seldom mention God's name but in oaths, and that rashly and sinfully: vile swearing, horrid, appalling oaths not to be named. Swearers, like mad dogs, fly in the face of heaven; and when they are angered, spew out their blasphemous venom on God's sacred majesty. When something runs against them, they run against God in oaths and curses. (4.) When we use our tongues in any way to dishonour God's name, or murmur at his providence, as if he has dealt hardly with us! We should speak of God only with the sacred reverence that is due to the infinite majesty of heaven.

Thomas Watson, *The Ten Commandments*, pp. 84-92

But grow in the grace and knowledge of our Lord and Saviour Jesus Christ.

2 Peter 3:18

A young Christian should be careful not to be too confident concerning their first understanding of difficult questions where Scripture is not very plain. Hold them modestly with due suspicion, being open to further investigation, supposing it is possible, or probable upon better instruction, evidence, and maturity, that you may, in such things, change your mind! Some take a position on issues along party lines, and hold to all that the party holds. The essentials of Christianity are received from divine, infallible revelation, but controversies about less necessary things cannot be absolutely settled by young beginners without hypocrisy. When it is certain that you have a dark, uncertain understanding of any point, to think it is clear and certain is to deceive yourselves by pride. To cry out against all uncertainty about it is to foolishly suppose that all men can be as wise and certain. Now reason and experience will tell you that a young understanding will not grasp the key points that a nearer examination may. If your conclusions are settled upon conceit, for all you know, you may be in error and are confident in it! And then how far may you go in seducing others? For a man to be confident in that which he does not know, is the way to keep him ignorant, and to shut the door of further information. When opinion is fixed by prejudice or conceit, there is no ready entrance for light. To be ungroundedly confident is to take up your teacher's word instead of faith and knowledge of your own. If you will never change your first opinions, how will you grow in understanding? You will be no wiser with age! Prejudice will make you resist the light and lose much truth. Hold fast the essentials well established on clear and certain truth, and for other matters allow time and study to alter younger opinions.

Richard Baxter, *Practical Works*, 1:49-50

No good thing does he withhold from those who walk uprightly.

Psalm 84:11

Adversity cannot be called absolutely an evil, as prosperity cannot be called absolutely a good. They are things indifferent because they may be used either for the honour or dishonour of God. Crosses are not excluded from being good when they may bring good. Our Saviour did not promise wealth and honour to his followers, nor did he think it worth suffering to bestow such gifts upon his children. He made heaven their happiness, and earth, their hell. The cross is their badge here, and the crown their reward hereafter. But God never leaves good men so bare, but that he provides for their necessities (*Psa.* 84:11). If anything is good, an upright man may expect it from God's providence. If it is not good, he should not desire it. The little that good men have is better than the highest enjoyments of wicked men (*Prov.* 16:8). Wicked prosperity is like a shadow that glides away in a moment. But God regards the state of the righteous and all that befalls them. God works all with respect to their everlasting inheritance. No righteous man in his right mind would exchange his sharpest afflictions for a wicked man's prosperity. It cannot be bad with the righteous in the worst condition. Would any but a madman exchange medicine for poison? It is better to be on a dunghill with intimate fellowship with God, than upon a throne without it. Crosses and sufferings fit good men for special service here, and eternal happiness hereafter. Fire refines the gold, which prepares it for service! Without crosses, how could you exercise heroic faith, and how could you believe against hope, if there was not something to contradict your hopes? In future glory, great will be their praise and public honour from God's mouth and a crown of honour set upon their heads. Every stroke only beautifies the crown that much more!

Stephen Charnock, *Works*, 1:34-36

Love the Lord, all you his saints!
The Lord preserves the faithful.

Psalm 31:23

We love God for the good things that we hope to receive from him. To love God for the hope of heaven is not a mercenary kind of love; not only may we love him for this, it is our duty, we must! Is it not an infinite kindness of God to make us promises? Our love for God will be perfected in heaven, but do we not now love him for our perfect freedom from sin, the perfection of grace, the society of saints and angels? We love him for all our temporal mercies, and how excellent is this love! Also, we love God for himself, because he is the most excellent good. Thus, the soul can rise and say, 'Lord, though I should never have a smile from you while I live, yet I love you.' There are few that can rise so high. In the case of sore temptations or long desertions, or when God smites them, they love him still! Does not grace work in the soul like medicine to the sick? The mother gives her child medicine that makes the child sick while it's working. The child, while sick, instead of being angry with the mother for the medicine, goes to the mother, hangs about her, lays its head in her bosom, and loves her though she gave him the medicine. So God deals with his children. Though some dealings make them heartbroken, they cling to him, fearing nothing but sin, and they can bear anything but his displeasure. These love God for himself. It is also true that God's love for them, all the while, is very great, though they do not perceive it. We should love him more than he loves us, but we never can. 'O Lord I beseech you, how much do you love me? Is it weakly and carelessly according to *my* goodness? That be far from you, Lord! You love your people incomparably more than you are loved by them!' O my soul, that you may be wholly filled and possessed with the sweetness of so great a love!

Samuel Annesley, *Puritan Sermons 1659–1689*, 1:598-604

God is love, and whoever abides in love abides in God, and God abides in him.

1 John 4:16

By faith we live *upon* God; by obedience we live *to* God; but by love we live in God! We live in God in some little resemblance to the child living in the mother's womb. What the mother loves, the child loves; what the mother longs for, the child longs for; in the mother's health, the child is well. The child lives in the womb in a far different manner from how he will live in the world. Though it cannot stir out of its enclosure, it never cries nor complains of its imprisonment. So is the soul that entirely loves God. He hates what God hates, and loves what God loves. His life is far above the life of others, and it desires no greater liberty than to be, as it were, imprisoned *in* God, to have no will of its own, but to only seek what God graciously concurs with. Yet it is so far from esteeming this a restraint, that it counts it the highest happiness of this imperfect state. He feels a sweetness in it beyond what the heathen who spoke of it ever thought of: 'In God we live, move, and have our being.' Love is a self-emptying and self-satisfying grace. It is a kind of pilgrimage from self. He that loves is absent from himself, doesn't think of himself, and does not provide for himself. But O, how great is the gain of renouncing ourselves, and by this receiving God and ourselves! We are, as it were, dead to ourselves, and alive to God; nay, more, by love we live *in* God. Love is a bold, strong, and constant grace of the Spirit of God. Nothing can stand before it. Though our love is not perfect, it can never be totally and finally extinguished. If you fear your love is not sincere, consider: Do you study to please him? Do you fear to offend him? Do you prize his presence and mourn in his absence? Do not be discouraged, your love for God is infallibly sincere.

Samuel Annesley, *Puritan Sermons 1659-1689*, 1:605-608

How then can I do this great wickedness and sin against God?

Genesis 39:9

There are a number of things that the mind of a believer is obliged to consider diligently for the preservation of the soul from the deception of sin. (1.) Sin is forbidden by a sovereign God, under whose absolute sovereignty I am. I am dependent upon him for life and eternity! Joseph focused on this in his great temptation (*Gen.* 39:9). The mind should always attend to this in all suggestions of the law of sin, especially when they gain advantage by some suitable or vigorous temptation. (2). Next, consider the punishment appointed unto sin in the law. We st keep in mind a due sense of the punishment that is due every sin. If men do not consider this, it aggravates their sins (*Rom.* 1:32). (3). Next consider the love and kindness of God against whom every sin is committed. This is a prevailing consideration, if rightly and graciously managed in the soul: 'God will be a Father unto us' (cf. *2 Cor.* 6:18), unto all eternity! If the mind is attentive to this consideration, there can be no prevailing attempt made upon it by the power of sin. Consider the privileges that we enjoy! And, besides the love and mercy we have in common, we also have special mercies and particular applications of covenant love to our souls! These provisions laid in by God may be borne in mind against an hour of temptation. (4). There is a constraining efficacy in the consideration of the blood and mediation of Christ, and the indwelling of the Spirit, the greatest privilege that we have on earth! The due consideration of how he is grieved by sin should be insisted on. These duties of the mind should be considered for particular sins and temptations. We should diligently and carefully attend to them and have them in a continual readiness to oppose all the lusts, acts, battles, attempts, and rages of sin.

John Owen, *Works*, vi:238-242

Those who live according to the Spirit set their minds on the things of the Spirit.

Romans 8:5

Consider three ways that sin seeks to draw the mind from due attendance upon spiritual thoughts, and to deprive the soul of this great preservative and antidote against sin's poison. (1.) *By sloth.* It draws the mind to be spiritually slothful and negligent in this duty. We are slothful if we are careless in our diligence, or make faint endeavours in the discharge of our duties, and do not continue. Where the slothful person was one day, there he is the next; yea, where he was one year, there he is the next! His endeavours are faint, cold, and vanishing. He makes no progress by them, but is always beginning and never finishing his work. He is content in his coldness and negligence. If the deceit of sin has once drawn away the mind into this frame, it lays him open to every temptation and incursion of sin. (2.) Sin seeks to draw away the mind from its watch and duty *by surprise.* It falls in conjunction with some urging temptation, and surprises the mind into thoughts quite of another nature than those which it ought to insist upon in its own defence. It lays hold of the mind as it suddenly thinks about the present sin. If spiritual thoughts are suggested, the mind is so filled with the thought of the sin that they make no impression on the soul and do not remain long. Here, therefore, lies the great wisdom of the soul: reject the very first motions of sin, because by parleys with them the mind may be drawn off from attending to its preservatives, and the whole person will rush into evil. (3.) The third way sin draws away the mind is *by frequent and persevering solicitations*, and finally at last making a conquest of it. But this does not happen without an open neglect of the soul. The failure to stir yourself up and give an effectual rebuke in the strength and by the grace of Christ against sin, is what results in its prevalency.

John Owen, *Works*, VI:242-244

But each person is tempted when he is lured and enticed by his own desire.

James 1:14

Indwelling sin seeks not only to deceive the mind, but to entice the affections. When a man is enticed, it is like being entangled as a fish deceived with the bait of a hook that holds him to his destruction. Consider three marks of being entangled with sin. (1.) The affections are certainly entangled when they stir up *frequent imaginations* about the proposed object to which the deceit of sin leads and entices them. Achan first saw the wedge of gold and Babylonian garment, and then he coveted them. He rolled them and the pleasures around in his imagination, and then fixed his heart on obtaining them. The heart may have a settled, fixed hatred of sin, but yet, if a man finds that the imagination of the mind is frequently solicited by it, his affections are secretly enticed and entangled with it. (2.) This entanglement is increased when the imagination can lodge these vain thoughts with secret delight. Such abiding thoughts of delight toward forbidden objects are greatly sinful even if the consent of the will is not obtained, and should be abhorred. These thoughts are messengers that carry sin to and fro between the imagination and the affections. These thoughts will more and more entangle the affections and so little by little the soul will break forth into sin. If the will parts with its sovereignty, sin is actually conceived. (3.) If you are ready to think little of sin, or justify it when it is committed, it is evidence that your affections are entangled with it. It is a great part of the deceit of sin to encourage thoughts that lesson sin before the mind. 'Is it not a little one?' or, 'There is mercy provided.' When the soul is willing, as it were, to be tempted and courted by sin, and to hearken to its dalliances and solicitations, it has lost its affection for Christ, and is entangled.

John Owen, *Works*, VI:245-247

Keep your heart with all vigilance,
for from it flow the springs of life.
Proverbs 4:23

Sin takes advantage to entice and ensnare the soul through its affections. It presents the sin as desirable and exceeding satisfactory to the corrupt part of our affections. This is the laying of bait. Bait is something desirable and suitable that is proposed to the hungry creature for its satisfaction, and by all of its craft it renders it desirable and suitable. Thus, sinful and inordinate objects are presented by the help of the imagination unto the soul for the affections to cleave to, and satisfy its corrupt lusts. It presents unto sensual and covetous persons, and in some degree to believers themselves, its 'wine sparking in the cup', the beauty of the adulteress, and the riches of the world. It seeks to prevail with the imagination to solicit the heart, by representing this false painted beauty or pretended satisfaction of sin, so that when Satan with any peculiar temptation falls in to its assistance, it often inflames all the affection and puts the whole soul into disorder! The deception of sin also hides the danger by covering the hook with the bait. Sin so possesses the mind and affections with the bait and the desirableness of sin that it diverts it from the contemplation of the danger. Sin will use a thousand wiles to hide from you the terror of the Lord and the outcome of sin: hopes of pardon, plans for future repentance, present importunity of lust, opportunities and occasions, and balancing duties with enjoyments of lust to the uttermost in pleasure, will hide the danger from you. It has a thousand wiles. If we would not be enticed and in danger of the conception of sin, let us take heed to our affections which are of so great a concern in the course of our obedience. Above all things, keep the heart so it is not entangled in sin. This is to be attended to with diligence. There is no safety without it! Watch the heart.

JOHN OWEN, *Works*, VI:247-249

But far be it from me to boast except in the cross of our Lord Jesus Christ, by which the world has been crucified to me.

Galatians 6:14

How do we protect our affections from sin's deception? First, set your affections upon heavenly things (*Col.* 3:2), which enables you to mortify sin. Let them enjoy the first place in your heart—God himself in his beauty and glory; the Lord Jesus Christ, who is altogether lovely and the chief of ten thousand; grace and glory, and the mysteries of the gospel. If our affections are filled with these, as is our duty, it is our happiness. What access could sin have to our souls with its painted pleasures, sugared poisons, and envenomed baits? We would loathe all its proposals as abominable things! Second, set your affections upon the cross of Christ. This is exceedingly effective in disappointing the whole work of indwelling sin. A heart filled with the cross of Christ casts death upon sin, making it undesirable with no seeming beauty. It crucifies me to the world and makes my heart, affections, and desires dead unto these things. It roots up corrupt lusts and affections, and leaves no principle to fulfil them. Labour therefore to fill your heart with the cross of Christ. Consider the sorrows he underwent, the curse he bore, the blood he shed, the cries he put forth, the love that was in all this to your souls, and the mystery of the grace of God in it! Meditate on the vileness, the demerit, and punishment of sin as represented in the cross, the blood, and the death of Christ. Was Christ crucified for sin, and shall not our hearts be crucified with him unto sin? Shall we give entertainment unto that, or hearken unto its trifling conversation, which wounded, pierced, and slew our dear Lord Jesus? God forbid! Fill your affections with the cross of Christ, that there may be no room for sin. The world once put him out of the house into a stable when he came to save us; now let him turn the world out of doors when he comes to sanctify us!

John Owen, *Works*, VI:249-251

A good name is better than precious ointment.

Ecclesiastes 7:1

The Old Testament often speaks of the advantage of a good name. A jewel set in iron does not have the lustre as when set in gold. A good name will make you more useful, and a blemished instrument is of little use. The priests under the law were to have no outward blemish or deformity. It is a qualification for a pastor to have a good reputation with those on the outside (*1 Tim.* 3:7): that is, an unstained life in the world. Who would drink from a dirty fountain or take food out of a leprous hand? We should be careful not to defame the good name of a believer, and cross God's ordination. How you ought to tremble when you go about to take off the crown which God has put on their heads! 'Why then were you not afraid to speak against my servant Moses?' (*Num.* 12:8). What? Against Moses! Did not your knees smite against each other in fear? A man should be afraid to dishonour those whom God will honour (*Esther* 6:9). You are the worst of thieves when you rob someone of their most precious jewel—there is no treasure like a good name! 'A good name is to be chosen rather than great riches' (*Prov.* 22:1). This is the very devil's sin. It is his proper work to be the accuser of the brethren and to frame mischievous insinuations against the children of God (*Rev.* 12:10). The devil does not commit adultery, break the Sabbath, or dishonour parents, but he does accuse the brethren. You are acting the devil's part while you are scandalizing those that are eminent in grace. They 'whet their tongues like swords, who aim bitter words like arrows' (*Psa.* 64:3). We should rejoice in the reputation of those with a worthy name, and not blemish it. We should preserve the reputation of others because it is a good means to keep our own. Take heed what you say about those more zealous than you. John the Baptist's head in a charger is an ordinary dish at many meals!

Thomas Manton, *By Faith*, pp. 63-65

Whoever would draw near to God must believe that he exists and that he rewards those who seek him.

Hebrews 11:6

The fountain of all obedience, gratitude, and service to God is a firm belief that he is a rewarder of those who seek him! God delights to manifest himself in acts of grace rather than in acts of judgment. Mercy pleases him. Goodness and grace are natural to him. Anger, wrath and justice suppose our sin, and are extorted from him. Therefore, if we would have a right notion of God, we must believe in his goodness. God is called the 'Father of mercies' (*2 Cor.* 1:3). When he proclaimed his Name, we hear first of his mercy, and still more of his mercy (*Exod.* 34:6-7). This draws the heart of the creature to him. Luther said this is the whole design of the scripture, to represent God in such a manner: as bountiful and ready to do good to his creatures that come to him. God is a rewarder, but how?—Out of his own bounty and the liberality of his grace, not out of our merit and desert. Our reward is principally in heaven. Now is the time for exercise and service, and hereafter—our enjoyment. Alas! All that we have here is not our wages: it is the overflow and additional supply that God gives beyond the better portion that we expect from him. 'All other things' shall be added (*Matt.* 6:33), but these are over and above the bargain! A Christian does not count it his reward if God should bless him with comfort or increase in this life. God may cast in outward things to commend our portion and to make it more amiable to us. We are both soul and body. But he adds these additional blessings as minor things; it is heaven that we consider our portion. We that are heirs according to the hope of eternal life expect better things in a better state. There will come a time when the Lord, as an infinite and eternal being, will give us a far more exceeding and eternal weight of glory (*2 Cor.* 4:17).

Thomas Manton, *By Faith*, pp. 322-327

O God, you are my God; earnestly I seek you; my soul thirsts for you.

Psalm 63:1

A wise man will not lay a broad foundation unless he intends to build a suitable structure upon it. Since God has laid such a notable foundation in the blood of Christ, the death of his Son, he certainly has a notable and worthy blessing to bestow upon those who diligently seek him. God would not go to such an expense for nothing! It is much more than the world has to offer! The fullness of what God has provided for us is in the world to come. But what does it mean to diligently seek him? Seeking implies that this is our aim and scope, and the business of our lives and action. It is to enjoy God now until we come fully to enjoy him in heaven. The whole course of a Christian must be the seeking after God, and getting more of God into the heart—'My soul follows hard after you!' It is not a slight motion or a cold wish. It will not easily be put off with discouragement or satisfied with other things. It is an earnest pursuit of him until he is found. Wicked men in a pang would have the favour of God, but they are soon put out of the humour, and are taken up with other things. This must be the scope of our whole lives. We must resolve that we will not go from him, without him. As Jacob said, 'I will not let you go except you bless me!' This is also seeking God in Christ. Without a mediator, guilty creatures cannot enjoy God. We cannot immediately converse with God—there must be a mediator between God and us. There is no getting to God but by Christ. Luther said—It is a terrible thing to think of God out of Christ. It is Christ's great work to bring us to God, for he died to that end. 'He is able also to save them to the uttermost that come unto God by him' (*Heb.* 7:25, KJV). This seeking is stirred up in us by the secret impressions of God's grace, and the help of his Holy Spirit.

Thomas Manton, *By Faith*, pp. 327-329

You will seek the LORD your God and you will find him, if you search after him with all your heart.

Deuteronomy 4:29

Seeking God is the great work of our lives upon earth. Many are convinced that they cannot be happy without the favour of God; their consciences tell them they must seek him, but their affections carry them to the world. If you are content to look after God by and by, with a few slight endeavours, and do not make this the great employment of your lives, you will never find him. We were made for God; it is the end of our creation. Therefore, this must be the business of our lives. God made us for himself, and man can never be happy without him. The purpose of God's gracious forbearance with sinful man, after punishing apostate angels, was that we would seek and find him (*Acts* 17:27). When we had lost God through Adam's sin, God might have cut off all hope that we should ever find him again. The fallen angels could never recover their first estate, but God deals with us upon more gracious terms that we might seek him. God did not need to seek his creatures: he had happiness enough in himself; but we needed such a Creator, and none shall seek him in vain! Though at first you do not find him, comfort yourself in the seeking way. Though you do not presently feel the love of God or the sensible comfort from his Spirit, continue seeking—this is your work. God will reward everyone that seeks him, without distinction. The door of grace stands open for all comers! God hearkens to the prayers of the poorest beggar as well as the greatest monarch. All will find him a rewarder; God makes good his promises. God does not look at the external splendour of our work, but to the honesty and sincerity of it. God will rather forget princes, lords, mighty men of the earth, and vain and sinful potentates, than pass by a poor servant that fears him. Whoever seeks him will be sure to find him a rewarder.

THOMAS MANTON, *By Faith*, pp. 330-332

Be still, and know that I am God.

Psalm 46:10

The more composed and contented your heart is under the changes which providence brings, the stronger your faith is. When God turns your health into sickness, your abundance into poverty, your honour into scorn and contempt: with what attitude do you now make your condition known to God? Is your spirit embittered into discontent and murmuring complaints? Or are you well satisfied with God's dealings so as to acquiesce cheerfully in your present portion, not because you don't feel the affliction, but because you assent to divine appointments? This shows that God has a throne in your heart and that you reverence his authority and own his sovereignty. When a servant strikes a child, he runs to his father and makes his complaint, but if his father does more to him, he seeks no redress because he honours his father. So does a strong faith comply with God and trust him. This acquiescence shows that you not only stand in awe of his sovereignty, but have comfortable thoughts of his mercy and goodness in Christ. You believe that soon God will certainly make you amends or you would not be able to easily part with these enjoyments. The child goes willingly to bed while others are going to a great feast in the family, when the mother promises to save something for him to eat in the morning. The child believes, and is content. Surely you have something in the eye of your faith that will recompense all your present loss, and you willingly fast while others are feasting, or be sick while others are well. Paul tells us why he and his brethren did not faint in affliction: they saw heaven coming to them while earth was going from them—'So we do not lose heart. Though our outer self is wasting away, our inner self is being renewed day by day. For this light momentary affliction is preparing for us an eternal weight of glory beyond all comparison' (*2 Cor.* 4:16-17).

William Gurnall, *The Christian in Complete Armour*, II:61-62

And let us not grow weary of doing good, for in due season we will reap, if we do not give up.

Galatians 6:9

The more able you are to wait long for answers to your prayers and desires, the stronger your faith is. It shows the tradesman to be poor and needy when he must have ready money for what he sells. A well-to-do merchant is willing to give time and able to forbear long for the payment. Weak faith is all for the present. If it does not receive its desires immediately, it grows impatient and lays down sad conclusions against itself—'My prayer was not heard', or 'God does not love me!' Thus, it is difficult to keep from fainting. But strong faith can trade with God and wait for his leisure. He knows his investment is in a good hand, and is not too quick to call for it, knowing that the longest voyages have the richest returns. Rich soil can go without rain longer than the sandy soil that needs regular rain to keep the corn from withering. A strong healthy man can fast longer without fainting than the sickly and weak—so the Christian of strong faith can wait longer for the returns of God's mercy and discoveries of his love than one weak in faith. Strong faith can also suffer upon the credit of a promise. If you see a man leave a fair inheritance, and leave his kindred and country, for hunger, hardship and a thousand perils that meet him on every hand, for a friend whom he never saw, but only knew upon the bare credit of a letter of invitation, would you not say that he had a strong confidence in that friend? Such gallant spirits we read of—'Whom having not seen, ye love' (*1 Pet.* 1:8, KJV). Faith enjoys God and Christ, whom it never saw or knew, except in the promise that the word makes of them. Faith can turn its back to the world's friendship and enjoyments, and embrace the greatest sufferings of the world when called to do it. This will prove the faith to be both strong and true.

William Gurnall, *The Christian in Complete Armour*, II:62-63

He entered once for all into the holy places, not by means of the blood of goats and calves but by means of his own blood, thus securing an eternal redemption.

Hebrews 9:12

Christ's death for us was so virtuous that, in the space of three days and nights, he reconciled to God in his flesh every one of God's elect. He presented himself to the justice of the law, standing in the stead, place, and room of all that he undertook for, and gave his life a ransom for many, abolishing death, destroying him that had the power of death, taking away the sting of death, obtaining for us the gift of the Holy Spirit, and taking possession of heaven for us! This heaven! Who knows what it is? This glory! Who knows what it is? It is called God's throne, God's house, God's habitation, paradise, the kingdom of God, the high and holy place, Abraham's bosom, and the place of heavenly pleasures. In this heaven is to be found *the face of God forever*, immortality, the person of Christ, the prophets, angels, the revelation of all mysteries, the knowledge of all the elect, and ETERNITY. This heaven we possess already. We are in it, we are set down in it, and we partake already of the benefits through our head, the Lord Jesus. It is fit that we should believe this, rejoice in this, talk of this, tell one another of this, and live in the expectation of our own personal enjoyment of it. And as we should do all this, so we should bless and praise the name of God who has put over this house, this kingdom, and inheritance into the hand of so faithful a friend, yea, a brother and blessed Saviour. All these things are the fruit of his sufferings, and his sufferings the fruit of his love which passes all knowledge. O how we should bow the knee before him and call him tender Father; yea, how we should love and obey him and devote ourselves unto this service, and be willing to be also sufferers for his sake, to whom be honour and glory for ever!

John Bunyan, *Works*, II:20-22

Your kingdom come, your will be done, on earth as it is in heaven.

Matthew 6:10

Hypocrites kneel down in church, and lift up their eyes to heaven and say, 'Your will be done', and yet have no care at all to do God's will! Others obey him in some things, but not in others. Jehu destroyed the idols of Baal, but let the golden calves of Jeroboam stand (*2 Kings* 10:28-29). Some make a high profession, but live idly. It is an evil thing not to do *all* of God's will! Let us examine all of our actions, to see whether they are according to God's will or not. The will of God is our rule and standard. It is the sundial by which we must regulate all our actions. Are our speech, words, and apparel according to God's will? Would Jesus do this? Misery always attends doing our own will. Our first parents left God's will and purchased a curse for themselves and all their posterity. Saul left God's will and lost the kingdom. Happiness always attends doing God's will. Joseph obeyed, and God raised him to be second in the kingdom. How may we do God's will properly? (1.) *Get sound knowledge.* We must know his will before we can do it! Knowledge is the eye to direct the foot of obedience. (2.) *Let us labour for self-denial.* Unless we deny our own will, we shall never do God's will. His will and ours are like the wind and tide when they are contrary: he wills one thing, we will another. (3.) *Get a humble heart.* Pride is the spring of disobedience. A proud man thinks it below him to stoop to God's will. The humble says, 'Lord, what will you have me to do?' He puts, as it were, a blank paper into God's hand, and bids him to write what he wills, and he will subscribe to it. (4.) *Beg the grace and strength of God.* I do not need to be taught to do my own will; I can do that fast enough. Teach me to do your will (*Psa.* 143:10). As the magnet draws the iron, God's Spirit will make it delightful to do God's will!

Thomas Watson, *The Lord's Prayer*, pp. 163-165

My Father, if it be possible, let this cup pass from me; nevertheless, not as I will, but as you will.

Matthew 26:39

When we pray, 'your will be done', we pray that we may have grace to submit to God in affliction. A good Christian, when under any disastrous providence, should lie quietly at God's feet, and say, 'Your will be done'. We may be deeply sensible of the affliction, and yet patiently submit to God's will. We may weep, for God allows tears; grace makes the heart tender. Weeping gives vent to sorrows. Job rent his mantle to express his grief, but did not tear his hair in anger. We may, when under oppression, tell God how we feel, and desire him to write down our injuries. Does not a child complain to his father when he is wronged? Holy complaint may agree with patient submission to God's will. But what is inconsistent with patient submission to God's will? (1.) *Discontentment with providence.* Discontentment mixes anger with grief and raises a passion in the soul. His thoughts run up and down in distraction as if he were undone! Jonah said, 'I do well to be angry!' (2.) *Murmuring.* Murmuring is the height of impatience, a kind of mutiny in the soul against God (*Num.* 21:5). When a cloud of sorrows gathers in the soul, if it drops hailstones of murmuring, this is far from patient submission to God's will. Murmuring springs from pride, thinking you deserve better at God's hand, and when the heart begins to swell, it spits poison. Murmuring also springs from distrust, for men do not believe that God can make medicine out of poison, and bring good out of all their troubles. Men murmur at God's providences because they distrust his promises. God has much ado to bear this sin. It is far from submission to God's will. It is a gracious frame of soul when a Christian is content to be at God's disposal, and acquiesces to his wisdom. 'It is the Lord; let him do what seems good (*1 Sam.* 3:18).

Thomas Watson, *The Lord's Prayer*, pp. 166-168

The Lord gave, and the Lord has taken away; blessed be the name of the Lord.

Job 1:21

Patient submission to God's will in affliction shows a great deal of wisdom, and piety. We must acknowledge God's hand in affliction, and trust his holiness and justice. Though he puts wormwood in our cup, we vindicate him, and confess he punished us less than we deserve. The skill of a pilot is most evident in a storm, and so is a Christian's grace in the storm of affliction. We now live in a valley of tears, and patient submission to God's will is much needed. Sometimes the Lord is pleased to exercise his precious ones with poverty, reproach, death, and infirmity, and sometimes he lets the affliction continue a long time. In all these cases we need patience and submissiveness of spirit to God's will. It is hard to learn 'Thy will be done', when the wind of providence crosses the tide of our will. To be displeased with God when things do not please us is a very bad temper of spirit. It is better to bring our will to God's, than for us to seek to bring God's will to ours! By judicious consideration we can learn 'Your will be done' in affliction. (1.) Consider that our present state of life is subject to affliction, as a seaman's life is subject to storms. The world is a place where wormwood grows. Troubles arise like sparks out of a furnace. (2.) Consider that God has a special hand in the disposal of all occurrences. It is vain to quarrel with instruments—wicked men are but a rod in God's hand. Whoever brings an affliction, God sends it! Shall we mutiny at that which God does? (3.) Consider that it is necessary for affliction: 'If need be' (*1 Pet.* 1:6, KJV). Corrections may be corrosives to eat out the proud flesh and keep us humble, or they may be instruments to display his power. If God did not sometimes bring us into affliction, how could his power be seen? Israel's bondage and deliverance glorified God!

Thomas Watson, *The Lord's Prayer*, pp. 168-172

When he calls to me, I will answer him; I will be with him in trouble; I will rescue him and honour him.

Psalm 91:15

God may prove us in affliction. Hypocrites can serve God in pleasure and prosperity, but when we keep close to him in times of danger, when we trust him in darkness, and love him when we have no smile, and say, 'Your will be done', that is the proof of sincerity! God is only trying us, and what hurt is there in that? Is gold worse for being tried? Our crosses have the kindness of God in them. There was no night so dark, but Israel had the pillar of fire to give light, so there is no condition so cloudy but we may see the light of comfort. It should make our wills cheerfully submit to God's, when we consider that in every path of providence we find his footsteps of kindness. There is kindness in affliction when God seems most unkind (*Heb.* 12:6). When God afflicts his people, and seems to sacrifice their outward comforts, he loves them. The husbandman loves his vine when he cuts it and makes it bleed, and shall we not submit to God? Shall we quarrel with that which has kindness and love in it? The surgeon binds the patient, and lances him in order to heal him. God deals with us as children (*Heb.* 12:7). God has one Son without sin, but no son without stripes. Affliction is a badge of adoption. It is God's seal by which he marks us for his own. When Munster, that holy man, lay sick, his friends asked him how he did? He pointed to his sores, saying, these are the jewels with which God adorns his children. Shall we not say then, 'Your will be done'? The rod of discipline is to prepare us for our inheritance! In the most cloudy providences, the promise 'I will be with him in trouble' (*Psa.* 91:15) appears. It cannot be ill with you if God is with you. He is with you to support, sanctify, and sweeten every affliction. I'd rather be in prison and have God's presence, than be in a palace without it!

Thomas Watson, *The Lord's Prayer*, pp. 173-174

Yes, we are of good courage, and we would rather be away from the body and at home with the Lord.

2 Corinthians 5:8

The grace of faith is such a grace that it carries a Christian through all the passages of this life. It enables him to hold out to the end, to suffer those things that he must suffer, and in the end, by faith, he dies. Everything else leaves him in death—his riches, his friends, his honour, his very breath—but his faith will never leave him until he is safe in full possession of heaven. Faith is then swallowed up in full enjoyment and vision for things now hoped for! Faith is a blessed grace that stands by us, goes along with us, and comforts us in all the passages of this life, and even in death itself, that dark passage. It never forsakes us until it has put us in possession of heaven. To die in faith is to die in the assurance of the forgiveness of sins. Faith looks upon Christ who on his own took the sting of death for us. We are reconciled to God through Christ. To die in faith overcomes the horror of death. Death is a terrible thing, and our faith is most exercised by it. There is the rottenness of the grave, the pain of death, the separation of body and soul, the parting of friends and loved ones with whom we have lived so lovingly and sweetly, the end of all employment in this world and the comforts of this life. But to die in faith is to conquer all of these! For all the enjoyments we have here, we shall have better friends, and we shall go to God and an innumerable company of angels. It is a blessed change for the better in every way. A better place, better company, better employment, better liberty, all better! All is ours! We die to be born to glory and happiness. The Lord will wipe away all tears from our eyes, and this happiness shall never end. So, indeed, faith sees that the day of death is better than the day of birth. By faith we overlook the grave, death and all, and see the conquering Christ, and ourselves already with him!

Richard Sibbes, *Works*, VII:415-417

Precious in the sight of the Lord is the death of his saints.

Psalm 116:15

The desire of God's children is to die in the faith of Christ. It is only faith, and nothing else, that will master this king of fears which subdues all mankind. Pagan answers are empty flourishes of speech. Their heart deceives them. Death is a terrible thing when it is armed with our sins and opens the doorway to the wrath of God. It is the end of happiness and the beginning of torment. It is a curse brought in by sin, and the end of all comfort. It is a terrible thing, and nothing can conquer and master it but faith in Christ. Oh, let us labour to get it while we live, that every day we may live by faith! It is not just any faith we can die by. It is a tried and proved faith that we must end our days with. If we have not learned to live by faith before, how can we end our days in faith? If you have not learned to trust God with your soul, your children, your estate while you live, how will you trust God for your body and soul and all, in death? You cannot do it! There must be a faith that is daily exercised and tried by which we trust him when we die. We can then say, 'All the days of my life I have experienced God's goodness, and I have depended upon him, and found him true in all his promises. I have committed myself and my ways to him and found him good and gracious in blessing me. I have found him work out all for good, and now I am strengthened to trust him since he has been so true to me all my lifetime. I will trust him now with my soul, that he will never fail me.' It doesn't matter if we die rich or great in the world, but only that we die in faith! Let us all labour for this faith. Even if a believer dies raging and in fits, they are not themselves in their sickness. They are safe—the covenant between God and them was made before, and it still remains. Their comfort may be reserved for heaven!

Richard Sibbes, *Works*, vii:418-419

Let us hold fast the confession of our hope without wavering, for he who promised is faithful.

Hebrews 10:23

God's promises are not empty shells, they are real things! He does not give us empty promises, but promises we may exercise our faith in until we have full possession. Blessings are wrapped up in promises. The faithful in Hebrews 11 'received not the promises' (*Heb.* 11:13). The meaning is, they did not receive the land of Canaan, or Christ in the flesh, right then. The soul does not look for fulfilment immediately, but in heaven! Faith looks to Christ, and heaven, and happiness as it is in-promise. It dares not expect anything from God but by a promise. God has engaged himself by promise. In his faithfulness, he will do it. The soul, then, looks to the promise, and in that it looks to Christ and grace, and heaven and happiness and all good things. Faith comes to God through his word and pleads his promise. Christ and heaven are wrapped in the promises. In the promises we are rich indeed, for God will perform them. Think of God's nature, his mercy, truth and justice. He must perform his promises. Think of his great name Jehovah, which gives being to the world and all things, nay, and that will turn all things that are now into nothing. This Jehovah has made these promises of life everlasting and grace to bring us there. He promised us perseverance and comfort under crosses and afflictions, and provision in our journey. That great Jehovah, which has given being to all, is faithful, he has bound himself, he has laid his faithfulness as security, he will make all good what he has promised! The soul, after it sees the promise, may rise up and look to God. All the promises of good things to come we cannot think of too often. We need to return to the promises again and again. Satan puts clouds and darkness before the soul every day, so we should every day repeat the promises and the hope of them.

Richard Sibbes, *Works*, vii:420-421

Count it all joy, my brothers, when you meet trials of various kinds.

James 1:2

Troubles befall us for our profit. Afflictions teach us. The school of the cross is a school of light. It shows us more of our own hearts. Sharp afflictions are to the soul as a soaking rain to the house. You don't know there is a leak until it rains. We don't know what unmortified lusts are in the soul until the storm of affliction comes, and then we find unbelief, impatience, carnal fear, and drooping down in many places. Affliction is a sacred eye-salve that clears our eyesight. It brings sins to remembrance that we have buried in the grave of forgetfulness. Joseph's brothers, for twenty years together, were not at all troubled for their sin in selling their brother, but when they came into Egypt, and began to be in straits, their sin came to their remembrance and their hearts smote them. Affliction also quickens the spirit of prayer. Jonah was asleep in the ship, but at prayer in the whale's belly. Perhaps in a time of health and prosperity we prayed in a cold and formal manner, we put no coals to the incense, we scarcely minded our own prayers, and how should God mind them? Then God sent some cross or other to make us stir up ourselves to take hold of him. When Jacob was in fear of his life by his brother, he wrestled with God, and wept in prayer, and would not leave him till he blessed him. In times of trouble we pray feelingly, and we never pray so fervently as when we pray feelingly, and is not this to our profit? Affliction also purges our sin. It is God's medicine to expel pride and the fever of lust. The water of affliction is not to drown us but to wash off our spots. We begin to look after our spiritual evidences and see how things stand between God and our souls. It takes us more off from the world, and calls us off the immoderate pursuit of earthly things that hinders us in our passage to heaven.

Thomas Watson, *The Lord's Prayer*, pp. 174-175

For I am sure that neither death nor life … nor anything else in all creation, will be able to separate us from the love of God in Christ Jesus our Lord.

Romans 8:38-39

Before we can understand the great love of Christ, we must know the nature of sin. Sin is worse than the devil. If you are more afraid of the devil than sin, you know little of its badness and thus little of Christ's love. If a man does not know the nature of his wound, how can he know the nature and excellence of the cure? Sin's filthiness goes beyond our knowledge, it pollutes us, and we are not even aware of it. There are aggravations attending sin against God's love and promises. Alas, our unwillingness to abide in affliction, and our secret murmuring under the hand of God. We may wonder why we are so chastised, and think our affliction should be removed sooner. Or we have slight thoughts of our guilt and take lightly our need for forgiveness. Who knows the utmost tendencies of sin and that which every sin drives at? This is plain: the least sin deserves hell! But this is not all: sin in us kills others. Good men think little about how many are hurt by their sin. How many unaware drive their own children down into the deep by not walking carefully? We easily blame the hard-hearted sinners who offered their children to devils, when it is easy to do worse ourselves! They but killed the body, but we body and soul in hell by our poor example! Do we know how our sins provoke God, and grieve the Holy Spirit? They weaken our graces and spoil our prayers. They tempt Christ to be ashamed of us. Alas, how short we fall from the knowledge of ourselves and of what is in us! Who has the perfect knowledge of all these things? I know that no one has a thorough knowledge of them all. And yet the love of Christ saves us from all, notwithstanding all the vileness and soul-damning poison that is in them.

John Bunyan, *Works*, ii:25-26

As the Father has loved me, so have I loved you. Abide in my love.

John 15:9

The love of Christ is exceedingly great, and its fullness beyond knowledge. It passes the knowledge of the wisest saint and the saints and angels in heaven! This is an eternal love! It is without beginning; the love of Christ was before the world, before we had being, for we were as yet uncreated. Though we were yet uncreated, we had the love and affections of Jesus Christ. The fullness of this love is unknown to man. Who can tell how many heart-pleasing thoughts Christ had for us before the world began? Who can tell how much he then delighted in us in his affections before we had our being? In general we may conclude it was a great love! There seems to be a parallel between the Father's delight in the Son, and the Son's delight in us. Yea, Christ confirms it (*John* 15:9). This love before the world began goes forward to an endless forever! The visions we shall have in heaven of this love will far transcend our utmost knowledge here, even as far as the light of the sun at noon goes beyond the light of a blinking candle at midnight. We shall immediately enjoy him with all the perfection of knowledge as far as is possible for a creature that is brought up to the utmost height that his created substance is capable of. But for all this perfection of understanding, we will come short of knowing the utmost of his love! All the enjoyments we will know of his love will be for all eternity! And this shall be our happiness. There will never be an end to our blessedness. Christ's love is infinite. This, if I may say so, will keep us employed even in heaven. It is not a burdensome employment, but dutiful, delightful and profitable. All things that were once burdensome in suffering and service shall be done away with, and that which is delightful and pleasurable shall remain.

John Bunyan, *Works*, 11:22-25

Be sober-minded; be watchful. Your adversary the devil prowls around like a roaring lion, seeking someone to devour.

1 Peter 5:8

We must watch *universally* to stand against the enemy. The honest watchman in his rounds walks the whole town; he does not limit his care to this house or that. So we must watch the whole man. We must watch every faculty of the soul or member of the body, lest the enemy endanger our spiritual welfare. Alas, how few set up such a full watch! We may be careful in one, but fail in another. You may set a watch at the door of your lips that no impure communication offends the ears of men, but do you guard the door of your heart? Is it defiled with lust? You may keep your hand out of your neighbour's goods, but do you envy his bounty? We need to watch in everything. No action is so small that we may do God or the devil a service, and so none are too small to carefully keep a holy watch over them. There is no creature so little among God's works, but his providence watches over it, even the sparrow or our hair. Let there be no word or work over which you are not watchful. We must watch *wisely* against the enemy. Pay careful attention where you need to keep the strictest watch. If a master charged his servant to care for his child, and repair the house while he was away, when he returns, will he thank that servant if he finds the house in good repair, but the child had fallen into the fire, and by it been killed or crippled through his negligence? He carried out the trivial that could have been left undone, while failing in his chief charge. We must watch over the areas in which we are weakest and have often failed. The weakest part of the city needs the strongest guard. Watch most carefully what you find to be the weakest. Is your weakness in passion? Watch over it as one that dwells in a thatched house watches over sparks from his chimney. And so also in any other particular as you find yourself weak.

William Gurnall, *The Christian in Complete Armour*, 1:289-290

For we do not know what to pray … but the Spirit himself intercedes for us with groanings too deep for words.

Romans 8:26

The Holy Spirit writes our petitions in the heart, and we offer them. If our prayer is the work of the Spirit, his voice, motion, and operation, we may believe our requests will be accepted. He joins with us in prayer, and supports us under infirmities with his own strength! He stirs us up, incites and inclines our hearts to pray. He puts us into a praying frame, and sometimes excites us so powerfully, that we cannot keep from pouring out our souls to God. Those that have the spirit of prayer often find by experience that the Lord is about to show them some special favour. The Spirit also teaches us what to pray for. We don't know what is seasonable or best, and are prone to ask for that which is unseasonable or hurtful. We seek ease, liberty, plenty, deliverance from troubles and suffering, and prefer joy, triumphs, raptures, and want them immediately. The Spirit better directs us to the most necessary, proper, and advantageous. He helps us by praying according to God's will. He is our advocate. An advocate is the comfort and encouragement of his client. He advises him, pleads for him, draws up his petitions and dictates the form of the words. Since much of prayer is the work of the Spirit, matter and form, expression and affection, and since he teaches us when, what, and how we should pray, this consideration affords great encouragement to faith. If prayer were our own work only, we might fear it would be rejected, but the work of the Spirit must be acceptable! If we ourselves only spoke, the Lord might shut his ear and refuse to hear sinners. But prayer is the voice of the Spirit he speaks in us and by us. The Lord will certainly listen to that voice. The voice of the Spirit in the court of heaven can never be rejected. The Lord can't deny him or he must deny himself.

David Clarkson, *Works*, 1:207-210

I was ready to be sought by those who did not ask for me; I was ready to be found by those who did not seek me.

Isaiah 65:1

God's providence affords many encouragements to faith. He hears those that cannot pray and answers that which cannot be called prayer. He hears the creatures and listens to their cries. He rewards their expectations and fulfils their desires though they cannot look up to him or desire from him: 'He gives to the beasts their food, and to the young ravens that cry' (*Psa.* 147:9), and 'The eyes of all look to you, and you give them their food in due season. You open your hand; you satisfy the desire of every living thing' (*Psa.* 145:15-16). They but open their eyes, and God opens his hand. They cry and look and God satisfies. Will the Lord hear lions and ravens, and not hear me? Will he satisfy their natural needs and not my spiritual desires? Will he regard them when their eyes are lifted up and not the lifting of my heart? Am I not much better than they? Shall he not much more hear me? 'If God so clothes the grass of the field . . . will he not much more clothe you, O you of little faith?' (*Matt.* 6:30). God also grants some things to men that they do not pray for. Some things, nay, the greatest are granted to those that do not pray. No prayer had any influence in election and our prayers did not contribute to the work of redemption. These fountains were dug without the help of any. The sweetest streams of love run freely. Pardon, regeneration, justification, adoption, reconciliation are bestowed on those who cannot or will not pray for them. Much precious fruit falls into our laps before we shake the tree by prayer. If the Lord is found when we seek not, opens when we knock not, answers when we call not, how much more will he open and answer when we knock and call! If the greatest is given before we have hearts to pray, how confident we may be that prayer can obtain the lesser things!

David Clarkson, *Works*, 1:210-211

The sufferings of this present time are not worth comparing with the glory that is to be revealed to us.
Romans 8:18

We must have a firm persuasion of a sure reward (*Heb.* 11:6). The Lord is righteous and will not forget your labour of love. Your work for the Lord may be hard work, ploughing or sowing, but we are sure of an excellent crop! When we feel nothing but trouble and inconvenience, sense may think lies about God, and we are apt to say 'I have cleansed my heart in vain' (*Psa.* 73:13, KJV). But the Lord will not forget the service you do for him. God looks upon himself as bound. We must have a living faith in God's reward. This trust in God's reward will ravish the affections, engage the heart, keep us from fainting under the cross (*2 Cor.* 4:16), and abate our pursuit after worldly things. A rich man with a vast inheritance would not be seen among the poor gleaning the grain that was scattered! A well-grounded confidence in God's reward will quicken our endeavours, moderate our desires, allay the bitterness of the cross, and help us onward on our way to heaven. We are apt to look upon God as a Pharaoh: harsh, and though he requires work, he will not give wages. Ay, but he is pleased to move us by reward and the bands of love. This quickens us in our duty, and makes us vigorous, cheerful and diligent in our service. The duty you do for him will return into your bosom, and will bring you a blessing. Let us who know this principle bless God that there is a reward, yea a great reward! In other things our fancy may overreach, but all of our thoughts of heaven will come short, for God himself will be our reward! All the difficulties of obedience, the sorrows of the cross, shall all be made up to you in this reward! If it is a painful race, remember the crown: we run for the everlasting enjoyment of the blessed God! We have the noblest work, the highest motives, and the greatest reward.

Thomas Manton, *By Faith*, pp. 332-335

Because the sentence against an evil deed is not executed speedily, the heart of the children of man is fully set to do evil.

Ecclesiastes 8:11

Denying God's providence gives liberty and occasion for unbounded licentiousness: For what may not be done when there is no government? All sin receives its birth and nourishment from this bitter root. Let the idea of providence be once thrown out, or the belief of it faint, and ambition, covetousness, neglect of God, distrust, impatience and all other bitter gourds will grow up overnight! Nothing can so discourage rising corruptions as an active belief that God takes care of human affairs. Denying God's providence destroys trust in his being and goodness. One doesn't worship a God who cares not, or pray to one believed to have no regard for his creatures. To believe in a negligent God is worse than to believe in no God at all! He that denies providence denies most of God's attributes: his omniscience is the eye of his providence; mercy and justice are its arms; his power is the life and motion of providence; his wisdom is the rudder by which it is steered; and his holiness is its compass and rule. In denying providence man seeks comfort from guilt. A city without a magistrate, a house without a governor, or a ship without a pilot, gives a brave liberty to passion and lust. Denial of God's providence gives security to prostitute one's conscience. Also, when we fail to pray we practically deny his providence. If we really believed there was a watchful providence he would hear from us more! Neglect shows we see no profit in prayer! We also deny his providence when we receive any good, and are more grateful for the instrument than for God, the principal author of it. Men are remiss when they ascribe their wealth to their own fortune, their health to their own care, or their learning to their own industry. Our thank-offering should be turned alone to the glory due only to God!

STEPHEN CHARNOCK, *Works*, 1:39-45

I delight to do your will, O my God; your law is within my heart.

Psalm 40:8

Affliction is for our profit and should make us submit to God and say, 'Your will be done'. There is kindness in affliction in that your case is not as bad as others, or not so bad that it couldn't be worse. When it is dusk, it might be darker. God gives gracious support in affliction. If he strikes with one hand he supports with the other. Without God's support we would sink under our trials. Christ bears the heaviest part of the cross! Affliction is sometimes sent for punishing sin, and at other times to prevent it. Prosperity exposes us to much evil; it is hard to carry a full cup without spilling, and a full estate without sinning. We are beholden to our affliction: we might have fallen into some scandal had not God set a hedge of thorns in the way to stop it. What kindness is this! God lets us fall into suffering to prevent one falling into a snare. Say then, 'Lord, do as it seems good in your sight; your will be done.' God mixes his providences; in anger he remembers mercy. Suffering is not pure gall, but honey is mixed with it, as the painter mixes with his dark shadows bright colours. So the wise God mingles crosses and blessings. The body is afflicted, but within is peace of conscience. Joseph was sold into Egypt and put in prison—the dark side of the cloud. Job lost all and was clothed with boils—a sad providence. But God gave testimony in heaven of Job's integrity, and afterward doubled his estate. God in kindness moderates his stroke by measure and sweetens it with divine consolation. After a bitter portion, he gives a lump of sugar. God comforts by his word and Spirit. He candies our wormwood with sugar and gives us grapes from thorns. Oh how much kindness there is in the cross! In the belly of the lion there is a honeycomb. This should make us cheerfully submit to God's will!

Thomas Watson, *The Lord's Prayer*, pp. 176-178

Behold, blessed is the one whom God reproves; therefore despise not the discipline of the Almighty.

Job 5:17

In kindness, God will not let affliction lie too long. The goldsmith will not leave his gold in the furnace after it is purified. Affliction has a sting, but will fly away. Affliction is a means to make us happy. It seems strange to flesh and blood that affliction should make us happy, but it is a means to bring us nearer to God. The magnet of prosperity does not draw us so near to God as the cords of affliction. When the prodigal was pinched with want, he said, 'I will go to my father.' Afflictions make us happy because they are safe guides to glory. The storm drives the ship into harbour. Blessed storm that drives the soul into the heavenly harbour. Is it not better to go through affliction to glory, than through pleasure to misery? Affliction leads to paradise where there are rivers of pleasure always running! This is God's ordinary course for his people it is the beaten path which all the saints have trod. The living stones in the spiritual building have all been hewn and polished! Christ's lily has grown among the thorns. 'All that will live godly in Christ Jesus shall suffer persecution' (*2 Tim.* 3:12, KJV). It has ever been the lot of saints to encounter sore trials. Saints of whom the world is not worthy passed under the rod. Those God saves from hell are not saved from the cross. Should we be exempt from trouble more than the prophets and apostles who marched through briars to heaven? Consider what Christ has already done for you—this should make us content to suffer anything at his hand and say, 'Your will be done!' We have been born from heaven; should we murmur at every slight cross? As a son or daughter to the king of heaven: are you troubled at these petty things? Quiet your spirit and bring your will to his, for he has given you honour, made you his son and heir, and will bestow a kingdom on you!

Thomas Watson, *The Lord's Prayer*, pp. 178-180

Come, let us return to the Lord;
for he has torn us, that he may heal us;
he has struck us down, and he will bind us up.
Hosea 6:1

God has given us Christ, a storehouse of all heavenly treasure; a pearl of price to enrich us and a tree of life to quicken us. He is the quintessence of all blessings; why then are you discontented at your worldly crosses? They cannot be as bitter as Christ is sweet. He can never be poor who has a mine of gold in his field, nor he who has the unsearchable riches of Christ! This should quiet the heart in afflictions. Grace is the seal of his love. When God intends the greatest mercy to any of his people, he brings them low in affliction. He seems to go quite cross to sense and reason, for when he intends to raise us highest, he brings us lowest. As Moses' hand before it wrought miracles was leprous, and Sarah's womb before it brought forth the son of promise was barren, so God brings us low before he raises us up. Water is at the lowest ebb before there is a spring tide. When God would bring Israel to Canaan, a land flowing with milk and honey, he first led them through the sea and wilderness. When God intended to raise up Joseph, he first cast him into prison and iron entered his soul. God usually lets it be darkest before the morning star of deliverance appears. When God intends to raise a soul to spiritual comfort, he first lays it low in desertion. As the painter lays his dark colour first and then lays his gold colour, so God first lays the soul in the dark desertion and then his golden colour of joy and consolation appears. Let the soul say, 'Your will be done; perhaps though now you afflict me, you are about to raise me up and intend a greater mercy than I can imagine.' It shows an excellent frame of mind to lie at God's feet and say, 'Your will be done'. This sweet temper of soul, which is melted in God's will, shows a variety of graces: faith, love, and humility.

Thomas Watson, *The Lord's Prayer*, pp. 180-181

For he will hide me in his shelter in the day of trouble; he will conceal me under the cover of his tent; he will lift me high upon a rock.

Psalm 27:5

Our comfort is altogether in the Lord. In darkness, he is our light, in danger he is our salvation, in weakness he is our strength, and in all our afflictions and straits, he is the strength of our life. In the greatest danger that can be, my heart shall not fear. King David's faith, after reflection on God's former assistance, broke out as fire out of smoke, or as the sun out of a cloud. He that sees God's greatness and power by a spirit of faith will see other things below as nothing. 'If God is for us, who can be against us?' (*Rom.* 8:31). King David had such sweet experiences of the goodness and power of God being his light, salvation and strength in confounding his enemies, that he studied how to be thankful to God. Therefore he said, 'One thing have I asked of the Lord ... that I may dwell in the house of the Lord all the days of my life' (*Psa.* 27:4). Holy David sought first the kingdom of God. God must have the whole sway of our souls. He will have no halting or the heart divided. The soul set upon many things can do nothing well; it must mind one thing. The soul is never quiet till it comes to God again. It must subordinate all things to this one thing. What is your desire? What is the bent of your soul? David used all means to enjoy communion with God sweetly above all other things whatsoever. When the desire is true, it stirs up all the powers and faculties of the soul to do their duty. If we find these holy desires, Oh! Let us take comfort in ourselves. Holy desires are the birth of God's Spirit, and not one of them shall be lost! The least thing stirred up by God's Spirit prevails with God in some degree, answerable to its value. If we have holy desires stirred up by God, God promotes those holy desires.

Richard Sibbes, *Works*, II:213-222

Take care lest you forget the Lord, who brought you out of the land of Egypt, out of the house of slavery.

Deuteronomy 6:12

Christians should exercise themselves to godliness in every condition. As the year has summer and winter, the day has light and darkness, the sea both ebbs and flows, our lives are a mixture of mercies and miseries, prosperities and adversities. Believers must know how to be in need and how to abound. If the world smiles or frowns, the Christian should move forward in their holy course and learn not to be exalted in prosperity, or be dejected in adversity. Extreme want and extreme wealth are both a temptation to wickedness. God in his wise providence is pleased to give some persons a large draft of sugared pleasures, and their cup overflows, but the fire made to warm us can also burn! A prosperous condition is a slippery place. When you have eaten and are full, beware that you do not forget the Lord your God (*Deut.* 6:10-12). Consider what a grievous sin it is not to serve God under the enjoyment of mercies. So many rich men, the more merciful God is to them, the more sinful they are against him. It is sad to sin under afflictions, but most base to sin against mercies. To abuse a friend upon whom you are dependent and from whom you receive your daily subsistence, is far worse than to abuse a stranger. Even beasts manifest some respect for them that feed and tend them. None sin at so dear a rate as they who sin against the riches of mercy. God, I am sure, may say of those he has exalted, 'I have lost seeming friends and got real enemies.' Too many serve the blessed God in poverty, disgrace or sickness, and when their afflictions are removed, and their health restored, then they can do well enough without him. We must be especially watchful against the sins of a prosperous estate. We must keep a strong guard, and let not earthly prosperity lessen our love or labour for heavenly things.

George Swinnock, *Works*, 11:46-54

As for the rich in this present age, charge them not to be haughty, nor to set their hopes on the uncertainty of riches, but on God, who richly provides us with everything to enjoy.

1 Timothy 6:17

For persons who enjoy a prosperous condition, one would think that if any in the world would praise God, these would! Alas! Bitter fruit grows on this sweet root. Who would not wonder at such wickedness, that blasphemy is the child of such heavenly bounty! What madness for blessings to shut one's heart against God. Reader, does not your heart rise against this abominable ingratitude? Take heed it is not your own case to fight against God with his own mercies. Beware, lest as the sunshine of your prosperity increases, your love to God should cool. In particular take heed of pride, carnal confidence, and insensitivity to others' sufferings. The prosperous are apt to be proud. Hearts also grow big with a herd. Like a peacock, they are proud of their feathers. How hard to keep a low sail in a high condition, and for a child of God not to think he deserves his Father's gracious dealings. Some think themselves better than others because they have better means. Reader, in the highest tide of earthly comforts, keep your heart within bounds. The more mercies you enjoy, consider, the more indebted you are to God! This should humble you that you are in greater debt than millions of others. There is also the danger of trusting in these blessings. That which is uncertain is no fit foundation for trust. The whole world is a sea of glass and yields no good footing. Trust must have a sure bottom; it must be the quiet repose of the soul in the hands of an almighty God and an immutable good. If I said to gold, 'you are my hope', I would have denied trust in God! Trust is the fairest respect we can give to God. We need to keep the world at a due distance. To trust God in adversity is honourable, but to trust him in prosperity is heroical!

George Swinnock, *Works*, 11:55-58

So that in the coming ages he might show the immeasurable riches of his grace in kindness towards us in Christ Jesus.

Ephesians 2:7

Do not value yourself by your estate, but by your inheritance in the other world. Grace teaches the saint in poverty to possess all things; and in plenty, to possess nothing. It is a sure sign of spirituality when a Christian who lives in bounty evaluates himself only by his estate in the covenant; and a sure mark of godliness for one with large possessions to overlook all and esteem himself wholly by his eternal portion. Grace is the cargo of spiritual riches in a vessel, and outward things but the ballast. Job's friends erred in judging Job wicked because afflicted, and so many err on the other hand in believing they are pious because they are prosperous. Some are foolish as children; they value themselves by their gay coats and gaudy cloths. A little grace, one drachma of God's special love in Christ, is worth millions. A painted face is no sign of a good complexion, so neither is a fair estate of a gracious or happy condition. One may be high with large earthly possessions whose portion shall be in the lowest hell. A monkey is still a brute, notwithstanding its golden collar and silver bells. Some live in a peaceful atmosphere and enjoy constant calm here, who must dwell hereafter amongst terrible tempests, and in an eternal storm. Alas! Reader, it is ill valuing yourself by the sunshine of common providence, when thousands who have it shall miss the undefiled inheritance. Esteem your value as you are related to the other world. Rate yourself by your treasure in heaven, by the pardon of your sins, by your interest in Christ, and by your durable riches and righteousness. These only are the mercies which are worth a thousand millions; all others are but painted cards and brass. Outward mercies serve the flesh, and last for a brittle life; but these mercies concern the soul and relate to eternity.

George Swinnock, *Works*, II:59-61

And Jesus … said to his disciples, 'How difficult it will be for those who have wealth to enter the kingdom of God!'

Mark 10:23

Jesus loved the young ruler who came to him to enquire about the way to heaven. He wished for the love of God, but loved this world too. He had a vain conceit of his own righteousness, and at the same time an excessive love of money. Rather than renounce the pleasant things of this life, he quit his pretences to a life to come, and went away grieved. Jesus called him to be his disciple, and gave him a promise of everlasting riches if he would comply with his proposal, but he made haste to wilful destruction. The young man's beauty and youth, strength and riches, and all this with the embellishments of many forms of godliness and shining outward virtues, could not obtain eternal life. If a man thus qualified and adorned prefers earth to heaven, and loves the possessions of this world above spiritual treasures, he abides in a state of condemnation and death. Grace is not a flower that grows in the field of nature, nor does it grow out of the heart of man. It is a divine seed. It is planted in our hearts by the Spirit of God (*John* 1:13). The young man sought eternal life, but not with all his soul; he could not take up his cross and follow Christ. He sought the kingdom of God for a season, but when he came to the hard work of self-denial, he would not venture into that thorny path, but turned back and went away sad. He sought justification and peace with God but not in the right way; he sought to establish his own righteousness. He loved heaven well enough, but he loved earth better. He chose his portion and happiness in this world, and lost his soul! In judgment Christ will discover one's secret love to sin. Wise and happy is the soul who doesn't build his hope of heaven on the sand. A wretched chain of gold withholds the soul from embracing the Saviour and his cross. He was *almost* a Christian!

Isaac Watts, *Works*, 1:72-94

I know, O Lord, that your rules are righteous, and that in faithfulness you have afflicted me.

Psalm 119:75

Faith believes God does all things in mercy, and corrects in love and faithfulness. This causes submission to the will of God. Love thinks no evil (*1 Cor.* 13:5), and considers all things in the best sense, and entertains good thoughts of God. 'Let God smite me', says love, 'it shall be a kindness.' The humble soul knows how much he has provoked God, and does not consider his afflictions great, but his sins great. He lies low at God's feet and says, 'I will bear the indignation of the Lord, because I have sinned against him.' This submissive frame of heart is full of grace. When God sees so many graces sweetly exercised, he says of such a Christian, as David of Goliath's sword, 'There is none like it.' To say 'Thy will be done' shows the strength of grace. As the body bears up in heavy weather, the soul that endures hard trials without fainting or fretting shows a more than ordinary strength of grace. You that can say you have brought your will to God's, let me assure you; you have outrun many Christians who perhaps may shine in a higher sphere of knowledge than you. To be content to be at God's disposal, to be anything that God will have us, shows a noble, heroic soul! It is reported that the eagle, unlike the ravens that cry for food, is never heard to make noise when it is hungry, because of the nobleness and greatness of its spirit. It is also proof of a great magnitude of spirit that, whatsoever cross falls upon a Christian in God's providence, he does not cry and whine as others, but is silent, and lies quietly at God's feet. There is much strength of grace in such a soul, nay, the height of grace! When God's grace bestows a crown on us, it is easy to say, 'thy will be done'. But when grace brings conflicts, and meets with crosses and trials, then to say, 'Thy will be done', is a glorious thing indeed!

Thomas Watson, *The Lord's Prayer*, pp. 181–182

Jesus, seeing that he had become sad, said, 'How difficult it is for those who have wealth to enter the kingdom of God!'

Luke 18:24

A prosperous condition is not always a safe one. A person is usually better in adversity than in prosperity. True, a prosperous condition is more pleasing to the taste, and everyone desires to get on the warm side of the hedge where prosperity shines, but it is not always the best. In a prosperous state there are more burdens, but many look at the shining and glittering of it, not at the burdens. A rose has its thorns, and so do riches. We see them happy that flourish in their silks and gold, but we do not see the troubles and cares that attend them. Disquieting care haunts the rich man. When his chests are full of gold, his heart is full of care. We must give account to God for our prosperity (*Luke* 12:48). The more talents we are entrusted with, the more we have to answer for. I have read of Philip, king of Spain, that when he was about to die, he said, 'O that I had never been a king! O that I had lived a private, solitary life! Here is all the fruit of my kingdom: it has made my accounts heavier!' Does this not quiet our hearts in a low, adverse condition, and make us say, 'Lord, thy will be done! As you have given me a less portion of worldly things, so I have a less burden of care, and a less burden of account'? A prosperous condition has more danger in it. Those at the pinnacle of honour are in more danger of falling, and are subject to many temptations. Millions are drowned in the sweet waters of pleasure. The great sails of prosperity overturn the vessel. It takes great wisdom and grace to bear a high condition. It is hard to carry a full cup without it spilling, and a full estate without sinning. When the tide rises higher, so do the boats. The world's golden sands are quicksands. Consideration of this should make us submit to God in adversity and say 'Thy will be done'. God knows what is best for us.

Thomas Watson, *The Lord's Prayer*, pp. 182-183

But God shows his love for us in that while we were still sinners, Christ died for us.

Romans 5:8

In the hour of temptation it is hard for the soul to hold fast to Christ's love. There is nothing that Satan sets himself more against than the shining forth of the love of Christ in its natural lustre. He assaults Christians with diverse thoughts to darken their judgment. He makes God out to be a fierce destroyer, and Christ a withholder of his love. But the true knowledge of Christ's love delivers us from all this. For this purpose Christ bids us to continue in his love (*John* 15:9). Faith in Christ's love disperses and drives away all such fogs and mists of darkness, and makes the soul rest in the promise of eternal life, yea, it helps us to grow up in him in all things. Here spring forth the riches of his love—that the eternal Word, for the salvation of sinners, should come down from heaven and be made flesh. This act of condescension displays such love that can never fully be understood. In this, his love was deep, broad, long, and high. That human nature was taken into union with God. By this very act of heavenly wisdom we have an inconceivable pledge of the love of Christ to man. He became a common person, and in his love he disabled our foes. When Satan, death, the grave and sin have done whatever they can do, we are still more than conquerors through him that loved us (*Rom.* 8:37). Christ in love is preparing a place for us, and has sent the Holy Spirit to strengthen us under all adversity. Christ is touched in our afflictions, and is laying himself out in intercession to preserve us from ruin. We will behold his glory and be partakers of it. He will come for us as a bridegroom and wrap us in the robes of glory. Then forever there shall be no death or sorrow. We know his great love when we consider all the glories, all the benefits, and all the blessings laid up in heaven. Who can understand his love?

John Bunyan, *Works*, 11:26-30

These all died in faith, not having received the things promised, but having seen them and greeted them from afar.

Hebrews 11:13

We do not see every promise fulfilled in our times. God may bring fulfilment in another age. The fathers didn't see the time of Christ in their day. This should help us in a common infirmity that Christians battle. We should be thankful for what we have though we do not have all we desire. The fathers didn't have the fulfilment—yet they were thankful and cheerful, and died in faith embracing the promise. We should be thankful for what we have, and content to wait for what we do not have. This is a proper temperament for a Christian. Covetousness and greed for what we do not have makes us miss the blessings of what we do have! The fathers saw the promises from afar, were persuaded of them and embraced them. Their fulfilment came generations after, yet they saw them by the eye of faith! Faith makes things present in regards to certainty and comfort. God also gives us grace to strengthen our faith during the interval between faith and actual possession. He gives us patience and hope and many other sweet graces so that we can comfortably wait for the accomplishment of the things believed. Faith has feet to go to Christ, arms to grasp Christ, ears to hear God's word and believe, and eyes to see things far off and invisible. Faith sees heaven, Christ, and our heavenly home. Faith breaks through with the most piercing beams. Faith sees the past: creation, and the punishment of Christ our surety. It sees the future: resurrection to life everlasting and happiness in heaven. It gives being to things, and pierces through difficulties. When our present estate seems contrary to promise as if God did not care, faith breaks through that. When we die, faith sees life. When we apprehend our sins, faith sees forgiveness. When we are greatly perplexed, faith sees happiness and glory!

Richard Sibbes, *Works*, VII:421–424

He considered the reproach of Christ greater wealth than the treasures of Egypt, for he was looking to the reward.

Hebrews 11:26

Faith is sometimes called sight. As the natural eye cannot see the invisible, so the natural man cannot see the things of God. This needs supernatural sight. Reason cannot see the resurrection of the body, the life to come, and such things as the word of God reveals to us. Nothing at all can be done in religion without a supernatural eye. A man may hear of heaven, forgiveness, and happiness, and think, 'Oh, these are good things', but notwithstanding he does not see them with a supernatural eye. He does not see them as holy and gracious. He desires them under his own conditions, but not in altering his disposition. He sees heavenly things with a carnal eye, as Balaam wished to 'die the death of the righteous' (*Num.* 23:10, KJV). Faith is able to see things afar off because it sees things in the power of God, and in the truth and promises of God. Faith is wrought by the mighty power of God in the soul. It takes great power to turn away from riches, honours, and pleasures, and to stand and admire the things that it cannot see. For a man to rule the course of his life upon reasons the world cannot see, because of a happiness to come, and because of an unseen God he believes in: it is a mighty power that plants such a grace in the heart. Faith is wrought by the mighty power of God, and thus faith lays hold upon the power of God that the promises shall be performed. This trust in the power and truth of God gives sight to faith. It is our duty to labour to have our faith clear, and to have this eye of faith giving us a strong sight. There are three evidences of strong sight: (1.) When we have it, faith is able to see things afar off. (2.) When there are clouds obscuring our hopes, faith's sight can pierce through them. (3.) When there is little light with many obstacles, faith yet breaks through to see things remote! Blessed are the poor in spirit, for theirs is the kingdom of heaven.

Richard Sibbes, *Works*, VII:424-425

Blessed are the poor in spirit, for theirs is the kingdom of heaven.

Matthew 5:3

What comfort the poor may have when they are also poor in spirit—those whose spirits are akin to their outward condition. Those who willingly submit to God in a poor condition honour him when they submit without murmuring. They may be encouraged by their share in the kingdom of heaven. Your King was poor in this world himself, and suffered hard things. If men in the army have only water to drink, yet it is as much as the general has; it is well with them! So Christ may well say, 'Are you dejected because of your poverty? Are you poorer than I was?' He was made poor that we might be rich! (*2 Cor.* 8:9). Ordinarily it is the poor of this world that are subjects of Christ's kingdom. The Lord has been very little beholden to the great ones of the world for the furthering of his kingdom. Poverty is no hindrance to the highest degree in the kingdom of heaven! It may be a hindrance to honour in the kingdoms of the world, but not in the kingdom of heaven. When it is time to choose officers in the church, there should be no consideration of a man's estate, but of spiritual power. The poorest of men may have more godliness and understanding in the kingdom of heaven than others, and are as qualified as any whatsoever. The poor have all the privileges of this kingdom! In this kingdom are spiritual riches that are infinitely beyond all outward riches! If you prize riches over the kingdom of heaven, and believe that given so much you would be a happy man, this shows a carnal heart. The kingdom of heaven makes you rich in faith, in holiness, in promises, in God and Christ, and in the enjoyments of the Holy Spirit and his gifts and graces. In the kingdom of heaven these spiritual riches are abundantly supplied. And, at last, the godly poor will posses all things! They will be as stones in a crown and shine as bright as the sun!

JEREMIAH BURROUGHS, *The Saints' Happiness*, pp. 29-32

And forgive us our debts, as we also have forgiven our debtors.

Matthew 6:12

Oh that we had a due sense of what it is to sin against God, against an infinite majesty! No debt to man can be so great as our debt to God, both in number and weight. Our debts stand on record. Our words and our actions cannot be forgotten. Many times we lose memory of what we have done, but it is all recorded, and your iniquities will one day find you out, though you have forgotten and think you will never hear of them any more. A day of reckoning will come, and all shall be called to give an account. The books at that day will be opened, and conscience by the power of God will recognize all our ways. O what it is to sin against God! God does not tell us when he will put the bond in suit against us; he may surprise us unawares (*Luke* 12:20). There can be no shifting to avoid the danger. When you fly from God as a friend, you fly to him as judge! All other debts cease at death, but here the law takes the sinner by the throat, and drags him to everlasting punishment. Death is God's arrest. As soon as the soul steps out of the world, it is seized and forfeited into the hands of God's justice. How many lie under this danger and never think of it! But Jesus Christ is a surety, and took the debt of man upon himself. He made full satisfaction by suffering the punishment due to us (*Isa.* 53:4). It pleased the Father to bruise him. Christ paid the full price which justice demanded. All who have an interest in his death are free from the wrath of God. God will not exact the debt twice; therefore, we go free! Christ not only satisfied the punishment, but also established righteousness for us. He is able to save to the uttermost those that come to God through him (*Heb.* 7:25). We come confessing our sins with a purpose to forsake them, pleading his propitiation and God's promise to blot out our offences.

Thomas Manton, *Works*, 1:167-173

If we confess our sins, he is faithful and just to forgive us our sins and to cleanse us from all unrighteousness.

1 John 1:9

Though the satisfaction for our sin is provided by another, and the surety is of God's own providing, God will have the creature to own so heavy a debt, and feel it in brokenness of heart. When we come with true remorse, and confess that we have offended so just, so holy, so merciful a Father, it must be grievous to us in the remembrance of it. You must not only confess sin as a wrong, but as a debt. Sin has wronged God, and it is a debt binding you over to a punishment you could never endure or make God any satisfaction for. The satisfaction of Christ must be pleaded by a sinner in the court of heaven, in a believing manner owning Christ's surety. God and Christ are agreed about the business of salvation. God has agreed to accept satisfaction from Christ, and Christ has agreed to make this satisfaction. All the business now is about the sinner's consent to accept Jesus Christ as his surety by the eye of faith. Christ Jesus tore the debt and handwriting that was against us, nailing it to the cross (*Col.* 2:14). We are required, in repentance, to own an unfeigned purpose to forsake sin. He that has been released of his debt must not keep running deeper into arrears. Christ never blotted out our debts that we might renew them, and go on upon a new course of offending God again. This is to dally with God and run into the snare he has broken for us. Shall we plunge ourselves into new debts from which he has given us an escape? We must purpose to forsake sin, otherwise we do not draw near to God with a true heart (*Heb.* 10:22). We do but deal falsely with God in all the confessions we make unless there is an unfeigned purpose to renounce all sin and cast it off as a thing that will undo our souls. All who call God 'Father' ought to humbly beg him daily to pardon their sins!

Thomas Manton, *Works*, 1:174-175

Repent therefore, and turn again, that your sins may be blotted out.

Acts 3:19

An impenitent and unpardoned sinner has a vast debt upon him that will surely undo him unless he is released in time. He is bound over to suffer the wrath of God for evermore, and no hand can release him but God's. Many times they do not consider this matter and cry, 'peace, peace' to themselves. But it is not the debtor which must cancel the debt, but the creditor. Have you a discharge from God? Poor creatures, what will you do? Many take care that they may owe nothing to any man. Oh! but what do you owe God? To live in doubt and fear of arrest, oh what a misery is that! When sin lies at the door ready to attack you every moment and haul you to the prison of hell: that is most dreadful. Think seriously, how do accounts stand between God and you? Sinners are loath to think about it. We are unwilling to be called to account; we shift and delay, and will not think of our misery. But putting off sin will not put it away! Failing to think about our misery will not help us out, and will not be a release or discharge. Our sin is an increasing debt, so that man is ever treasuring up wrath against the day of wrath. This should press us to be careful to get out of this condition. Flee as a deer from the hand of the hunter. Oh, it is a sad thing to lie in our sins! If you are in this debt, do not give sleep to your eyes; make peace with God speedily. We need to beg our pardon which is an exercise of faith, looking unto Christ. Christ taught us to pursue the discharge of our debts. God has set forth Christ to be a propitiation through faith in his blood (*Rom.* 3:25). He that confesses and forsakes his sin shall have mercy (*Acts* 3:19). And certainly it is God's way that we humbly beg. The exercise of repentance includes mourning for sin, and the confession, and the forsaking of it.

THOMAS MANTON, *Works*, 1:175-176

As one trespass led to condemnation for all men, so one act of righteousness leads to justification and life for all men.

Romans 5:18

The imputed righteousness of Christ is the only true basis for a believer to build his happiness, joy, comfort, peace and quiet of his conscience upon. If a judge acquits the prisoner at the bar, he cares not if the jailer or fellow prisoners condemn him. There are no accusers that a believer needs to fear since it is God, the supreme judge, that absolves him. The consideration of this should arm us, comfort us, and strengthen us against all the terrors of conscience, guilt, accusation of the law, or cruelty of Satan. If God justifies, none can reverse it. If any come against you, true or false, they shall never hurt you. He from whom there is no appeal has fully acquitted you, and none can take your peace. Ah! What a strong cordial to all the people of God if they would just live in the power of this glorious truth. Christ's righteousness is real, sure, and a solid foundation upon which a believer may safely build his peace, joy, and everlasting rest. It will help him to glory in tribulations, and to triumph over all adversities. Seek Christ who was crucified, and you do not need to fear anything, for God's justice has already received satisfaction for your sin. The day of judgment is the most dreadful day that ever was in the world to all the ungodly, but the faithful shall lift up their heads! The law looks for perfect obedience, and because the sinner cannot come up to it, it pronounces him accursed. The sinner seeks hard for mercy, yet the law shows none! When the believing sinner casts his eye upon the righteousness of Christ, it is a perfect and exact righteousness. God imputes to me the perfect holiness and obedience of my blessed Saviour. He has clothed us with the robe of his Son's righteousness. By this means we recover more by Christ than we lost by Adam. It is far more glorious than that which we lost by the first Adam!

Thomas Brooks, *Works*, v:240-244

Be faithful unto death, and I will give you the crown of life.

Revelation 2:10

The imputed righteousness of Christ is the highest reason in the world to rejoice. Every believer is in a more blessed and happy estate in Christ's righteousness than Adam was in his innocence. Adam's righteousness was uncertain and possible to lose. But the righteousness of Christ is more firm and sure to us. It is a noble portion that shall never be taken away. Adam sinned away his righteousness, but a believer cannot sin away the righteousness of Christ Jesus! The gates of hell shall never be able to prevail against the soul clothed in Christ. What higher ground of joy and triumph can there be than this? Adam's righteousness was in his own keeping, but righteousness in Christ is in our Father's keeping. We are kept as in a garrison. Though the saints may meet with many shakings in this world, it is certain we will come to full possession of eternal life. God is so unchangeable in his purposes of love, and so invincible in his power, that neither Satan, nor the world, nor our own flesh shall ever be able to separate saints from the crown of life (*Rev.* 2:10). The power of God is so far above all created opposition, that it will certainly maintain us in a state of grace. Adam's righteousness was a mere man's righteousness. How can that be compared to the righteousness of Christ? His righteousness is far more excellent, absolute, glorious, and in every way all-sufficient. It is the righteousness of God (*2 Cor.* 5:21). If all created excellencies, all the privileges of God's people, and all the kingdoms of the earth and the glory of them were presented in one view, they would be nothing to the fullness in Jesus Christ! The world rejoices in barns, money, honour, and pleasures, but the joy of a Christian that keeps a fixed eye on Christ and his righteousness cannot be expressed.

Thomas Brooks, *Works*, v:244-246

It is good for me that I was afflicted, that I might learn your statutes.

Psalm 119:71

Take notice what unteachable creatures we are by nature. We will not set our hearts to receive instruction until we are whipped to it by the rod of correction, and then, hardly. Unless God multiplies stripe upon stripe, and affliction upon affliction, his multiplying precepts are in vain. We are like a child that will be taught only when the rod is upon his back! But the whip, the rod, the prison, the wilderness: anything is precious that brings instruction with it. Ah, but what if you find yourself by the patience and forbearance of God free from affliction, and the candle of the Almighty shines in your tabernacle, and your steps are washed in butter? How might you avoid chastisement and keep off the strokes of divine displeasure from yourselves and families? Study the word of God well. Neglect of the word forces God to turn us over to a severer discipline. Set your hearts to all the truths and counsels God has revealed to you. We should prize our creature comforts more and indulge in them less, and be more thankful and less sensual. We need to prize the gospel by its worth and study self-denial and meekness of spirit; and labour to discover the hidden corruptions of our own heart, a bottomless pit. Labour to maintain sweet communion with God, and make God your choice, not your necessity. Labour to maintain such constant fellowship with him, that when you die, you may change your place only, not your company! Study to know God more, and love him better! While you are in your strength and peace, there is but one thing necessary. There are many maybes, but one must-be. O take heed of industrious folly, and the pursuit of trifles; mind your work! Redeem the time; the days are evil. O that Christians would study the worth of time, and value a day, an hour, a moment!

THOMAS CASE, *Select Works, A Treatise of Afflictions*, pp. 135–142

Remember those who are in prison, as though in prison with them.

Hebrews 13:3

If you would prevent your own discipline, labour to set your mind in heaven, looking for the hasting and coming of Christ. Say, 'Come Lord Jesus, quickly.' Study thoroughly the sinfulness of sin, the emptiness of the creature, and the fullness of Christ. Resolve with Paul to know nothing but Jesus Christ and him crucified. A due contemplation of the cross will heighten Christ's love, and lessen your own sufferings. Learn in the time of your peace and tranquility to lay to heart the sufferings of your brethren. Think of those whose feet are hurt in the stocks and irons as if you were bound in chains with them. Learn to sympathize with all the people of God whatever their adversity. Hide not your eyes and shut not up your heart of compassion from any that are in a suffering condition. We should grieve in their sorrows, weep with their tears, and sigh with their groans. Show compassion, that you may not need compassion, or, if you need it, you may find it. Also, labour to learn from God's judgments you see on other men. The world's judgments are the church's instructions! His severity to strangers was his tender mercy towards Israel. He did not spare the nations, that he might spare Israel. Israel's chastisements should have been Judah's warning (*Jer.* 3:8). Judah should have felt Israel's rod. So we should fear God and receive instruction. We sin worse than others when we sin the very sins others have been punished for before our very eyes. If we are not bettered by God's warning, he may aggravate their plagues on us. Remember Lot's wife; her pillar of salt should season our hearts when the judgments of God are in the earth. When a father is correcting one child, the whole family should fear and tremble. If we would learn by other men's sufferings, we would prevent our own!

THOMAS CASE, *Select Works, A Treatise of Afflictions*, pp. 137-146

He disciplines us for our good, that we may share his holiness.

Hebrews 12:10

Take notice, O afflicted soul, of God's design in afflicting you, and make it your own design, namely, that correction may be turned into instruction. Hear the rod, and who has appointed it. It is a great mistake to make haste to remove your afflictions instead of being sanctified by them. Men would leap out of the window before God opens the door, but this is folly. Deliverance belongs only to God. When God delivers, no obstruction can stand in the way. He is the Lord of hosts, and has all the armies of heaven and earth at his command! Men look to the creature for deliverance and neglect God, or cry only for deliverance without learning. But God sends captivity to teach us, humble us, prove us, and to make known what is in our heart. Learning is the shortest way to deliverance. God will own his people. If they seek him, they will not wait long for their deliverance! Make more haste to be taught than to be delivered, and choose to have your afflictions sanctified more than removed. If you cross God's design, it is just for God to cross yours. If you will not let God have his way in instruction, he will not let you have your end in enlargement. The only way to retard deliverance is to make too much haste to be delivered. Bare deliverance is not a blessing, but the fruit of common bounty. Bare deliverance may be the fruit of the curse. A man may be delivered from wrath, but not in love; deliverance from one affliction may but make way for a greater affliction! The blessing of correction is instruction; O let not God go, till he blesses you. It is sad to have affliction but not the blessing of affliction; to feel the wood of the cross, but not the good of the cross; to taste the bitter root, but not the sweet fruit; to know the curse, but not the cordial. Persevere to be taught by God, that you might be holy as he is holy!

Thomas Case, *Select Works, A Treatise of Afflictions*, pp. 146–149

I appeal to you, brothers, by the name of our Lord Jesus Christ … that there be no divisions among you.

1 Corinthians 1:10

If controversies cause any divisions among you, look first to the interest of common truth and good in love. Do not become a passionate contender for any party in the division, but join more with the moderate and peacemakers than with the divisive. Division tends to ruin the church, and is condemned in the Scriptures greatly. It is usually the exercise of pride and passion, and the devil is pleased and gains the most by it. Those that would draw you into a contentious zeal will tell you that their cause is God's, and that you desert God if you are not equally zealous. They claim moderation and peace as a mark of being lukewarm and carnal. This may be true if the cause is of God. But upon great experience, I must tell you that of the many zealous contenders who claim the cause of God, few know what they are talking about. Some cry out 'the cause of God' when it is a brat of a proud mind. Some are rashly zealous before careful consideration. Some are misguided or captivated by others, and some are hurried on by passion and discontent. Many of the ambitious and worldly-minded are blinded by their own carnal interests. They proudly glory in their own opinions and think they know more than ordinary men. But it is not God's cause, but their own! What mischief is done for lack of knowledge. Souls should not be so lightly endangered! As far as I have seen, moderation is the most judicious course among good Christians. Those that furiously censured these as lukewarm have been men that had the least judgment and the most passion and pride. From my observation, ignorant and self-conceited wranglers who think they are champions for the truth are venting their passions and own fond opinions. These with formal enemies have caused the most suffering to the church down through the ages.

Richard Baxter, *Practical Works*, 1:50-51

There is no fear in love, but perfect love casts out fear.

1 John 4:18

True godliness is the best life on earth, and the only way to perfect happiness. In the end we please and glorify our Maker, and enjoy everlasting happiness. The nature of man is not capable of a more noble, profitable and delightful life than what God has called us to by his Son. If we but rightly knew it, we would enjoy continual cheerfulness and delight. It is a principal design of the devil to hide the goodness of God from you, to turn you back to the world so that you seek your pleasure somewhere else. One of his ways is to overwhelm you with fear and sorrow. He seeks to persuade you that religion only consists in an excess of sorrow, and that you will only spend your time in trouble and grief, and that this course is the most acceptable to God. Satan takes advantage of those fearful and passionate by nature, and so makes every thought of God to be a torment by raising some overwhelming fears. To weak and melancholy persons this temptation takes such an advantage in the body, that the holiest soul can do but little in resisting it. Even when there is a sincere love to God and his ways, fear plays the tyrant in them so that they perceive almost nothing else. But, alas! God has commanded you to a sweeter work! It is a life of love, and joy, and cheerful progress to eternal joy, with no more fear or grief than is necessary to separate you from sin. The gospel presents to you abundant matters for joy and peace, that these may become the very make-up of your souls, if you receive them as intended. Fears that are inordinate and hurtful are sinful, and must be resisted with other hurtful passions. Get better acquainted with Christ and his promises, and you will find enough in him to pacify the soul and give you confidence and holy boldness in your access to God (*Heb.* 4:14; *Rom.* 8:15).

Richard Baxter, *Practical Works*, 1:51-54

No one can serve two masters, for either he will hate the one and love the other, or he will be devoted to the one and despise the other. You cannot serve God and money.

Matthew 6:24

'Love not the world…' (*1 John* 2:15, KJV). Love is to be taken here in a strict sense, proceeding from the full bent of the heart and the fullness of the will carrying the whole soul with it. The love of the world and the love of the Father are perfectly opposite and inconsistent with each other. Love in this sense belongs to God alone. This love for the world is none other than lust, and so altogether inconsistent with love of the Father. There is a regular and lawful love of the world in an inferior degree, and in subordination to God, but here 'the world' is used in a narrow sense as the fuel for lust, and contrary to God. 'The world' here is the irregular and inordinate love of the world; the lust of the flesh, the lust of the eyes, and the pride of life; the grandeur, pomp, glory, riches, pleasures, honours, or whatever else may captivate the hearts of degenerate men. Alas! Are not the world and the Father perfectly opposite? They both require the whole heart, yea, the whole man. Both 'loves' cannot consist together in the same heart. Love is the most vigorous, domineering, sovereign affection of the human soul. This love seated in the will governs the whole soul. What you love determines what you are. If the object loved is absent, love goes forth to meet it by desire; if it is present, love takes comfort in it and delights in it; if it is in danger, love faints with fear; if its enjoyment is obstructed by others, love grows angry; if it is lost, love sorrows; if there is the possibility of its return, then love hopes! Thus, love takes different forms or affections according to the state of its beloved. If love sets its heart on God it becomes spiritual, noble, and divine; but if it loves the world it becomes carnal, base, and worldly.

THEOPHILUS GALE, *Puritan Sermons 1659-1689*, 1:642-646

In the last days there will come times of difficulty. For people will be ... lovers of pleasure rather than lovers of God.

2 Timothy 3:1-2, 4

God never appointed worldly goods to be our chief good, but worldly men put the crown upon the heads of pleasure, profits, and preferments. The worldly man's trinity is the lust of pleasure, riches, and glory (*1 John* 2:16). The lust of the flesh is the inordinate delight in sensual pleasures of any kind: recreations, eating, drinking, or any unclean objects. O what seeds of sorrow there are in sensual pleasures! O how the pampering of the flesh tends to the starving of the soul! The lust of the eyes sets itself on riches as the choicest good. O how greedy is the covetous man's eye after gold and silver! The pride of life looks for any worldly grandeur as its best good. These worldly men may scorn sensual pleasures or riches, yet are not without violent and impetuous lustings after the pride of some human excellence. Love to the world is a violent bent of the heart toward the world making it the centre of gravity. O what an infinite weight is love to this dirty world! It presses the heart downward, even unto hell! O how the sensual man's heart is bent toward his pleasures, the greedy toward his riches, and the ambitious toward his honours! These become their gods. What a vile, profane wretch was Esau, to part with his birthright and dignity for a mess of such coarse pottage! Do not let your thoughts and affections run so deep into the world as to become one with it! O what a tyrannic sovereignty has the world over those that love it! It takes away all sense of divine concerns. When a man's thoughts, inclinations, affections, studies, and cares pay tribute to the flesh, what is he but a slave to the flesh? God must be our supreme object of satisfaction above all lower goods, the object of our strongest passions. Our love should be active, pure, generous, abiding, vigorous, infinite and boundless!

THEOPHILUS GALE, *Puritan Sermons 1659-1689*, 1:647-654

Good and upright is the LORD; therefore he instructs sinners in the way.

Psalm 25:8

If you find yourself freshly out of affliction or fiery trials, sit down and reflect upon yourself. Does the world seem vain and as nothing in your eyes? Do you grasp divine truth more inwardly, more clearly, more experimentally, more powerfully, more sweetly than ever? Does it have a more abiding impression upon your heart? It is good that you have been afflicted! Study to be thankful. When God loads us with mercy we should load him with our praises! Your Patmos has been made a paradise. God changes the nature of affliction, he turns your water into wine, a prison into a temple. Let the lips of prayer be turned into praise. Labour to preserve what you have learned in affliction. Work their impressions on your heart. It is sad to consider how corruption will lie as if quiet and dead while danger and death are before us, and how suddenly and powerfully it will revive when the danger is over. Remind yourself of the sharpness and bitterness of the affliction, and the sorrows of a suffering condition. Remember the fears and tremblings that were yours during times of distress. Call to mind your impatience, murmuring, unbelief, and hard thoughts of God during your tribulation. Yet God was pleased to teach you by his Spirit; not because you were good, but because he is good; not because you pleased him, but because mercy pleases him; not because you were upright before him, but because he is upright, true and faithful to his own promises. But no sooner is the trial over than we are apt to forget God's teachings and our own vows and return to the same course. Remember your vows and spread them out before the Lord. Attend upon the ministry of the word. The word and the rod teach the same lessons. Attention to the word will revive and sanctify the teachings of the rod!

THOMAS CASE, *Select Works, A Treatise of Afflictions*, pp. 149-162

For the mind that is set on the flesh is hostile to God.

Romans 8:7

Note three ways Satan makes religion grievous: (1.) He encourages you to retain unmortified sensual desires. If you keep up your lusts, they will strive against the gospel and against all the works of the Holy Spirit (*Gal.* 5:17). Every spiritual duty will become unpleasant to you since it is opposed to your carnal inclinations and desires. Away with your beloved sickness, and both your food and physician will be less grievous to you. Mortify the flesh and you will more enjoy the things of the Spirit. The carnal mind is at enmity with God. (2.) Another cause of confounding and wearying you is your actual sins, when you deal unfaithfully with God, wound your conscience, and renew your guilt. If you keep the bone out of joint, and the wound unhealed, it is no marvel you are loath to work or travail in spiritual duties. But it is your sin and folly that should be grievous to you, and not that which is contrary to it. If you would remove the cause of all your troubles, resolve to forsake your wilful sinning, and come home by 'repentance towards God, and faith towards our Lord Jesus Christ'. (3.) Lastly, the tempter seeks to make religion unpleasant to you by keeping the substance of the gospel unknown and unobserved by you. He would hide the wonderful love of God revealed in our Redeemer, and all of the riches of saving grace. He hides the great deliverance and privileges of believers, and the certain hope of eternal life. He hides the kingdom of God which consists in righteousness, peace, and joy in the Holy Spirit. He seeks to show these as errors, trifles, and shadows. If ever you would know the pleasures of faith and holiness, you must labour above all to know God as revealed in his infinite love in the Mediator, and in every duty draw near to God as a reconciled Father, the object of your everlasting love and joy.

Richard Baxter, *Practical Works*, 1:54

I count everything as loss because of the surpassing worth of knowing Christ Jesus ... not having a righteousness of my own ... but that which comes through faith in Christ.

Philippians 3:8, 9

The righteousness of Christ cannot be painted. No man can paint the sweetness of the honeycomb, or the sweetness of a cluster of grapes, or the fragrance of the rose of Sharon. So the joy of the Holy Spirit cannot be painted, or the joy that rises in a Christian's heart when he keeps up a daily converse with Christ and his righteousness. This cannot be painted or expressed! Who can look upon the glorious body of our Lord Jesus Christ, and seriously consider that even every vein of that blessed body did bleed to bring him to heaven, and not rejoice in Christ Jesus? Who can look upon the glorious righteousness of Christ imputed to him and not be filled with an exuberance of spiritual joy in God his Saviour? There is not the pardon of the least sin, nor the least degree of grace, nor the least drop of mercy, but it cost Christ dear. He must die and be made a sacrifice. He must be accursed that pardon may be ours, and grace and mercy ours: oh, how this should draw out our hearts to rejoice and triumph in Christ Jesus! The work of redemption sets both angels and saints rejoicing and triumphing in Christ Jesus (*Rev.* 5:11-14). We especially should rejoice who have received infinite more benefit by the work of redemption than ever angels have. A beautiful face is at all times pleasing to the eye, but then especially when there is joy manifested in the countenance. Joy in the face puts a new beauty upon a person and makes that which before was beautiful to be exceeding beautiful. It puts a lustre upon beauty. So does holy joy and rejoicing in Christ Jesus put, as it were, a new beauty and lustre upon Christ. Let us rejoice and triumph in Christ Jesus and his righteousness, even if the times are ever so sad.

Thomas Brooks, *Works*, v:246-247

A person is not justified by works of the law but through faith in Jesus Christ.

Galatians 2:16

The imputed righteousness of Christ comforts and supports the people of God from fainting under the sense of weakness concerning their own righteousness (*Isa.* 64:6). When a Christian keeps a serious eye upon the spots, blemishes, infirmities and follies that cleave to his own righteousness, fears and tremblings arise to the saddening and sinking of his soul. But when he casts a fixed eye upon the righteousness of Christ imputed to him, his comforts revive and his heart bears up. Though he has no righteousness of his own by which he may stand accepted before God, he has God's righteousness which infinitely transcends his own. In God's account, sinful man has exactly fulfilled the righteousness which the law requires. Faith wraps itself in the righteousness of Christ, and is justified. Christ exactly fulfilled the law for all who close savingly with him! O sirs! None can be justified in the sight of God by a righteousness of their own making. The righteousness of Christ is infinitely better than our own—'Jehovah Tsidkenu'—The Lord our righteousness. When a sincere Christian casts his eye upon the weaknesses, infirmities, and imperfections that daily attend his best services, he sighs and mourns; but if he looks upward to the imputed righteousness of Jesus Christ, this brings forth his infirm, weak, and sinful performances as perfect, spotless, sinless and approved according to the tenor of the gospel, and he can rejoice! As there is imputation to our person, there is also to our services and actions! Our works are dipped in the blood of Christ! Though the Lord's faithful have eminent cause to be humbled and afflicted for the weakness that cleaves to their best duties, they have wonderful cause to rejoice and triumph that they are made perfect through Jesus Christ!

THOMAS BROOKS, *Works*, v:247-248

And this is the name by which he will be called: 'The Lord is our righteousness.'

Jeremiah 23:6

The Sun of Righteousness has healing enough in his wings for all our spiritual maladies. His imputed righteousness gives us the greatest boldness before God's judgment-seat! There is an absolute and indispensable necessity of perfect righteousness for us to appear before God. The holiness of God's nature, his righteous government, the severity of his law, and the terror of his wrath calls aloud upon the sinner for a complete righteousness. No righteousness below Christ's is able to stand the trial of God's justice. Christ's righteousness is a crowning comfort to believers. Christ's righteousness is full, exact, perfect, complete, matchless, spotless, peerless and acceptable. There is an indispensable necessity that lies upon the sinner to have such a righteousness. We may bear up with the greatest cheerfulness and boldness in the great day of account if Christ's righteousness is imputed to us! This righteousness is of infinite value and worth. It is an everlasting righteousness that can never be lost. It is an unchangeable righteousness. Though times change, and men change, and friends change, and providences change, and the moon changes, yet the Sun of Righteousness never changes. In him is no variableness, nor shadow of turning. It is a complete and unspotted righteousness. In this righteousness the believer lives, and dies. In this righteousness the believer stands before the judgment-seat, to the deep admiration of all the elect angels, and to the transcendent terror and horror of all reprobates, and to the matchless joy and triumph of all on Christ's right hand who shall then shout and sing! O how will Christ be admired and glorified in all his saints in that great day! Every saint will be wrapped up in this fine linen, the robe of Christ's righteousness shining more than ten thousand suns!

Thomas Brooks, *Works*, v:249-250

For by a single offering he has perfected for all time those who are being sanctified.

Hebrews 10:14

Suppose we saw a believing sinner standing before God's bar of justice. The books are opened, the accuser present, and the witnesses are ready. The Judge speaks: 'You stand before me for millions of sins of commission and omission. You have broken my holy laws, and have been proven guilty. What do you have to say for yourself as to why you should not be eternally cast out?' Upon this, the sinner pleads guilty and earnestly desires liberty to plead for himself as to why this dreadful sentence should not be passed upon him (*Matt.* 25:41). Given opportunity, the sinner pleads: 'Jesus Christ has, by his blood and sufferings, given full and complete satisfaction to divine justice, and has paid down upon the nail the whole debt at once, and it can never stand with the holiness and unspotted justice of God to demand satisfaction twice.' If the judge shall further object, 'Ay, but sinner, the law requires an exact and perfect righteousness; where is your exact and perfect righteousness?' the believing sinner very readily, cheerfully, humbly, and boldly replies, 'My righteousness is there on the bench; in the Lord I have my righteousness. Christ, my surety, has fulfilled the law on my behalf. Christ, by his active and passive obedience, has fulfilled the law for righteousness, and this active and passive obedience of Jesus Christ is imputed to me. His obeying the law to the full, his perfect conforming to its commands, his doing as well as his dying obedience, is by grace made over and reckoned to me for my justification and salvation. This is my plea by which I stand before the judge of all the world.' Upon this, the sinner's plea is accepted as good in law and accordingly he is pronounced righteous, and goes away glorying and rejoicing, triumphing and shouting it out—Righteous!

Thomas Brooks, *Works*, v:251

And the tempter came and said to him, 'If you are the Son of God, command these stones to become loaves of bread.'

Matthew 4:3

Men deny providence when they turn to dishonest ways to gain wealth or honour. This is to leave God and seek relief at hell's gates. It adores the devil's providence over God's. When God does not answer us, like Saul, we will go to the witch of Endor, and have our desire by hell when heaven refuses. This is covenanting with the devil and striking up a bargain with hell. When a man commits sin to gain his ambition or covetousness, does he not covenant with the devil? He hopes to attain those things by sinful means that are only in the hands of God. This is the devil's design. He tempted Christ to distrust his Father's care (*Matt.* 4:3), as though God would not provide for him! This is to prostitute providence to our own lusts and to pull it down from the government of the world. To use means which God prohibits is to set up hell to govern us since God will not govern our affairs in answer to our greedy desires. It seeks to obtain by the curse of God that which we should only desire by God's blessing. This is to slight God's wisdom and adore our folly. When we go out of God's way, we go out of God's protection. To do evil is not to trust in God or have any regard to his providential care. To distrust God detracts from his power as if he had undertaken a task of government too hard for him, or as if he had grown weary of his labour, or as if he were unfaithful and not walking by rules of unerring goodness. But his care for us is a principal argument to move us to cast our care upon him (*1 Pet.* 5:7). If we do not cast our care on him we deny his care for us. He that trusts in anything else besides God denies all the powerful operations of God, and perceives him lacking in strength! How unreasonable it is not to trust his powerful goodness and question whether he can or will do this or that for us.

Stephen Charnock, *Works*, 1:46-47

Flee youthful passions and pursue righteousness.

2 Timothy 2:22

Be very diligent to mortify the desires and pleasures of the flesh. Keep a continual watch upon your senses, appetite, and lusts. Do not cast yourself upon temptations or opportunities for sinning. The lusts of the flesh and the pleasures of the world are common enemies of God and souls. Some by natural make-up have a special inclination to lust and they need a great deal of diligence, resolution, and watchfulness for their preservation. Lust is not like a corrupt opinion that vanishes as soon as truth appears, but is a brutish inclination that continues even in light of the best reasoning. It is constantly with you. It will allure when objects are presented by sense or fantasy. It is like a headstrong horse that must be restrained at first, or it will hardly be restrained when it breaks loose and gets the advantage. You may think you may walk without a guard if you have been brought up in temperance and modesty, but when the baits of lust abound and the devil's snares inflame your lusts, you may find to your sorrow that you have need for watchfulness, and that all is not mortified just because it is quiet. As a man that walks among gunpowder with a lighted candle, you should never be careless since you are in a constant danger. You are never out of danger with such an enemy to watch. If once you suffer the fire to kindle, alas! What work it may make before you are even aware (*James* 1:14-15). Little knows the fish when he is nibbling at the bait that he is swallowing the hook that will lay him soon on the bank. When you are looking on the cup, or gazing on alluring beauty, or wantonly dallying and pleasing your senses with things unsafe, you little know how far beyond your intentions you may be drawn, and how deep the wound may prove, how great the smart, or how long and difficult the cure. Keep a full distance from the bait, and always watch, and avoid temptations.

RICHARD BAXTER, *Practical Works*, 1:54-55

Not neglecting to meet together ... but encouraging one another, and all the more as you see the Day drawing near.

Hebrews 10:25

We must call the Sabbath a delight, and prefer it as our greatest joy as all the saints of God in all ages have done (*Psa.* 122:1). We must observe it as a holy time. It is a day in which God bows the heavens and comes down and offers himself in ways of sweet and friendly communion with his people. By reserving one day in seven for his own immediate worship, we actually acknowledge him as Sovereign Lord of ourselves and of our times. In this we seek things of eternity and enjoy spiritual rest for the soul. Thanks be to God for this unspeakable gift! We are not to account the Sabbath as an ordinary and common thing, but to place a high and precious valuation upon it, the joy and rejoicing of our hearts, a day wherein all our comforts and pleasures centre. Our delight springs principally from the presence of God. He is pleased graciously to come in, and to fill our soul with his own presence; he convinces, enlightens, converts, quickens, strengthens and comforts by his presence. To grow in holiness is our design in sanctifying the Sabbath: to come down from the mount with our faces shining with the savour of Christ and with his sweet ointment upon our garments, and to have others notice that we have been with Jesus! It is sad when men come out of a Sabbath just as they came in, just as vain, loose, proud, worldly, and lovers of pleasure rather than lovers of God, fit for sin as they were before. But it is the golden spot of the week: graces triumph in it, the ordinances enrich it, the Father rules it, the Son rose upon it, and the Spirit overshadows it! It is heaven in a glass, and the first fruits of an everlasting blessed harvest. This calls for a solemn preparation of the heart and affections for communion with God, that we might go forth to meet him whom our soul loves, and bring him home with us.

Thomas Case, *Puritan Sermons 1659-1689*, II:26-46

Like newborn infants, long for the pure spiritual milk, that by it you may grow up into salvation.

1 Peter 2:2

Holy Scripture is a golden epistle sent to us from God. We are commanded to search the Scriptures. We must search as for a vein of silver, or as a child reading over his father's will and testament. Scripture is our Magna Carta for heaven. Scripture being translated in our language is the sword of the Spirit unsheathed, and enables us to diligently search into holy mysteries. What will become of them who are strangers to Scripture? They who slight the word written, slight God himself, whose stamp it bears. Nor is it enough to read alone, but it should be our care to get spiritual profit by our reading. God gave his word not as a landscape to look at, but as a father delivers money to his son to improve. How shall we read the Scriptures with most spiritual profit? This is a momentous question! First we must remove any hindrances. We must remove the love of every sin. If a patient were to take poison, it would hinder the effect of medicine prescribed by the doctor. Sin, lived in, poisons scriptural prescriptions. The soul cannot thrive under the heat of lust. Also, cares of the world may choke the word. Is a man likely to profit with his eye on the word but his heart upon the world? Next, we must read the Scriptures with reverence: think of every line you read as God speaking to you. Pray for understanding since there are knots in Scripture that are not easily untied. Read the word with seriousness. If you received a letter in which your whole estate were concerned, how serious would you be in the reading of it! Seek to remember what you have read; Satan desires to steal it out of your mind. Meditate on your reading. Reading without meditation is barren. The bee drinks from the flower and then in the hive works it into honey. So we must warm our reading at the fire of meditation.

Thomas Watson, *Puritan Sermons 1659-1689*, II:57-62

The law of your mouth is better to me than thousands of gold and silver pieces.

Psalm 119:72

We must read the word of God in humility. How unworthy we are that God should reveal himself to us. God's secrets are with the humble. We must cherish every word to be from God, and prize this book above all other books. Scripture is the library of the Holy Spirit, and the standard of truth. It is the north-star to direct us to heaven. It is the compass by which the rudder of our will is to be steered. It is the field in which Christ, the pearl of great price, is hidden. It is a rock of diamonds, and the eye salve to mend our eyes. It is the mirror on which the glory of God shines, and it is the universal medicine for the soul. It is the leaves of the tree for the healing of the nations, and the breeder and feeder of grace. It warns us of the rocks of sin to avoid, and is the antidote against error and apostasy. It is our bulwark to withstand the force of lust. 'Take away the word, and you deprive us of the sun', said Luther. The word is a voice from heaven. Get a strong love for the word. It is a storehouse of truth to adorn the inner man of the heart. It is the true manna with an abundance of sweet tastes. Seek the whole counsel of God so no truth is concealed. Read it to be made better by it. Let it pierce the rock of your heart and make you fruitful in grace. Apply the word personally. Say, 'God intends me in this', when it presses any duty or thunders against sin. Notice the precepts of duty as well as promises. Focus on passages with the greatest sweetness and that speak to your particular case. Take notice and be warned of examples in Scripture as living sermons to you. Read till you find your heart warmed, and labour to be inflamed by it. Implore the guidance of God's Spirit, and beg his anointing.

THOMAS WATSON, *Puritan Sermons 1659–1689*, II:62–69

For this light momentary affliction is preparing for us an eternal weight of glory beyond all comparison.

2 Corinthians 4:17

Great regard is to be made to those paragraphs of Scripture that are most beneficial to one's present case. Has God made your chain heavy? Consider passages that speak to this (*Heb.* 12:7). The sun may hide itself in a cloud, but not out of the firmament; God may hide his face, but he is not out of covenant. God is like a musician: he will not stretch the strings of his lute too hard, lest they break. A saint's comfort may be hid as seed under the dirt, but at last it will spring up into a harvest of joy. When God's Spirit joins himself to the word, it will be effectual to salvation. Through God's blessing his word becomes engrafted into men's hearts, sanctifies them and makes them bring forth the sweet fruits of righteousness. When you have profited by reading the holy Scriptures, adore God's distinguishing grace. Bless God that he has brought light to you so you can see. He has unlocked his hidden treasure and enriched you with saving knowledge. Some perish by not having Scripture, others by not improving it. That God should pass by millions in the world, and that his electing love should fall upon you; that the Scripture, like the pillar of cloud, should have a dark side to others, but a bright side to you; that his word is a dead letter to others but a savour of life to you: how you should be in a holy ecstasy of wonder and wish that you had a heart of burning love to God and the voice of an angel to make heaven ring with God's praises! But some godly may fear they do not profit by the word they read. Ah, you will profit though you come short of others. There is variation in the produce of the good ground. The apostles were but slow in understanding! The Holy Spirit will bring to your remembrance that which you are in most need of!

Thomas Watson, *Puritan Sermons 1659-1689*, II:67, 70-71

Now the Lord is the Spirit, and where the Spirit of the Lord is, there is freedom.

2 Corinthians 3:17

When cases of prayer are uncertain, observe the frame and temper of your spirit in prayer, for the heart may indicate a positive outcome. (1.) A liberty of spirit in prayer like a bubbling fountain is an excellent sign of a positive outcome. The heart is sometimes locked up that it cannot pray, and it finds a straitness, as if the Lord had spoken as to Moses, 'Speak no more to me about this matter.' In this case the bow of prayer does not abide in strength, but when the Lord graciously grants enlargement of heart, it is a notable sign of success. (2.) A blessed quiet calmness of spirit in times of prayer, especially when the soul was troubled and clouded at first, is an indication of a positive outcome. At length, the sun shines forth brightly, and the heavens look serenely and cheerfully upon the soul in prayer. Prayer chases away dark thoughts from the heart, eases the conscience, and fills the soul with the peace of God. (3.) Sometimes God makes his people joyful in the house of prayer. When we look upon God with an eye of faith, it enlightens our faces with heavenly joy. This joyful light of God's countenance is like the sun rising upon the face of the earth; it chases away the dark fears and discouragements of the night. Such heavenly joy shows the strength of faith in prayer and the radiant appearances of God, yea, to this end all prayer should be directed (*John* 16:24). (4.) A sweet affection to God is a positive indication of success. Clouds of suspicion of divine mercy, as if God were a hard task-master, are unbecoming a soul that goes to God as Father. When the soul perceives that all flows from the fountain of his eternal love, it makes prayer to be filled with holy delights and joys. As answers of prayer flow from the love of the Father, so suitable workings of holy affections flow from the hearts of his children.

Samuel Lee, *Puritan Sermons 1659–1689*, II:183–185

From the first day that you set your heart to understand … your words have been heard.

Daniel 10:12

It is a dangerous state to carry on public duties only and neglect secret duties. It is a suspicious token of hypocrisy, for the soul of religion lies so much in the heart and the closet! God's eye is open to you in the closet, and if your eye is open to his, you may see his glorious beauty. The excellency of grace lies in making conscience of secret sins and of secret duties. Would you live delightfully? Would you translate heaven down to earth? Then keep up communion in secret prayer—to know him, to discern his face, to behold the lustre of his eyes that shines in secret. Remember the glorious person that meets you in your closet. All the world cannot yield the beauty you may see when you are in a happy frame in secret prayer. Shut your eyes when you come out, for all other objects are but vile and sordid, and not worth the glances of a noble soul. O the sweetness and the hidden manna that a soul tastes when in living communion with God! Its ecstasies allure and draw the heart from earthly vanities. Prayer stands on Mount Zion and foretells great things to the church's joy and its enemies' terror. The prayers of Christians confounded the nations. When the spirit of prayer is once poured out, it brings deliverance to Mount Zion. Let us never be discouraged—prayer awakens Christ in the ship of the church, and her storms will cease in a great calm. Nothing revives and cheers the spirit so much as answers of love and mercy from heaven. Our closets cast an influence upon our shops, our ships, our fields, and all we enjoy, so that they smell of divine blessing! O you that fear the Lord, be diligent to observe secret prayer, for the life and joy of a Christian is improved by it. God is graciously pleased with secret prayer, and with great account esteems his praying people!

Samuel Lee, *Puritan Sermons 1659–1689*, II:191–194

Addressing one another in psalms and hymns and spiritual songs, singing and making melody to the Lord with your heart.

Ephesians 5:19

When the saints rejoice in God, he hears their music. A singing saint—how triumphant! Is not singing a taste of the joy reserved for us within the veil, in concert with angels singing to their glorious Creator? Singing is the triumph of a gracious soul joying in the praises of his Father. In praise the heart takes wings and mounts up with the celestial choir. Singing takes its proper rise from the heart. We magnify the true God by our singing. Moses sang a holy song (*Exod.* 15), David wrote songs, and Hezekiah appointed them to be sung (*2 Chron.* 29:30). Our dearest Jesus practised this sweet duty (*Matt.* 26:30). Singing is the soul's spiritual recreation, and puts the soul in a sweet meditation. It elevates us to a higher degree in communion with God. There is not a greater resemblance of heaven upon earth than a company of God's people singing psalms together. In singing, the soul rejoices in the divine goodness, exults in divine excellencies, and meditates on divine promises. If we sing of God's goodness, it inflames our hearts to love and admiration. When we sing of his power it stirs our faith and confidence. Singing is the music of nature—the mountains and valleys sing, the trees sing, and the birds chant their musical notes. The saints sing in their greatest straits and their greatest deliverances. Singing is the music of angels and the music of heaven. God's holy prophets sang, and in all ages God's people have sung praises. Singing, like praying, can work wonders (*Acts* 16:25-26). Singing is the expression of a gracious soul. Wicked men only make a noise. Singing is joy expressed. There is no joy comparable to what we have in Christ! As we pray in the Spirit, so we should sing in the Spirit! Singing sweetens a prison, prepares us for suffering, and lightens and exhilarates the soul.

JOHN WELLS, *Puritan Sermons 1659-1689*, II:72-85

And they were singing a new song before the throne.

Revelation 14:3

Rejoice in God by singing. It is prompted by the Holy Spirit and a joyful heart; singing follows joy! The Psalms provide an abundance of matter for meditation. A gracious spirit may find sweet contemplation from them. The themes of David are comprehensive and suitable for every condition! How they are full of sweet counsels, divine raptures, humble complaints, and hearty expressions of love to God! Sometimes we may find David swimming in his tears, and sometimes ravished with his joys. He is sometimes eclipsed with distrust and at other times raised with confidence in times of distress. The Psalms are a Christian's choicest oracle to fly to in times of distress. Was not the Psalmist guided by an infallible Spirit? How often are the Psalms quoted by Christ and the apostles to establish divine truth! Let us embrace and pursue this holy duty of singing the praises of the Psalms which is the very suburbs of heaven. No one thrives so well as those who sing the Psalms. Don't turn your back on this joyous and sweet ordinance! Let us sing the praises of the great Jehovah, and in our homes may our children be little birds to sing praises to our Creator. It might behove us to ponder how much of heaven we lose in neglecting this service! In singing Psalms we begin the work of heaven. There, they are singing the song of Moses and the Lamb (*Rev.* 15:3), and the angels use their voices to sing the praises of the Most High! Jerome exclaims that we should sing not only with a sweet voice, but with a melting heart. Bernard says we must sing purely, without any vain thoughts, and strenuously, heartily, and energetically. As Christ perfumes the prayers of saints, he makes our tune a precious melody. He raises our voice to a pleasing elevation. Though we have Esau's garments, he can give us Jacob's voice.

JOHN WELLS, *Puritan Sermons 1659–1689*, II:85–88

He who keeps Israel will neither slumber nor sleep.

Psalm 121:4

Consider the care of providence for your body. With great tenderness God has carried you in his arms through innumerable hazards and dangers in this world. How great a wonder it is that our lives have not been extinguished in some of those dangers! Have not some of us fallen into very dangerous sicknesses and diseases, in which we have approached to the very brink of the grave? Have we not often had the very sentence of death in ourselves? Our bodies have been like a leaky ship in a storm. Yet God has preserved and launched us out again, just as well as ever. O what a wonder that such a crazy body should be preserved for so many years and survive so many dangers! It is like a delicate glass that has been in use for fifty years without being broken. If you enjoy health, or have recovered out of sickness, it is because the Lord is your physician. And how many deadly dangers has God's hand rescued you from in battle, when the sword was bathed in blood and made a horrid slaughter? And many have seen the wonders of salvation in the deep when God has stretched forth his hand for their rescue from danger! O what cause we have to adore our great preserver. Many thousands of our companions have gone down, and yet we are here to praise the Lord among the living. How innumerable are the hazards God has carried us all through! Many thousands we never saw, but our God did! Consider what you owe to his providence for your protection since you came out of the womb. Consider how every member of your body has been tenderly kept even when you were an instrument of sin against the Lord before salvation. We have provoked him to afflict us, but how great was his compassion and his patience! All this, that we might employ our bodies for God. Shall they not then be cheerfully employed in his service? Is this not reasonable?

John Flavel, *Works*, IV:402-405

Before I was afflicted I went astray, but now I keep your word.

Psalm 119:67

An eminent favour of divine providence for saints is God's assistance in the great work of mortification. In believers, there is yet a strong inclination to sin, and every believer finds it so daily to his grief. God is our safety in the hour of temptation. Our fitness for service depends much upon it. The Spirit works internally as the principal agent, and providence assists externally. His providence lays bars and blocks in our way to hinder and prevent sin. Basil was sorely grieved with a prolonged headache, and he earnestly prayed that it might be removed: but no sooner was he freed from this clog, but he felt the inordinate motions of lust, which made him pray for his headache again. So it might be with many of us if our clogs were cut off! One design and aim of afflictive providences is to purge and cleanse us from the pollutions into which temptations have plunged us. The blood of Christ is the only fountain opened for the purging of sin, but sanctified affliction may in virtue of Christ's blood produce blessed effects upon the soul. Though a cross without a Christ never did any man any good, yet thousands have been beholden to their crosses by virtue of Christ's death. The best of hearts, if bestowed with comfortable enjoyments, become overheated in their affections and are too much taken up with them, and their hearts are drawn away from the Lord. Thus, he may use his providence to wean us from these excessive and inordinate affections! God will prepare a worm to smite Jonah's excessive delight in his gourd. How many husbands, wives, and children has providence smitten upon this very account? It might have spared them longer if they had been loved more moderately. This has blasted many an estate and hopeful project, and it is a merciful dispensation for our good!

John Flavel, *Works*, IV:405-409

The living creatures give glory and honour and thanks to him who is seated on the throne, who lives for ever and ever.

Revelation 4:9

That I may in good earnest stir up your souls to thankfulness, consider these things: (1.) *There is more need of praises than there is of prayers.* For our mercies outweigh our needs. What multitudes of mercies we enjoy, both temporal and spiritual. Also, our needs and miseries are deserved by our own sins. But all of our mercies are unmerited and undeserved; they all flow in upon us from the free love and favour of God. O that the high praises of God were more in our mouths. (2.) *Thankfulness is a sure evidence of our sincerity.* Thanksgiving is a self-denying grace. It takes the crown from ourselves, and sets it on the head of our Creator. It is a grace that gives God supremacy in our hearts, thoughts, desires, words, and works. Thankfulness is a free-will offering. Nothing so clearly and fully speaks of your sincerity. The little birds, after a sip of water, never fail to look up as if they meant to give thanks. So we should give thanks for every drop of grace! (3.) *A thankful soul holds community with the music of heaven.* By thankfulness we join in unity with the angels who are singing hallelujahs to him that sits upon the throne (*Rev.* 4-5). In heaven, there are no prayers, but all praises. There cannot be a clearer argument of a man's right to heaven, and readiness for heaven, than his being much at the work of heaven here on earth! Remember one thing more—that there is no better way to get more grace than to be thankful for a little grace. He who opens his mouth wide in praises will have his heart filled with graces. Ingratitude stops the ears of God and shuts the hand of God, and turns away the heart of the God of grace! Unthankfulness is a great injustice. O do not give God an occasion by your ingratitude to write upon your forehead—'ungrateful children'!

Thomas Brooks, *Works*, III:76-77

Sing praises to the Lord, O you his saints, and give thanks to his holy name.

Psalm 30:4

Will you be thankful, O Christian, for the least courtesy of men, and not be thankful for the little measure of grace that is bestowed upon you by God? The least measure of grace is of more value than a thousand worlds! Do you remember that most men do not have the least measure of saving grace, and free grace has knocked at your door while it passes by thousands? Free grace has tossed the pearl of price into your bosom, and others are left to wallow in their blood forever! And will you not be thankful? Oh do but consider how notoriously wicked you would have been if the Lord had not bestowed a little grace upon you! Look around and hear the cursing and blaspheming of God to his face. Had not the Lord given you a little grace, ten thousand to one but you would have been one in wickedness among these monsters of mankind. Had not the Lord given you tastes and sips of grace, you might have been as vile as the vilest among them. Ah, weak saints! Do you know what an awakened conscience would give for a little of that grace that the Lord has given you? Were all the world a lump of gold, and in their hand to give, they would give it for the least spark of grace, and for the least drop of mercy! I have heard of a man, who being in a burning fever, professed that if he had all the world at his disposal, he would give it all for just one drink. So would an awakened conscience for one dram of grace. Oh! Says such a soul, 'when I look up and see God frowning and feel my conscience gnawing and accusing, when I look down and see hell open to receive me and devils standing ready to accuse me, oh! Had I a thousand worlds I would give them all for a little drop of grace!' Oh! What would not a damned soul that has been in hell an hour give for a drop of grace. Think seriously of this, and be thankful!

Thomas Brooks, *Works*, III:75-76

I write these things to you who believe in the name of the Son of God that you may know that you have eternal life.

1 John 5:13

A weak saint may say, 'Sir! There is weight in what you say, to provoke us to thankfulness for small grace, if we but knew we had true grace; but we live between fear and hope. One day we hope for heaven and another day we are fearing hell! We are up and down, backward and forward. We have a little light, and then the sun is clouded. I desire to put an end to this controversy in my soul.' Well, speak on, poor soul, and let me hear what you have found in your own soul; I find—(1.) *A holy restlessness in my soul*, like Simeon, until I have Christ in my heart. I am like Noah's dove: I cannot rest until I am back in the ark. I cannot be quiet till I know that I am housed in Christ. My soul is like a ship in a storm, that is tossed hither and thither; oh, how shall I find him who is the chiefest of ten thousand? What are honours to me, riches to me, and the favour of creatures to me so long as I go mourning without my Christ!—(2.) *I have strong desires.* The poor man desires bread to feed him, the wounded desires medicine to heal him, but I have holy and heavenly desires. Oh that I had more of God! Oh that I were filled with Christ! Oh that I had his righteousness to cover me, his grace to pardon me, his power to support me, his wisdom to counsel me, his lovingkindness to refresh me, and his happiness to crown me! But, (3.) Though I dare not say that Christ is mine, yet I can truly say that Christ, his love, his works, his grace, his word, are the main objects of my contemplation and meditation. Oh I am always best when I am most meditating and contemplating Christ, his love and his grace. I can truly say that the lack of Christ's love is a greater grief and burden to my soul than the lack of any outward thing in this world. The discovery of his favour is better than life! *(Continued)*

Thomas Brooks, *Works*, III:77-79

We know that we have passed out of death into life, because we love the brothers.

1 John 3:14

(4.) 'I know there was a time when my greatest care and fear was to please myself. I can remember with sorrow and sadness how often I have displeased Christ to please myself, but now it is quite otherwise with me. My greatest care is to please Christ, and my greatest fear, to offend him. I would not willingly nor resolvedly sin against Christ, for a world. (5.) Though I dare not say that Christ and heaven is mine, yet I can truly say that I dearly love the people of Christ that have the Lord for their portion, and for the image of Christ I see stamped upon them. The poorest, most neglected and despised saint in the world is more precious and dear to my soul than the greatest and richest sinner in the world. (6.) Though I lack assurance, my soul weeps for the dishonour done to Christ by myself and others. I could look the Lord in the face, were I now to die, and say, "Lord! You know my eyes run down with rivers of tears because men do not keep your word." I prize persons and things according to the holiness and spirituality that is in them. Thus, I prize Christ above all. Oh that I might be filled with the fullness of Christ. Let the ambitious man have the honours of the world, the sensual man his pleasure, and let the covetous man tumble up and down in all the gold and silver of the world, but if I have Christ, it shall be enough for my soul! When he gives me a little light through a crevice and a little power to walk close, this gives me more joy, sweet peace and comfort to my soul than all the riches, honours, friends, and favours in this world! I wouldn't change my position with the profane men of this world for ten thousand worlds!'—*Well then, weak saint, these things undeniably speak out of the truth and strength of your grace. So, bless God and walk thankfully and humbly before him!*

Thomas Brooks, *Works*, III:79-82

Do not be deceived: 'Bad company ruins good morals.'

1 Corinthians 15:33

Be exceedingly wary with what company you familiarly converse. These have great advantage to help or hinder your salvation. They have the advantage of an interest in your affections as well as familiarity. They may be powerful instruments of your good or hurt. If you have a familiar friend that will defend you from error, help you against temptations, lovingly reprove your sin, feelingly speak of God and the life to come, and they do this from the inward power of faith, love, and holy experience, the benefit of such a friend may be more to you than of the most learned or greatest in the world. How sweetly will their speeches relish of the Spirit from which they come! How deeply may they pierce a careless heart! How powerfully they may kindle in you a love and zeal for God and his commandments. How seasonably may they discover a temptation, prevent your fall, reprove an error, and recover your souls. How faithfully will they watch over you! How profitably will they pray with you fervently when you are cold, and remind you of the truth, duty, and mercy which you have forgotten. It is a very great mercy to have such a judicious, solid, and faithful companion in the way to heaven. But take note of familiar company that is lukewarm or profane. If your ears are daily filled with folly and curses, is this likely to leave a pleasant or wholesome relish on your minds? Before you are aware, it may so cool and damp your graces, that your decay is seen by others. First you will hear with less offence, then with indifference, then you will begin to laugh at their sin and folly, and then you will begin to speak as they, and grow cold and leave off prayer and other holy duties. But to have a companion to open your heart to, and join with in prayer and edifying conference, is a mercy worldlings do not value!

Richard Baxter, *Practical Works*, 1:55-56

The word of God is living and active, sharper than any two-edged sword, piercing to the division of soul and of spirit.

Hebrews 4:12

We must prepare for reading or hearing the word of God. Before you go to hear, labour to affect your heart with the necessity, excellence, and efficacy of the word. There was half an hour's silence in heaven before the seventh trumpet sounded. Mary minded 'the one thing necessary'. Urge your soul with this: The word I am going to hear is ordained of God to be absolutely necessary for my spiritual and eternal good. If I am dead, it must enliven me; if I am blind, it must enlighten me. It is necessary to open my eyes to see Christ. My soul is sinful—the word must sanctify it; my soul is sick—the word must heal it; my soul is hungry—the word must feed it. Whatsoever condition of misery I am in, it is the word that must give suitable exhortation to support me. Consider its excellence: it is God's word—it is the voice of God. It enjoys divine operation. What wonders God has wrought by his word. It has given eyes to the blind, feet to the lame, ears to the deaf, and life to the dead. God is the author, Christ is the matter, and eternal life is its end. The word will work one way or another, for salvation or damnation. It will either convert or confound you. The sea sinks some vessels, and lands others safely. Entreat God to bless it to you: 'the Lord opened the heart of Lydia'. Paul might have preached his heart out before Lydia's heart opened to let the word in, if God had not undertaken to work. If the sword of the word is to pierce your soul, and slay your most beloved sins, the arm of the Lord must wield it. The voice of thunder must come from heaven, which can pluck up the strong trees of unbelief, and pull down the high towers of pride and self. He that made the word can make it strike home, even 'to the dividing of soul and spirit'.

George Swinnock, *Works*, 1:145-152

Therefore whoever wishes to be a friend of the world makes himself an enemy of God.

James 4:4

The love of the world is inconsistent with the love of God. The world and God are contrary lords, who require each the whole heart of man. The world commands you to engage no further in matters of religion than may consist with its interest, but Christ commands you to part with all worldly interest for himself. The world commands you to take your fill of the world, to enjoy the sweets of it, and feed your heart with it, but Christ commands you to use this world only as if you used it not. The world commands you to endeavour to make your names and reputations great, while Christ commands you to glory only in his cross, and to account abasement for Christ your greatest honour. The world commands you not to worry about small sins, but to take your liberty, but Christ commands you to dread the least sin more than the greatest suffering. How contrary are these masters! When the heart is full of the world, how soon is all sense of love to God choked! O how the mind is blinded and charmed with the painted heart-bewitching shadows of the world! Love to the world turns the heart from God, and so bids adieu. Love of the world is a god-maker. Lust makes pleasure its god. Worldlings lose the true God in the crowd of false gods! Acts of lust that arise from sudden passion, though violent, may consist with the love of God, but a deliberate bent of heart towards the world as our supreme interest cannot! Love to the world makes us servants to it. He that cannot part with the world will soon part with God. The flesh-pleasing sweets of the world make the delicacies of heaven seem bitter. Love to the world is the devil's throne, the helm of his ship where he sits and steers the soul hell-wards. What made Judas or Demas fall, but love for the world? Love for God is the best good!

THEOPHILUS GALE, *Puritan Sermons 1659-1689*, 1:654-659

Anyone who does not love does not know God, because God is love.

1 John 4:8

The love of God excels and transcends the love of the world. The more noble and spiritual love's object, the more perfect that love. Is not God the most perfect being? He is our choicest good, and in every way desirable for himself. O what an excellent thing is love to God, who is so amiable! But the world, what a dirty, heart-ensnaring thing it is! The love of God is pure and unspotted, but how filthy and polluted is love to the world. The love of God amplifies and widens the heart, but the world confines and narrows it. By love to God we become lords over all things beneath us, but love to the world brings us into subjection to the most base of persons and things. Love to God is tranquil and serene, but the world, tempestuous and turbulent. Love to God gives repose and quiet to the soul, but the world, perpetual agitation without end. Love to God is an angelic life, a taste of heaven, and a living mark of God's children. It is a dismal contemplation, how many follow Christ in profession, but have the mark of worldlings on their foreheads. O how much love to the world lies hidden under the mask of a professed love to God! Their tongues are tipped with heaven, but their hearts drenched in the earth. They mention God in name, but exalt the world in heart. Is not God greatly dishonoured? O that painted shadows and dirty clay should run away with our love! O what a transient thing is the glory of this perishing world. Why rejoice in but fetters and chains? Keep your love in heaven while living in the world. Don't let worldly cares choke your sense of God. Bring your natural desires into a narrow compass, and let your hearts be enlarged toward God. Let us love nothing greatly but what we shall love forever, and let us labour after the highest strain of love to God.

THEOPHILUS GALE, *Puritan Sermons 1659-1689*, 1:659-665

We appeal to you not to receive the grace of God in vain ... Behold, now is the day of salvation.

2 Corinthians 6:1-2

By *'the grace of God'*, Paul means the message of the gospel. The gospel is called 'grace', because it is the instrument, under the Spirit of God, of bestowing the benefits of free grace upon us. To receive it in vain is to receive it unprofitably. God has assigned a certain time and day for the bestowment of his grace, and Paul seeks for the Corinthians to respond to this season. Neglect of this season hazards one's eternal salvation! When time and means meet together in conjunction, they produce opportunity. The day of salvation is the time in which God will by free grace accept man out of his free good will. We may easily let this time slip between our fingers. It is needful therefore to instantly lay hold upon it! Embracing this opportunity is a wisdom that God alone must teach us. Opportunity is so very short and sudden, and men are blinded by pleasures, prejudices and vain hopes. Opportunity must be presently embraced. The neglect of the opportunity is the greatest destroyer in the world. It is not only flat denial that ruins, but delay! All that the devil pretends to desire is your now, your present opportunity. He will offer God your tomorrow—'Let me have the present time, and give God all the future!' Few deny, but most delay. The present opportunity is a short time; don't waste it; it cannot be recalled when spent. It is an irrecoverable loss. Esau lost his day, and the foolish virgins could not break open the shut door of heaven. Time hurries you to the grave. You have no assurance of another opportunity. Death may knock without warning. Hell is not so full of souls as it is of delayed purposes. What would a lost soul give for a crumb of time wasted! Nothing can recompense for the neglect of salvation, yet salvation can recompense for our neglecting all other things.

William Jenkin, *Puritan Sermons 1659-1689*, 1:665-688

Look carefully then how you walk, not as unwise but as wise, making the best use of the time.
Ephesians 5:15-16

Opportunity must be presently embraced and improved, and this is man's greatest wisdom! Brute creatures are far wiser than he that neglects opportunity. We are fully accountable for every opportunity. If the sparrows are awake and chirping, is it fit for pastors to be sleeping? Men of the world of all employments, yea, the sons of violence, embrace their season and are up early! Shall professors be asleep when these are awake and active? Work, work! Work apace, you that have the sunshine of the gospel. Are you idle while time hurries you to the grave? Time has wings, your hourglass needs no shaking, there is no stopping the stream of time, and the sun is going down. Lazy Christians, if the sun must not go down upon your anger, surely it must not go down upon your loitering! You do not see your time going, but shortly you will see it gone. It is like a clock; you may not see the hands moving, yet you can see that they have moved. It is bad to say, 'It is too soon', but it is worse to say, 'it is too late'. Morning is your golden hour, and the fittest for your employment, but the evening time is better than no time at all. If God will help us, much work may be done in a little time, but God must step in almost with a miracle to make up fifty years in an hour or two. We must redeem our time out of the clutches of vain employments that have so often taken us captive! It is miserable for our work to be undone for lack of time when we are dying, when it is undone because of the waste of time while we are living. Let the lashes of divine severity that have fallen on others quicken you in your pace as you travel to heaven. There are many thieves in your candle of time that waste it—sleeping, employments, and enjoyments. There are many tasks that take time on our journey. The longer we delay, the harder it is to begin!

WILLIAM JENKIN, *Puritan Sermons 1659-1689*, 1:675-683

Live for the rest of the time in the flesh no longer for human passions but for the will of God.

1 Peter 4:2

Sin is as deceitful to detain us as it is to draw us into sin. Lust and delay know no measure. The further you travel, the more difficult it is to go back. The deeper the engagement, the more difficult is the retreat. Neglect can become unwillingness and obstinacy. The habit of sin will at length turn into necessity. Antidotes against poison must not be delayed. The longer a tenant fails to pay his rent, the harder it will be for him to make it up. A nail driven into wood is more difficult to draw out when it is driven up to the head! The longer wood lies in water, the harder it is to burn. The longer Satan's possession has been, the more difficult will be his ejection. Every delay makes your return to God seem more impossible. Goliath must be smitten in the forehead and Satan opposed often. The sooner you begin, and the faster your work in this day of grace, the sweeter will your sleep be in the evening. How sweet it is in older age to feed upon the comforts of a well-spent youth. Early beginnings in godliness make an easy deathbed. Salvation is a work of absolute necessity. Other things are maybes at the best, but salvation is a peremptory and indispensable necessity. A work of necessity must not be put off to a time of uncertainty. You may be excused in the day of judgment for leaving anything in the world undone besides the getting of salvation. You may be excused if you had no time to get riches and honours of the world. But what if you have not looked after eternal life? Can you say you had another employment more necessary? Can you say you were taken up with something more needful or useful? If you delay, delay in looking for riches and honour, and the vanities of the world! O, but now, now, now pursue salvation! It is a must-be. If the present time is gone, you may be undone forever.

William Jenkin, *Puritan Sermons 1659-1689*, 1:683-686

For my iniquities have gone over my head; like a heavy burden, they are too heavy for me.

Psalm 38:4

I dreamed, and behold I saw a man clothed with rags, standing in a certain place, a book in his hand, and a great burden upon his back. I looked, and saw him open the book, and as he read he wept and trembled and broke out with a lamentable cry, saying, 'What shall I do to be saved?' A man named Evangelist came to him and asked, 'Why do you cry?' He answered, 'I perceive by the book in my hand that I am condemned to die, and that this burden on my back will sink me lower than the grave.' Then said Evangelist, 'Flee from the wrath to come. Go up directly to the shining light at the wicket gate, and it will be told you what you should do.' His wife and children began to cry after him to return, but the man ran on crying, 'Life! Eternal life!' So in the process of time Christian got up to the gate, and over the gate there was written, Knock, and it shall be opened unto you. He knocked, saying, 'May I now enter? I have come from the city of Destruction and am going to Mount Zion, that I may be delivered from the wrath to come.' Mr Goodwill, at the gate, said, 'Do you see this narrow way? That is the way you must go. You may distinguish the right from the wrong by this—the right way is only strait and narrow.' The highway on which Christian was to go was fenced on either side with a wall, and that wall was called Salvation. Up this way did burdened Christian run, but not without great difficulty, because of the load on his back. He ran thus till he came at a place somewhat ascending, and upon that place stood a cross, and a little below, a sepulchre. So I saw in my dream that just as Christian came up to the cross, his burden loosed from off his shoulders and fell from off his back and began to tumble until it came to the mouth of the sepulchre where it fell in, and I saw it no more.

John Bunyan, *The Pilgrim's Progress*, pp. 1-36

Behold, I have taken your iniquity away from you, and I will clothe you with pure vestments.

Zechariah 3:4

Then was Christian glad and lightsome, and said with a merry heart, 'He has given me rest by his sorrow, and life by his death.' Then he stood still a while to look and wonder, for it was very surprising to him that the sight of the cross should thus ease him of his burden. He looked therefore, and looked again, even till the springs that were in his head sent the waters down his cheeks. Now, as he stood looking and weeping, behold, three shining ones came to him and saluted him with 'Peace be to you.' So the first said to him, 'Your sins be forgiven.' The second stripped him of his rags and clothed him with a change of raiment. The third set a mark on his forehead, and gave him a roll, with a seal upon it, which he bid him look on it as he ran, and that he should turn it in at the celestial gate. So they went on their way, and Christian gave three leaps for joy, and went on singing:

> Thus far did I come laden with my sin;
> Nor could aught ease the grief that I was in,
> Till I came hither: What a place is this!
> Must here be the beginning of my bliss?
> Blest Cross! Blest sepulchre! Blest rather be
> The Man that there was put to shame for me!

Then Christian espied two men come tumbling over the wall—Formalist and Hypocrisy. Christian said, 'Know you not that he that cometh not in by the door is a thief and a robber?' They looked at each other and laughed. But when they came to the Hill of Difficulty, which was steep and high, they chose two other ways which were called Danger and Destruction. These were full of dark mountains and there they stumbled and fell and rose no more!

John Bunyan, *The Pilgrim's Progress*, pp. 36-41

Now to him who is able to keep you from stumbling and to present you blameless before the presence of his glory with great joy, to the only God, our Saviour, through Jesus Christ our Lord.
Jude 24-25

When Pilgrim came to the house built by the Lord of the hill to entertain such pilgrims, they gave him something to drink and began discourse until supper was ready, for the best improvement of time. Prudence asked a few questions—'Are you not yet troubled by the influence of the things of the country from where you came?' 'Yes,' said Christian, 'but greatly against my will. I am troubled especially by my inward and carnal thoughts that I once delighted in, but now all those things are my grief. If I might choose mine own things, I would choose never to think of those things any more, but when I desire that which is best, I find that the worst is yet with me.' Prudence: 'Do you not find sometimes as if those things are vanquished, which at other times are your perplexity?' Christian: 'Yes, but that is seldom, and they are golden hours.' Prudence: 'What means have you found to be of help?' Christian: 'When I think what I saw at the cross—that will do it. When I look upon my embroidered coat—that will do it. When I look into the roll that I carry in my bosom—that will do it, and when my thoughts wax warm about whither I am going—that will do it.' Prudence: 'What is it that makes you so desirous to go to Mount Zion?' Christian: 'I hope to see him alive that did hang dead on the cross; and there I hope to be rid of all those things, that to this day are an annoyance to me. *There* they say there is no death, and *there* I shall dwell with such company as I like best. For, to tell you truth, I love him, because I was by him eased of my burden, and I am weary of my inward sickness. I would desire to be where I shall die no more and with the company that shall continually cry—"Holy, Holy, Holy!"'

JOHN BUNYAN, *The Pilgrim's Progress*, pp. 47-51

For we do not wrestle against flesh and blood …

Ephesians 6:12

Pilgrim had gone but a little way before he espied a foul fiend coming over the field to meet him. His name was Apollyon. Pilgrim resolved to venture, and stand his ground. The monster was hideous to behold, and coming up to Christian, he beheld him with a disdainful countenance. Apollyon: 'I perceive you are one of my subjects.' Christian: 'I was born in your dominion, but your service was hard, and your wages, the wages of death.' Apollyon: 'Go back, and what our country will afford, I promise to give you.' Christian: 'I have let myself to another, even to the King of princes. I have given him my faith and sworn my allegiance to him, and how can I, with fairness, go back with you?' Apollyon: 'Consider what you are like to meet with in the way: for the most part his servants come to an ill end because they transgress my ways! Many have been put to shameful deaths!' Christian: 'Present deliverance we do not expect; we wait for glory!' Apollyon: 'You fainted at your first setting out!' Christian: 'All this is true, and much more, but the Prince whom I serve and honour is merciful and ready to forgive.' Then Apollyon broke out into a grievous rage, saying, 'I am an enemy to this Prince, I hate his person, his laws, and people, and I am come out on purpose to withstand you!' Christian: 'Beware what you do, for I am in the King's highway—the way of holiness; therefore, take heed to yourself.' Apollyon straddled the whole way and said, 'Prepare to die, I will spill your soul!' With that he threw a flaming dart at his breast, but Christian had a shield in his hand. While wrestling with him, Christian began to despair of life, but, as God would have it, while Apollyon was fetching his last blow, Christian grasped his sword and gave him a deadly thrust, and Apollyon spread his dragon's wings and sped away, and Christian saw him no more.

John Bunyan, *The Pilgrim's Progress*, pp. 58-63

Even though I walk through the valley of the shadow of death, I will fear no evil, for you are with me; your rod and your staff, they comfort me.

Psalm 23:4

Christian needed to pass through the Valley of the Shadow of Death because the way to the Celestial City lay through the midst of it. It was a wilderness, a land of pits and droughts. At the border of the land, Christian met two men who brought an evil report of the land, crying, 'Back! Back!' Men: 'We heard howling and yelling as from unutterable misery in affliction and irons. There were clouds of discouraging confusion, and death spread its wings over it. It is in every way dreadful and without order.' So they parted. The valley had a deep ditch on the right, and on the left a dangerous bog. The pathway was exceedingly narrow. In the dark it was difficult to avoid the bog and ditch. Thus he went on. In the midst of the valley he perceived the mouth of hell was close by the wayside. There were flames and smoke in abundance, and hideous noises, so Pilgrim called on the weapon of prayer. Thus he went on, the flames reaching towards him, and distressed voices coming and going; he thought of going back, but resolved to go on. Christian was so confused that he didn't know his own voice. Wicked ones from the pit whispered blasphemies of the One he loved so much before. But he thought he heard the voice of a man saying, 'Though I walk through the valley of the shadow of death, I will fear no evil, for you are with me.' Then he was glad for these reasons: (1.) Others who feared God were in the valley as well as himself. (2.) God was with them in that dark and dismal state though he did not perceive it! (3.) He might have company by and by if he could overtake the voice he heard! As morning broke, Christian could look back and see more clearly the hazards he had gone through in the dark and the narrow way through the danger.

JOHN BUNYAN, *The Pilgrim's Progress*, pp. 64-69

But I, O LORD, cry to you; in the morning my prayer comes before you.

Psalm 88:13

They had not journeyed far, and the way became rough, and their feet tender, and the souls of the pilgrims were much discouraged because of the way, and they wished for a better way. Now a little before them, over the stile, was a meadow called By-Path Meadow. Christian said to Hopeful, 'Let us go over into it; there is the easiest going.' Hopeful: 'What if this path should led us out of the way?' Christian: 'Does it not go along the wayside?' Hopeful being persuaded by his fellow they went over the stile, and found it very easy for their feet. Walking before them was a man called Vain Confidence, who affirmed this was the way to the Celestial City, but the night came on and it grew very dark, and they heard Vain Confidence fall into a deep pit, and be dashed in pieces with his fall. It began to rain and thunder in a dreadful manner, and Hopeful groaned, 'Oh that I had kept on my way!' The way was now dangerous by reason of the rising water, and they realized it is easier going out of the way when you are in, than getting back in when you are out! Nearby was Doubting Castle, and the owner Giant Despair, who was stronger than the pilgrims, forced them into a dark dungeon. It was nasty and stinking to the spirit of these men. Here they lay for days without bread or a drop of water. They were frightened here and far from friends, and Christian knew double sorrow because he had led them out of the way! They began to pray, and Christian, as one half amazed, said, 'What a fool am I. I have a key in my bosom called Promise, and I am persuaded it will open any door in Doubting Castle.' Christian pulled it out, and the door flew open with ease; then they went on and came to the King's Highway again, and were safe.

> Out of the way we went, and then we found
> What 'twas to tread upon forbidden ground!

JOHN BUNYAN, *The Pilgrim's Progress*, pp. 124-134

His master said to him, 'Well done, good and faithful servant … Enter into the joy of your master.'

Matthew 25:23

So I saw in my dream that they came within sight of the gate of the city, but before them was a deep river with no bridge to cross. Until the trumpet will sound, only Enoch and Elijah have been permitted access to the city without passing through the river. The pilgrims began to despond, for no way could be found to escape the river. The river was found to be deep or shallow, as one believes in the King of the place. Entering, Christian began to sink. Hopeful: 'Be of good cheer, my brother, I feel the bottom, and it is good.' Christian: 'The sorrows of death have compassed me.' With that, a great darkness and horror fell upon Christian. Hopeful endeavoured to comfort him, saying, 'I see the gate, and men ready to receive us! Be of good cheer, Jesus Christ makes you whole.' With that Christian broke out with a loud voice, 'Oh, I see him again! And he tells me, when you pass through the waters, I will be with you.' And they both took courage. Thus they got over. On the other side two shining men were waiting to lead them to the gate of the city. While they were drawing near the gate, behold, a company of the heavenly host came out to meet them: 'These are the men who have loved our Lord, and have left all for his Holy Name!' Then the heavenly host gave a great shout! Thus they came to the gate. Written over the gate in letters of gold was: *'Blessed are they that do his commandments, that they may have right to the Tree of Life, and may enter in through the gates into the city.'* Enoch, Moses, and Elijah looked over the gate to see the pilgrims coming from the City of Destruction. The King commanded to open the gate, and when the two men entered, they were transfigured. They were met with harps and crowns, and the bells of the city rang out for joy—'Enter into the joy of our Lord!'

John Bunyan, *The Pilgrim's Progress*, pp. 181-189

Delight yourself in the Lord, and he will give you the desires of your heart.

Psalm 37:4

We are not ashamed to open up holy desires to God in prayer. What a Christian desires he prays for, and what he prays for he desires. Otherwise, he is a hypocrite. If a man prays to be free from temptation, yet is unwilling to have his loving bait taken from him, he prays but does not desire. There are many that pray, 'lead us not into temptation', and yet run into temptation; they feed their eyes, and ears, and senses with vain things. Their lives are nothing but a satisfying of their lusts. And there are many persons that desire that for which they dare not pray, since it is so bad. But a Christian, what he desires, he prays for. When we have holy desires stirred up by God, we should turn them into prayers. Prayer is more than a desire. It is a desire put up to God. Let us turn our desires into prayer; this is the way to have them speedily. The reason we should pray for our desires is to keep our acquaintance continually with God. We have a need of mortification, continual grace, and of freedom from this and that evil that is upon us. As many desires as we have, let there be so many prayers. Turn your desires into prayers and so maintain your acquaintance with God. We shall never come from God without a blessing and comfort. He never sends any out of his presence empty that know what they desire and come with a gracious heart. And it brings peace with it when we make our desires known to God by our prayers (*Phil.* 4:6-7). If God does not grant what we ask, his peace that passes understanding shall keep our hearts and minds. So when we put up our requests to God with thankfulness for what we have received, the soul will find peace. Therefore, let us turn all our desires into prayers, to maintain perpetual communion and acquaintance with God. Oh! It is a gainful and comfortable acquaintance!

Richard Sibbes, *Works*, II:222-223

Then he said, 'Let me go, for the day has broken.' But Jacob said, 'I will not let you go unless you bless me.'

Genesis 32:26

One qualification of prayer—it must be with perseverance and importunity. God loves importunate suitors (*Luke* 18:1-8). Will not God regard his children whom he loves more than the unrighteous judge? We are exhorted in Scripture not to keep silent, and to give God no rest. As Jacob with the angel wrestled with God, do not leave him till you have a blessing. As the woman of Canaan, let us follow him still, and refuse to take no for an answer. Oh this is a blessed violence, beloved, when we can set upon God, and will have no nay, but renew suit upon suit, and desire upon desire, and never leave till our petition is answered. Can a hypocrite pray always? Sometimes he will pray, but if God does not answer him presently, he gives up. But God's children pray always until it is gotten, if there is good reason, if it is an excellent thing, a necessity, and amiable. When they see the excellency, the necessity, and that it is attainable, they need no more, they will never give up. He that is guided by the spirit of prayer will not give God rest, but pray, till all his prayers are answered, even in heaven. Thus we ought eagerly, and constantly, to persevere in our desires in prayer, till they be fully satisfied. Let us make conscience, I beseech you, of this duty more than we have done. Let us not give up in prayer for grace, strength against our corruptions, for his church, for the prosperity of the gospel, and for those things we have grounds for. Let us never give up till we see he has answered our desires. And when he has answered our desires, let us go on still to desire more, for this life is a life of desires! Full accomplishment will be in heaven. Then all our desires shall be accomplished, and all promises performed. We must be in a state of desires and prayers till we're in heaven!

Richard Sibbes, *Works*, 11:223-224

She said, 'Yes, Lord, yet even the dogs eat the crumbs that fall from their masters' table.'

Matthew 15:27

Why does God not immediately accomplish our desires? (1.) He loves to hear the desires of his servants when they come, because he knows it is for their own good. It is music to his ears to hear a soul come to him with a request, especially for spiritual things which he delights to give, and that he knows is most useful and best for us. This pleases him so marvellously, that he will not presently grant it, but leads us along and along, that still he may hear more and more from us! (2.) And then to keep us in a perpetual humble subjection and dependence on him, he does not grant all at once, but leads us along by yielding little by little, so that he may keep us in a humble dependence. (3.) The spirit of prayer exercises all graces. We cannot pray without exercising faith, love for God and his church, a sanctified judgment as to the best things to pray for, and mortification. A spirit of prayer puts all these into exercise; therefore, God keeps us in the exercise of prayer by not answering at the first. (4.) When he would have us to set a high price upon what we desire, he doesn't answer at first so we would esteem its price. (5.) Then, that we might better use it when we do have it. We use things as we should when we have achieved them with great effort. When we have won them from God with great importunity, we will keep and preserve them as we should. Therefore, let us not be offended with God's gracious dispensation if he does not answer our desires presently, but pray still. And if we have the spirit of prayer continued in us, it is better to us than the thing we beg for. Often God answers us in a better kind. What particular grace would you have? In increasing a spirit of prayer in us he increases all graces in us, and so answers better than we asked. He will answer in one kind or another.

Richard Sibbes, *Works*, II:224-225

When you received the word of God … you accepted it … as what it really is, the word of God.

1 Thessalonians 2:13

When you hear or read the word of God, set yourself seriously as in the presence of God. God sits before you in his word and offers life or death, blessing or cursing, his infinite favour or fury, heaven or hell; and, friend, are these things to be jested with? When Cornelius heard Peter, he said, 'We are all here present before God, to hear all things that are commanded you of God.' When the heart is awed with the awareness of the divine presence, the iron gates of the ears will fly open, and give the word a free passage. We must diligently hearken to the speech of God, on whose breath depends life and death, when we see him immediately before our eyes. Erasmus: 'There is little good received by Scripture, if a man hears it carelessly, but if a man hears it out of conscience, and as in the presence of God, he shall find such an efficacy in it, as is not to be found in any other book.' Setting yourself seriously as in the presence of God is like the fire of a blacksmith on the iron to shape it and strike it while it's hot into the form and mould he is pleased with. The Thessalonians received Paul's message as the very word of God. When Senaclaeus heard Diaruis the martyr preach, he heard the Holy Spirit himself preaching to him! The devil's great design is to render the word fruitless lest the strongholds of his kingdom are broken down. As a jailer he will let the hands free so long as the doors of the prison are barred. He will give liberty for acts of charity so long as your ears and heart are locked fast. Christ waits at the door of your ear for access to your heart to deliver you—a poor captive—out of his hands. The devil will seek to hinder you from hearing as in God's presence by finding other work for you to do. He may get you to play and toy or do some business or other to keep you from hearing with a serious heart as in God's sight!

GEORGE SWINNOCK, *Works*, 1:156-157

Teach me, O Lord, the way of your statutes; and I will keep it to the end.

Psalm 119:33

After we hear or read the word, we need to be very watchful, for many birds are waiting to eat the seed after the farmer has sown it (*Matt.* 13:19). A farmer travelling home after the sale of his cattle is in danger of being robbed. So when a Christian has had a good meal, the devil tries all his wiles and tricks so he will lose it. After hearing and reading the word, we need to pray for a blessing upon it, and give thanks for its blessing. We need to pray for the influence of heaven for the seed's harvest. Go to God, and say, 'Teach me, O Lord, the way of your statutes, and give me understanding, and I shall keep your law with my whole heart.' Then, with thanksgiving, consider what a distinguishing mercy and treasure the word of God is. Without it, you would have been unholy and unhappy, but now you may eternally be both gracious and glorious. Bless the giver for this gift! What honour God deserves for this favour! We have both the Old and New Testaments in our mother tongue that is suitable medicine for every malady, seasonable comfort in all our miseries, and the costliest cordials and choicest comforts without price. Surely all this deserves thanks and praise. Do you realize the misery of those who lack the word? How many starve for lack of the bread of life! We sit at a full table, but millions famish for lack of spiritual food. How can they walk without the word to direct them? O reader, what infinite cause you have to bless the Lord that you are not in their condition! What shall we render to the Lord for this benefit? We sit by the fire of his word while many poor souls are freezing. We sit in the light of his word while many sit in darkness. Our table is spread with all sorts of food, both for necessity and delight, while millions starve and famish. Oh, that men would praise the Lord for his goodness!

George Swinnock, *Works*, 1:162-166

But be doers of the word, and not hearers only, deceiving yourselves.

James 1:22

When the preacher is done in the pulpit, the hearer must begin his practice. He hears a sermon best who practices it most! A Christian's life should be a legible commentary on God's law. Christ said, 'Blessed are they that hear the word of God and keep it!' Saints must be ready to die for the gospel, but a Christian may defend it just as truly by a holy life. A scandalous life is an offence to religion, and opens the mouths of its enemies. A fire is a good defence in a wilderness against ravenous beasts, so the heat of grace flaming, and the light of holiness shining in the lives of professors, will also defend the word against opposition. A sermon practised is a sermon in print, and teaches all week long. When the life and the word preached are one, others can see the word in every leaf, line, and volume of his life. An obedient hearer is the man who builds upon a rock and stands firm in the midst of wind, waves, and weather. Suppose you are never so great a hearer, yet if you are not a doer, you deceive your own soul. Alas! What will become of the frequent hearer, when the non-doer is to be thrown in hell? I read a story of two men who, walking together, found a young tree laden with fruit. Both gathered enough to satisfy, but one took all the remaining fruit. The other took the tree. The former had enough for the present, but the owner of the tree knew fruit every year. So it is with the one who plants the word in his heart! When the sermon is at an end, that is not an end of the sermon. A good husband having a bag of money will lock it up in a safe. As the occasion arises, he takes some out to pay for food, clothes, rent, and some for this and that as his necessities require. So, friend, lay up the precious treasure of the word, safe in the cabinet of your heart, and bring it out as occasions call for it in your life.

George Swinnock, *Works*, 1:166-168

Oh how I love your law! It is my meditation all the day.

Psalm 119:97

A good wish about the word of God: The Holy Scriptures have authority as from the heart and handwriting of God himself. By this star, I am directed as the wise men to Jesus Christ. I desire to set a high price on every part of God's word. I esteem the law of his lips above gold and silver! O that I may cry mightily to my God that he would open my heart to receive the word with all affection, and that the arrow of the preacher from the quiver of Scripture may hit and pierce my dearest corruptions. I wish that the weight of the word may sink so deep into my heart that I might cleanse my ways, and that the noise of the world may never hinder me from hearing the voice of God. I pray that the gospel may come to me not in word only, but also in power, that I may go to it with a blank sheet for any inscription, or soft wax for any impression which my God shall be pleased to make upon me. Oh that I might behold the Lord so effectually in that glass as to be changed into his image, from glory to glory. In special, I wish that my sins may be placed, by me, in the front of this spiritual battle, as Uriah, purposely to be slain, that the smooth stones from the streams of the sanctuary will be thrown so skilfully, and by a powerful hand, to sink deep into the foreheads of these to their death and destruction. I wish that after the seed of the word is sown, there will be showers of heaven's blessings springing up in the fruits of righteousness to the glory of God, and good of my soul. Because the gospel is a dish not set on every table, but through free grace bestowed on me, I wish that I may never rise from this spiritual food before I have given thanks to the master. I desire not only to hear the word, but to live like a saint and to be known by this ear-mark to be one of Christ's sheep, following him wherever he goes.

George Swinnock, *Works*, 1:170-171

Have nothing to do with irreverent, silly myths. Rather train yourself for godliness.

1 Timothy 4:7

Make careful choice of the books you read, and let Holy Scripture always have the preeminence. After Scripture, enjoy solid, living, heavenly treatises that best expound and apply Scripture. Next, consider credible histories, especially of the church. Take heed of the poison of false teachers which would corrupt your understanding, and of vain romances, plays, and false stories which may bewitch your fantasies and corrupt your heart. They are powerful baits of the devil to keep more necessary things out of the mind, since they are read with more delight and pleasure. Scripture is better than any other book whatever to convey the Holy Spirit in power to make us spiritual by imprinting itself upon our hearts! It will acquaint us more with God and bring us nearer to him, and make the reader more reverent, serious, and divine. Let Scripture be first and foremost in your hearts and hands, and let other books be subservient to it. The devil seeks to keep it from you. The divines are nothing more than a preaching of the gospel to the eye, as the voice of preachers to the ear. Vocal preaching moves the affections more, but books have the advantage in other ways; you can read an able preacher when a good one is not available. Every congregation cannot hear the most powerful preachers, but they can read them! Preachers may be silenced while books may be at hand. We may choose books that treat every subject, but we cannot choose the subject of the preacher. Books are at hand every day and hour, while preachers are but seldom and at set times. If sermons are forgotten they are gone, but books can be read over at our pleasure and leisure. Good books are a mercy to the world. The Spirit can preserve writing to all generations. Books are present, powerful sermons and of great use to our salvation.

RICHARD BAXTER, *Practical Works*, 1:56-57

How precious is your steadfast love, O God! The children of mankind take refuge in the shadow of your wings.

Psalm 36:7

The reward of God is freely dispensed by grace upon those who seek him (*Heb.* 11:6). We can hardly believe God's readiness to do good to his creatures, and reward our slender services. The comforts we have in well doing in this world are gifts of God, and an assurance that God will give us more. They are a taste of how good, and a pledge of how sure our reward shall be. Let us bless God that there is a reward, a great reward, a reward so freely dispensed. This gives us the joy of the Spirit, and hope and encouragement to go on in well doing upon this ground. So few seek after God. None at first (*Rom.* 3:11); we are busy seeking our own fancies and never think of returning to God, our chief good, until a thousand disappointments scourge us home to him! But alas, some do not seek him at all. Some are ever running from God to get away from his presence. Others do not seek him diligently with their whole hearts. Oh what a sorry use most of us put to our lives! We hunt after the profits of the world and the pleasures of our senses. How little is our delight in God. How seldom we speak of him and how cold our affections are. How dead and careless are our prayers. We must seek him till we find him. To enjoy God is the centre of our rest and the fountain of our blessedness and the chief end for which we were made (*Psa.* 73:25). It is our business to seek him, and our happiness to enjoy him. God refreshes our sense and taste with his goodness with new experiences every day. The devil says there is no need to seek God, especially when former endeavours did not succeed. Oh, but seek him. If there is nothing in hand, there is much hope; seeking brings an everlasting reward! If we do not sensibly find him, we may comfort ourselves, we are still in pursuit in a seeking way! It's better to be a seeker than a wanderer.

Thomas Manton, *By Faith*, pp. 335-339

By faith Noah, being warned by God … in reverent fear constructed an ark for the saving of his household.

Hebrews 11:7

The destruction of the old world showed God's displeasure against sin, and the preservation of Noah the privileges of the godly. Moses could not write about it without tears. The whole world perished—men, women, infants, and beasts. For forty days nothing but rain. It would have melted a heart of stone to hear the cries and shrieks of parents, women, and children. All things in the world were afloat. The foolish world thought it was just the dream of a foolish man, but the Lord made good Noah's word. We mark God's justice and his truth. Fire and water are at God's beck and call. He that punished the old world with water will punish the new world with fire in the latter days. Those living in Noah's day were secure and nourished their hearts with pleasure. So it will be in the last days: men secure in their luxury scoffing at ministers of the gospel. It was said of men in Noah's day, 'they did not know, till the flood took them all away.' Noah warned, but they took no notice. The waters rose. They ran to and fro: higher still the waters increased. They desired the despised ark for refuge. So the wicked in the great day: 'Who shall hide us from the wrath of the lamb?' They shall cry out, 'Oh, that I had accepted Christ and gotten into the ark!' God is pleased to give warnings! God is slow in his judgments! The pace of mercy is swift and earnest, yet judgment walks with leaden feet and comes on by degrees (*1 Pet.* 3:20). The father ran to meet the prodigal. Judgment seldom takes the world by surprise; first there is notice. Take notice of the rich mercy and patience of God! Whenever you are warned of the evil of your ways, lay it to heart. But when warning is neglected, wrath is exasperated. This will be your great torment in hell, to think you were warned and would not regard it.

THOMAS MANTON, *By Faith*, pp. 341-346

Sanctify them in the truth; your word is truth.

John 17:17

God usually revealed himself to holy and righteous persons. They are his familiars, and you know that it is a part of friendship to communicate secrets. The Lord will communicate his secret to them that fear him (*Psa.* 25:14). God looked upon it as a violation of friendship to conceal the matter of Sodom from Abraham. So a holy man has a greater insight into truth than a carnal man, for lusts are the clouds of the mind. He that is encumbered with lusts is blind. Revelation is the ground of our faith. What we know by reason is knowledge or opinion, but not faith. Faith supposes a revelation. Revelation can only be the object of faith because it is infallible truth and cannot deceive us. In times past God spoke in various ways—voice, visions, dreams, miraculous inspiration, urim and thummim, angels and signs from heaven—but in these last days he has spoken in his Son (*Heb.* 1:1-2). God speaks today through his word and the light of his Spirit. Let us be content with this dispensation. Chrysostom said, 'the saints should never complain of the darkness of the word, but of the darkness of their own heart!' If things are dark to you, do not accuse the Scriptures as if they were an uncertain rule, but desire the Lord to open your eyes that you may look into them. Some desire to have Christ speak from heaven as to Paul. Neglecting the word, they desire miracles, to save them the pains of study, prayer, and discourse. If men were not drowned in lusts and pleasures, all would be clear. Today, the mind of God is exceedingly open to us when his providence, word, and Spirit are taken together. The apostles laid the foundation and canon by miracles; our duty is only to build upon that foundation. Be content with the word, which is confirmed by miracles, sealed by the blood of martyrs, and manifested to your conscience by divine force.

THOMAS MANTON, *By Faith*, pp. 347-350

Justified by his grace as a gift, through the redemption that is in Christ Jesus.

Romans 3:24

Rules for understanding the Ten Commandments: (1.) The moral laws of God include the heart. They require not only outward actions, but inward affections. They forbid not only the act of sin, but the desire; not just adultery, but lusting; not only stealing, but coveting. Man's law only binds the hand; God's law binds the heart! (2.) There is more intended than what is spoken. When sin is forbidden, the contrary duty is commanded. When we are forbidden to take God's name in vain, reverence for his name is commanded. When we are forbidden to wrong our neighbour, we should do him good. (3.) When sin is forbidden, the occasion is also forbidden. If murder is forbidden, envy and rash anger are forbidden that may give occasion for it. If adultery is forbidden, then also the lust of the eyes. He who would be free from the plague must not come near the infected house. The Nazarite was forbidden not only wine, but grapes. (4.) When greater sins are forbidden, lesser sins are also. When idolatry is forbidden, so is innovation in God's worship as Aaron's sons offering up strange fire (*Lev.* 10). (5.) Both parts of the law stand together—piety to God and equity to our neighbour. If you hold to one and neglect the other, your heart is not right before God. (6.) God's law forbids not only our own sin, but being an accessory to the sins of others! David sinned in the murder of Uriah. Eli was guilty in not suppressing the sins of his sons. He that suffers an offender to pass unpunished makes himself an offender! Ahithophel's counsel to Absalom brought guilt upon himself. It was Paul's sin to consent to the murder of Stephen. A person is an accessory by example. A child learns to swear by a parent! (7.) We are not able in our own strength to fulfil these commandments, but we are accepted in the Beloved our Surety by virtue of his blood!

Thomas Watson, *The Ten Commandments*, pp. 44-48

You shall have no other gods before me.

Exodus 20:3

The sum of this commandment is that we should sanctify God in our hearts; we must have God for *our* God! He is God to us when we are persuaded in our hearts, confess with our tongues, and subscribe with our hands that he is the only true God, and that there is none comparable to him, and we enter into solemn covenant with him. This follows mature deliberation of his attributes: his glorious holiness, his riches of mercy, and his faithfulness to his promises. To have God as our God is to give him adoration and reverence. It is to fear him, and always have him in our eye, and know he is looking on as judge, weighing all our actions. We need a holy awe of God upon our hearts, that we dare not sin. Bid me to sin, and you bid me to drink poison! Anselm: 'If hell were on one side, and sin on the other, I would rather leap into hell, than willingly sin against my God.' He who fears God will not sin, though it is ever so secret. To have God as our God is to trust him, to rely on his power as a Creator, and on his love as a Father. It is to commit our chief treasure to him. A good Christian believes that if God feeds the ravens, he will feed his children. If God gives us heaven, he will give us daily bread. Can we trust God in our fears? When adversaries grow high, can we display the banner of faith? (*Psa.* 56:3). Faith cures the trembling heart and gets above fear. Oil swims above the water. To have God to be God to us is to love him. In the godly, fear and love kiss each other. It is only right that we cleave to him from whom we receive our being. Who has a better right to us than he that gives us our breath? It is unjust, yea, ungrateful, to give away our love or worship to any but God. If we cleave to the Lord as our God then he shall bless us with inward peace and a smiling conscience which is sweeter than the dropping of honey, and turn all evils to our good!

Thomas Watson, *The Ten Commandments*, pp. 49-53

You shall not make for yourself a carved image … You shall not bow down to them or serve them.

Exodus 20:4, 5

No sooner was Nebuchadnezzar's golden image set up, but all the people fell down and worshipped it (*Dan.* 3:7). If anyone should make an image of a snake or a spider, saying it represented his prince, would not the prince consider it in contempt? What greater dishonour is there to represent the infinite God by that which is finite; the living God by that which is dead; and the maker of all things by that which is made? It is absurd and irrational, for the workman is better than his work! He who builds the house has more honour than the house! (*Heb.* 3:3). How absurd to bow down to the work of one's hands, when God himself is everywhere present! The Jews have a saying, that in every evil that befalls them, there is an ounce of the golden calf in it. Senesius calls the devil a rejoicer at idols, because their worshippers help to fill hell (*Rev.* 22:15). For Israel's idolatry their army was routed, priests slain, and the ark taken. The idolatrous are enemies not to their own souls only, but to their children! How sad it is to be the child of an idolater! How sad to have been one of Gehazi's children, who had leprosy entailed upon them (*2 Kings* 5:27). The child of an idolater is exposed to heavy judgments. But what a privilege it is to be the children of good parents. Parents who are in covenant with God lay up mercy for their posterity (*Prov.* 20:7). A religious parent helps to keep off wrath from his child. He seasons his children with religious principles, and he prays down a blessing on them. He is a magnet to draw his child to Christ by good counsel and example. Oh, what a privilege to be born of godly parents! Augustine says that his mother Monica travailed with greater pain for his new birth, than his natural birth. The wicked entail misery on their posterity, but godly parents a blessing.

Thomas Watson, *The Ten Commandments*, pp. 59-67

Do not withhold discipline from a child; if you strike him with a rod, he will not die. If you strike him with the rod, you will save his soul from Sheol.

Proverbs 23:13-14

God counsels parents to do with their children as he does with his—to wisely use the discipline of the rod before vicious dispositions grow into habits and folly so deeply rooted that the rod of correction will not drive it out (*Prov.* 19:18). 'Folly is bound up in the heart of a child, but the rod of discipline drives it far from him' (*Prov.* 22:15). Error and folly, said one very well, are the knots of Satan, by which he ties children to the stake to be burnt in hell, and these knots are most easily cut early! Do not spare for his crying, for it is not only foolish, but cruel pity to forbear correction for a few childish tears. Pity to the flesh is cruelty to the soul. Foolish indulgence of the parent may be, and often is, the eternal death of the child! Abraham feared not so much to sacrifice his son as such parents fear to chasten theirs. The Holy Spirit says not to fear correction, for, behold, the strokes of the rod are not the strokes of death; it is but a rod, and not a serpent—take it into your hand; it may smart, but it will not sting. It may be that by divine blessing accompanying it, it may prevent the first and second death to which a child is exposed by the sinful indulgence of the parent. The rod on the flesh shall be a means to save the soul in the day of the Lord Jesus. Correction is a kind of medicine. For lack of disciplinary love, some have accused their parents on their death bed, yea, at the gallows! O it would grieve the heart of the most unnatural parent to hear such complaints or the hideous yellings of poor children in hell fire whom their fondness has sent there. O that parents would awaken themselves to follow the pattern and precept of their heavenly Father who corrects whom he loves, and so commands them to correct if they love their children!

Thomas Case, *Select Works, A Treatise of Afflictions*, pp. 168-172

Fathers, do not provoke your children to anger, but bring them up in the discipline and instruction of the Lord.

Ephesians 6:4

Parents, if you would have your children happy, add instruction to correction. Let chastisement and instruction go together. This the Holy Spirit urges upon you (*Eph.* 6:4). The goal of discipline is to admonish in the Lord! While we chasten the flesh, we should labour to form the mind and spirit by infusing right principles, pressing and urging upon their tender hearts counsel, reproof, and instruction as the matter requires. A dumb rod is but a brutish discipline that will leave them more brutish than it found them. Chastisement without teaching may sooner break the bones than the heart—it may mortify the flesh, but not the corruption, extinguish nature, but never beget grace. The rod and reproof give wisdom (*Prov.* 29:15). Instruction added to correction makes excellent Christians and good children. There are parents severe enough to their children, they spare no blows, but instead of breaking them of their wills by a wise and moderate correction, they are ready to break their bones, and their necks, too, sometimes, in their moods and passions. But they never mind the other branches of paternal discipline—instruction and admonition. There is more passion than judgment, more lust than love. The rod and reproof give wisdom! The rod without reproof will harden the heart, and reproof without the rod will leave no impression. It is divine truth that works saving grace in the heart. Every parent is a prophet, priest, and king—a king to govern, a prophet to teach, and a priest to offer prayer and praise for the family. What greater delight is there than to see your children walking in the truth! Then add prayer to your instruction. Means are ours, but success is in God's hands. Therefore let us put the rod into the hand of instruction, instruction into the hand of prayer, and all into the hand of God!

Thomas Case, *Select Works, A Treatise of Afflictions*, pp. 174-177

Rejoice with me, for I have found my sheep that was lost.

Luke 15:6

Christian's wife and children played the fool at first and by no means would be persuaded, either by tears or entreaties, to go with him on pilgrimage from the City of Destruction. But after her husband was gone over the river, her thoughts began to work in her mind. She was much broken with calling to remembrance how she hardened her heart against his entreaties and loving persuasions to go with him. There was not anything he said while his burden did hang on his back but that they returned upon her like flashes of lighting, and rent the depths of her heart, especially that bitter outcry, *'What shall I do to be saved?'* Christiana: 'Sons, we are all undone. I have sinned away your father and hindered you of life.' With that, the boys fell all into tears and cried out to go after their father. Christiana: 'Oh! That it had been our lot to go with him; then it would have fared well with us.' The next night she had a dream with a parchment opened before her with the sum of her crimes, and she cried out loud in her sleep, 'Lord, have mercy upon me a sinner', and the children heard her. Then she thought she saw her husband in a place of bliss with a harp, playing it before the one sitting on the throne, and thanking him for bringing him to this place. Next morning, one named Secret knocked hard at the door and said: 'It is told that you are aware of the evil you have done to your husband in hardening your heart against his way. The merciful one has sent me to tell you he is a God ready to forgive, and that he takes delight to multiply the pardon of offences. He invites you to his table and presence, where he will feed you with the fat of his house. Do as your husband, for that is the way into his presence with joy forever, through yonder Wicket Gate.' Her children burst out into tears for joy that their mother was so inclined, and they began to prepare for their journey.

John Bunyan, *The Pilgrim's Progress*, pp. 201-210

But he gives more grace. Therefore it says, 'God opposes the proud, but gives grace to the humble.'

James 4:6

Now I saw in my dream that they began to go down the hill into the Valley of Humiliation. It was a steep hill, and the way was slippery, but they were careful and got down pretty well. Great-heart: 'We need not be so afraid of this valley, for here is nothing to hurt us. This valley is a fruitful place. But it is easier going *up* than *down* this hill, which can be said of few hills in these parts. It is the best and most fruitful piece of ground in all these parts. It is a fat ground, and, as you see, consists much in meadows and is a delight to the eyes. Behold how green this valley is and how beautified with lilies. I have known many labouring men that have got good estates in this Valley of Humiliation. (For God resists the proud, but gives *more, more* grace to the humble.) It is a very fruitful soil and brings forth by the handfuls. Living in the valley is a merrier life and gives your heart more ease than those clothed in silk and velvet. In this valley our Lord had his country house, and he loved much to be here. He loved to walk in these meadows, for he found the air was pleasant. Here a man shall be free from the noise and hurryings of this life. All other states are full of noise and confusion; only this valley is a solitary place. Here man is not hindered in contemplation. Only pilgrims walk in this valley. In former times men have met with angels here, have found pearls here, and found the words of life. To the people that live and trace these grounds, the Lord has left a yearly revenue to be faithfully paid them at certain seasons for their maintenance by the way, and for their farther encouragement to go on in their pilgrimage.'

He that is down, needs fear no fall; he that is low, no pride
He that is humble, ever shall have God to be his Guide!

John Bunyan, *The Pilgrim's Progress*, pp. 278-283

And if I go and prepare a place for you, I will come again and will take you to myself, that where I am you may be also.
John 14:3

I beheld until they came to the land of Beulah. They tasted of the water of the river over which they were to go, and they thought it tasted a little bitter, but it was sweeter when it was down. It was much discussed how the river to some flowed heavy while others knew an ebbing flow when they passed over. For some it was in a manner dry, while it had overflowed its banks for others. While they waited, there was a noise in town that a letter came from the Celestial City with a matter of great importance to Christiana: *Hail good woman! I bring you tidings, that the Master calls for you, and that you should stand in his presence in clothes of immortality within the next ten days.* The messenger read the letter with a token of love which by degrees worked its way easily into her heart. When Christiana saw her time was come, she called Great-heart for advice how to prepare for her journey. He said that those remaining would accompany her to the river. She called her children and gave them her blessing and told them that she was comforted that she would see them there. Now the day drew on that Christiana must be gone. So the road was full of people to see her take her journey. And behold, all the banks beyond the river were full of horses and chariots which were come down from above to accompany her to the city gate. So she came forth, and entered the river with a beckon of farewell to those that followed her to the riverside. The last word she was heard to say was, 'I come, Lord, to be with you and bless you.' So her children and friends returned to their place, for those who came for Christiana had carried her out of their sight. So she went and called, and entered in at the gate with all the ceremonies of joy that her husband had done before her. It is glorious to see the welcome of pilgrims at the gate.

John Bunyan, *The Pilgrim's Progress*, pp. 368-379

They will perish, but you will remain; they will all wear out like a garment … but you are the same, and your years have no end.

Psalm 102:26-27

How foolish to set our hearts upon that which shall perish. Perishing things can be of no support to the soul. If we would have rest, we must run to God and rest in God. How unworthy are other things to be the centre of our souls. They change in the very using of them, and slide away while we are enjoying them. 'You are the same.' The essence of God, and all the perfections of his nature, are the same without any variation from eternity to eternity. Not only is he eternal in duration, he is immutable in that duration. What endures is not changed, and what is changed does not endure. God is always the same in his nature, will, and purpose. There is no shadow of change though ever so slight. Jehovah—I am! All other things are tottering like water flowing by, while he remains fixed and immoveable. His wisdom, power, and knowledge are always the same. There is no alteration either by itself or by any external cause. He lacks nothing, loses nothing, and uniformly exists by himself, without any new nature, new thought, new will, new purpose, or new place. All of his perfections are immutable without the least shadow of imperfection. How cloudy would his blessedness be if it were changeable! if his wisdom could be obscured or his power languish! How mercy would lose its lustre if it could change into wrath! Jehovah is everlasting strength, and his mercy and holiness endure forever. He never could, nor ever can, look upon iniquity. He is a rock in the righteousness of his ways; he is the truth of his word, and the holiness of his proceedings. God is holy, happy, wise, and good, by his essence. Men are made holy, wise, happy, strong, and good, by the gift and grace of God.

STEPHEN CHARNOCK, *Existence and Attributes of God*, pp. 103-106

Every good gift and every perfect gift is from above, coming down from the Father of lights with whom there is no variation or shadow due to change.

James 1:17

The immutability of God is grounds and encouragement for worship. If he is God, he is to be reverenced, and the more highly reverenced because he cannot but be God! But certainly, since his unchangeableness in knowing and willing goodness is a perfection, adoration and admiration is due God upon this account. What comfort would it be to pray to a god that, like the chameleon, changed colour every day, every moment? What encouragement could there be to lift up our eyes to one that is of one mind today, and of another mind tomorrow? But God is a prince whose promise is sure, and oh what blessings he has promised upon the condition of seeking him! If he were changeable in his mind, this would be a hindrance to our seeking him and would frustrate our hopes. Isn't this excellence of his nature the highest encouragement to ask of him the blessings he has promised? It is a beam from heaven to fire our zeal in asking! God has willed everything that may be for our good, if we perform the condition he has required. If we do not seek him, by our neglect and folly we imply he is not sincere and means not as he says. If we ask according to his revealed will, the unchangeableness of his nature will assure us of the grant! (What a presumption it would be for a creature dependent on his sovereign to ask that which he knows is against his will.) Our Saviour joins the promise and our petition together, the promise to encourage the petition, and the petition to enjoy the promise. He does not say, 'perhaps it shall be given', but, 'it certainly shall', for your heavenly Father is unchangeably willing to give you those things! We must depend upon his immutability for the thing, and submit to his wisdom for the time being.

Stephen Charnock, *Existence and Attributes of God*, pp. 131-132

Trust in the Lord for ever, for the Lord God is an everlasting rock.

Isaiah 26:4

God's immutability is the greatest encouragement to prayer. Prayer is an acknowledgment of our dependence upon God. Our dependence could have no firm foundation without God's unchangeableness. Prayer does not desire any change in God, but is offered to God that he would confer those things that he has immutably willed to communicate. But God willed them with prayer as the means of bestowing them. The light of the sun is ordered for our comfort, for the discovery of visible things, and for the ripening of the fruits of the earth. But withal it is also required that we use the faculty of our seeing, and that we employ our industry in sowing and planting to expose our fruits to the view of the sun, that they may receive its influence. If a man shut his eyes, and then complained that the sun had changed into darkness, it would be ridiculous. Nor is God changed in not giving us the blessings he has promised through prayer because we do not pray. God's immutability is also a strong ground of consolation. The fear of change in a friend hinders a full reliance upon him, but an assurance of stability encourages hope and confidence. Immutability is the strongest prop for faith. It is not a single perfection but the glory of all attributes that belong to God's nature. He is unchangeable in his love and his truth. It is the basis and strength of all his promises. His goodness cannot be distrusted when his unchangeableness is well apprehended. All distrust would fly before it as the darkness from the sun. It only gets the advantage of us when we are not grounded in his name. If ever we have trusted in God, we have the same reason to trust in him forever, for God is perpetually unchangeable. 'The Lord *Jehovah*, I am, is an everlasting rock!'

Stephen Charnock, *Existence and Attributes of God*, pp. 132, 136

Jesus Christ is the same yesterday and today and forever.

Hebrews 13:8

If God is immutable, it is sad news to those that are resolved in wickedness. Sinners must not expect that God will alter his will, make a breach upon his nature, and violate his own word to gratify their lusts. No, it is not reasonable that God should dishonour himself to secure them, and cease to be God that they may continue to be wicked, by changing his own nature that they may be unchanged in their vanity. God is the same; goodness is just as amiable in his sight, and sin as abominable in his eyes, now as it was at the beginning of the world. God is the same enemy of the wicked, and the same friend to the righteous. He is the same in knowledge, and cannot forget sinful acts; he is the same in will, and cannot approve of unrighteous practices. Goodness is always the object of his love, and wickedness is always the object of his hatred. As his aversion to sin is always the same, as he has been in his judgments upon sinners, the same he will be still. The perfection of immutability belongs also to his justice for the punishment of sin. Though Adam and Eve were the only rational creatures in the world, God subjected them to that death he had assured them of, and from this immutability of his will arises the necessity of the sufferings of the Son of God for the relief of the apostate creature. His will in the new covenant is as unchangeable as that in the penalty; only repentance is settled as the condition of acceptance in Christ. Without repentance, the sinner must irrevocably perish, or God must change his nature! There must be a change in man; there can be none in God: 'If a man does not repent, God will whet his sword; he has bent and readied his bow' (*Psa.* 7:12). Atheists, hypocrites, and the profane, can sooner expect the sun to stand still at their order, than that God should change his nature!

Stephen Charnock, *Existence and Attributes of God*, pp. 135-136

But as it is, they desire a better country, that is, a heavenly one. Therefore God is not ashamed to be called their God, for he has prepared for them a city.

Hebrews 11:16

Faith has a strong eye: it can see things afar off. Faith flew over thousands of years in a moment and saw Christ the Messiah, and heaven itself, typified in Canaan. So the strong eye of faith mounts over all in a moment, and sees Christ in heaven! Faith looks through difficulties. Abraham was willing to slay his son, a command one would think against reason, against affection, against hope. His faith knew hope against hope, and he saw God raising Isaac from the dead. His faith saw more comfort, joy, benefit and blessing in the promises and in the word of God than in Isaac. Faith would rather part with the dearest thing on earth than part with God. To strengthen the eye of faith, let us take heed of Satan, that he doesn't dim our sight with the dust of the world. The soul led by lusts cannot see. When death, danger, and damnation are near, the devil provides glasses to make these appear distant; 'I may live many years and enjoy my pleasure and my will', but this is a false glass. Let us take heed that Satan does not blind us! Faith is like binoculars—to see afar off. Open your eyes every day to the promises, that you may see Christ. Let us beg daily that God would take away the things that hinder, inward and outward, that we might see afar off. Let us take a fresh look at our corruption and sin every day to humble us. What a corrupt heart we carry about us. Men loathe to look in the book of their consciences, lest they be disturbed from their pleasures. But a view of our corruptions makes us glad to see a better object. It makes us turn our eyes to Christ, to the promises, and all the things we have by Christ. If we grasp the dimensions of our corruptions, we delight to see God's love in Christ, the height, breadth, and depth of it all.

Richard Sibbes, *Works*, VII:425-427

Save others by snatching them out of the fire.

Jude 23

The physician is most concerned for those patients whose case is most hazardous. So, unconverted souls call for earnest compassion and prompt diligence to pluck them as brands from the burning. How shall I win them? O that I could tell! I would write to them in tears, and weep out every argument. I would petition them on my knees. O how thankful I would be if they would repent and turn. There is no entering into heaven but by the strait passage of the second birth. Set yourself to seek the Lord Jesus now! The devil has many counterfeits, and cheats one with this, and another with that. *Conversion is not taking up a mere profession of Christianity.* It is more than a name. Are there not many that name the name of the Lord Jesus, that do not part from iniquity, or profess they know God, but in works deny him? And will God receive these for true converts? What! Converts from sin when they still live in sin? It is a visible contradiction. *Conversion is not through Christian baptism.* This would fly directly in the face of Scripture. If this were true, we should no more say, 'Strait is the gate, and narrow is the way', but, 'Wide is the gate, and broad is the way.' *Conversion does not lie in moral righteousness.* Unconverted Paul was blameless according to the law. You must have more than this, or else, however you may justify yourself, God will condemn you. There is more needed than going to church, giving alms and making use of prayer, to be a sound convert. There is no outward service but a hypocrite may do it. Jehoash was no more than a wolf chained up, and when Jehoiada died, he fell into idolatry! Why build your hopes on the sand? Let the word convince you in time. O repent and be converted, break off your sins, and fly to Christ for pardon and renewing grace. Give yourselves to him to walk in holiness. If not, you must die!

JOSEPH ALLEINE, *A Sure Guide to Heaven*, pp. 15-25

Therefore, if anyone is in Christ, he is a new creation. The old has passed away; behold, the new has come.

2 Corinthians 5:17

Conversion lies in the thorough change of the heart and life. The author of conversion is the Spirit of God (*John* 3). It is a work above man's power. Never think you can convert yourself. If ever you would be savingly converted, you must despair of doing it in your own strength. It is a resurrection from the dead, by free grace alone (*Titus* 3:5). The means is the merit and intercession of the blessed Jesus. The instrument is the word of God, and the end is the glory of God! This change extends to the whole man. A carnal person may have some shreds of good morality, but he is never good throughout the whole cloth. Conversion is not a repairing of the old building, but it takes down the whole building, and erects a new structure. It is not the sewing on a patch of holiness, but holiness is woven into all his powers, principles, and practice. He is a new creature. It is a deep work, a heart work. It makes a new man. His judgment is changed, so that God and his glory outweigh all carnal and worldly interests. Before, he saw no danger in his condition—now he is lost and undone. He sees sin as the chief of evils. God is all with him: he has none in heaven or earth like him. The will is altered: the man has new ends and designs. He chooses Jesus as Lord. His testimonies are not his bondage, but his heritage; not his burden, but his bliss; not his cords, but his cordials. They are the desire of his eyes and the joy of his heart. O happy man, if this is your case! His affections run in a new channel. Christ is his hope and prize. He would rather be the holiest man on earth than the most learned, famous, or most prosperous. Augustine poured his love upon Christ: 'Let me love you, O life of my soul, my sweet comfort: let me find you, hold you, embrace you, O heavenly bridegroom! O gladden my heart.'

JOSEPH ALLEINE, *A Sure Guide to Heaven*, pp. 26-34

And we desire each one of you to show the same earnestness to have the full assurance of hope until the end.

Hebrews 6:11

In true believers there may be full assurance, or a not-so-full assurance that is yet growing. We may grow stronger and stronger, even as the eye of faith grows clearer. The Spirit of God may give such assurance that may be shaken, ay, but one recovers oneself presently. The tenor of a Christian's life is usually a state of sight and persuasion. Sometimes it falls out that a Christian may be convinced of the truth of the word, and that the promises of salvation are true, yet, notwithstanding, he may not feel the particular persuasion of his own sins forgiven and his own interest in Christ. A newborn Christian is not so persuaded of his own good estate as he is after he is grown. A soul that stretches forward for entire satisfaction of assurance will be satisfied. He that hungers and thirsts after assurance of God's love in Christ, forgiveness, and life everlasting, is satisfied by God at length, for the most part, in this world, but certainly in the world to come forever. Hungering and thirsting is a mark that a man is in a state of grace. A Christian does not know his own estate at all times, but he may be in the state of grace notwithstanding. God may allow this state to humble us, and make us careful and diligent. But how do people know they are God's children?—Are they conscientious of heavenly duties, and striving and labouring to be persuaded of God's truths while attending to the means and moving forward in spiritual duties? Do they labour to obey God in all things? Such will find peace at length. They should never give their hearts rest till they attain to it. We ought to labour for it, for the soul is never in such a frame as it ought to be, until it has gotten some assurance of God's love. We must labour, however, that this persuasion is supernatural, by the Holy Spirit, lest we be deceived.

Richard Sibbes, *Works*, VII:429-432

So that the name of our Lord Jesus may be glorified in you, and you in him.

2 Thessalonians 1:12

True believers are persuaded by the Spirit of God, together with Scripture. The Spirit works in our nature a holiness suitable to God's word. A man that only has human knowledge without the Spirit may hear the commands of Scripture with a kind of scorn. He never makes scruple of these things. The Spirit has not sealed these truths to his soul. He knows nothing of conversion, the mortifying of his corruptions, being raised up when cast down, wonders worked in his conscience, or bringing all into a spiritual subjection. If he has not felt the word work this way, regardless of his general knowledge by education, breeding, and reading, he may be a disobedient wretch, and live and die a rebel, a strong contrast to the power of grace. What does one think of scholars, men of great knowledge, perhaps pastors that preach to others, that are just as carnally disposed as others? Those who preach the word should live their lives by its rule. It is no wonder, for the devil himself has knowledge enough. So a man may be a devil, having knowledge of these things, and yet no true divine. But he that is taught by the Spirit the things of the word of God, the Spirit works the taste of Scripture in them! True believers also hold on in times of peril and temptation. A carnal man will not hold out in the hour of death! When afflictions and persecutions arise, we see many excellent learned men give up their profession. When such men in persecution are to lose their position, or their friends, or their life, they fall away altogether because these were their only motives. But then we see a man in a lower position, whose knowledge was wrought by the Spirit and the word; he will not move. He holds out in persecution, because he has felt the work of divine truth in his soul, and has found the Spirit of God raising him up in comfort, and he holds on in all trials.

RICHARD SIBBES, *Works*, VII:432-433

Our gospel came to you not only in word, but also in power and in the Holy Spirit and with full conviction.

1 Thessalonians 1:5

The Spirit works in the soul together with the word of God. All men in the world cannot persuade the soul without the work of the Spirit. Paul preached, but God opened Lydia's heart. God's Spirit must open our eyes, persuade and convict our hearts. The persuasion that carries a man to heaven must come from the Spirit of God. The Spirit enlightens the understanding. He presents arguments and motives from the excellency of the things promised and the good things we have by Christ. He strongly works upon the disposition, the will, and upon the affections to persuade and convince. He who framed the soul knows how to work upon it to draw it sweetly but strongly to embrace the things revealed. He persuades sweetly by the truth by showing a man the goodness of it, and its suitableness to our condition. He does not force the soul, but strongly persuades the soul so that for all the world he would not be of any other mind. The persuasions of the Spirit and the promises are stronger than the temptations of Satan and corruptions of the flesh. It is infinite mercy and goodness of God to reveal to our souls such excellent things. There is such inward rebellion and distrust in the soul, that these things seem to be too good to be true. Considering our unworthiness, and the excellency of these things, our unbelief is the greatest sin. Let us labour then that our knowledge is spiritual knowledge. With reverent and humble hearts let us implore the teaching of the Spirit to remove the veil as we read or hear the word of God. Pray that the outward teaching will include the inward teaching of the Spirit, that he that has the key of David may open, incline, and persuade the heart. Every day labour more and more to be spiritual-minded, and beg God to give his Holy Spirit (*Luke* 11:13).

Richard Sibbes, *Works*, VII:434-437

Open my eyes, that I may behold wondrous things out of your law.

Psalm 119:18

When we come to hear or read the word of God, let us pray, 'Lord, open my eyes! Persuade my soul! Bow the neck of my soul, the inner man of iron. Take away my hard heart, and teach me!' God opens the eyes and then persuades. He persuades the inner man with enlightening. The devil keeps the soul in darkness and ignorance. He persuades by fleshly allurements to draw away. God opens our eyes of understanding to persuade us. The devil persuades with carnal objects to bewitch the affections while keeping us in the dark. Those who are enemies to the means of salvation fear God's people should know too much. The Holy Spirit persuades by opening the mind to truth. If we attend upon the means, and go to church, yet continue in a course of sin, it is evidence that we are not persuaded by God. If the covetous were persuaded, would he not leave that course? Light and persuasion always rule the actions! We act according to insight. A mule bears burdens as nature framed him, but you can't drive the silly creature into the fire—he knows it will consume him! Men lead a life in a course wherein they see a pit before them, and yet they run on. Certainly they are not persuaded! We may know the truth of our persuasion by the power it has to rule our lives and conversations. What is the reason that a simple man lives Christianly and dies in the faith he lived by, while a great man, conceited in knowledge, lives wickedly and dies worse? The poor man lived by the knowledge he received by the Holy Spirit! The great man had book knowledge without the illumination of the Holy Spirit. Only God has the power to deal with the heart! Let us desire God, that we may do things from reasons of Scripture, to please God in a holy, sanctified affection, and that we may be persuaded by the Holy Spirit.

RICHARD SIBBES, *Works*, VII:437-438

Because your steadfast love is better than life,
my lips will praise you.
Psalm 63:3

They 'embraced them' (*Heb.* 11:13, KJV). They embraced the promises—Christ's coming, Canaan a type of heaven, and heaven itself. They were not in hand; they embraced the promises of them. That is the nature of faith! When they were persuaded of the truth of the promises, the will and affections joined and embraced them. The will chooses them and cleaves to them, the affection of desire extends itself to them, the affection of love embraces them, and the affection of joy delights in them. We may know whether the Spirit of God has wrought anything in us by our embracing of good things. Faith is first persuaded that things are good, and then the heart opens itself to let in those things. We can test the state of our faith by our affection. Do we joy and delight in them? Is there a holy wonder at them? When the soul stands in admiration of God and good things, and welcomes Christ and heavenly things, and says, 'Now, away all former vanities! Away all lusts of youth! Away confidence in beauty, strength, and riches!', the soul has discovered better things. There is an attractive, drawing, magnetical power in heavenly things. What a man loves, he often thinks of. True faith carries the whole soul to Christ; the understanding to see, the will to choose and cleave, the affections to joy, delight and love—it carries all. If a man has knowledge of holy things, but does not prize them above earthly things, does not rejoice in them as his best portion, does not embrace them, there is no true faith at all. God has made the soul for these heavenly things. When the soul and these close together, there is a sweet embracing. The soul is raised above itself. It is quieted, stilled, and satisfied. Our souls are made for them, our desires to embrace them, our love to delight in them, and our wills to cleave to them above all things.

Richard Sibbes, *Works*, VII:438-441

Therefore I love your commandments above gold, above fine gold.

Psalm 119:127

Four things I observe God works in every sound convert with reference to the laws and ways of Christ: (1.) The mind is brought to like the ways of God. He thinks of them as best, and looks at them not only as tolerable, but desirable, yea, more than fine gold. He is fully determined that it is best to be holy. (2.) The desire of the heart is to know the whole mind of Christ. He would not have one sin undiscovered or one duty unknown. An unsound convert is willingly ignorant and does not love to come to the light. He is willing to keep such and such a sin, and is loath to know it to be a sin. The gracious heart is willing to know the whole latitude and compass of his Maker's law. (3.) The free and resolved choice of the will is for the ways of Christ, before the pleasures of sin and prosperities of the world. His consent is not from anguish or hasty resolve, but is deliberate and purposed. True, the flesh will rebel, yet the prevailing part of his will is for Christ's laws and government. They are not a burden, but bliss. The unsanctified go in Christ's ways as in chains and fetters; the true convert heartily, and counts Christ's laws his liberty, and delights in the beauties of holiness. When God touches the heart of his chosen, they presently and freely run after him, and willingly devote themselves to his service. (4.) The bent of his course is directed to keep God's statutes. It is the daily care of his life to walk with God. He aims at perfection and desires it and reaches after it. He does not rest in any degree of grace until he is perfected in holiness. Here the hypocrite's rottenness may be discovered. He desires holiness only as a bridge to heaven and seeks the least that will serve his turn. He desires only enough to get to heaven. But the sound convert desires holiness for holiness' sake, and not merely for heaven's sake.

Joseph Alleine, *A Sure Guide to Heaven*, pp. 46-48

For now we see in a mirror dimly, but then face to face.

1 Corinthians 13:12

The way to increase in grace is to increase in the knowledge of Christ (*2 Pet.* 3:18). Christ is the fountain of all grace. It highly concerns all sincere Christians to grow and increase in the knowledge of Christ. Who would ever have thought of God's being manifested in the flesh to redeem the church with his own blood? These are the deep things of God revealed by the Spirit. Moses saw Christ (*Heb.* 11:26), and Abraham rejoiced to see his day (*John* 8:56), and though the New Testament helps us to understand in a far more glorious light than ever shined before, Paul himself saw as through a glass darkly (*1 Cor.* 13:12). What is it to grow in the knowledge of Christ? (1.) *A fuller apprehension of his Godhead.* Here is majesty, immensity, and glory—that may presently amaze and overwhelm us. Alas! It is but a small portion of this that we can understand: but this must be known—the selfsame perfections which are in the Father are likewise in the Son, for he and his Father are one. Christ is 'the true God and eternal life' (*1 John* 5:20). He is over all, God blessed forever (*Rom.* 9:5). All things were created by him, visible and invisible (*Col.* 1:16). This truth—that Christ is God—is more and more to be looked into! He who denies it, loses his Christianity and the foundation of his faith. Here is the rock upon which the church is built, so that the gates of hell shall not prevail against it. This makes his blood a price of infinite value! (2.) *A clearer sight of his humanity.* God manifest in the flesh is a great mystery. Christ has a true body. The Holy Spirit took care that his human nature should not be in the least defiled, and his whole life was perfectly free from sin, his heart always pure! Let saints search into this truth, and they will find matters of unspeakable encouragement.

NATHANAEL VINCENT, *Puritan Sermons 1659-1689*, III:294-299

He was foreknown before the foundation of the world but was made manifest in the last times for the sake of you …

1 Peter 1:20

Growing in the knowledge of Christ implies—(3.) *A full persuasion that he was foreordained to be a Redeemer.* Christ was the person marked out from eternity to be the Saviour of the elect of God. There was a compact and agreement made between the Father and the Son. The Son agreed in the fullness of time to be made of a woman, to take a body, to offer up himself without spot to God; and the Father promised eternal life and salvation, and that Christ should have a church given him out of the world fallen into wickedness, and upon this church eternal life should be bestowed. And when the saints behold that Christ is the person from eternity designed to be a Saviour, they may conclude that God has a love to them, a care of them, and a purpose of grace toward them from everlasting. How securely and sweetly may they rest upon the blessed Jesus, not doubting that he is a person in every way fit and sufficient to finish the work of redemption, which he undertook according to the appointment of his Father! (4.) *A greater insight into his sufferings.* All four evangelists record them. There is much in his crucifixion that concerns believers to pry into. The sufferings of Christ were great, both in body and soul! He was full of heaviness and sorrow and agony before he was condemned and fastened to the cross. His death was violent and accursed, and before he breathed his last, his Father hid his face. The sins of the whole church were laid upon him. None shall be laid to the charge of them who believe in the blood of God! By the cross we climb up to the throne of glory. The more the death of Christ is studied, the more the spirit will be broken, the heart become clean, and the conscience become calm and quiet. The death of Christ puts sin to death, and delivers the sinner from it!

NATHANAEL VINCENT, *Puritan Sermons 1659-1689*, III:299-300

That I may know him and the power of his resurrection, and may share his sufferings, becoming like him in his death.

Philippians 3:10

Growing in the knowledge of Christ implies—(5.) *A more fruitful consideration of his resurrection.* The justice of God arrested Christ, and cast him into the grave as into a prison. If Christ were not risen, our faith would be in vain, and the guilt and power of sin would remain. Christ being raised, he triumphed over death and Satan, and true believers are delivered from sin's punishment and power! For believers, there is a very great power and virtue to be derived from the resurrection of our Lord. There is power to raise a drooping spirit (*John* 20:17); power to make carnal affections to be spiritual, and set the affections on things above (*Col.* 3:1-2); power to confirm and establish the soul in grace (*Rom.* 6:9). Those once given life by Christ shall never again be dead in sin, and shall continue faithful until death, and shall expect a joyful resurrection. Christ is the firstfruits of those that sleep (*1 Cor.* 15:20). There will be a harvest at the end of the world, and the bodies of the saints that were sown in corruption shall be raised in incorruption, and those sown in dishonour shall be raised in glory! (6.) *A greater satisfaction about Christ's imputed righteousness.* Paul declares his desire to be found in Christ's righteousness (Phil. 3:9). Christ is Jehovah, the true God, or else his obedience and sufferings would not have been sufficient to justify us. Christ is called 'the Lord our righteousness' (cf. *Jer.* 33:16). The guilt we contracted can be removed out of God's sight only by the righteousness and blood of his Son. O the completeness and perfection of this righteousness of Christ! There is no need of any addition. He is called 'the sun of righteousness' (*Mal.* 4:2); therefore, in the business of justification, all other righteousness should vanish as the stars do at sunrise. Let Satan rage—Christ's imputed righteousness must stand!

NATHANAEL VINCENT, *Puritan Sermons 1659-1689*, III:300-302

He is able to save to the uttermost those who draw near to God through him, since he always lives to make intercession for them.

Hebrews 7:25

Growing in the knowledge of Christ implies—(7.) *A more constant trust in Christ's intercession, pity and compassion.* Believers should better know this friend and advocate in the court of heaven, who always appears for them there. Though the head is in heaven, he is mindful of his members on earth, and is ready to plead for them. Here is the ground for boldness in prayer! Here is the reason the saints' prayers are so mighty and prevailing—they are backed with the intercession of Christ. (8.) *A better acquaintance with his great power and presence with his church.* Behold!—All power is given to him in heaven and earth (*Matt.* 28:18). At his name every knee shall bow (*Phil.* 2:10). He is King of kings, and Lord of lords (*1 Tim.* 6:15). He has all the reprobate angels in a chain, and the key of hell is in his hand. In heaven, the elect angels are his ministers to fulfil his pleasure. He is exalted above all principality, power, might, dominion and every name, in this world and in that which is to come! (*Eph.* 1:21). He will be with his church, his body to the end of the world (*Matt.* 28:20). The church, in spite of earth and hell, shall last while the world lasts! Let fear give way, and faith increase. Believers may condemn their proudest adversaries. (9.) *A better understanding of Christ as mediator of the new covenant.* On this covenant is promised pardoning mercy, renewing grace, and eternal glory! Earth, heaven, and God himself are made over to believers. Promises are all 'yes' in Christ (*2 Cor.* 1:20). The covenant stands good in Christ's blood for eternity! (10.) *A more earnest looking for Christ's appearing.* The day of his appearing is appointed and draws near. If Christ were better known, this day would be more longed for by the saints, for the whole church to be glorified.

Nathanael Vincent, *Puritan Sermons 1659–1689*, III:302–303

Fear not, Abram, I am your shield; your reward shall be very great.

Genesis 15:1

Abraham is called the 'friend of God' (*James* 2:23). The Lord spoke with him familiarly, in secret counsel. God said, 'I am your superabundant, very exceeding much reward!' Nothing on earth can be our reward. God never intended that we should dig happiness out of the earth which he has cursed. God sends away the wicked with riches and honour, but makes over *himself* to his people. They not only have the gift, but the giver. And what can be more? The saint's portion lies in God! God is his people's reward through the blood of Jesus Christ. The 'blood of God' has merited this glorious reward for us. Without this, the portion would never have come into our hands. God is an exceedingly great reward. He is '*a satisfying reward*'. God is a whole ocean of blessedness. While the soul is bathing in it, it cries out, 'I have enough'. Here is fullness. God is all marrow and sweetness, and such a reward exceeds our faith! God is '*a suitable reward*'. The soul is spiritual and must have something suitable. He is '*a pleasant reward*'. God is the quintessence of delight, all beauty, and love. Holy meditation draws out his sweetness like a bee drinking nectar from a flower. God is a '*transcendent reward*'. The whole world put in the balance with him is like the weight of a feather compared with a mountain of gold. He is better than the world, better than the soul, and better than heaven. He is the original cause of all good things. Nothing is sweet without him; he perfumes and sanctifies our comforts. God is '*an infinite reward*'. Every believer possesses the whole God to himself. Throw a thousand buckets into the sea, and there is water enough to fill them. Though there are millions of saints and angels, there is enough in God to fill them! His glory is imparted, not impaired—it is a distribution without a diminution.

Thomas Watson, *Puritan Sermons 1659-1689*, III:67-70

Tell the next generation that this is God, our God for ever and ever. He will guide us for ever.

Psalm 48:13-14

God is '*an honourable reward*'. Honour is the height of men's ambition. Alas! Worldly honour is but a 'pleasing fancy'. It often has a speedy burial. But to enjoy God—this is the top honour. What greater dignity than to be taken into communion with the God of glory, and to possess a kingdom with him, bespangled with light, and seated above all the visible planets. We shall be clothed with white robes and sit with Christ upon his throne. God is '*an everlasting reward*'. Mortality is the disgrace of all earthly things. Eternity can't be measured by years. Eternity makes glory weighty. God is our God for ever and ever. A Christian cannot say, 'I have an estate in the world and I will have it for ever', but he can say, 'I will have God for ever!' O saints of God, your repenting and faith are but for a while, but your reward is for ever. As long as God is God, he will be rewarding you. God marries himself to his people, and this admits of no divorce. God's love to his elect is as unchangeable as his love to Christ! Our portion is for ever. It can never be spent, because it is infinite. It can never be lost, because it is eternal. We read of a river of pleasures at God's right hand (*Psa.* 36:8). If God is such an immense reward, then see how little cause the saints have to fear death. Are men afraid to receive rewards? Christians would be clothed with glory, but are loath to die. They pray, 'your kingdom come', and when God is leading there, they are afraid to go. What makes us desire to stay? There is more in the world to wean us from it than to entice us. Is it not a valley of tears? And do we weep to leave it? Are we not in a wilderness among fiery serpents? Are we loath to leave their company? Is there a better friend we can go to than God? Are there any sweeter smiles or softer embraces than his? The pangs of death bring us to glory!

THOMAS WATSON, *Puritan Sermons 1659-1689*, III:70-74

If then you have been raised with Christ, seek the things that are above, where Christ is, seated at the right hand of God.

Colossians 3:1

If God is such an exceeding great reward, let us endeavour that he may be our reward. He who says, 'he is *my* God', is the happiest man alive. We are undone without him. Beware of the Laodicean temper, 'I am rich and have need of nothing'. Live every day in the contemplation of this reward. Live in the heights. Think what God has prepared for those who love him! O that our thoughts could ascend. The higher the bird flies, the sweeter it sings. If one could look for a while through the crack in heaven's door, and see the beauty and bliss of paradise, or if he could but lay his ear to heaven and hear the ravishing music of the angelic spirits, and the anthems of praise which they sing, how would his soul be exhilarated and transported with joy! O Christians, meditate on this reward. Slight, transient thoughts do no good—they are like the breath upon steel, which is presently off again. But let your thoughts dwell upon glory till your hearts are deeply affected! O the love of God to sinners! Stand at this fire of meditation till your hearts begin to warm. Reflection on this immense reward conquers temptation and beheads those unruly lusts that have conspired against us; 'What! Is there a reward so sure, so sweet, so speedy? And shall I forfeit it by sin? Shall I lose my crown to please my appetite? All ye pleasures of sin, be gone with your sugared lies, wound me no more with your silver darts! Though stolen waters are sweet, the water of life is sweeter!' There is no stronger antidote to expel sin than forethoughts of heavenly remunerations. When the future reward is long out of mind, then we set up some idol-lust in our hearts which we begin to worship. When Moses was long out of sight, Israel made an idol to worship (*Exod.* 32:1-6).

Thomas Watson, *Puritan Sermons 1659-1689*, III:74-77

Draw near to God, and he will draw near to you.

James 4:8

Let us beg God to be our reward. Be earnest suitors, and God can't find it in his heart to deny you. Prayer is the key of heaven, which, being turned by the hand of faith, opens all God's treasures. If God is our reward, this may teach us contentment. If we have but little oil in the cruse, and our estate is almost boiled away to nothing, our great reward is yet to come! Though your pension is small, your portion is large. If God is your deed of gift, this may rock your hearts quiet. God lets the wicked have their pay beforehand, but the saints' reward is given later; the robe and the ring is yet to come. May not this tune our hearts into contentment? Christian, though God does not give you a goat to make merry with, you can be content with 'all I have is yours!' How can you complain of the world's emptiness when you have God's fullness? Is not God reward enough? Does a son have any grounds to complain if a father denies him a flower from the garden when he makes him heir to his estate? So Christian, if you do not have much of the world, you do have God, an inexhaustible treasure! Who should be content if not he who has God for his portion, and heaven for his haven? If God is so great a portion, let those who have an interest in him be cheerful. Let the birds of paradise sing for joy. Shall a carnal man rejoice whose hope leans on earthly crutches? Shall not he rejoice whose treasure is laid up in heaven? Be serious, yet cheerful; a dejected, melancholy temper unfits for duty, especially praising God. Will others think God is a great reward when they see Christians drooping? It is a sin not to rejoice as much as not to repent! Let God take away what he will, he will at last give you better! Be not too much troubled at the diminishing of earthly things—heaven is yours. There you shall tread upon stars, make friends with angels, and commune with the holy Trinity.

THOMAS WATSON, *Puritan Sermons 1659-1689*, III:76-78

My desire is to depart and be with Christ.
Philippians 1:23

If God is our exceeding great reward, let us long to take possession of it. Though it should not be a burden to stay on earth and serve him, we should long to have our portion in hand! This is a becoming temperament in a Christian—content to live, desirous to die (*Phil.* 1:23-25). When we consider our earthly condition, we are compassed with a body of sin; we cannot pray without wandering; and we cannot believe without doubting. Should not this make us desire to be gone? Think how happy in God the saints above are, beholding the smiling face of God. While we drink wormwood, they swim in honey. While we are perplexed between hope and fear, they are enrolled in the book of life. While we are tossed upon turbulent seas, they have arrived at their harbour. If we really knew what a reward God is, and what the joy of our Lord means, we would need patience to be content to stay here any longer! If God is our exceeding great reward, let us be a living organ of his praise. When we consider the greatness of this reward, let us present him with our thank-offering, for many are passed by, and the lot of free grace has fallen upon us! Saints look comely in the garments of praise, and praise is the work of heaven. Let us break forth into doxologies and triumphs. Long for the time when you shall join in concert with angels sounding forth hallelujahs to the King of glory. Monuments of mercy should be patterns of thankfulness. If we lose on earth, as long as God lives, our reward is not lost. I cannot be poor as long as God is rich. Whatever we lose for God we shall find again in him. The disciples left all and followed him. Alas! What had they left? A few small boats and tackling! What are these to the reward? They parted with movable goods for the unchangeable God. All losses are made up in him. We may be losers *for* God, but we shall not be losers *by* him.

THOMAS WATSON, *Puritan Sermons 1659-1689*, III:78-80

We love because he first loved us.

1 John 4:19

It is the duty of every child of God to keep himself in the love of God (*Jude* 21). This proposition is grounded upon a threefold supposition—(1.) That some are in the love of God, really and eternally, (2.) That this love, in which God loves his chosen, is a special love, a particular and distinguishing love, and (3.) That it is a duty as well as a privilege to keep ourselves in the love of God. Our love to God is the effect, and not the cause, of God's love to us. He that will keep himself in the love of God must mind and meditate on four attributes and properties of God's love, which will have a great influence upon his heart and love. First—Consider the eternity of God's love to you. Yea, before all time God has been your friend. Election is the effect of God's eternal love. His love is as eternal as himself! Second—Consider the freeness of God's love. God's free love is called grace. Paul, the great champion of free grace, says, 'Not because of our works but because of his own purpose and grace, which he gave us in Christ Jesus before the ages began' (*2 Tim.* 1:9). O, meditate on this! O how the consideration of this should keep us in the love of God! Mark and mind this well: free grace and love sent Jesus Christ into the world with all the train of spiritual blessings. O, meditate and mind the infinite, free love of God in all the sweet streams of it. Dwell on it, be ravished with it, and give the God of grace and love the glory for it forever! Third—Consider the immensity of God's love. It is as vast as the ocean, but without bounds or bottom. It passes all knowledge (*Eph.* 3:17-19). Consideration of this alone has so amazed some devout souls that they have been in an ecstasy, above and beside themselves. Fourth—Consider the unchangeableness of God's love. This gives a sure anchor and comfort to a true believer in a storm! It is an everlasting, inseparable, invincible, and unquenchable love.

WILLIAM COOPER, *Puritan Sermons 1659-1689*, III:130-134

For all that is in the world—the desires of the flesh and the desires of the eyes and pride of life—is not from the Father but is from the world.

1 John 2:16

He that will keep himself in the love of God will seek to know what is the will and pleasure of God and to conform to it. The will of God is the sovereign will for all the world. Who can say to God, 'What are you doing?' When your will comes in conflict with God's, you know what you must do. We can never keep ourselves in the love of God but by doing that which is agreeable to his holiness. We must keep ourselves free from the love of the world. The love of the world is contrary to the love of God. The love of the world is a heart-thief: it steals the heart away from God as Absalom did from David by his kisses and flatteries. To love the world is to make an idol of it (*Col.* 3:5). The Lord says, 'Take care, and be on your guard against all covetousness' (*Luke* 12:15), a double caution! Luxury, sensuality, drunkenness, and the love of pleasure more than the love of God, are of this nature; they are belly-gods. Inordinate love of children likewise can become an idol, as with old Eli, honouring his sons above God (*1 Sam.* 2:29). Love of the world chokes all that is truly good. Do we not see what mortal enemies worldly men are to divine things? The devil is the prince of the wicked world, and rules the children of disobedience. The world feeds the flesh and is not subject to the law of God (*Rom.* 8:7). Yea, it is a deadly thing to the soul. When once men drink of the world's cup, they are intoxicated. The greatest witch in the world is the world! Her honours are bewitching honours, her delights and pleasures are bewitching, and her riches and profits are bewitching. Love of the world makes men apostates from Christ—so Demas (*2 Tim.* 4:10), and many thousands more! How then is the love of the world consistent with God's love?

William Cooper, *Puritan Sermons 1659-1689*, III:132-136

The words of him who has the seven spirits of God and the seven stars. I know your works. You have the reputation of being alive, but you are dead.

Revelation 3:1

Watch diligently against the most discernible decays of grace, and against the degenerating of it into some carnal affection, or some counterfeit of some other kind. We are no sooner warmed by the celestial flames, but our natural corruption is inclining us to grow cold. Hot water loses its heat by degrees unless a fire is continually kept under it. Who does not feel that his heart is prone to cool after a sermon, or prayer, or holy meditation has begun to warm it? As soon as it is gone, we are so prone to return to our former temper, and neglect our duty, and return to thoughts or business about the world, and we presently grow cold and dull again. Be watchful, therefore, lest it declines too far. Be frequent in the means that must preserve you from declining. You are rowing against the stream of fleshly interests and inclinations. Do not wait too long, lest you go down faster by your ease than you go up by your labour. The decay of grace is a very common form of backsliding that is too little observed. God does not value men by their places and dignity in the world, but by their graces and holiness of life. The most common way of degenerating in all religious duties is to adopt a dead formality. How apt men are to corrupt and debase all duties of religion. If the devil can but get you to cast off your spirituality and life of duty, he will give you leave to seem very devout with outward action, words, and beads. Thus you will have much zeal for a dead religion, or the corpse of worship, and he will make you think it is indeed alive. By all means take heed of turning the worship of God into mere lip service. It is the work of a saint, and a diligent saint, to keep the soul itself both regularly and vigorously employed with God.

Richard Baxter, *Practical Works*, 1:59-60

In your book were written, every one of them,
the days that were formed for me, when
as yet there was none of them.
Psalm 139:16

Do not promise yourself a long life or prosperity and great matters in the world, lest it entangles your heart with transitory things, and engages you in ambitious or covetous designs, and steals away your heart from God, and destroys all your serious apprehensions of eternity. The approach of death greatly influences the mind of most, and so, if we do not count on a long life, it greatly helps us in our preparation and work of holiness through our lives. Come to a man that lies on his death bed, or a prisoner that is to die tomorrow, and test him with riches, or honours, or temptations to lust, or drunkenness, or excess, and he will think you are mad or impertinent to talk of such things. Oh how serious we are in repentance and casting up our accounts when we see that death is at hand! Every sentence of Scripture has life and power in it, and time seems precious! If you ask such a man if it is better to spend time in needless recreations and idleness, or in prayer and holy conversation, the word of God and the life to come, he will be easily satisfied with the truth, and dispute frivolous temptations to sensual time-wasting. Expectation of a speedy approach into the presence of an eternal God has much in it to awaken the powers of the soul. If anything will make you serious, this will, in every thought, speech, and duty! It is a great mercy of God that in this short life there are frequent dangers, sicknesses, and uncertainties, that cause us to look about us and be ready for our change. The sick who are looking at death are most considerate, and it is a great part of the duty of the youth in good health to consider their frailty and the uncertainty of their lives, and always live as those that wait for the coming of the Lord. Since time is so swift, common reason teaches us to live in a constant readiness to die.

Richard Baxter, *Practical Works*, 1:60

Do not boast about tomorrow, for you do not know what a day may bring.

Proverbs 27:1

If youth and health ever makes your departure seem a long way off, this will do much to deceive and dull the best, and take away the power of every truth and duty. You will hardly be able to keep the faculties of your soul awake if you do not think of death and judgment as near at hand. The greatest change or joy or misery in eternity will not keep our stupid hearts awake unless we look at them as near as well as certain. Among men, there is a common difference in their thoughts of death in health and when they are dying. In health, they can speak of death with laughter, or lightly without awaking the soul. When they come to die they are oftentimes much altered, as if they had never heard they are mortal. To live in the house of mirth is more dangerous than to live in the house of mourning, and the expectation of a long life is a grievous enemy to the operations of grace, and the safety of the soul. This greatly strengthens our temptations to luxury, ambition, worldliness, and almost every sin. When men think they have many years of leisure to repent, they are apt to transgress more boldly! When they think they have yet many years to live, it tempts them to pass away time in idleness, to loiter in their race, to trifle in their work, and to overvalue the pleasures, honours, and shadows of felicity that are here below. He that makes his life about house or land or inheritance will give more importance to it than one that must go out of it the next year. He that thinks of living many years will feel it a great matter to obtain an estate, name, family, and the accommodations and pleasing of his flesh, while self-denial will seem a very hard work. Though health is a wonderful mercy, it is perhaps a great snare to the heart to turn it from duty. Take heed, if you love your souls, of falling into the snare of worldly hopes.

RICHARD BAXTER, *Practical Works*, 1:60-61

In the last days there will come times of difficulty. For people will be lovers of self, lovers of money, proud, arrogant …

2 Timothy 3:1-2

(1.) He that will love God and keep himself in the love of God *must not love self.* There is no greater enemy to the love of God. 'Lovers of self' leads the list in Paul's description of the last days. Where this principle prevails, it opens a flood-gate of sin, and shuts the door upon all holy motions. If self is loved, admired, and idolized, it is the worst idol in the world. This is an idol in a secret place continually adored. This sets men upon God's throne, and un-gods him by deifying themselves. Self-denial is the first lesson to be learned to take away this great stumbling block to God's love (*Matt.* 16:24-25). (2.) To keep yourselves in the love of God, you must *be very shy of sin's risings and temptations*, for the love of God and the love of sin are more contrary to each other than heaven and hell! O, mind this, we must keep God's commandments if we love him (*John* 14:21)! We keep ourselves in the love of God when we walk closely with God in ways of strict holiness. God's favourites had this characteristic: Abraham (*Gen.* 17:1), Enoch (*Gen.* 5:22), Noah (*Gen.* 6:9), Caleb (*Num.* 14:24), and David (*Psa.* 73:28). God is love, and he that dwells in love dwells in God (*1 John* 4:16). O sweet dwelling! You will find that the holiest persons were always the highest favourites of God: Job (*Job* 1:1), Zechariah (*Luke* 1:6-7), Mary (*Luke* 1:28), Simeon (*Luke* 2:25), and Anna (*Luke* 2:36-37). Holiness and purity bring us to the sight of God. This is the soul's highest happiness and ultimate end! (3.) We also keep ourselves in the love of God when we cherish in our hearts the pardon of sin. What wonderful love it is for the Lord to pardon the great and many sins of a poor sinful soul! We cannot but choose to express our great love to the Lord for it! Forgiveness of sin is an act of the greatest grace, condescension, and kindness of God to a poor soul!

William Cooper, *Puritan Sermons 1659-1689*, III:136-140

If anyone loves me, he will keep my word, and my Father will love him, and we will come to him and make our home with him.

John 14:23

To keep ourselves in the love of God we should keep up our love to its height. The Lord commands our love toward him to the most intense degree of affection: 'With all your heart, and with all your soul, and with all your might.' You can never be excessive in your love to God. It should know no bounds or measures. Let us blow and stir up the dying embers of divine love in our souls. Consider that the Lord is incomparably the most lovely object in the world. He is the chief of all good and goodness. If we love a drop of good in the creature, how we should be ravished with an ocean, many oceans, in God! Happy is he that enjoys this fountain of good! God is purely good without mixture, infinitely good without measure, absolutely good without dependency, communicably good without failure, eternally good without end! O consider this! This good, this God—is ours forever and ever. May every believer say, 'O, let this inflame our love to this good!' God most deserves your love. All the world cannot vie with God in loving us. The world is not worthy to be a rival with him. It is a horrid and an amazing thing that the glorious God should be provoked by such rivals, and have to bear with them so long. This is true of the greatest part of the world; one silly idol or other courts all of them! Yet they never did any man any good, nor can! If you love them, they cannot love back. They cannot save us in our trouble. They cannot hear us when we cry. Our love is lost upon them. Augustine: 'O poor soul, how you debase yourself when you love earthly things. You are better than them! Only God is above you and you were made to love him only!'

WILLIAM COOPER, *Puritan Sermons 1659–1689*, III:140–149

All Scripture is breathed out by God and profitable for teaching, for reproof, for correction, and for training in righteousness.

2 Timothy 3:16

God warned Noah about the judgment to come. Note: God's threatening of judgment is the object of faith as much as the promise of his mercy. Every part of divine truth is worthy of trust and reverence, because it is the word of God. We read of faith in the promises, faith in the command, and faith in the threatening. Faith is a loose presumption if it doesn't include the threats as well as the promises. In all right belief there is a mixture. Men that look only to be honeyed and oiled with grace, and feasted with love, mistake the nature of God and the manner of his dealing with the world. God is just, as well as merciful. We are bound to believe that God will condemn the obstinate as well as save the penitent. Threatenings are necessary: (1.) *To beget humility for past sins.* In threatenings we see the deserts of sin. You will never understand how displeasing things are to God till you read the curses; then the soul will say, 'Oh, what have I done? We deserved to be cast into hell, but grace has saved us!' Your hearts will be enlarged in praises and thanksgiving to God that he has delivered you from the lowest hell. When we think of the evil of sin, how we will bless God for Jesus Christ—'No condemnation!' (*Rom.* 8:1). (2.) *Threatenings make us vigilant and watchful.* When we see the danger, we shall not be so secure. When a bird sees the snare he will not venture upon the bait. So the soul will be more careful and will not dally with sin. (3.) *Threatenings check indulgence to carnal pleasure.* Pleasure and delight are dearly bought if they cannot be enjoyed but with the danger of our souls. There is no way to counterbalance delight but by fear—to consider the wrath of God that shall come on sinners. Take a view of the land of darkness as well as the land of promise!

THOMAS MANTON, *By Faith*, pp. 351-354

But Noah found favour in the eyes of the LORD.

Genesis 6:8

The strength and force of Noah's faith is revealed in these words—'Of things not seen as yet' (*Heb.* 11:7, KJV). The coming flood and Noah's preservation in the ark were in no way able to be tested by sense! They were difficult, strange, and likely to entertain the scoffing and opposition of the world, yet he prepared an ark. The flood was a thing never before seen and so difficult to believe. The world was newly created, and it seemed unlikely to the men of that age that God would destroy it presently. By the grant of God himself the world enjoyed the respite of a hundred and twenty years, and all besides Noah were utterly secure. Though Noah only had the naked word of God, he believed. Also, the means of an ark was an improbable and incredible way of safety. The ark was made like a coffin where Noah was to be buried with all kinds of living creatures for many days. Certainly so great a work was done at great expense and labour. It was a work that was likely to meet with many mocks and scoffs in the world. The wicked looked upon Noah as a vain person, and mocked and laughed at the design every day. He had a thousand discouragements, yet being moved with fear, he prepared an ark. These things being so remote from sense, and only certain in God's word, show the great force and virtue of his faith. He was persuaded of the world's ruin, and his own preservation. It is the property of faith to be moved by such things that are not open to sense. When things are seen and known, there is no room for faith. Faith gives over its work when its object is seen. If we were in a dungeon, we might believe the sun was up when someone told us, but if we are out in it, it cannot be properly said we believe because we feel and know it. Faith and sense are opposed (*2 Cor.* 5:7). Now, heaven and the glory of God are not matters of sight, but faith. Feeling is left for the next life.

THOMAS MANTON, *By Faith*, pp. 357-358

The fear of the Lord is the beginning of wisdom.

Proverbs 9:10

When Noah's world was given up to pleasure and marrying and giving in marriage, who would believe that within a few years the rain and waters should cover the whole earth? Today, also, the despisers of the gospel shall surely meet with an unexpected judgment. The power of every threatening stands upon two feet—the irresistibleness of God's power, and the immutableness of his counsel. Do you do as Noah did? In fear, he made serious preparation for things to come and yet unseen. Though the flood was yet a great while to come, he presently set about it with great labour and trouble. Can you wait in God's leisure for the accomplishment of God's promise? And during the time of your pilgrimage wait, and be followers of them 'who through faith and patience inherit the promises'? (*Heb.* 6:12). The Israelites were long in the wilderness ere they came to Canaan, and endured a tedious march. So David was anointed king a long time before he reigned. This is Christ's bargain—whatever you lay out on earth, he will pay it in another country! Noah no doubt wasted himself and his all, but what did he lose by it? Noah and his sons had the possession of all the world when they came out of the ark. Noah was moved with fear. Godly fear is a fruit and effect of faith. Faith works upon the promises, and begets love and hope. Faith works upon God's threatening and begets fear. Love, fear, and hope are not contrary: they stand together and proceed from faith. They walked 'in the fear of the Lord, and in the comfort of the Holy Spirit' (*Acts* 9:31). This is a double remedy—fear to keep from sin, and comfort to keep them from sinking under affliction. On earth we still need this mixture. In heaven there is all joy, and no fear of punishment. Love would grow secure without fear, and fear slavish without love. Both bring reverence and sweetness.

Thomas Manton, *By Faith*, pp. 359-364

Work out your own salvation with fear and trembling.

Philippians 2:12

What is godly fear? There are three effects by which it may be discerned—*caution*, *diligence,* and *reverence.* Caution concerns sin, diligence concerns duty, fear and reverence concern God himself. (1.) Faith fears lest we should dash the foot of our faith against stumbling blocks that are in the world. The children of God know what a precious treasure they have about them, that they have a soul that cannot be valued, and that the world is a rough passage with many stones of stumbling. The main grace that maintains the fire of religion in the soul is a cautious fear. They consider their own hearts, look for direction from the word, and call in the help of the Spirit. (2.) Godly fear ends in duty. It stirs up the soul to use all the means to prevent the danger. If Noah had not feared, he would never have prepared the ark. The fear of the wicked ends in irresolution, perplexity, and despair, but the fear of the godly sets them a-work. (3.) Godly fear knows reverence and a dread of God—his holiness, majesty, power, and justice. The wicked stand in fear of hell, wrath, and their own danger, but not God as God. Godly fear is always coupled with love, for there is harmony between the graces. Godly fear arises from a humble sense of God's goodness. The wicked have hard thoughts of God and could wish there was no God to punish them. A godly man is afraid of losing God, and the carnal man is afraid of finding him. The wicked are afraid to burn, but not afraid to sin. If they do leave off sin, it is not out of hatred to sin, but out of fear of punishment. Godly men not only forbear to sin, but abhor it. The wicked do not fear God as an act of faith, but as a mere judicial impression. Godly fear rises naturally out of faith and tenderness of spirit. The godly are under fear not by fits and pauses, but they bear a constant respect to God by seeing him that is invisible!

Thomas Manton, *By Faith*, pp. 364-368

And this is eternal life, that they know you the only true God, and Jesus Christ whom you have sent.

John 17:3

Eternal! What sound this word makes in my ears! What workings it causes within my heart! What casting about of my thoughts! O! That eternal world, now unseen and yet to come! My trembling heart desires to know to which word *eternal* is prefixed as to myself. Shall it be *eternal damnation*? O dreadful words! Can more terror be contained or misery comprehended in any two words than in '*eternal damnation*'? But we in time are praying, hearing, repenting, believing, conflicting with devils, mortifying sin, weaning our hearts from this world, that we might find life and salvation added to 'eternal'. *Eternal salvation!* These are words as comfortable as the others were terrible, and as sweet as they were bitter. This word *'eternal'* is the horror of devils, the amazement of lost souls, and it causes desperation for all in hell. It wounds, like a dart sticking in them, as they certainly know they are lost to all eternity. *Eternal!* It is the joy of angels, the delight of saints. While saints are made happy in the beautiful sight, and are filled with perfect love and joy, they sit and sing, 'All this will be eternal!' *Eternal!* This word—it is a loud alarm to all yet on earth, a serious caution to make it our grand concern, that when we go out of this life, our eternal souls might obtain eternal salvation. God gives time in this world to prepare for eternity. You have time to repent, to get an interest in Christ, to mortify sin, to pray for grace, to make your peace with God, to get the pardon of your sins: all this, that you might be fitted for eternity. God doesn't lengthen his patience so you might labour for temporal riches or live a life of carnal pleasures. He doesn't support your being, and keep you from the grave, to scrape together things temporal, and neglect eternity! O the years that you have had to improve for eternity!

Thomas Doolittle, *Puritan Sermons 1659–1689*, iv:1–2, 32

But God, being rich in mercy, because of the great love with which he loved us ...

Ephesians 2:4

The degree of the love of Christ may be known in that he passed by angels, and took a hold of us. We are both fallen, but angels are far more noble than we. Jesus Christ chose to take us up, and pass by them to their eternal destruction. O love in high degree to man! The depth of Christ's love is seen in his unwearied work to bring men to that kingdom which Christ obtained for them by his blood. While man was an enemy, and by no means willing to be saved through Jesus Christ, the good shepherd went to look for his sheep that was lost in the wilderness. He took her and lay her upon his shoulder and brought her home rejoicing. This is love in a great degree. Christ's great love is seen also in his patience. When Christ has made man to come to himself and willingly accept his salvation, man cannot be trusted and left alone, because of the corruptions that are still scattered up and down in his flesh. How often saints are found playing truant, and lurking like thieves in one hole or other. Yea, when found in such decayings, how commonly they hide their sin with Adam, and David, until their Saviour fireth out of their mouths a confession of the truth of their naughtiness. When the sins of saints are so visible and apparent to others, and God must punish for the sake of his name, he but chastises them with rods to do them good in the end, that they may not be condemned with the world. This is great love. The great degree of Christ's love can be seen by the sort of sinners he most rejoices in—sinners of the 'biggest size'—and he proportions examples of his love to encourage those who would trust in him. Christ's fullness of grace, which is necessary for our salvation, continues after salvation, for us to hold out to the end. That Christ should be such to us with gladness shows his great love!

JOHN BUNYAN, *Works*, II:31-32

Pray without ceasing.

1 Thessalonians 5:17

It is our duty to persevere in prayer. It is sinful and foolish to give up this duty. It is a high crime for one trusted with a castle for his prince to deliver it cowardly into the enemy's hand, especially if he has provision to defend it. Has not God provided sufficiently for us to maintain this duty against all armies of men and devils, and affliction and temptations that can oppose it? Prayer is a duty that is hard laid at by Satan, and many other difficulties render it no easy matter to be constant at it. God understands and provides help. He gives his Spirit to lift with us in the work. While the Spirit is ready to pray in us, Christ is as ready in heaven to pray for us. And the precious promises of the gospel are sent as messengers to a besieged town, to assure that soul relief is coming from heaven no matter how formidable the affliction or temptation is. Now to faint in the work, and give over the duty, opens the city gate of the soul for Satan to enter and triumph over God with his insulting blasphemies. O what gracious soul, that has any spark of loyalty in his breast to his God, does not tremble at the thought of such a treasonable action! We cannot cast off prayer, but we cast some dishonourable reflection upon God. The causes of fainting in prayer are evil and bitter, and by and by will appear. It is dangerous to faint in prayer. It is the way to bring some stinging affliction upon us. Expect a storm to bring you back to work. Are you a child and play the truant? Your heavenly Father will send you to school with a rod at your back. Cease to pray, and you will begin to sin. Prayer is a means to prevent sin—'Pray that you do not enter into temptation.' After sleeping, the disciples were defeated when the tempter came. Saul gave up prayer to God and sought a witch. He that casts off prayer, it would be a wonder if you did not find him ere long cast into some foul sin!

William Gurnall, *The Christian in Complete Armour*, II:517-518

But she came and knelt before him, saying, 'Lord, help me.'

Matthew 15:25

Sometimes fainting in prayer comes from pride—'why should I wait any longer for the Lord?' Pride does not like to wait. Your heart begins to grow discontented that God makes you stay so long for a mercy. Discontent softens the heart to receive sinful impressions from the tempter. But remember what it is to pray. It is a begging for alms, not the demand of a debt. Is it becoming to be short with God? Should we not wait patiently for his pleasure? Who are we praying to? Is he not the great and glorious majesty of heaven and earth? Would it not be insufferable sauciness in a servant to complain that his master sat too long and required too much waiting at his hands? Is he not a righteous, holy God? Surely he does you no wrong to make you pray, and that long, for a mercy which you do not deserve when it comes at last. Is he not wiser to know how to time mercies? Will you have God overthrow the course of providence, which he thinks fit, to gratify your impatient spirit? Surely this is to charge God foolishly with some error in his government. Is he not a faithful God, though he does not come as soon as you like for your relief? Where did he give you leave to date his promises and set the day of payment? No, he has promised to answer his children's prayers, but conceals the time of performance. This keeps us in a waiting posture. He does not break his promise when he detains a mercy. It is our duty to wait. Look at the generation of seekers, and you will find that God exercised their patience as well. Shall God raise a bridge for us when thousands took weary steps through deep sloughs of affliction? Did not Christ himself, an example beyond all examples, wait, even to heaven itself, for answers to his prayers? Did God wait on you at last to be gracious, and is it too much for us to wait on him in prayer?

WILLIAM GURNALL, *The Christian in Complete Armour*, II:518-520

He grew strong in his faith as he gave glory to God.

Romans 4:20

Unbelief often keeps us from persevering in prayer. We pray, God is silent, and no answer comes. Now, thinks Satan, is my time for mischief. And he labours to persuade us that there is no mercy to be expected from God. 'If', says the tempter, 'God had meant to come, he would have been here by now. So many days are now gone, and there is no news of his approach. You have waited too long to meet with disappointment at last; give over and take some other course.' This is his way. He lets them alone while he thinks they are being softened into compliance by long standing on duty, and hopes their ammunition grows low. Then he comes to parley with them, and take them off from waiting upon God by planting many fears and doubts in their thoughts concerning the power, mercy, and truth of God, so that the poor Christian is at last put to a stop, and does not know whether he should pray or not. Or if he holds up the duty, his heart is not in it, and he prays faintly with a kind of despair—like the widow that made ready her last handful of meal with no other thoughts than of dying when she had eaten it. Thus he prays, but nothing but death and misery are to follow it. O this is sad praying, to expect no good from God in the performance! Unbelief is a soul-enfeebling sin. It is to prayer as the moth to wool, which bites the threads asunder, and it crumbles to nothing. It wastes the soul's strength, and cannot look up to God with any hope. Resist, therefore, Satan, and be steadfast in the faith. Never let your heart suffer the power, mercy, or truth of God to be called into question. You might as well question whether he can cease to be God! Rest on his attributes as Moses on the stone; they will sustain your spirit. O this waiting is pleasing to God, and never puts the soul to shame! Seek Christ in faith, and he will at last be with us, though we do not presently see him!

William Gurnall, *The Christian in Complete Armour*, II:520-521

Ask, and it will be given to you; seek, and you will find; knock, and it will be opened to you.

Matthew 7:7

Some do not persevere in prayer because they have their eye on something other than God, from whom they expect help. It is no wonder that one will give up praying if he thinks he has another string for his bow. While the carnal heart prays for deliverance, he has other possibilities in his head to wiggle himself out of the briars in which he is caught, and on these he lays more stress and weight than on God to whom he prays! At length, he gives up praying and turns to these. Another, who looks for all from God, and sees no way to help himself but calling on God for his aid, will say, as Peter to Christ, 'Lord, to whom shall we go but unto you? You have the words of eternal life.' 'I do not know another door to knock at but yours,' says the poor soul. 'The creature does not have anything to give, but you have. I will never leave you!' 'We do not know what to do, but our eyes are on you,' said good Jehoshaphat. Also, some do not persevere in prayer because they lack inward rest and communion with God. Men do not call upon God because they have never cordially delighted in him. We can easily let go of that which we take no great effort to enjoy. The sincere soul is tied to God by the heart-strings. His communion is founded in love. Love is stronger than death, and many waters cannot quench it. A stranger may have an errand that brings him to a man's house, but that done, the visit ceases. But a friend would come and sit a while and delight in his company. Get your affections on God as your chief good and you won't forget the way to your God in prayer. Hypocrites use prayer as medicine, not because they like the taste of it. The sincere soul finds it sweet to the taste, and cries out with David, 'It is good for me to draw near to God!' (*Psa.* 73:28). Never will such a soul part with it.

WILLIAM GURNALL, *The Christian in Complete Armour*, II:521

Far be it from me that I should sin against the Lord by ceasing to pray for you.

1 Samuel 12:23

The Spirit, which stirs us up to pray for ourselves, will, if we do not quench him, send us on the same errand for others. In praying for others, get your heart deeply affected with their state and condition. Pouring out your soul shows greater love than drawing out your purse. Be sure your soul is poured out, or else you are a deceiver, and wrong God and those you pray for. Christ was troubled at the grave of Lazarus, and those about him said, 'Behold how he loved him!' You will pray fervently when your heart is warmed with sympathy. A lawyer may show rhetoric in pleading a man's case in court, but a dear friend will show more affection. And when you pray for others, prefer spiritual blessings over temporal. If health is all you beg for, you are not faithful to your friend. He may have that and yet be worse for it. Ask of Christ grace and glory for him, and you have something significant! Our Saviour used this method with the paralytic (*Matt.* 9:2). First, he brought him news of a pardon, which is of infinitely more worth than life or limbs. For the nation, aim at more than deliverance from outward judgments. The carnal Jews could ask for water, but didn't think about repentance for sin or pardon. The beast can bellow in a drought! Do not be discouraged in your prayers when the answer does not presently come, if a rebellious child or carnal friend continues to be so. Don't give up the work! Don't take them out of your prayers, or think they are past grace because you see no sign of spiritual life in them. It is not too late for God to breathe life into them! A father's labour is not lost if his son receives the benefit of it! He may die before the ship he prays for comes home, but his child lives to have the gains of that adventure paid into his purse. One generation sows prayers, and another reaps the mercy prayed for!

William Gurnall, *The Christian in Complete Armour*, II:522-527

For who in the skies can be compared to the LORD? Who among the heavenly beings is like the LORD?

Psalm 89:6

It is certain that our happiness in heaven will consist in part in our perfect knowledge of the blessed and boundless God. And it is as certain that our holiness in this world depends a lot upon our knowledge of him. They who know his beauty and bounty cannot but love him, and they who know his power and faithfulness cannot but trust him! To know God affectionately as our chief good is spiritual life here, and the beginning of our eternal life hereafter. Who is like you, glorious in holiness, fearful in praises, doing wonders? God is incomparable. There is none among the highest, the holiest, in heaven or earth, like Jehovah. His being is from himself. No other being is its own cause. He is an absolutely perfect being, and nothing can be added to him or taken from him. Man is in need of continual additions to sustain him. He needs air to breathe, food to strengthen him, raiment to cover him, fire to warm him, sleep to refresh him, righteousness to justify and save him. He is a heap of infirmities, a hospital of diseases, and a bundle of imperfections. God is unchangeable in his being, incapable of the least alteration. He is the same yesterday, today, and forever (*Heb.* 13:8). God is an eternal being. Men and angels have a beginning and no end, but God is eternal with no beginning, succession, or end! From everlasting to everlasting he is God! (*Psa.* 90:2). There is no succession in his duration—he dwells in one indivisible point of eternity. There is no past or 'to come' with God. He enjoys his whole eternity every moment. Nothing in the least has been added to his duration since the world was. His Name is *I Am* (*Exod.* 3:14), not, *I was or shall be*. Christ told the Jews, 'Before Abraham was, *I Am*' (*John* 8:58). It seems false grammar, but it is the most proper true divinity. Past and future are all his present!

GEORGE SWINNOCK, *Works*, IV:381-396

If I take the wings of the morning and dwell in the uttermost parts of the sea, even there your hand shall lead me, and your right hand shall hold me.

Psalm 139:9-10

God is an infinite being that knows no bounds, no limits. All the heavens cannot contain him. He is in heaven, earth, sea, hell, and infinitely more. Oh, what a being is the blessed God, who is boundless in duration, boundless in all his perfections and attributes, and boundless in his essence and being. No place can confine him. He is neither shut up in any place nor shut out of any place. He is above place, without place, yet in all places. Men and angels are finite—less than drops to this ocean. Man cannot comprehend God or perfectly understand him. The sea may be contained in a nutshell sooner than God can be contained in man's limited understanding. The heathen know somewhat of him (*Rom.* 1:20-21), his saints much much more, and the perfect spirits in heaven even more, and yet by all these a very little portion is known! The being of God passes our understanding. The knowledge of God is higher than the heavens and deeper than hell. It is longer than the earth and broader than the sea. Though he is not far from you, yet he is far above you, and far beyond you—far above your thoughts, and beyond your conceptions. He dwells in unapproachable light, whom no one has ever seen or can see (*1 Tim.* 6:16). Try to reach the nearest planet with your arm, yet the knowledge of God is above and beyond. What a fool would he be thought, who would attempt to climb to the stars. Yet to find out God to perfection he must climb much higher. The heavens are high, yet their height is finite; hell is deep, yet its depth is determined; the earth is long, yet its length is limited; the sea is broad, yet its breadth is bounded; but God is infinite, boundless, and beyond all these!

GEORGE SWINNOCK, *Works*, IV:397-402

For everyone who has been born of God overcomes the world. And this is the victory that has overcome the world—our faith.

1 John 5:4

The more easily that a Christian can repel desires and resist temptations to sin, the stronger is his faith. The snare or net, which holds the little fish fast, is broken by a stronger fish. The Christian's faith is strong or weak as he finds it easy or hard to break from temptations to sin. When an ordinary temptation holds you by the heel, and you are entangled in it like a fly in the spider's web and there is much ado to get it off and persuade your heart from yielding, truly this indicates a very feeble faith. Peter's faith was weak when a maid's voice dashed his composure, but it was well amended when he could withstand, and, with a noble consistency, disdain the threats of a whole counsel (*Acts* 4:8-20). Christian, compare yourself with yourself, and pass honest judgment on yourself. Do your lusts now powerfully allure and captivate your heart, and carry you away from God as they did some months or years ago? Or can you say your heart has gotten above them? Since you know more about Christ and have had a view of his spiritual glories, can you now pass by lust's door and not look in? Yea, when they knock at your door in temptation, can you shut it upon them and disdain the desire? Surely your faith has grown stronger. When you see that clothes that fit a year ago will not fit now because they are too small, you may easily be persuaded that you have grown since that time. If your faith has not grown, those temptations which fit you then, will still fit you now! If you find that the power of sin is declining, you may know that your faith is more lively and vigorous. The harder the blow, the stronger the arm that gives it. A child cannot strike as strong a blow as a man, and weak faith cannot give a knockout blow to sin as a strong faith can.

WILLIAM GURNALL, *The Christian in Complete Armour*, II:63-64

Jesus immediately … took hold of him, saying to him, 'O you of little faith, why did you doubt?'

Matthew 14:31

Can there be true faith, and yet doubting? Yes, there is a doubting that shows the strength of faith. The doubtings of a true faith are attended with much shame and sorrow of spirit for those doubtings. I appeal to your conscience, poor doubting soul—does the consideration of this sin cost you many tears and a heavy sigh? Where does this come from? Will unbelief mourn for unbelief? Or sin put itself to shame? Certainly not! This shows that there is a principle of faith in the soul which takes God's side, and cannot see his promises and name wronged by unbelief, without protesting against it and mourning under it, though the hands are too weak at present to drive the enemy out of the soul. The gospel will clear you who sincerely mourn for your unbelief! How many times do we find unbelief questioning God's mercy and faithfulness—which should be beyond all dispute in our hearts? We might as well question whether there is a God! We must acknowledge this folly. 'O my unbelief, the enemy of God and my soul, will you puzzle me with needless fears, and make me think so unworthily of my God?' Doubtings of a true believer are also accompanied with a burning desire after the very things you doubt! The weak believer questions God's love, but desires it more than life. He doubts if Christ is his, yet he sets great value upon Christ, and would consider no price too great if he were to be bought. This is a judgment only of a believer. It is very ordinary for excessive love to beget excessive fear, and that groundless. The wife who loves her husband dearly, who's traveling abroad, fears his harm, and thus torments herself without just cause. Passion, when strong and violent, disturbs our reason. The weak Christian's doubting is like the wavering of a ship at anchor—he is moved, yet not removed from his hold on Christ.

William Gurnall, *The Christian in Complete Armour*, ii:66-69

And then will I declare to them, 'I never knew you; depart from me, you workers of lawlessness.'

Matthew 7:23

I shall lay down three characteristics of a presumptuous faith. (1.) *A presumptuous faith is an easy faith.* It has no enemy of Satan or our own corrupt hearts to oppose it, and so, like a stinking weed, shoots up and grows proud all of a sudden. The devil never has the sinner surer as when he is trusting vain hopes of Christ and salvation, like a man walking in his sleep. The devil draws the curtains about him, that no light or noise will break his rest. A thief in the night won't wake the master of the house! Sleep is his advantage. True faith finds Satan to be a sworn enemy against it. The devil pours out a flood of wrath as soon as true faith is born and cries after the Lord. (2.) *A presumptuous faith is lame in one hand.* It has a hand to receive a pardon and heaven from God, but no hand to give itself up to God. True faith has the use of both hands. True faith takes Christ: 'My beloved is mine', and then surrenders to his use and service: 'and I am his'. The presumptuous soul, like Ananias, lies to the Holy Spirit, and keeps back the chief part instead of laying it at Christ's feet. This lust, or that enjoyment, he hides when he should deliver it up to justice. His life is bound up in it, and if God will have it from him, he must take it by force. If this is a true picture of your faith, you mistake a bold face for a believing heart. If you count it as a great privilege that Christ should have the throne of your heart as that you should have a place in his mercy, you prove yourself a sound believer. (3.) *A presumptuous faith is a sapless and unsavoury faith.* The one who pretends to have great faith will taste little sweetness in Christ. He still has the relish for gross food of sensual enjoyments over spiritual dainties. If he could freely speak, he would prefer the scraps of the carnal treasures of the world over the spiritual pleasures in Christ, his promises, and his holy ways.

William Gurnall, *The Christian in Complete Armour*, II:69-71

When I look at your heavens, the work of your fingers ... what is man that you are mindful of him, and the son of man that you care for him?

Psalm 8:3, 4

I desire you to stand with me in holy amazement, and wonder at the dealings of God with poor worms as we are! Surely God deals familiarly with men, and his condescension to clay is astonishing. God is transcendent and infinitely above us and all of our thoughts. The heavens cannot contain him. He is glorious in holiness, fearful in praises, doing wonders. The nations are as a drop in the bucket. The holiest men of God have addressed themselves to him, 'Woe is me, for I am undone, I am a man of unclean lips ... for mine eyes have seen ... the Lord of hosts!' (cf. *Isa.* 6:5). Then consider the baseness, vileness, and utter unworthiness of man; yea, the holiest and best of men before God are altogether vanity! By nature we are children of wrath (*Eph.* 2:3). The blood that runs in our veins is just as tainted as that of those now in hell! What offensive and God-provoking corruptions daily break out in the best hearts! Let us consider and admire that this great and blessed God should ever be so much concerned about such vile, despicable worms as we are! He does not need us, but is perfectly blessed and happy in himself without us. We can add nothing to him. No, the holiest of men add nothing to him, and yet see how great account he makes of us! His electing love speaks of the dear account he made of us. How ancient, how free, and how astonishing is this act of grace! This is the design of his providence, which will not rest until it is accomplished. Consider the gift of his Son out of his bosom that God has made for us in a state of enmity with God. Consider his providential care for us. He keeps us night and day; no, not a moment does he withdraw his eyes, or a thousand mischiefs in that moment would rush in upon us and ruin us!

John Flavel, *Works*, iv:410-412

And why are you anxious about clothing? Consider the lilies of the field, how they grow: they neither toil nor spin.

Matthew 6:28

It is the unquestionable duty of God's people at all times to reflect upon the performance of God's providence, but especially in times of trouble. We are called to consider it, that we may prop up our faith by these considerations. In Scripture, the Holy Spirit has affixed our attention to the narratives of the works of providence, which invites men to a due and clear observation of them. We see the great and celebrated work of providence in delivering Israel out of Egyptian bondage, and when the daring enemy Rabshakeh put Hezekiah to such consternation, we see he was defeated by providence. Without due observation of the works of providence, no praise can be rendered to God for any of them. Giving praise and thanksgiving for mercies depends upon this. Psalm 107 is spent in narratives of God's providential care of men. God will be defrauded of his praise if this duty is neglected. Without this, we lose the usefulness and benefit of all the works of God for us, or others, which would be an unspeakable loss indeed to us. This is the food our faith lives upon in days of distress! From providences past, saints used to argue to fresh and new ones to come! So David (*1 Sam.* 17:37)—'The LORD who delivered me from the paw of the lion and from the paw of the bear will deliver me from the hand of this Philistine.' If these are forgotten, the hands of faith hang down! Jesus called the disciples to remember divine providence (*Matt.* 16:9). Saints can draw arguments in prayer for new mercies from this fountain. When Moses prays for a new pardon for the people, he argues from what was past—'Please pardon the iniquity of this people, according to the greatness of your steadfast love, just as you have forgiven this people, from Egypt until now' (*Num.* 14:19).

JOHN FLAVEL, *Works*, IV:413-415

I will ponder all your work, and meditate on your mighty deeds.

Psalm 77:12

Oh that we were acquainted with the heavenly duty of reflecting on the providence of God! How sweet it would make our lives! How light it would make our burdens! Ah sirs! If you neglect this duty, you will live estranged from the pleasure of the Christian life. Labour to get as full a recognition of God's providence to you as possible. Fill your hearts with the thoughts of him and his ways. Search back through your lives as did Asaph (*Psa.* 77:11-12). He laboured to recover ancient providences and get fresh sweetness out of them. Ah, there is not a more pleasant history than our own lives. If you would but sit down and review, from the beginning, what God has been to you, and done for you. Consider the special manifestations and out-breakings of his mercy, faithfulness, and love in the conditions you have passed through. Let your thoughts dive as far as you can to the bottom, to plumb the depths of providence, and admire them, though we can't touch the bottom. Ponder the seasonableness of the mercies. Exact timing makes a mercy a thousand-fold more considerable, and enhances the value of such a mercy. Ponder his peculiar providence for you among others. This particular attention heightens the mercy and endears it even more to us. When a general calamity comes upon the world, and we are exempted by the favour of divine providence, and living under the shelter of his wings, how endearing are such providences! Consider, also, leading providences. These may seem slight and trivial in themselves, but they rank first among providential favours to us. These may usher in a multitude of other mercies, and draw a train of happy consequences after them, like Jesse sending David to his brothers at the battle-front. Thus every Christian may furnish himself out of his own stock of providential experiences.

JOHN FLAVEL, *Works*, IV:416-418

'Now I am sure that the Lord has sent his angel and rescued me from the hand of Herod' ... he went to the house of Mary ... where many were gathered ... praying.

Acts 12:11, 12

As you reflect on the providence of God, consider the instruments employed for you, for the finger of God is clearly seen when we pursue this meditation. Sometimes great mercies are conveyed to us by very improbable means, while more probable ones are laid aside. A stranger might be stirred up to do for you what a near relation by nature has no power or will to do for you! Jonathan, a mere stranger to David, was closer to him, more friendly and useful to him, than his own brothers who despised and slighted him. Ministers have found more kindness and respect from strangers than from their own people; 'A prophet is not without honour, except in his home town' (*Mark* 6:4). Sometimes God uses the hand of enemies. He has bowed the hearts of many wicked men to show great kindness to his people (*Acts* 28:2). Sometimes God makes use of instruments for our good that were intended for evil and mischief. Joseph's brothers designed his ruin, but God used it for his advancement. The design and scope of providence must not escape our thorough consideration. Above all others, this is the most warming and melting consideration—'And we know that for those who love God all things work together for good, for those who are called according to his purpose' (*Rom.* 8:28). A thousand friendly hands are at work to promote our happiness. Consider also the relation providence bears to our prayers! This is sweet meditation. Prayer honours providence and providence honours prayer! Great notice is taken of this in Scripture (*Gen.* 24:45; *Dan.* 9:20; *Acts* 12:12). You have had the very petitions you asked from him. Providences have born the very signatures of your prayers upon them. O how affectingly sweet are such mercies!

JOHN FLAVEL, *Works*, IV:418-419

I will never leave you nor forsake you.

Hebrews 13:5

The word of promise assures us that whatever wants and straits the saints fall into, he will never leave or forsake them (*Heb.* 13:5), and he will be with them in trouble! (*Psa.* 91:15). Consult the various providences of your life up to this point, and, I believe, you will find the truth of these promises confirmed as often as you have been in trouble. Ask your own hearts, where and when was it that your God forsook you, and left you to sink and perish under your burdens? I do not doubt that most of you have been, at one time or another, plunged into difficulties out of which you could see no way of escape by the eye of reason. Yea, it may be that it staggered your faith in the promise, like David: 'David said in his heart, "Now I shall perish one day by the hand of Saul"' (*1 Sam.* 27:1). And yet notwithstanding all, we see him emerge out of that sea of trouble, and the promises made good in every jot and tittle to him! Doubtless you may observe your own case and be satisfied, and ask your own soul the question, 'Did God abandon or cast you off in the day of your trouble?' Certainly you must deny your own experience if you should say so. It is true there have been times you were overwhelmed with difficulties you have met with, in which (1.) You could see no way of escape, and concluded you must perish in them. (2.) Difficulties have staggered your faith in the promises, and made you doubt whether the Fountain of all sufficiency would let out itself for your relief. (3.) Yes, difficulties have provoked you to murmuring and impatience, and thereby provoked the Lord to forsake you in your straits, but yet you see he did not forsake you. He either strengthened your back to bear them, or, lightened your burden, or opened an unexpected door of escape, according to that promise (*1 Cor.* 10:13), so that the evil you feared did not come upon you!

JOHN FLAVEL, *Works*, IV:423-424

Not one word has failed of all the good things that the Lord your God promised concerning you.

Joshua 23:14

In all your observation of providence, take special note of the word of God, which is fulfilled and made good to you. This is a clear truth, that all providences have relation to the written word. Solomon acknowledges that the promises and providences of God went along step by step with his father David all his days; that his hand fulfilled whatever his mouth had spoken (*1 Kings* 8:24). So also Joshua (*Josh.* 23:14), who observed the relation of the works of God and his word. He found them in exact harmony. Let us consider, therefore, the word of God in our review of providence. There is a two-fold advantage: (1.) It greatly confirms the truth of the Scripture, when we see truth manifest in events. O what a great confirmation is here before our eyes! (2.) This will abundantly instruct us in our present duties under all providences. The word interprets the works of God. Providence in itself is not a perfect guide. It often puzzles and entangles our thoughts, but bring them to the word, and your duty will be quickly manifest. Bring the providences you have passed through, or are now under, to the word of God, and you will find yourselves surrounded with a marvellous light! The word of God is the only support and relief to a gracious soul in the dark day of affliction. Is this not a proven truth attested by a thousand undeniable experiences? From here, the saints fetched their cordials when fainting under the rod. One word of God can do more than ten thousand words of men to relieve a distressed soul. When providence directs you to such promises as—The Lord is with you in trouble (*Psa.* 91:15), or, God's inward peace (*John* 16:33), or, blessed fruit in all things (*Rom.* 8:28)—O what sensible ease and relief ensues! How light is your burden compared with what it was before.

John Flavel, *Works*, iv:419-420, 424

Blessed be the God and Father of our Lord Jesus Christ, the Father of mercies and God of all comfort.

2 Corinthians 1:3

In all your observations of providence, be sure that you eye God as the author of them all. Without the direction of God, no mercy or comfort can come into your hands. It is not enough to acknowledge him in a general way, so take special notice of the following particulars. (1.) Eye the care of God for you: he cares for you (*1 Pet.* 5:7); he knows what you need (*Matt.* 6:32); don't worry (*Phil.* 4:6). (2.) Eye the wisdom of God in the way of dispensing his mercies to you. Note how suitably and seasonably they are ordered to your condition. When one comfort is removed, another is raised up in its place. Thus Isaac was comforted in Rebekah after his mother's death (*Gen.* 24:67). (3.) Eye the free grace of God in his providences, yea, see riches of grace in every bequest of comfort to so vile and unworthy creatures as we are. See yourself overwhelmed by the least of all your mercies (*Gen.* 32:10). (4.) Eye the condescension of God to your requests for those mercies (*Psa.* 34:6). This is the sweetest part in any enjoyment—that God has answered our prayers. This greatly enflames the soul's love to God (*Psa.* 116:1). (5.) Eye the design of God in all your comforts. They are not sent to satisfy the cravings of your sensual appetite, but to quicken and enable you for a more cheerful discharge of your duty (*Deut.* 28:47). (6.) Eye the way that your mercies are conveyed to you; they flow to you through the blood of Christ and covenant of grace. Mercies derive their sweetness from the channel through which they run to us. (7.) Eye the distinguishing goodness of God in all the comfortable enjoyments of your lives. How many thousands—better than you—are denied these comforts? (8.) Eye them all as comforts appointed to refresh you in your way to a far better mercy—the best mercies are still reserved till last!

John Flavel, *Works*, iv:425-426

Blessed be the God and Father of our Lord Jesus Christ, the Father of mercies and God of all comfort.

2 Corinthians 1:3

In the sad and afflictive providences that befall you, eye God as the author of these also. Consider, (1.) God is sovereign and infinitely superior to you. At his pleasure, you, and all you have, came into being, and it is natural that we should be in submission to his will. His sovereignty is gloriously displayed in his eternal decrees and his temporal providences. He might have put us as a worm, or as the most miserable among men. We might have been lost for eternity and miserable forever. Shall not this quiet us under the common afflictions of this life? (2.) Set the grace and goodness of God before you in your affliction. See him passing by, proclaiming his Name, *'the Lord, merciful and gracious'*. There are two mercies that are seldom eclipsed by the darkest affliction that befalls the saints in their temporal concerns, namely—*sparing mercy* in this world, and *saving mercy* in that to come. It is not as bad as it might be, or as we deserve, and it will be better hereafter. Has he taken something? He might have taken all. Are we afflicted? It is a mercy we are not destroyed. O! If we consider temporal and spiritual mercies we would admire mercy rather than complain of severity. (3.) Eye the wisdom of God in all your afflictions: the *kind* of your afflictions—this, and not another; the *time*—now and not at another season; the *degree*—in this measure only, and not in a greater; the *supports*—you are not left altogether helpless; the *outcome*—for your good, not ruin. We see great reason to be quiet and well satisfied under the hand of God. (4.) Under the saddest providence, set the faithfulness of the Lord before you, and eye his all-sufficiency. See enough in him still, whatever else is gone. His fountain is full as ever! Look on him as the rock of ages, always the same. God is what he was, and where he was!

John Flavel, *Works*, iv:426-428

Peter answered him, 'Though they all fall away because of you, I will never fall away.'
Matthew 26:33

Man changes, and what an infinite distance between man and an immutable God! This should cause us to lie down under a sense of our nothingness in the presence of the Creator. In the fall, man was wounded in his head and heart; the wound in the head made him unstable in the truth, and that in his heart, unsteadfast in his affections. He is like a ship without pilot or sails, or a weathervane that is turned by every breath of wind. We waver between God and Baal. While we are resolving, we look back at Sodom. Sometimes we are lifted up with heavenly intentions, and presently cast down with earthly cares. Our resolutions are like letters written on water. With John we love Christ today, and as Judas tomorrow we betray him. We are resolved to be holy as angels in the morning, and the evening beholds us as impure as devils. Peter vowed allegiance, and almost with the same breath swore against him. The flesh sets its desire against the Spirit, and the Spirit against the flesh. In a good man, how often there is a spiritual lethargy! Though he does not openly defame God, yet he does not always glorify him. He does not forsake the truth, but he does not seek to rest in it. How hard it is to make our thoughts and affections keep their stand! Place them on a good object, and they will be flying from it like a bird from branch to branch. This ought to trouble us! Though we may stand fast in the truth, and spin our resolutions into a firm web, and though the Spirit may triumph over the flesh in our practice, we ought to bewail the inconstancy of our nature. The stability we do have is from grace. How contrary we are to the unchangeable God, who is always the same! And he would have us the same in our religious promises and resolutions for good!

Stephen Charnock, *Existence and Attributes of God*, pp. 132-135

Now there is great gain in godliness with contentment.

1 Timothy 6:6

What is contentment? (1.) It is *self-fullness*, and so is opposed to dissatisfaction of mind that arises from emptiness and deficiency. A man is content when his soul is full because he possesses that which is adequate for all his desires and wants. Inherent self-sufficiency belongs only to God, but there is a dependent, derived, and borrowed self-sufficiency that every gracious person has. Having God for his God, and so possessing the universal good, he has everything he can desire or need, and so, in a borrowed sense, he is self-sufficient! We become self-sufficient through a covenant interest in God, and then improving and living upon God. Until this is done, there is no self-fullness—only want and emptiness, with no contentment or satisfaction. The only good in the creature is a finite, defective good, that cannot answer the desires of the soul. The heart is restless and unsatisfied. But God is a perfect, complete, comprehensive good. If man is once brought to possess God, he is satisfied, and all his desires answered. Having God, he has all, and thus contentment. We can be content under the least of creature comforts, but a man without God will not be content with all. (2.) Contentment lies in *restricting and moderating* our desires after earthy possessions, so that the heart is not craving more and more, but is well content with the present proportion allotted by God. It is opposed to covetousness. The covetous never thinks he has enough; the more he has, the more he wants. Contentment suppresses these exorbitant and extravagant desires, and cheerfully enjoys what he has! (3.) It is a calmness of mind in every condition and occurrence of providence; when he likes whatever God does with him, and quietly submits without fretting and murmuring, even when he crosses our natural desires. Always think well of God, and of every state he is pleased to bring you in.

Thomas Jacombe, *Puritan Sermons 1659–1689*, II:550–552

I have learned in whatever situation I am to be content.

Philippians 4:11

Paul learned contentment, a rare and excellent lesson that is harder than almost any other lesson in the whole compass of Christianity! How admirable was this blessed man in this difficult piece of practical knowledge. Surely he that can master such a lesson as this may well be set in the highest place in Christ's school! Learning this lesson is both *supernatural* and *mysterious*. This knowledge doesn't come from natural light; it must be infused by God, and taught by the Holy Spirit. There must be a divine light beamed into the soul, a special grace from Christ, and the supernatural working of God's Spirit in the heart, or else there can be no true contentment. Then, in a subordinate sense, it is taught by prudent observation, Christian experience, and daily, constant exercise. All of these, when blessed by God, contribute to making the heart quiet in every condition. It is the sincere Christian only who indeed lives this way. This lesson is also mysterious, as a great secret that lies out of the common road, and is not so easy to be understood. It is not open and obvious to every person, but is a hidden mystery that few discern. It carries a holy art and skill in it, such that, when one learns it, one becomes one of the greatest artists in the world. Here is a man that has very much, and yet is not content, and here is another that has little or nothing, and yet he is content. Surely this is a mystery! The question then will come to this: How may we get this excellent frame, to be contented under anything that may befall us? He that would learn to live content must be (1.) a considering man, (2.) a godly man, and (3.) a praying man. Consideration will do much, grace or godliness will do more, and prayer will do most of all. In consideration, we have the strength of the man; in grace, the strength of the Christian; and in prayer, the strength of God! These being united do the work effectually.

Thomas Jacombe, *Puritan Sermons 1659-1689*, II:546-549, 553

My times are in your hand; rescue me from the hand of my enemies and from my persecutors!

Psalm 31:15

The first help to learn contentment is consideration. Few consider, and so few are content. More consideration would bring less murmuring. Men are hasty and do not ponder things, and passion and discontent prevail over them. When we meet with anything which runs cross to our desire, we should sit down and consider the matter; this would tend to quiet our spirits. Consideration is an excellent help to contentment. Consider who it is that orders our state: surely the supreme, sovereign, all-disposing God. There is a hand above that directs all events here below. He numbers our hairs and orders our state. Anytime your heart begins to storm and fret, sit down and seriously consider who it is that orders that condition. Let your thoughts dwell upon it. What! Believe that providence is carving out every condition, and yet be discontent? That is very sad. Shall clay dispute with the Potter? I do not know a more effectual help to still the spirit than this consideration. Consider *how* all things are ordered by him—(1.) All is ordered by God *irresistibly!* This is true for every person in the world. 'I work, and who can turn it back?' (*Isa.* 43:13). God will do his pleasure. Christian, if you passionately desire a mercy, you will not receive it sooner because you desire it. If you desire an affliction removed, and if God takes it away from you, that's the end of it, but if not, you must bear it still. Humble contentment may do much, but proud contending will do nothing. Pray, therefore, whenever passion begins to rise in the soul; think of this speedily. The tide of providence will have its course, and there is no hindering of the almighty and sovereign acting of God! He does whatever he pleases (*Eccles.* 8:3), and works all things according to his will (*Eph.* 1:11). It is best to submit to God what we cannot alter!

Thomas Jacombe, *Puritan Sermons 1659–1689*, II:553–555

The LORD is righteous in all his ways and kind in all his works.

Psalm 145:17

To further learn contentment, consider also—(2.) God orders our estate *righteously!* He is righteous, and does nothing but what is righteous! Shall not the judge of the earth do right? (*Gen.* 18:25). This is an excellent subject for our thoughts to dwell upon, when anything troubles us. We may well be content in every state. Providence may sometimes be dark and mysterious, yet it is always just and righteous. God may sometimes cross us, but he never wrongs us! He does not see it good to gratify us in all our desires; but it is good for us to justify him in all his dispensations. Does he remove a mercy we desire, or lay an affliction on us that was not prompted by our sin? Is it not becoming to us to be silent before him? We provoke God to afflict us, and then are angry with him, whereas we have reason only to be angry with ourselves, since our own sins are the cause of our miseries. We too often have just grounds of being troubled with our own hearts, because of their pride, carnality, unthankfulness, unbelief etc.—but this is a good discontent. But we never have any just grounds for being disturbed at what God does, seeing that all of his actions are holy and righteous. Consider this: 'Such a good I want, and such an evil I feel, but is God unrighteous in either? Surely, no! For do I deserve the one, and do I not deserve the other? Why then should I quarrel or fret against God?' Discontent is a bold impeachment of God's righteousness. This is a thing of a very heinous nature, grounded upon the greatest falsehood that is imaginable! Take heed of it. When wronged, then complain, but not until then, and I am sure you will never complain. In a word, let this heart-quieting consideration be much upon your thoughts; all is righteously ordered by God, and must be accepted with contentment!

THOMAS JACOMBE, *Puritan Sermons 1659-1689*, II:555-556

O Lord, how manifold are your works! In wisdom have you made them all.

Psalm 104:24

To further learn contentment, consider also—(3.) God orders our estate *wisely!* The windings of providence are full of wisdom. God made all things with infinite wisdom, and so also disposes and governs all things with infinite wisdom. And this holds true, not only with respect to the whole of creation, but also with respect to every part and parcel of it, especially to man, and every individual man, in the world. If this was believed and considered, it would greatly help to teach us contentment in every condition. Certainly it must be the most absurd folly to find fault with or dislike that which is done by God in admirable wisdom! In our worldly affairs, we quietly acquiesce to the advice of men we apprehend are endued with understanding. The patient takes the medicine prescribed by a skilful physician, even though it makes him nauseous, and the pilot of a vessel is trusted by the passengers. Why do we not rest with contentment in God, whose wisdom and faithfulness infinitely transcend what is in man? Shall we not rest in that which he thinks best? Vain man thinks he can order things better than God, and finds fault in God's disposal of him, but this attitude is the highest folly. God always makes a wise choice for man. The saints shall see it when they come to heaven, if not before. May we not rest quietly in his wisdom? On the other hand, what a sad choice do men make for themselves when in their discontent, they insist on their own way. Rachel must have a child, but it cost her life. Jacob couldn't wait God's time for a blessing, and by his hastiness knew a world of troubles. Poor creature, you need no more to undo you, than to be left to choose your own condition! He that has the wisdom to steer the vessel of the world has wisdom to direct your life! He won't make a mistake!

Thomas Jacombe, *Puritan Sermons 1659-1689*, II:556-557

Godliness is of value in every way, as it holds promise for the present life and also for the life to come.

1 Timothy 4:8

The second help to learn contentment is grace or godliness. Godliness and contentment go together (*1 Tim.* 6:6). Godliness causes this blessed frame of heart. True contentment requires a divine principle within, and a divine assistance from above. All outward motives cannot keep the heart quiet under crosses, unless there is a work of saving grace there. The true and only way to be content is to be godly. Contentment is the daughter of godliness! How does godliness produce contentment? (1.) *It transforms the faculties of the soul.* The *understanding* is enlightened, so fancy and imaginations do not carry it away. Thus the heart is more quiet. Agitations of the mind are founded in the power of fancy. Fancy perceives things wrong, which causes us to fret. Grace sets up sound judgment of things. An enlightened mind promotes a submissive heart. Grace also transforms the *will.* Grace melts our will into God's. When the wind and tide are contrary, the waters are rough and boisterous, but when they go the same way, all is calm. So here, when God's will and ours differ, the storms of passion rise, but when they agree, there is nothing but stillness in the spirit. O! We are never discontent unless our wills clash with God's. Grace also transforms the *affections*. Grace removes the inordinate love of earthly things and keeps it in bounds, and so works contentment. Where love of earthly things is too great, there is danger of discontent and impatience. Grace also makes the *conscience* good. A good conscience is the ark that holds the manna of contentment and joy, and is not easily moved at trouble. If your leg is sore, you cannot touch it without pain, but if it is sound, it can bear a smart blow without complaining. When the conscience is sound, a man can bear anything.

Thomas Jacombe, *Puritan Sermons 1659–1689*, II:580–582

It is my eager expectation and hope that … Christ will be honoured in my body, whether by life or by death.

Philippians 1:20

How does grace or godliness produce contentment? (2.) *It makes a person have a powerful sense of God's glory, so as always to rest in that as his ultimate end and most desirable good.* Grace produces this glorious effect in the heart, and so effectually produces a quiet spirit in every condition. Selfishness is the foundation of discontent. The selfish look no higher than sensual ease, delight, and satisfaction, and if these are crossed, they storm and become angry. But the godly man who is living up to his godliness sets an eye on the glory of God as his chief aim and central focus. Such a one says, 'Let my state be what it will, God will glorify himself by it. It must be the best state that most tends to his glory, otherwise he would not have put me into it! O! Therefore, I will like it, yea, rejoice in it, since it is the most conducive to that which is better than all my little comforts, namely, the glory of God.' He will live in contentment who knows and considers these two things—all occurrences tend to the promoting both of God's honour and our own good! Only the godly can mind these, and so godliness is necessary for contentment. (3.) *Grace further establishes contentment through special graces.* (a.) *Humility.* The humble man is a contented man and submits to God. Pride makes us think we are wiser than God, and can order our conditions better than he. The proud man cannot bear a low state, and sees himself wronged if he is not chief. Humility accepts the lowest condition and the lowest mercy. Pride charges God, and humility admires God. Pride disquiets the heart, while humility is a heart-quieting grace. It is never well enough for the proud. It is always well with the humble. How does godliness work contentment?—By rooting out pride and planting humility in the soul.

Thomas Jacombe, *Puritan Sermons 1659-1689*, 11:582-583

I believe that I shall look upon the goodness of the Lord in the land of the living!

Psalm 27:13

Another special grace that eminently helps to promote contentment is (b.) *Faith.* How readily it rises upon all occasions to keep down turbulent risings in the heart. If a man begins to worry, 'What will become of me and mine?'—'Be still,' says faith, 'God will provide for you and yours.'—'O, but such and such blessings are denied me.'—'Yet be still, you have all in God. These and these blessings are yours, for God is yours,' says faith.—'But the providences of God toward me are very bitter.'—'Yet be still, there is abundant sweetness in the promises to take off that bitterness,' says faith.—'But it is at present very ill with me.' 'Yet be still, wait a little while, and it will be better,' says faith.—'But what have I to comfort me?'—'Why,' says faith, 'enough and enough; the unchangeable love of God, the pardon of all your sins, the covenant-state, eternal life.' They have never felt God's love or tasted forgiveness, who are discontent. Faith answers all objections that tend to disturb the spirit. It is a grace that keeps you from fainting and fretting. (c.) *Repentance.* He that mourns for sin does not easily murmur because of some outward cross. When sin is heavy, nothing besides, comparatively, is heavy. This is contentment by diversion—the sinner would be grieving of poverty, sickness, etc., but his focus is on the naughtiness of his heart: pride, passion, and unbelief! (d.) *Heavenly-mindedness.* The more a man minds things above, the less he is concerned about things below. A heart set on heaven doesn't concern itself about what befalls him on earth! (e.) *Self-denial.* This takes men off their own wisdom, will, and affections, to be fully resigned to the gracious disposal of God. 'O,' says the self-denying Christian, 'I am not fit to be my own chooser; God shall choose for me! I desire nothing but what God sees good to give me.'

Thomas Jacombe, *Puritan Sermons 1659-1689*, 11:583-584

Is anyone among you suffering? Let him pray.

James 5:13

The third and final help to learn contentment is prayer. Prayer is essential; without it, considerations and godliness are not enough. Humility, faith, repentance, heavenly-mindedness, and self-denial are the heart-quieting graces, and prayer is the heart-quieting duty. He that has not learned to pray, will not learn to be content. There must be a good striving with God in prayer, or there will be a striving against discontent. O sirs! Are you afflicted? Pray (*James* 5:13). Do you meet with crosses? Pray. Does your estate decay, your family die, or is the body consumed by pain and sickness? Pray. The best way to be content in every state is to pray in every state. We study this hard lesson best upon our knees. Prayer furthers contentment—(1.) *By giving vent to the mind under trouble.* Full vessels are apt to burst! Prayer is the best vent. We can go to God and pour out our hearts before him, and a heart ready to break is now greatly relieved. Hannah prayed, and wasn't sad anymore (*1 Sam.* 1:18). (2.) *By obtaining grace and strength from God that enables contentment.* He that stills the sea when it rages can also still the soul in all its passions and discontents. The calming of an inward storm is a thing in every way as marvellous as Christ calming the storm (*Matt.* 8:24-27). Paul was content 'through Christ who strengthened him'! This was a supernatural quietness of his mind. If you desire to be content in every condition, then go to God often and beg for it from him. Say, 'Lord, I am beside myself, and have a discontented heart that is ready upon every cross to fret against you. This is my burden: I cannot get the victory over my passion, I cannot bring myself to a calm, submissive frame. Blessed God, do help me through the power of your grace to have a contented mind in me!' O, do but pray thus, and in due time God will give you what you pray for!

Thomas Jacombe, *Puritan Sermons 1659-1689*, 11:585-586

Blessed are those who mourn, for they shall be comforted.

Matthew 5:4

Certainly, those who mourn for sin as the object of their mourning—their own sins and others'—are blessed indeed, and they shall be comforted. What is mourning for sin in a gracious manner? When it mourns—(1.) Because it is against God. David prayed, 'Against you only have I sinned' (*Psa.* 51:4). David had sinned against Uriah, his kingdom, and his own soul, but above all, he sinned against God! (2.) Because sin is the greatest evil. Paul's greatest sorrow was for sin (*Rom.* 7:24). Paul never cried 'O wretched man that I am' because he had suffered so much affliction, but only for his sin! (3.) Because it agrees with the law. Many men are afflicted for sin, but in their spirits, they are against the holiness of the law that forbids the sin. They don't want to be troubled for their sin and wish there was no such law that forbids it, and that there was no threat of God against it! Gracious mourning delights and approves of the law as good. (4.) To carry the heart to Jesus Christ. Many men and women who are troubled for their sin think God will be satisfied by their mourning. But mourning your heart out for a thousand years will never satisfy the justice of God. Mourning will come to nothing, unless it leads you to Jesus Christ for satisfaction of God's justice. Mourning that leads to Christ is blessed mourning. (5.) When the heart becomes set against sin. Gracious mourning doesn't mourn for sin and still live in it! It breaks the league it had with sin before. The soul is made so sensible of the evil of sin that it breaks with sin forever! Sin becomes bitter, and the soul bids it adieu. Though sin may overcome through weakness, yet I will renounce it, and set the soul forever against it. (6.) When it is a free work in the soul. The soul freely and willingly yields to Scripture, delights to hear any truth of God, and blesses God that opened his eyes to understand the evil of sin!

Jeremiah Burroughs, *The Saints' Happiness*, pp. 48-50

Today, if you hear his voice, do not harden your hearts as in the rebellion.

Hebrews 3:15

Those who mourn for sin are blessed, for it is a means to prevent eternal sorrow. There is no sinner upon the face of the earth but at some time or other must come to understand what sin means. As it is determined in heaven that all men must once die, so it is determined that all men must once sorrow. This is a certain rule; you must have sorrow for sin and repent. How much better it is to sorrow for sin while it may be pardoned, than to sorrow for sin when there can be no help! If it happens that you pass your days away in mirth here, and never come to feel the weight of sin upon your spirit, you are reserved to have eternal sorrows to be your portion, and to have the load of sin to lie upon you to all eternity! But blessed are they that mourn *now*, that feel the burden of sin now! They feel it in such a time in which they have hope of being delivered from the evil of sin to all eternity. How many thousands of men and women have lived securely, and have spent all their lives in the hardness of their hearts, and have never been made sensible of their sin, and have cried out upon their deathbeds, but the Lord has withdrawn himself from them. Now I would appeal to such a one, would you have thought it a blessed thing to have had the weight of sin upon your soul, in the time of your strength? You can hear them cry, 'Happy if I knew the evil of sin before, and spent my time not in mirth, but in mourning for my sin! Now on this sick bed I would know comfort and peace. I was led by sense and the flesh, and now the weight of sin comes upon me! Now I feel it as a heavy load. The Lord be merciful to me! It would be better for me to have been a mourner before!' Mourning fits us to receive the grace of God in Christ! How sweet is one drop of mercy! It is worth more than ten thousands of worlds.

Jeremiah Burroughs, *The Saints' Happiness*, pp. 50-51

Come now, let us reason together, says the Lord: though your sins are like scarlet, they shall be as white as snow.

Isaiah 1:18

Those who mourn for sin are in a blessed condition! They shall be forgiven for all the sins that cause them to mourn, which shall never be charged to their soul! Be assured of it. The pardon is sealed in heaven already. Also, your mourning for sin will be blessed to you to help you against the very sin you are mourning about! This is certain—either a man's sin will make an end of his mourning, or a man's mourning will make an end of his sin. If a man goes on sinning, he will leave off mourning, but if he keeps mourning, he will leave off sinning. The bitter aloes of mourning is the means to help against the crawling worms of sin. Mourning for sin shall one day wholly deliver you from sin, and you will never sin more against God. What will become of those that rejoice and laugh in their sin? Many have no greater delight in this world than satisfying themselves in their sinful ways. Oh, dreadful condition, and dreadful is the wickedness of your soul! Have you no joy but that which strikes at the blessed God, and caused Jesus Christ to be heavy unto death? Here is one reserved for eternal sorrows! The lusts in which you find so much pleasure will be bitter one day. Take head of rejoicing in sin. If a child that has a loving and merciful father and mother should go into a room, and fall down wringing his hands, mourning, and lamenting, 'Oh that I could please my father and mother more, and not do anything to grieve them'; if the parents were watching through a keyhole, would not this go right to the heart, and would not your hearts yearn towards this child? Your love is a drop compared to the infinite ocean of God's mercy. He holds every tear of your mourning in a bottle! Mourners are blessed; Jesus Christ has made a sufficient atonement for sin; that is, he has atoned for all the wrongs that sin has ever done to God.

Jeremiah Burroughs, *The Saints' Happiness*, pp. 51-53

Have mercy on me, O God, according to your steadfast love; according to your abundant mercy blot out my transgressions.

Psalm 51:1

The way to the valley of blessing is by the way of Baca, the valley of tears. It is good for men whose hearts begin to be troubled for their sin to get alone out of the way to consider their sin, and lay the rule to their heart alone between God and their soul. When Christ looked at Peter after Peter's great sin, Peter went out and wept bitterly. When he fell to mourning, he got alone. Do you feel the Spirit begin to stir and work in your heart? Cast yourself out from company and labour to work upon your thoughts to affect you further. Consider that you are dealing with an infinite God in all your ways. Call yourself to account. Some think that once they are believers, why then should they mourn? The truth is, there is more mourning: required after the pardon of sin than before. After Nathan had come to David, and he knew he was forgiven, he prayed the fifty-first Psalm. He laments his sin and cries to God to restore the joy of his salvation! The assurance of pardon is no hindrance to mourning. It makes our mourning sweeter than before. Look up to the Spirit of mourning, 'I will pour out the Spirit of grace ... and they shall mourn' (*Zech.* 12:10). 'But Lord, I have a hard heart!' Look up to God and plead the promise: the promise is infinite! And then plead this promise: 'I will take away the heart of stone, and give them a heart of flesh' (*Ezek.* 36:26). If you cannot mourn, then mourn that you cannot mourn—this will be acceptable unto God. Oh, and then take heed of sinning after mourning. If God begins to break your heart and help you to mourn, do not sin wilfully after mourning. At all times, you have need to be watchful and careful over yourself! Do not give way and liberty to your soul to commit the same sin again!

Jeremiah Burroughs, *The Saints' Happiness*, pp. 54-60

Blessed are the meek, for they shall inherit the earth.

Matthew 5:5

Meekness is easy to be entreated, and has a gentle spirit. Its nature consists especially in a gracious moderation of the passion of anger. Sometimes there is a natural meekness from a person's natural constitution, while others have a more choleric temperament. These are not so prone to anger naturally as other men are. But this blessed meekness goes beyond natural meekness. This natural meekness may not be as angry as others in some outward thing, but it quenches zeal for God. Spiritual meekness is a grace of the Holy Spirit that includes zeal as well as patience. Grace will teach men and women to be meek and gentle when they are personally crossed, but grace will never teach them not to be angry when God is dishonoured. In Scripture, those marked as the most eminent for meekness in their own cause, when it came to God's cause, were the most eminent in zeal! Moses was the meekest in all the earth, but when he came down from the mountain and saw the people worshipping the golden calf, he was all on fire! Jesus, our pattern of meekness, when he saw the moneychangers in the temple, took a cord, and whipped them out of the temple. And so Paul, who was very meek, and taught Timothy so (*2 Tim.* 2:25), set his eyes upon Elymas, who sought to draw away Sergius Paulus from the faith, and said, 'You son of the devil, you enemy of all righteousness, full of all deceit and villainy, will you not stop making crooked the straight paths of the Lord?' (*Acts* 13:10). What! Does any man speak more terribly than he did to Elymas? This meekness is mixed with zeal. When a man or woman can be weak in their own cause, and can moderate their anger, but yet, when it comes to the cause of God, they can be all on fire, this is the right meekness that is pronounced blessed!

Jeremiah Burroughs, *The Saints' Happiness*, pp. 70-71

Be angry and do not sin; do not let the sun go down on your anger.

Ephesians 4:26

Meekness moderates the *object* of its anger. It doesn't get angry for just anything. If it must get angry, it can justify its anger before God; 'Lord, I was angry, but no more than you would have me to be, and upon such and such grounds.' Meekness also moderates the *time* of anger, so it is not too sudden. If anything provokes you to anger, first weigh and consider the thing; then, if there is sufficient cause, let out your anger. Sudden anger has a gunpowder spirit, and a little spark puts all on fire in an instant. Meekness keeps anger from being *unseasonable*. When we are going to prayer, many times the devil will lay some temptation to provoke your passion, for he knows your prayer will be spoiled if he can get you into a passion. The grace of meekness can overpower anger, and make anger your servant and not your lord. Thus you can frustrate Satan's design. Oh it is dangerous to give way to passion at any time, but especially upon the Lord's day! If you are put into a passion, ten to one but you will lose the Sabbath. Your thoughts will be considering how you have been wronged and how to get revenge. Meekness keeps anger from lasting *longer than it should*. Much anger is like hell being once kindled, it is never quenched. Some, if something falls out in their family, and they are worked into a fit of passion, continue day after day in that fit of passion. Sometimes even a man and wife will not speak for days. This sinful anger is far from meekness! Meekness also moderates the *measure* of anger. If I am angry, meekness will be angry no more than needs be. It keeps it from being violent, fierce and cruel. One that has a meek spirit may be angry sometimes, ay, but his meekness will measure out his anger—this much, and no more!

JEREMIAH BURROUGHS, *The Saints' Happiness*, pp. 71-72

A man of wrath stirs up strife, and one given to anger causes much transgression.

Proverbs 29:22

Anger grows from the ground of pride in your hearts, or some other lust or weakness. Oh the woeful, evil effects that come from the anger of men and women! Oh what acts of sin can be committed in just one hour when you have given way to passions! Sometimes there is more sin committed in one day by a man or woman when they are in an unreasonable, hostile humour, than you may do in a year, and it will take a lifetime to repent of. Oh, sin is multiplied almost infinitely when we come into a passion! Passion and anger heat the lusts that are in the hearts of men and women. Those in a passion are active in sin. People in their sinful passions break both tables of the law by their woeful distempers and sinful actions, like Moses when he came down in his holy zeal smashing the tables on which the law was written. What reviling speeches, what revengeful thoughts, what words and desperate resolutions are there in times of anger! But when there is meekness in the heart, it pulls anger back, and will not allow it to proceed in any sinful effects. Nay, says meekness, 'what has the Lord given me these affections in my soul for? Is it not for his glory? What! Is it for the producing of such base and sinful effects as these are? The Lord forbid it.' Oh the evil of anger! Oh remember in the days of your humiliation to be humbled for the wicked effects of your sinful anger.—'Oh, let me have only holy ends and holy aims in my anger. You know all things, Lord; you know if I let out my anger against any man or woman or child, whether I aim at seeking their good, or not. If being gentle would do them more good, why, may they never see me angry.' This should be the resolution of every godly parent. Blessed are the meek—they overcome their passions!

Jeremiah Burroughs, *The Saints' Happiness*, pp. 72-73

Take my yoke upon you, and learn from me, for I am gentle and lowly in heart, and you will find rest for your souls.

Matthew 11:29

There is much to be said for the grace of meekness, and the blessedness of it, as for almost any grace I know. Next to faith itself, it is the great mother-grace. Why, you that are meek are like God the Father! When God showed his glory to Moses (*Exod.* 33-34), was not this a great part of his glory? And this is the glory of Jesus Christ to be so: 'Learn from me, for I am meek!' Christ doesn't call for any other grace that he would have his disciples follow him in, but humility and meekness. Why, blessed Saviour, do you not speak of your other excellent graces? You have grace without measure, and when you would have your disciples learn of you, why do you not mention your confidence, your heavenly-mindedness, your despising the world, or any other graces? 'No', says Christ, 'if you desire to be my disciples, I commend this to you—I am humble and meek.' Why was this the great commendation of Christ? Because the Lord accounted it his glory to be meek! Shall Christ reckon it to be his glory to be a meek man, and shall you not account it to be your glory? O blessed are those that are like God the Father and God the Son! They also have much of the Spirit of God. What was the Holy Spirit compared to more than meekness? When the Holy Spirit appeared on the head of Jesus Christ, he appeared in the form of a dove (*Matt.* 3:16). They say of the dove that it has no gall, and is the emblem of meekness. Therefore, if you would be like the Father, Son, and Holy Spirit, you must be a man or woman of a meek and gentle spirit. God directed the sacrifices to him to come not from lions and tigers, but doves and lambs! Oh may the Lord give us meek spirits, that we may be blessed!

Jeremiah Burroughs, *The Saints' Happiness*, pp. 73-74

But let your adorning be the hidden person of the heart with the imperishable beauty of a gentle and quiet spirit, which in God's sight is very precious.

1 Peter 3:4

God does not prize the rich things in the world—gold, silver, land, possessions and crowns. What are these to God? He does not regard the nations of the world with all their pomp and glory, but a meek and quiet spirit is high in God's esteem. Most of the words listed as fruit of the Spirit (*Gal.* 5:22-23) are synonyms of meekness. These graces are near akin—love, joy, peace, patience, kindness, goodness, faithfulness, gentleness, self-control. Passion and anger are fruits of the flesh, the fruit of the devil in the heart. The Lord looks upon the meek as the most brave and excellent spirits. He that is slow to wrath is better than the mighty (*Prov.* 16:32). If you think you cannot do great service for God, consider ruling your spirit with this grace of meekness. It is a braver exploit, and more honourable in the sight of God, than if you were able to overcome a city! Do you desire to walk worthy of your calling? Walk in meekness (*Eph.* 4:1-2)! The meek are not given to wrangling as other men are; they love to be quiet and enjoy their estates with comfort here on the earth, though it is little. The meek are more attractive than others. If you hire a servant, wouldn't you desire one that is of a meek and quiet spirit? If a man is seeking a wife, the first important quality is a meek spirit; without that, let her have whatever else she will, she is often rejected. If you are travelling, wouldn't you rather stay in an inn where the host and servants are of a quiet spirit? Whatever wrongs a meek man has in this world, he yields his cause to God, and keeps his heart quiet, and this interests God in his cause. When you once have interested God in your cause, you are likely to do well enough!

Jeremiah Burroughs, *The Saints' Happiness*, pp. 74-77

Now the man Moses was very meek.

Numbers 12:3

Is there any cause you desire to have success here on this earth? It may be that you will try to gain success yourself by wrangling and quarrelling, and think you can gain the victory by your own strength, and by making certain friends, but this will not do it, and it is a hundred to one that you will not succeed. But now, if you can by meekness give it up to God, turn it over to him, and interest God in this cause; certainly you will have success in it and obtain your desire. Ambrose says that all of Moses' great works did not make him as honourable as his meekness. Chrysostom says his extraordinary meekness is the reason why God spoke to him face to face. The Jews have a tradition, that when Moses was to die, God came to him, embraced him, and drew out his soul. If God would ever draw out a soul this way, it would be Moses'. In Exodus chapter twelve, Miriam and Aaron spoke against Moses for marrying a Cushite woman, and the Lord heard. They came and wrangled with Moses: 'What is this Moses?' As if to say, 'Has the Lord spoken to Moses alone? Would he lift himself above others?' Moses did not cry against them. His meekness drew God's attention to his cause. The Lord spoke suddenly; he breaks, as it were, forth from heaven. As if God should say, 'What! Is my meek servant Moses wronged? I will quickly appear for him.' Note, Moses was not suddenly in a passion, and therefore God was sudden. Moses' passion was not stirred, but God's was. You think how others have wronged you and your anger is stirred presently. Ay, you do not interest God in your case. If you are meek, God's anger will be kindled for you! God will sooner right your cause than when your own anger is kindled! The less you hear when you are wronged, the more God will hear. Oh that we had such a spirit as Moses.

JEREMIAH BURROUGHS, *The Saints' Happiness*, pp. 77-78

And do not grieve the Holy Spirit of God, by whom you were sealed for the day of redemption.

Ephesians 4:30

The lack of meekness is as contrary to true grace as almost any corruption that can be named. Without meekness you cannot see the stamp of the Spirit of Christ upon you. Labour for meekness, that the Spirit of God may delight in you, for meekness is very suitable to the Holy Spirit. An angry spirit is contrary to true grace, and there may be reasonable suspicion whether there is any true grace in those lacking meekness, and prevailing in passion. Grace reveals our vileness. What! Do you see yourself as a vile worm, and yet cannot bear anything against you? If you are crossed, is your heart presently aflame? Giving way to passion will grieve the Holy Spirit. The first lesson Christ teaches us is self-denial. Ay, an angry heart is a self-seeking heart. The principal work of grace is to subdue our hearts to God. Sinners are naturally stout and rebellious against God, and go on in a stubborn way until grace lays them under, and this is quite contrary to passion. The heart that is subdued to the Lord and his authority yields presently, but not a man in a passion! The Spirit of God enters when grace enters, and passion is opposite to the Spirit of Jesus Christ. The light of grace brings light and wisdom to the soul, not the darkness of passion. The promise of the gospel is to make men meek. I beseech you that profess godliness to consider that there is more danger in an angry, passionate spirit, than you are aware of! And though you may think you have grace because you make a profession, come to hear the word preached, and spend much time in prayer and fasting—you may be mistaken, and the anger of your heart may be your destruction forever! How often have you been drunk with passion? Look upon it as a greater evil than you are aware of!

Jeremiah Burroughs, *The Saints' Happiness*, pp. 80-81

The fruit of the Spirit is love, joy, peace, patience, kindness, goodness, faithfulness, gentleness, self-control.

Galatians 5:22-23

Let us all learn to have a meek and quiet spirit. It is unbecoming to have an angry, passionate heart. We ought to be meek towards our brethren, one another, and our neighbours. There are many that are so used to anger and passion towards their servants, their children, or wives, that even when they deal with God they show themselves angry and passionate. My brethren, let us learn to be in love with this amiable and lovely grace of meekness. Consider several ways to get the habit of meekness, and to behave yourselves meekly and gently in the places where you live, that you may be the blessed ones of Christ. (1.) *Learn to set a high price upon the quiet and sweetness of your spirit.* It is a rich jewel of great worth. One way to get it is to consider the rest to your spirit that meekness will give to you. Put a high price on the rest and quietness of your spirit. When you are tempted to passion, ask, 'Am I willing to lose the sweetness that I have in my spirit to have my will in such and such a matter? I can deny myself, and exercise meekness; oh the quiet of my heart! It is worth a world. Shall I lose this for a trifle now, for a toy?' Oh the poor trifles and toys that men and women cast away the quietness of their spirits for! If a man had a ball made of solid gold in his hand, and someone on the street cast dirt upon him, would it not be great folly to throw his golden ball at them for revenge? Truly, this is what you do when you cast away your meekness for passion to revenge yourself, when someone crosses your will, or does things to displease you! You cast your golden ball at them when you lose the quietness and meekness of your spirit to gain revenge upon them. Account meekness at a high rate, and do not lose it even for a little while!

JEREMIAH BURROUGHS, *The Saints' Happiness*, pp. 81-82

We have sinned and done wrong and acted wickedly and rebelled, turning aside from your commandments and rules.

Daniel 9:5

(2.) A second rule to help against passion, and to exercise meekness, is *to make a covenant with God often*, yet in the strength of Christ. Why not, when you rise in the morning, consider this: 'Today, there may perhaps fall to me something that will stir my passion, and take away the comfort of meekness I have enjoyed; well, I will covenant, through God's enablement, that today, whatever else shall befall me, I will be quiet at least until the evening. I am resolved to curb my passion and my will for this one day.' If that seems too long, purpose until noon. Though this does not mortify our passion, there is great benefit in keeping down your passion for a while. A fire can be put out by smothering it for a time. If a man can overcome himself for one day, he may find such sweetness that day, that he will begin to think, 'Why not covenant for tomorrow too?' Oh, if you could but overcome yourselves for one day, you might find so much good that it would exceedingly help you against another day. (3.) *Humble yourself for past failures.* If you resolve to set upon a duty, and are not humbled for your failures before, it is not likely that you will gain much good by your resolutions. Humbling yourself for the distempers of passion is a special means to purge out passion and to tame and quiet the spirits of men and women. Unless you are humbled for what you have done, you will fall to it again. It is a rule in other things, that if you resolve to amend in any particular, if you are not humbled for that which is past, you will fall to sin again. Israel failed time and time again for not humbling themselves for past failures. Oh get alone and apply the salt tears of humiliation for your anger, and it will be a special help for times to come!

Jeremiah Burroughs, *The Saints' Happiness*, pp. 82-83

The beginning of strife is like letting out water, so quit before the quarrel breaks out.

Proverbs 17:14

If you would have a meek and quiet spirit, (4.) *Take heed of the first beginnings of passion.* In a fire, you do not wait to quench it until the house is engulfed in flames! When the fire is first discovered, or just smoke, you seek it out and will not rest until you have put it out. So should it be when passion begins to rise and your soul begins to catch fire. Set yourself to quench it when it first begins. Perhaps a dish of water may quench it now, but later many pails will not do it. So it is with passion. If you are careful at first, you may quench the passion with little ado. But if you stay a while, passion cannot be measured, and you can't go near the man. So it is with poison. The sooner the antidote is administered the greater the hope of healing. Oh, look on passion as a poison, and take the remedy immediately. There have been the most fearful distempers of passion rise from very small beginnings, which have broken out to the most fearful outrages. How often in our families does a little spark kindle a great fire! First a word is spoken amiss, but that word begets another, and another, and thus grows into a most hideous flame. Take heed in the beginning. A friend thinks another's countenance is not as friendly as before, then comes suspicion, then misinterpretation, then estrangement, then gossip and hard words, and then violent contention. It could all have stopped in the beginning! (5.) *Consider beforehand that you will meet with things that will cross your will.* Being prepared helps against passion. Your servant will certainly do things to displease you. In marriage you will displease one another. Resolve beforehand that our wills will not be satisfied with everything, and this will be a means to quiet your heart when it comes. Mariners expect to meet with storms!

Jeremiah Burroughs, *The Saints' Happiness*, pp. 83-84

Do not take to heart all the things that people say, lest you hear your servant cursing you. Your heart knows that many times you yourself have cursed others.

Ecclesiastes 7:21-22

Further to promote meekness, (6.) *Consider your own frailty.* You will surely meet with provocation from others, but, in a little while, they will meet with things amiss in you. They offend you, but you offend them too! We seek pardon, and we give it. This is a marvellous help to quiet the spirits of those who are truly gracious. Do others cross you? Be meek towards them as you would like them to be to you. When we are weak, we can bear the weakness of others. But some are like the gouty leg—they need a lot of attention, but are useful for nothing. They have a proud spirit, and expect everybody to please them, but do not seek to please anybody. (7.) *Labour to keep your peace with God.* There is no greater means to promote meekness than to keep your heart quiet and at peace with God. This will calm you when you meet with crosses. That which most stirs up the heart is the corruption inside, and not so much the temptation outside. (8.) *Convince yourself that nothing can be done in anger that may be done better out of it!* If you need to reprove a man, reprove him in meekness. A doctor does not give medicine with scalding hot water. When you correct your children, it is much better out of passion than in. Ay, the truth is, those that have power over their passion have a great advantage over those that contend about everything. When your heart is up in anger, it desires to act presently, but keep down your passion, and call in grace and meekness. Consider that you can act as well without passion, yea, even better. If your passion continues to stay a while, it will at least be moderated. Anger is like medicine: if too much is given, it does no good, but the right dose heals. So with passion.

Jeremiah Burroughs, *The Saints' Happiness*, pp. 84-85

A soft answer turns away wrath, but a harsh word stirs up anger.

Proverbs 15:1

To promote meekness, (9.) *When you feel your passion rise, labour to turn your passion upon another object.* If you feel anger begin to arise against your brother, or wife, or husband, labour instead to exercise mourning. Before you give way to anger, get alone and bemoan their sin. Then come out and see how your passion fares. You will find this rule of very great use. If there is no sin before God, there is no great matter for your anger, but if there is sin in it, be sure to mourn for it. Before God let out your passion and so turn anger into love. The Christian that can turn his affections has a great bit of skill, wisdom, and strength. Now I will exercise anger, now love, now sorrow, now joy, and now hope, whichever way he desires. It is a good thing in dealing with children. Don't fall on them in a rage if they are in an ill humour; turn their thoughts to something else, and you will sooner repair their mood than by opposing it. So it is with us. Many times we have an angry mood on our hearts. Instead of opposing it directly, put some object before it to turn the stream of the heart. (10.) *To help against anger do not multiply words.* Many passages warn of the danger of multiplying words in a passion. Words are wind, ay, but they are the wind that blows up the fire to a mighty heat. Those who would behave themselves will take heed of loud speeches, and then add word upon word. The best way is to be silent, or give some gentle answer, and resolve not to multiply words at such a time as this. (11.) *Don't become busy with business where God did not call you.* Men with too many irons in the fire—more than God calls them to—will get burnt. When you know you are doing the business God has called you to do, you can expect the blessing of God to quiet you.

Jeremiah Burroughs, *The Saints' Happiness*, p. 85

Christ also suffered for you, leaving you an example, so that you might follow in his steps.
1 Peter 2:21

To further meekness and overcome passion, (12.) *Take heed of too much curiosity.* If you pry into everything in the family, it is a thousand to one that you will find something to cause your passion to rise. Don't take notice of every little fault in a servant, nor every small offence in a wife or children; but you must see and not see, if you will have a meek spirit. (13.) *Consider passion a temptation of the devil.* Are you in a fit of passion? The devil intends to do you some mischief. The fowler throws stones in the bush to scare the birds into the trap. So in passion, the devil intends to draw you into some sin. He leads you into passion to lead you into some vile sin. (14.) *Set the example of Christ and his saints before you.* This is a mighty help against passion and anger. Consider how meek the Lord is. When God dealt with Cain and Jonah in their sin and anger, he used such meekness and gentleness! Consider how God deals with his poor creatures; and it is no dishonour for you to deal so with your servants and children that are not so injurious to you as you are to God! A wife asked her husband how he was able to overcome himself when he had such wrongs and injuries offered him. 'Why, truly, I go and meditate on the wrongs Jesus Christ had, and how he was a lamb, and I never leave meditating until I get my spirit quiet.' Consider his wounds, and his wrongs, and how gently and meekly he bare them. Oh, this is a special means. In a rage, set the meek lamb before you! He did not revile when reviled, and when he suffered, he did not threaten. He entrusted himself to the Father who judges justly (*1 Pet.* 2:23). Read this text, and set the example of Christ Jesus before you, and it will be a special means to quiet your spirits.

Jeremiah Burroughs, *The Saints' Happiness,* pp. 85-87

God is faithful, and he will not let you be tempted beyond your ability, but with the temptation he will also provide the way of escape, that you may be able to endure it.

1 Corinthians 10:13

If you would like to exercise this grace of meekness, though you forget the other rules, lay up this one—(15.) *Take heed to the next temptation*, and go away with this resolution: The Lord has shown me the excellency of the grace of meekness, how it is commended by Christ, and has excellent promises. He has shown me the evil of an angry spirit, that is so contrary to it, and has given me rules to help me live more quietly in my family. Well, I go away now after I have heard all of this, and it may be that a temptation will come to me this night, for that is the way of the devil. After you have heard about some sin, there will come a temptation to that sin. And when you have been put on some duty, there will come a temptation to take you off that duty. So now that you have heard about meekness, it may be that this very night, or tomorrow morning, there may come a temptation to anger and passion in your spirit, for a hundred to one you will meet with something. If you will but have a heart now to realize that this temptation is coming, and that it is the devil's work to take away all the profit of the sermons on meekness, by God's grace you can take heed of the temptation! You can't imagine what a great deal of good it will do to resist the very next temptation. If tonight, or in the next few days, the first temptation overwhelms you and prevails, I have lost my labour concerning you. Therefore look to yourselves, that you will not lose the word. Go away with the resolution that by God's grace you will take an account of these truths for the ordering of your heart and life in your family, so that all that live with you shall see by your life that you have heard a sermon on meekness!

Jeremiah Burroughs, *The Saints' Happiness*, p. 87

For what will it profit a man if he gains the whole world and forfeits his soul?

Matthew 16:26

Godliness ought to be everyone's principal business, but this calling is so exceedingly neglected. Why do you stand idle all day from this heavenly trade, while the flesh flocks to its fancies? The lawyer is filled with clients, the doctor with patients, and the tradesman with customers, while Jesus Christ is left alone! Heaven and happiness, Saviour and salvation are near, but men go sleeping to hell. They trample this pearl under their feet, and love to wallow in the mire. There are many men, but few soldiers—many nominal, but few real Christians. Godliness has few faithful friends that wait upon her daily. Pretenders are like the sand of the sea—numerous—but faithful servants rare and precious. Many court her, but few marry her! Soldiers who pretend to fight under Christ's banner are sleeping. Weariness without some apparent cause is a sign of a sick body, and so laziness speaks of an unsound soul. The worldling is eager for earthly things. What labour and industry the farmer uses for profit—he rises early, sits up late, denies himself, runs to and fro, embraces all opportunities, and all for earthly mammon! Men laugh at danger and trample on difficulties in the pursuit of earthly treasures. Their whole life is a laborious loitering. Is it not sad that so noble a being as man's soul should be wholly taken up with such low and sordid things? Ah, how costly is that treasure which makes you a beggar for all eternity! The profit of godliness is invaluable above all price. Gold and pearls cannot equal it. The favour of God, the promises of the gospel, the covenant of grace, the blood of Christ, the embroidery of the Spirit, the life of faith, the hope of heaven, and the joy in the Holy Spirit are overlooked! He is a beast to love silver above his soul! What, shall worldlings labour for trifles more than we for concerns of eternity and the affairs of God?

George Swinnock, *Works*, 1:66-72

O man of God, flee these things. Pursue righteousness, godliness, faith, love, steadfastness, gentleness.

1 Timothy 6:11

The true Christian needs to increase his godliness in all company, and in the whole course of his life. Every day he should be careful to keep his soul clean and his conscience clear. But, when he draws near to God, he should take special care and extraordinary caution. The time of sacred duty calls for his greatest diligence. The hours of praying, reading, and hearing are the saint's opportunities and seasons of grace. If he is not careful and conscientious to plough up the fallow ground of his heart, and sow to the Spirit, his return will be very inconsiderable and a thin crop. God is a glorious and jealous Majesty, and esteems it a dishonour for any to wait upon him without their best attire. Though Uzzah is dead, he still speaks to you to take heed how you touch the ark! Godliness should be our special work when God is near. The saints' holiness and godliness are appropriate garments in our approach to a holy God. God is more honoured or dishonoured in our religious actions than in all other actions of our life. In these we directly and immediately pretend his honour and service, and therefore if we do not walk in them watchfully, and attend them seriously, the greater is our sin. God cares how men carry themselves in his courts. The tabernacle was made of the best wood, the purest gold, and the finest linen. The sacrifices must be without blemish. The substance of all these shadows teaches us that God will be served by holy men in the purest and holiest manner. We must be very exact both in our persons and performances when we are in his presence. He expects the best of living sacrifices in the hearts of men, nay, the best of the best, and all the heart, and all the soul, and all the strength. Oh how much is an ordinary, slight performance unsuitable to so great a prince!

GEORGE SWINNOCK, *Works*, 1:87-89

For all the people were hanging on his words.

Luke 19:48

The blind heathen were devoted in the service of dumb idols. They had a higher respect for these lies than many have for the true God! Were they so careful in the service of their dunghill deities, and will not you, my friend, be conscientious and circumspect in the service of the living God? Did they think that nothing was too expensive for their inanimate creatures, and will you offer to the Lord your God that which costs you nothing? Can your box of precious ointment be bestowed any better than on your dearest Saviour? Can your labour and love be employed any better than in his service? Make godliness your business in the ordinances of God, and you may get much spiritual good, and meet Christ in them, and receive grace through them, and thrive as a healthy nursing baby. But if you, like the horse in the mill, only go around in religious duties, without considering the true purpose in them, your prayer will be an abomination. Be watchful over yourself in your religious duties. Heedless service is fruitless service. The comfort we receive is in measure to the care we give! The heart is prone to wander in the worship of God, so we need to keep a strict hand over it. Parents set their children before them at church, and keep their eyes on them, because otherwise they will be toying and playing. So will your heart if you do not watch it! There is a bottomless depth of deceit in your heart that is unwilling in duty (*Jer.* 17:9). How many pretences will it have to make you omit holy performances! It will fill you with cares and thoughts of the world to purposely choke the seed of the word. If you do not watch at the altar, the birds will devour the sacrifice. When Nehemiah was building, he worked and watched, because of his enemies. When you pray, temptations outside are waiting, and corruptions within are working—therefore it is important for you to be watching!

George Swinnock, *Works*, 1:89-93

Oh come, let us worship and bow down; let us kneel before the LORD, our Maker!

Psalm 95:6

There are two special graces to be performed in our approach to God: namely, fear and faith. (1.) Fear and awful apprehensions of God's infinite majesty are required in our religious actions. God allows a humble familiarity, but will always have the children of men to know their distance. When God gave the law to Israel, the Jews sanctified themselves for three days. There was thunder and lightning, and a thick cloud upon the mount, and the voice as a loud trumpet. Smoke ascended like a furnace, and the whole mountain quaked greatly. Why was all this? The possessor of heaven and earth appeared in such a state of magnificence and royalty to assure us that he is not open to disrespect, and to be slighted by any. He is not powerless to revenge himself on all that affront him, and to teach us that he will be feared and reverenced in all them that draw near to him. What reverence is due from poor dust and ashes to the God of all flesh, King of kings, and Lord of lords! Ah, with what humility should a poisonous, polluted toad crawl out of a ditch into the presence of so glorious and dreadful Majesty! Especially when saints approach him, they must stand in awe of him. Jacob at Bethel cried out, 'How dreadful is this place!' (*Gen.* 28:17, KJV). Abraham, God's friend, fell on his face when God spoke to him (*Gen.* 17:3). Moses, who was high in the heart of God, humbled himself, and bowed his head to the ground and worshipped (*Exod.* 34:8). When you pray, put up your petitions too with awful apprehensions of him. We are at best beggars, and a proud heart will not suit a beggar's purse. The elders fell on their faces and worshipped (*Rev.* 4:10), and so did the Lord Jesus himself in prayer! (*Matt.* 26:39). If angels veil their faces in his presence, much more do we with fear and trembling!

GEORGE SWINNOCK, *Works*, 1:95-98

Let us draw near with a true heart in full assurance of faith, with our hearts sprinkled clean from an evil conscience.

Hebrews 10:22

(2.) The second grace to be performed in our approach to God is faith. Fear keeps the heart reverent, and faith will make it cheerful in the service of God. Faith is the instrument to justify both our person and performance, because it looks up to and lays hold on Christ, through whose merit we are justified. God is of purer eyes than to behold iniquity, and there are many sins in our best services; therefore we must carry all our sacrifices to our high priest, who will take away the iniquity of our holy things, and procure their acceptance with the Lord. Christ purges away the dross from our duties, and then they shall be pleasing to God. It was a sacred law among the Molossians, that whosoever came to the king with his son in his arms should be pardoned, whatsoever offence he was guilty of. The Athenian general, therefore, when banished from his country, fled to Admetus, king of the Molossians, his dreadful enemy, and prostrated himself before him with his son in his arms—and found favour! God and man are enemies, and there is no use appearing before this dreadful King without his Son in our arms! With Christ, there is no fear of rejection! (*Eph.* 3:12). Christ makes us friends with God. Whatever you do, whatever you pray, or hear, or sing, or read, do all in the name of Christ (*Col.* 3:17). The admission into God's presence is Christ! (*John* 14:6). It is his blood which has purchased you this great privilege. He alone has turned the seat of justice into a throne of grace. When you approach God, he would be a fire to consume you, and not a Father to embrace you, were it not for his Son! Faith in Christ pleases the heart of God. Therefore, when you go to God, be sure to take Christ along with you! Let your prayers be in his name, with an eye to his promise (*John* 14:13).

George Swinnock, *Works*, 1:98-100

Just as sin came into the world through one man, and death through sin, and so death spread to all men …

Romans 5:12

When God caused his everlasting decree to fall into labour to give birth, he delivered it by bringing the world into being, and by infinite design he formed man to be his viceroy over all the works of his hands. God equipped man with all the abilities needful for such a voyage, as the grounds for the covenant of works. Adam set forth fully furnished with skill, and richly laden with all the fortunes, hopes, and happiness of mankind. Satan, who knew very well the worth of the prize, and envying man and the haven of bliss to which he was sailing, and envying God, the one to receive honour in such a venture, raised a storm before Adam had scarce launched out of sight. The vessel, through the unfaithfulness of Adam, the pilot, ran upon a rock and miscarried. Oh what a joyful spectacle was that to Satan! What a depressing sight to Adam, to behold himself and all his posterity sinking into the bottomless ocean of destruction and misery, through his unfaithfulness and treachery! Then, lo, all of a sudden, the glorious God, out of the superabundant riches of his mercy, resolving that the devil should never rob him of the honour of his manifold wisdom, and unsearchable goodness, and almighty power, which had been manifested in the work of creation, did provide and cast out the covenant of grace—a plank sufficient for his poor shipwrecked creature to swim safe to shore. As all the rivers meet in the sea, all the comforts of mankind meet in this covenant. All our mercies are contained in it, all our hopes are sustained by it, and heaven at last is attained through it. The precious blood of Christ was the costly price of man's redemption, and the only path to eternal salvation. It was promised to Adam, believed by the patriarchs, shadowed in sacrifices, foretold by the prophets, and witnessed in Scripture!

GEORGE SWINNOCK, *Works*, 1:172-173

And when he had given thanks, he broke it, and said, 'This is my body which is for you. Do this in remembrance of me.'

1 Corinthians 11:24

When the blessed Saviour was taking a solemn farewell to an ungrateful world, as a living symbol of his sufferings for his people, and an undeniable evidence of his love, he instituted the Lord's Supper. A crucified Christ is the sum of the law, and the substance of the gospel. Knowledge of him is worth no less than eternal life. Banquets are costly, but oh, what did this feast cost! The Lord of life was put to death that he might be food for our starving souls. A little bread and a spoonful of wine are in themselves of very small value, but when received according to Christ's institution, they are of unspeakable value. The Lord's Supper is like a medicine, which is small in quantity, but is great in value. In it is the spirit of many excellent things. Most of the other ordinances are invited to this feast—the word, prayer, and singing all meet at the table—and contribute their help to carry the Christian up to heaven. We need to be wary in reverence. You should be serious at the table, as a dying man preparing to go into the other world. On Mount Sinai, if a beast touched the mount, it was to die. What will become of you if you touch the table of the Lord with a brutish heart? With great affection the Father gave the Son, and the Son knew grievous passion to satisfy God's justice for sin. The Lord's Table, which represents this, is the most serious thing man's heart can conceive. Oh it is sad jesting with the sufferings and ordinances of Christ. Cyprian speaks of a woman who had denied the faith, and yet ventured to this heavenly feast, and as soon as she received the elements, she fell down dead. Friend, let others' woe be your warning! The Lord Jesus will take special notice of your respect for his body and blood! We need serious preparation for this ordinance.

George Swinnock, *Works*, 1:173-175

Let a person examine himself, then, and so eat of the bread and drink of the cup.

1 Corinthians 11:28

The Lord takes notice of the manner in which you come to the Lord's Table. Do you examine your regeneration to prove yourself one of the family? Do you measure yourself by the standard of Scripture? When you seek pardon for past sins, do you come with a resolution against sins to come? Do you come to the heavenly feast with deep sorrow for sin, seeking mercy with a mouth of faith? We should seek to be holy to honour Christ Jesus. Would you trample on the picture of a dear friend before their face? Will you tread under foot the precious blood of the Son of God as if it were the blood of a malefactor or a dog while he himself stands by? Think this way: 'I am now to sit down at the table of the Lord, among his children. I know the King will come in to see his guests, even that King who is too just to be bribed, too great to be slighted, too wise to be deceived, and too good to be forfeited. O my soul, how will I prepare for his sacred presence?' If at any time of your life you would be extraordinarily serious, this is the season! Oh let your preparation be such for this glorious supper, that the Master of the feast may see that you are sensitive to his honour, watchful of his eye, and fearful of his anger! Consider the dreadful condition of those who receive the table unworthily (*1 Cor.* 11:27-29). They are guilty of the body and blood of the Lord, and eat and drink their own judgment! They offer indignity to Christ's person. Jesus Christ is your king, and will you stretch out your hands against your sovereign? Will you put to death the author of life? When Satan, or your own heart, persuades you to be slight in examination of your heart, let your conscience cry out, 'God forbid that I stretch out my hand against the Lord's anointed!' Therefore, take time to commune with your heart before you go to the table!

George Swinnock, *Works*, 1:176-179

Therefore let us leave the elementary doctrine of Christ and go on to maturity.

Hebrews 6:1

Take heed that you do not rest satisfied only with the knowledge of Christ you have attained, but go on to perfection. It is the sin even of the best of saints, when they see how deep the knowledge of Christ lies, to throw away the shovel of duty, and cry, 'dig we cannot'. To your work, O Christians, to your work! Let not your candle go out, and devote yourselves to this study; cherish the blessed communications of light and grace from on high; count all things but dross in comparison with the excellency that is in the knowledge of Christ! Consider the unspeakable felicity of the original state of Christ. Before his incarnation he knew the highest and most unspeakable delight and pleasure in the enjoyment of his Father. He was in the bosom of the Father (*John* 1:18). The Father delighted in the Son (*Isa.* 42:1). The Son, being equal with the Father, had all the glory and marks of his majesty (*John* 17:5). He was then abased to the condition of a creature, which was a low step indeed! For God to be made man, and to appear in true flesh, but also to appear in the likeness of sinful flesh (*Rom.* 8:3), O what is this! Before his incarnation he was not liable to any of the sorrowful consequences of the frail state of humanity, which he afterwards assumed. There was no sorrowing, and he was not pinched with poverty, nor did he lack a place to lay his head. He never knew reproach or shame in heaven. He never knew temptations, and the assault of demons. He was never sensible of pain and torture of the body, nor did he groan and sweat under them. The Father embraced him from eternity and never wounded him till he stood in our place under the Father's wrath. There was no death as he lay in the Father's bosom, and then, for our sakes, he voluntarily subjected himself unto all these!

John Flavel, *The Fountain of Life*, pp. 21-26

In the beginning was the Word, and the Word was with God, and the Word was God.

John 1:1

Christ's primeval state was of matchless happiness, if we consider the persons enjoying and delighting in each other. God is the fountain, ocean, and centre of all delights and joys—'In your presence there is fullness of joy' (*Psa.* 16:11). To be wrapped up in the soul and bosom of all delights, as Christ was, must needs be a state of bliss transcending understanding. Consider the intimacy, dearness, yea, oneness of those great persons, and the nearer the union, the sweeter the communion (*John* 10:30). Oh what matchless delights must flow from such a blessed union! The best of creatures are mixed and debased delights, but the embrace of Father and Son is a pure delight. No stream flows so purely, and no light so unmixed, as Father and Son embrace with a most holy delight and love! This delight was from everlasting and eternity; it has never suffered one moment's interruption. The overflowing fountain of God's delight and love has never stopped in its course, and has never ebbed. Christ was daily his delight, rejoicing always before him. Any comparison falls infinitely short. Jacob was bound up in Benjamin's love, and David's soul was knit to Jonathan, but these are finite and cannot equal the delights between the Father and Son. The Lord takes pleasure in his saints, but not like he does in his Son! Thus, what an astonishing act of love was this, for the Father to give the delight of his soul for poor sinners! All tongues must pause and falter to express his grace! What an outcry did David make for Absalom, yet never did any child lie so close to a parent's heart as Christ to his Father's. And yet, he willingly parted with him to a cursed death for sinners. Christ consented to leave such a bosom for worms as we are! O the heights, depths, lengths, and breadths of unmeasurable love. Christ denied himself for us!

JOHN FLAVEL, *The Fountain of Life*, pp. 26-29

I made known to them your name ... that the love with which you have loved me may be in them, and I in them.

John 17:26

Do you desire to be in the favour and delight of God? Get an interest in Jesus Christ, and you will presently be there! In heaven, persons are preferred according to their interest in the Beloved (*Eph.* 1:6). Christ is the great favourite there. How worthy is Jesus Christ of all our love and delight! The Father delights in him; shall not we? Why do you lavish away your precious affections upon vanity? None but Christ is worthy of them! When you spend your affections upon other objects, what is this but to dig dross with a golden shovel. May the Lord direct our hearts into the love of Christ. O, that our hearts, loves, and delights would meet with the heart of God in this most blessed object. O, let him that left the Father's bosom be loved by us! He deserves it! Consider what a grievous thing it is to the Father, to see his dear Son despised, slighted, and rejected by sinners. What a serious word is this—'If any man love not the Lord Jesus Christ, let him be Anathema!' (*1 Cor.* 16:22, KJV). O sinners, you shall one day know the cost of this sin! O, that you would slight him no more. O that this day your hearts might fall in love with him. There is no love so valuable as his. If Christ lay eternally in the bosom of the Father's love, and yet was content to forsake it for you, then, Christians, should we not be ready to forsake all the comforts we have on earth for Christ? Moses left the glory of Egypt, and Peter and the other apostles left all! What we have to leave is of no comparison to what he left for us. Christ is the highest pattern of self-denial for us. Sinners, embrace the bosom-Son of God. Poor fellow-mortals, whatever you are or have been, under whatever guilt or discouragement you lie, embrace Christ, who is freely offered to you, and you shall be as dear to God as the most eminent believer in the world.

John Flavel, *The Fountain of Life*, pp. 29-31

He poured out his soul to death and was numbered with the transgressors; yet he bore the sin of many.

Isaiah 53:12

The business of man's salvation was transacted upon covenant terms, between the Father and the Son, from all eternity (*Isa.* 53:10-12). The elect, though not yet in being, are here considered as existing, yea, as fallen, miserable, forlorn creatures. How these may again be restored to happiness without prejudice to the honour, justice, and truth of God, is the business that lay before them. The Father promised to anoint Christ with a threefold office—Prophet, Priest, and King—and to crown his work with success, and bring it to a happy issue, and reward him highly. In like manner, Jesus Christ yielded to the Father upon these terms, and was content to be made flesh, empty himself of his glory, come under the malediction of the law, and not to refuse the hardest sufferings it should please the Father to inflict upon him (*Psa.* 40:8). The Son thus consented to the discharge of his work, took a body, and in it he fulfilled all righteousness and was made an offering for sin, having fulfilled all the parts of his active and passive obedience, cheerfully and faithfully! Before the world was, he delighted in us, before we had our existence, except in the infinite mind and purpose of God, who had decreed this for us in Christ Jesus (*2 Tim.* 1:9). This gives abundant security for God's people. Happy would it be, if Christians, in perplexity and distress, would turn their eyes from the defects in their obedience to the fullness of Christ, and see themselves complete in him! Consider the unquestionable success of Christ's intercession in heaven for believers! (*Heb.* 7:25). That his blood shall obtain what it pleads for in heaven is undoubted. The things he now asks of his Father are the very same things he promised him, and covenanted to give him, before the world was! Our happiness was secure before the world, and is most free!

John Flavel, *The Fountain of Life*, pp. 32-40

For God so loved the world, that he gave his only Son.

John 3:16

The gift of Christ is the highest manifestation of the love of God to sinners ever made from eternity. 'Giving' implies a parting. There was parting for a time when the Son took upon himself flesh (*John* 16:28). There was also a parting when Christ was pierced and wounded (*Psa.* 22:1-2). 'Giving' also implies the delivering of Christ over into the hands of justice, to the sentence of law and execution (*Acts* 2:28). Consider how near and dear Jesus was to the Father. A writer tells us that, in a famine in Germany, a poor family was about to perish, and the husband proposed to sell one of the children for bread for the rest. The wife at last consented, and they considered which of the four should be sold. They refused to part with the eldest, their firstborn, and they could not yield the second, who looked like his father. The third resembled the mother, and the youngest was their Benjamin, the child of their old age—so they decided to perish rather than to part with a child for relief! You know how Jacob mourned when Joseph was rent from him. What is a child but a piece of a parent wrapped in another skin! And yet our dearest children are but as strangers to us in comparison to the unspeakable dearness between the Father and Christ! His love in sending the Son will be admired to all eternity! Christ was made a curse for us, and knew scorn and contempt. It breaks our heart to see our children suffer. The Father saw Christ struggle under agony, falling to the ground crying for the cup to pass. He was delivered to the wrath of an infinite God! And for whom—angels? No, but for men. For his friends?—No, for his enemies! This is love. It came freely; it wasn't wrestled out of his hand by our importunity. We didn't desire it or deserve it. And, if God has given us his own Son, we can expect any other temporal mercies from him! (*Rom.* 8:32). Oh love unspeakable!

John Flavel, *The Fountain of Life*, pp. 41-50

Since therefore the children share in flesh and blood, he himself likewise partook of the same.

Hebrews 2:14

Jesus Christ assumed the true nature of man into a personal union with his divine nature, and still remains true God and true man, in one person forever. This is one of the deepest mysteries of godliness. Apply yourself to these truths with the greatest attention of mind! The second person in the Godhead took human nature into a personal union with himself, yet without confusion, both natures making but one person—Immanuel, God with us. Though we truly ascribe a twofold nature to Christ, yet not a double person. The human nature was united to the second person miraculously and supernaturally framed in the womb of the virgin by the overshadowing power of the Highest. Christ took a complete and perfect human soul and body with its faculties. In his human nature he assumed natural infirmities such as hunger, thirst, weariness, bleeding, mortality, etc. The natures are so united that each nature retains its own essential properties, but are united in one person. It is proper to say the Lord of glory was crucified (*1 Cor.* 2:8), and the blood of God redeemed the church (*Acts* 20:28). However, it is not proper to say the divine nature suffered, or that the human nature is omniscient, omnipotent, or omnipresent. Let all Christians understand this truth of so great a moment, and hold it fast. Do not divide Christ's person or confound his natures. Adore the love of the Father and Son, who valued your souls so highly! A council of angels could not devise so great a plan to recover poor sinners. Oh, how wisely is the method of our recovery laid! Oh, happy are they that have dropped anchor on this ground and know peace. How wonderful a comfort that he who dwells in our flesh is God! God will never divorce the believing soul and its comfort, after he has married our nature to his own Son!

John Flavel, *The Fountain of Life*, pp. 51-61

For on him God the Father has set his seal.

John 6:27

Jesus Christ did not of himself undertake the work of our redemption, but was solemnly sealed unto it by God the Father. When I say 'not of himself', I do not mean that he was unwilling, for his heart was as fully engaged in it as the Father's (*Psa.* 40:7-8). But the meaning is, he came not without a due call and full commission from his Father! (*John* 8:42). On account of these sealed credentials, Christ was sent forth by the Father's authority. He was sealed as mediator for us to recover and save all whom the Father had given him (*John* 17:2). Since this was done by commission and authority of the Father, it encourages a believer's comfort and security. Christ was eminently qualified and fit to carry out the Father's design for our recovery. He is faithful like none other (*Rev.* 1:5). For zeal, there is none like him (*John* 2:16-17). He was so intent upon his Father's work that he wasn't hungry (*John* 4:32). Yea, love to his Father carried him on through all of his work, and made him delight in the hardest piece of his service. For self-denial, there was never any like him. He sought not his own glory, but the glory of him that sent him (*John* 8:50). The Lord filled him with the Spirit without measure! (*John* 3:34). Believers are engaged to love the Father because he was the spring of their redemption, so all men are bound to ascribe equal glory and honour to both Father and Son (*John* 5:23). This calls us to admire the grace and love both of the Father and Son. The Father sealed the commission for the death of his Son for us instead of a sentence for our damnation, and no less is the love of Christ to be wondered at, that he would accept such a commission as this for us, understanding fully the contents of his commission. Oh then, love the Lord Jesus all you saints. Draw forth comfort from the Father's sealing Christ for you. The Father will make good all he has promised!

John Flavel, *The Fountain of Life*, pp. 62-73

And for their sake I consecrate myself, that they also may be sanctified in truth.

John 17:19

Jesus Christ, being fitted with a body, and authorized by a commission from the Father, now sets himself apart for the work of our salvation. His consecration as a sacrifice implies the great dreadfulness of the breach that sin has made. No less than Christ himself is sufficient to make atonement. The magnitude of the remedy shows the greatness of the wound. Christ sanctified himself freely and voluntarily to undertake the work. No one took his life; he laid it down freely. He offered himself in pure and perfect holiness. There was no spot or blemish in him. He hung upon the tree as a curse in our place. He was buried for us, and rose for our justification. He ascended into glory to prepare a place for us. He ever lives to make intercession for us, and will come for us too. He sanctified himself for us to die vicariously, in our place. His name is well called 'Wonderful'. He was sanctified in keeping with both natures. His human nature was the sacrifice upon the altar of his divine nature. For it is the altar that sanctifies the gift. We may say, 'Lord, condemnation was yours, that justification might be mine; agony was yours, that victory would be mine; pain was yours, and ease mine; the curse yours, but blessing is mine.' If Jesus Christ wholly set himself apart for believers, how reasonable it is that believers should consecrate themselves apart wholly for Christ! Is he all for us, and shall we be nothing for him? What is a Christian, but a holy dedicated thing to the Lord? Is Christ all for you, and you all for him? Blessed exchange! Such as it is, I am yours: my soul, faculties, body, gifts, time, and talents. It is not I, but Christ; not my will, but Christ's; not my ease, lusts, credits, but Christ—Christ! O wretched idol, myself, be wholly expelled, and Christ wholly put in your room!

JOHN FLAVEL, *The Fountain of Life*, pp. 74-86

There is one mediator between God and men, the man Christ Jesus.

1 Timothy 2:5

There is only one mediator between God and men! Christ, clothed in our flesh, paid our ransom. We can safely trust him who tenderly regards all our wants and miseries as our faithful high priest. A mediator is a middleman, or one who interposes between two parties at variance to make peace between them. Christ as our mediator has the same nature both with God and us—true God, and true man. Our need for a mediator reveals a most dreadful breach between God and men! Once there was sweet friendship between them, but it was quickly dissolved by sin. That first sin was a heinous and aggravated evil. Adam was an upright, perfect man, created in the image of God, who thus sinned. He sinned when his mind was most bright, clear, and discerning; his conscience pure, active and undefiled; his will was free, and able to withstand any temptation. He well knew that the happiness or misery of his numberless offspring was involved in him. The condition he was placed in was exceedingly happy. No necessity or lack could arm or sharpen the temptation. He lived amidst all natural and spiritual pleasures and delights. The Lord delightfully conversed with him; yea, he sinned while as yet his creation mercy was fresh upon him. His sin was the most horrible ingratitude; yea, a casting off the yoke of obedience almost as soon as God had put it on him. Christ as mediator reveals the necessity of satisfaction to the justice of God. For any to imagine they can be reconciled to God by anything but by faith in the blood of this mediator is vain and destructive to the soul. To imagine this is to murder the truth. God's law being violated by man requires either the penalty levied on the delinquent, or satisfaction made by the mediator. What infinite value is in his blood and sufferings!

John Flavel, *The Fountain of Life*, pp. 87-91

If you are insulted for the name of Christ, you are blessed, because the Spirit of glory and of God rests upon you.

1 Peter 4:14

Matthew 5:6—Part one: Hungering and thirsting for righteousness clearly expresses an earnest desire for righteousness. This desired righteousness may include, (1.) The proof of our righteousness in a crooked world, (2.) Righteousness exhibited in the world, (3.) The imputed righteousness of Christ, and (4.) Our personal holiness. *First*—(1.) Christians are likely to meet with many unrighteous dealings in the world, and blessed are you that are content to submit to such a condition while sending up your desires to heaven to clear your righteousness. The world may accuse and revile you for being troublesome, factious, and turbulent among them, but blessed are you that appeal to God to judge your righteous cause! 'Blessed are you,' says Christ; 'I have my eye on you.' When others say you are false, do not be troubled now; the Lord will manifest your righteousness yet before the world. If the world accuses you of self-seeking, you can appeal to God of the righteousness of your hearts. God will reveal the secrets of all men's hearts and your motive will be justified. There is nothing more common in the world than for the wicked of the world to cast aspersions upon the saints of God for some evil or other to darken them in their holy profession. If you bear what is cast upon you patiently, and long for the time when the righteous God will appear to manifest your righteousness, blessed are you when you thus hunger and thirst after this righteousness. You have the testimony of your own heart and God! He is working for you all the while you lie under these accusations. One day you shall be cleared and satisfied, for God will make it break forth as the noonday! Now you are bespattered, but then you will be clothed with white linen!

Jeremiah Burroughs, *The Saints' Happiness*, pp. 87-90

The eyes of the Lord are toward the righteous and his ears toward their cry.

Psalm 34:15

P*art two:* Hungering and thirsting for (2.) *Righteousness exhibited in the world, among men in general.* That is, a desire for righteousness to prevail in the world. Blessed are those who are grieved when they see unrighteousness abound, and cry out to God that he would set up righteousness to reign. The people of God are grieved to see unrighteous dealings, because the honour of God is eclipsed. Unrighteousness is unsuitable to their spirits, since the Lord has put righteousness in their hearts. When they see men in a public responsibility, or men that make profession of religion, act unrighteously, this grieves them. They see how the godly suffer and are trodden under foot while the wicked and ungodly shine and prosper. They long for the time when righteousness prevails, which would give them joy. In unrighteousness they see the kingdom of Satan set up, and the righteous kingdom of Christ hindered. 'Why, Lord, does the kingdom of Satan prevail in the world? O Lord, when shall the righteous sceptre of Jesus Christ have sway among the children of men? Oh that God would hasten those times! How long shall it be?' For their own part, they would rather suffer any misery in the world than countenance or join in any unrighteous ways! They would rather lose the advantage of their places, than meddle with any unrighteous actions. A righteous heart hungers for righteousness, and will shake his hands of all unrighteousness. Though he loses friends, estate, and outward enjoyments, he will keep his conscience right, and be a friend to righteousness as long as he lives. He will not dally and trifle with God in hungering and thirsting after righteousness, and yet be unrighteous himself. He will labour to promote righteousness in the world.

Jeremiah Burroughs, *The Saints' Happiness*, pp. 90-91

For I am not ashamed of the gospel, for it is the power of God for salvation to everyone who believes ... For in it the righteousness of God is revealed from faith for faith.

Romans 1:16-17

P*art three:* Hungering and thirsting for (3.) *Imputed righteousness.* The righteousness of Christ enables us to stand before the infinite righteousness of God. This righteousness is the righteousness of justification, for without this, our God is a consuming fire! The righteousness of Christ is a perfect satisfaction to divine justice in whatever it requires, either in punishing sin, or in obedience to the law. Seeking this righteousness is a matter of great moment and consequence in comparison to the others we have considered. Sin, having made a dreadful breach between God and man, requires God's justice to be satisfied, or none of the children of men could be saved. God cannot forgive without his justice being satisfied. Man is in such a condition that he has lost all righteousness—he cannot think a thought, speak a word, or do an action that is righteous and acceptable to God! What a dreadful condition! Thus, angels could not imagine how man's salvation would be possible; man must perish! But Jesus came and showed how the justice of God may be satisfied, the law kept, and wretched, sinful, corrupt man saved! This gives as much glory to God's justice as if all men were damned. Wretched sinners come to be made righteous in Christ, their sins transferred upon him, and Christ's righteousness transferred upon them. This is a most glorious righteousness. Blessed are the souls that are enlightened by the Holy Spirit to see the reality, the certainty, the beauty, the necessity, and the glory of this righteousness, and set their hearts hungering and thirsting after a part in it! They shall be filled with this righteousness, and their souls shall have enough.

JEREMIAH BURROUGHS, *The Saints' Happiness*, pp. 96-97

Woe is me! For I am lost; for I am a man of unclean lips.

Isaiah 6:5

Part three continued: From where does this hungering and thirsting for imputed righteousness come? It rises from the clear apprehension and thorough conviction of the soul of four things. (1.) *The soul is thoroughly convinced of its need for a righteousness to stand before a holy God.* Men going along in the common way don't consider that God is a righteous God, and they must trust solely on his mercy! They don't realize that no unrighteous thing shall enter into the kingdom of heaven, and that all the mercy in heaven can't save them. But when their conscience reveals their ungodliness, and that they must appear before a righteous God to receive the sentence of eternal doom, they realize their need for this imputed righteousness. (2.) *The soul comes to be convinced of the insufficiency and imperfection of its own righteousness.* Let me look into my heart, and ways, and life for my own righteousness. I am not as bad as others! I am not an adulterer, or drunkard, or swearer, or blasphemer! I may stand before a holy God! Oh, but this is a mistake. Certainly they do not know God or themselves as they think. But when the Lord works graciously by his Spirit in the soul, he sees nothing but dirty rags—'I have no righteousness at all!' (3.) *The soul sees that there is another righteousness available beyond its own.* The gospel tells me that the Son of God was made sin for atonement, and that believers are made righteous in him! The fullness of that righteousness is sufficient to satisfy God for whatsoever sin I have been guilty of, however great. Here is a righteousness that satisfies infinite justice! (4.) *This righteousness is bestowed freely upon our believing!* Upon faith, as it were, the soul launches forth into this infinite ocean of righteousness, and all sin is swallowed up, little or great, whatsoever!

Jeremiah Burroughs, *The Saints' Happiness*, pp. 97-98

You will seek me and find me, when you seek me with all your heart.

Jeremiah 29:13

P*art three continued:* The manner of God's working upon the soul to bring it to this righteousness is to make it hunger and thirst for it, until it is satisfied. A starving man would venture through fire to get meat rather than not have it. The soul that understands what a God he has to deal with, and the infinite necessity of this righteousness to stand before him, cannot but faint without the assurance of this righteousness. Come to a hungry man with bags of gold, or a fine suit of clothes when he is ready to perish, and though you give him all the possessions in the world, they are nothing to satisfy his hunger! So it is with the soul—'If I do not have this righteousness, I die! I am ready to perish eternally without this righteousness.' We used to say that hunger will beak through stone walls. There is no work too difficult for a man to get bread. One who hungers and thirsts is determined—whatever the condition—to yield in submission to God. Here is where the hypocrite fails. Many men or women has a beginning of the work of God upon them, and begin to see a need for righteousness. They may fall to prayer and attend upon the word for a while, but soon are wearied and tired. The devil persuades them to live somewhat better than before, and that this is righteousness enough, and they are satisfied! The soul that God works savingly upon hungers and thirsts for his righteousness, and nothing in the world will satisfy without it. Luther said that righteousness between men is a very sweet thing, and that being a good citizen, a chaste husband or just merchant is good, but making these your righteousness before God is an abomination. Take heed of this mistake—it is a dangerous rock! Don't miss the righteousness of Jesus Christ!

Jeremiah Burroughs, *The Saints' Happiness*, pp. 98-101

But if anyone does sin, we have an advocate with the Father, Jesus Christ the righteous.

1 John 2:1

P*art three continued:* This righteousness of Christ is so desirable. There is no need for despair for our lack of righteousness! When we realize and consider the unrighteousness left in our hearts before an infinitely great God, our despair is taken away because of his righteousness. Without it, we would give ten thousand times ten thousand worlds to be delivered from the anguish and trouble of those sinking and despairing thoughts and temptations we are afflicted with. His righteousness makes up for all the wrong ever done to God by our sin. Is this not desirable? His righteousness also fully satisfies all the claims of the law on us for any breach of it. I stand before the law of God with dreadful charges upon me, but his righteousness delivers my soul! With this righteousness, the hazard of miscarrying is quite over, and there is absolute safety and blessed security. The unrighteousness that might remain in me shall never hazard the eternal miscarrying of my soul. You are certainly safe in Jesus Christ! He will certainly bring you to eternal life. There is no condemnation to them that are in Christ Jesus. It is impossible for a soul that God the Father shall look upon him in the righteousness of his Son yet miscarry to eternity. It can never be! In his righteousness we have bold access to the throne of grace before God's infinite holiness and justice. We stand before his judgment seat fully pardoned in the court of justice! We are clothed with a glorious robe of righteousness. When Jesus Christ shall appear, and God the Father, and the holy angels, this robe shall cover the souls of believers. Christ's robe will adorn and beautify the saints in the day of judgment before God. This robe takes away all the terror of that day.

JEREMIAH BURROUGHS, *The Saints' Happiness*, pp. 101–102

The Spirit and the Bride say, 'Come.' … let the one who desires take the water of life without price.

Revelation 22:17

Part three continued: If your heart thirsts after Christ's righteousness, consider several things for comfort and consolation. (1.) *Your thirst and Christ's thirst are the same!* Christ thirsts after souls as much as souls thirst after him. It is a great satisfaction to Jesus Christ to see his righteousness applied to sinners. No soul can be more content for this assurance than Christ is content in bestowing it on those who thirst for it. There is nothing in the world that can satisfy the soul of Christ more than to have poor sinners come to him for his righteousness. (2.) *The great design of God in the world to glorify himself is found in applying the righteousness of his Son to sinful souls.* The Father is honoured when the righteousness of his Son delivers souls from the guilt of their sin and sets them righteous before him. The Lord takes delight in no work like this work. This is the masterpiece of God and his glory! (3.) *There is nothing offered more freely than the righteousness of Christ.* It was never given to any soul but freely as a gift from God (*Rev.* 22:17). Four times in one verse we are invited to come! There is nothing more free than the water of life. Former unrighteousness shall never be a hindrance. If it were, it would not be free! May not I have my portion as well as another? It is true I am a vile, unrighteous wretch, but the Lord gives this water freely! (4.) *Nothing can give any right to any soul to apply this righteousness but this free offer.* The soul must believe and cast itself upon it! Do not fear, but come hungering and thirsting for it. Open your mouth and heart wide that it may be filled. Take heed that you do not satisfy yourself with any righteousness beneath this. The blood of Christ alone satisfies the hungry soul.

Jeremiah Burroughs, *The Saints' Happiness*, pp. 106-108

But as he who called you is holy, you also be holy in all your conduct.

1 Peter 1:15

M*atthew 5:6—Part four:* Hungering and thirsting for (4.) *The principle of personal holiness.* This is a righteousness consistent with the word, which acts as God himself acts. 'Oh that it were so with me', says this soul; 'I feel an abundance of corruption, and the Lord is worthy of more. I was made for him, and oh that my heart could be taken off of other things and enjoy him alone to be my portion. If his will were the rule of my life, happy would I be! This righteousness is lovely and excellent in itself, and I long after it.' He that hungers for this righteousness seeks it to the highest degree, and not just enough to keep him from the danger he fears. It is a ruling desire. Any desire contrary to this overruling desire must go. Unruly corruptions of the heart grieve his soul. Did you ever hear Paul cry out for any of his sufferings, 'Oh wretched man that I am'? No! But in his lack of righteousness, he gives such a dreadful shriek. This desire is a mighty, earnest desire, and an industrious desire. It follows hard after God in the use of all means to gain it. It is an abiding desire and will continue, and never be quiet, until the thing is done. 'Lord, let me have the righteousness of your Spirit for my sanctification, to overcome my corruptions, and to enable me to live to your praise. And, Lord, you know these desires have been earnest, and not a passing whim, but are constant and settled and industrious. Lord, you know the pains my soul has taken, and is still willing to take. I don't care what it takes for me that I might overcome such corruptions and be enabled to walk with you in holiness. I am resolved to continue through your grace. If I should perish, I will perish crying to you for the righteousness of your Son and the righteousness of the sanctification of my heart!' If you can so appeal to God, you are blessed!

Jeremiah Burroughs, *The Saints' Happiness*, pp. 108-112

Worship the LORD in the splendour of holiness.

Psalm 96:9

Part four continued: What excellence is in this personal holiness that causes a soul to hunger and thirst for it? It is excellent because the soul is enabled to glorify God, and honour him as the infinite first being of all things. This righteousness is the right temper of the soul! A sick man is unable to enjoy life and work, and so desires health above all outward blessings. Also, sin is the sickness of the soul, and takes away the excellence of all it might enjoy. This righteousness is also a sparkling of the divine nature! It is the very image of God in the soul. Holy creatures have the footprints of God upon them. When we behold a saint, we see the glory of God in them. God's image in us was defaced and blurred by the fall, but grace in the heart shows the image of God reflected, as a father sees himself in the face of his children. The soul acting as God acts, is living the life of God. The glory of God is the ultimate end of all his actions; he drives all his designs to this end. This is an excellent life, and though he is not able to reach the very highest of this glory, every saint in some measure attains this end. Oh how we ought to desire God's glory. This shines in the souls of the saints according to the measure of grace received. Oh that a poor wretch should hold forth the glory of God to the world! Here is a great mystery! Every action with this righteousness in it is worth more to God than heaven and earth. This righteousness raises the soul above all earthly enjoyments and makes it acknowledge no supreme but God himself. The soul is enlarged infinitely, and can be satisfied with nothing but God! Before, it was satisfied with every lust and filthy vanity, but now only God can fill up the cravings of the soul. The soul now enjoys that which is worth more than a thousand worlds! This righteousness is the beginning of heaven, and your desire for it the breathings of the Spirit of God!

JEREMIAH BURROUGHS, *The Saints' Happiness*, pp. 112-116

It is written, 'You shall be holy, for I am holy.'

1 Peter 1:16

Part four continued: Those who hunger for personal holiness are blessed in comparison with those who seek no higher excellency than to eat and drink and give contentment to the flesh. Those who hunger for righteousness see its excellence as the greatest blessing under heaven—next to the imputed righteousness of Christ. According to the greatness of the object you love is the greatness of your spirit. A poor base spirit is content with poor base things. Some are content with money enough to drink with their companions and look no higher for a blessed life. Those hungering for righteousness will not be satisfied with anything else. Such a desire is the seed of righteousness that is already there. No soul can thirst for righteousness unless it has some righteousness already. Everything desires things suitable to its nature. The ox desires grass, and the fish desires water. So a covetous man desires riches, a sensual man desires pleasure, and an ambitious man desires honour, because they are suitable to their natures. So where there is a desire for righteousness it has already begun in the soul. Though they do not feel the righteousness they desire, they are blessed, because, in the covenant of grace, God accepts the desire for the deed! Their righteousness is manifest by their desire. Thirst after righteousness is an indication of being in the covenant of grace, and this helps the soul in the midst of all infirmities. This thirst for holiness quenches sinful and base desires. We mortify sinful desires by gracious desires. The way to get base, sordid love in the soul to be mortified is by love to God and love to Jesus Christ. Replace sinful joy with the joy of the Holy Spirit. Set your desires on the life of God and upon the principles of union and communion with him and this will take off your desires for vain and base things. Thirsting for righteousness quenches base, sinful desires.

Jeremiah Burroughs, *The Saints' Happiness*, pp. 117-118

What the wicked dreads will come upon him, but the desire of the righteous will be granted.

Proverbs 10:24

Part four continued: Hungering souls are blessed because they shall be satisfied. (1.) They shall find such contentment in the ways of righteousness that their hearts shall never turn quite out of those ways, whatever temptations they meet with. This is a comfort to the soul to know that no temptation can possibly draw you out of the way. If a bee has fastened itself upon a flower, and is sucking honey, and cannot be removed, it is certainly because it finds sweetness there. All who have the beginnings of true grace, though they are hungering for more, find enough satisfaction that they will never leave the paths of God. It may be you have been desiring for many years, 'Oh that I might overcome such a corruption, and that I might serve God with more freedom of spirit and cheerfulness', but you grow little. You labour, strive, desire, and pray—it seems to no avail. 'Give up, and return to your former course,' says temptation. 'God forbid,' says the gracious soul; 'I will never turn to my former ways. Though I don't have what I desire, I have a thousand times more peace and contentment than ever I had in my former ways.' (2.) Those who thirst after righteousness shall also have grace growing. More shall always be coming in. Perhaps you may not always be sensible of it, but grace is coming in just the same! There will at least be upholding grace, if not as much as you desire. Your spirit will find something to uphold it, even though not so fully to comfort you as you would. (3.) There is a time coming when all hungering souls shall be satisfied to the full: a time when you will sin no more, when you shall never be troubled with that wretched, proud, stubborn, carnal, distrustful heart. There is coming a time when you shall serve God as much as you desire, and have as much grace as you desire to have!

Jeremiah Burroughs, *The Saints' Happiness*, p. 120

And from his fullness we have all received, grace upon grace.

John 1:16

Part four continued: Souls who hunger for righteousness may be encouraged, for—(1.) This is a sign of spiritual life! This is a sign that, at the very least, you are a newborn babe. Why do you hunger? Is it not for your growth, and to have more power over your corruptions, and to serve the Lord in holiness? (2.) It is also a sign of a thriving Christian. As a good appetite for food is a sign of physical health, so is a desire for more righteousness a sign of spiritual health. Others' desires are clogged with the lusts of the flesh, and desires for the world, preferments, honours, riches, and pleasures! (3.) Christ offers an infinite fountain of grace to satisfy poor souls! There is enough bread in your heavenly Father's house for hungering souls. (4.) The desires of hungering souls come from none other than the Holy Spirit himself, and the Father understands the meaning of the Spirit's desires. (5.) There is nothing in the world that God desires more freely to bestow than righteousness, and so his desires match ours! God's desire for you to overcome sin and serve him in holiness meets together with your desire for personal holiness. (6.) If God hears the ravens who cry to him for food, will he not fill the hungering soul? Shall not our desire for the grace of the Spirit be satisfied, that we might bear the image of God? (7.) If we are to feed our enemies, shall not God himself, the infinite fountain of all mercy, give his children who thirst for righteousness spiritual food and drink? (8.) This hungering and thirsting will make you a praying Christian! Prayer that comes from this hungering soul is worth a hundred prayers that come from mere memory. (9.) There is a time coming when Jesus Christ will satisfy your soul immediately. We thankfully enjoy grace for the present, but in heaven—immediate satisfaction!

Jeremiah Burroughs, *The Saints' Happiness*, pp. 120-122

Blessed are those who keep his testimonies,
who seek him with their whole heart.
Psalm 119:2

Part four continued: Directions for souls that do not find all the righteousness they desire—(1.) Be sure you renounce ALL unrighteousness: 'Lord, through your mercy, I want to purpose in my heart not to meddle with anything that appears to be unrighteous, or have anything to do with it!' Many seek for righteousness—at least they think so—and yet, in the meantime, they give in to some other form of unrighteousness. They flatter themselves for the desire, and think that God will be pleased. Take heed of justifying any form of unrighteousness. (2.) Often express your thirsting for righteousness before God. (3.) Make sure it is God's righteousness you are seeking, and freely express to God that he knows your heart's desire for his righteousness, whatever it is, and that you long after all his ways and commandments. Tell him that you will not give liberty to yourself in anything that is not according to his ways. (4.) Often examine if you have gained the victory over your corruptions. This is a matter for praise, and, if not, a matter for humbling. (5.) Manifest your desire by using all means possible. If ordinary means will not do it, use extraordinary means. If your heart is set upon a thing, it will leave no means untried. The Syrophoenician woman, being affected with the misery of her daughter, resolved, one way or the other, to find Christ who could heal her. So, if the Lord is pleased to withdraw himself from the soul in one means, the soul that desires righteousness will follow hard after God in one means or another, and will never rest until it obtains the ways of righteousness it desires. (6.) Set your faith on Christ, the fountain of all grace. Cast your soul on him for both justification AND sanctification. (7.) Keep your heart resolved not to turn from this desire until it is satisfied!

JEREMIAH BURROUGHS, *The Saints' Happiness*, pp. 124-126

I am the bread of life; whoever comes to me shall not hunger, and whoever believes in me shall never thirst.

John 6:35

Part four continued: Many men and women have good desires stirred in them for a time, but they vanish away and turn their desires to other things. It is of very great consequence for you to labour to keep your appetite continually after righteousness. Take heed of those things that will take away your desire for righteousness. Giving in to corruptions will take away your desire for holiness. In times past, some may have run to the word, and earnestly prayed as if they would rend the heavens, but they have allowed fearful stuff into their hearts that has defiled their souls. Others give themselves up to the world and delights of the flesh, and this takes away their desires. Others keep themselves from the sins of the times, and satisfying the flesh in carnal things, but they grow dull and sluggish and negligent. They do not exercise their faith, and they have no stirrings of their heart after God. If you would keep your heart warm, every morning pray until you get your heart warm again. In your desire for more righteousness, do not forget what you already have. Take notice of it, and bless God for it! Bless him for every good motion and inclination, and so expect more! 'Lord, I find the beginning of your work of grace sweet to my soul; oh that I had more!' Be willing to go through all discouragements that you meet with in your hungering. Trample down all difficulties and hindrances that lie in your way. You may meet with more temptations than ever, or more corruptions. Don't let this discourage you. You will be satisfied at last. Thousands have had good beginnings, but have been taken off by discouragements. The hungry soul says, 'Oh that I might have grace, or else I am undone. Whatever hindrance there is, I do not care; I am willing to part with all, so I may have grace!'

Jeremiah Burroughs, *The Saints' Happiness*, pp. 126-128

My sheep hear my voice, and I know them, and they follow me.

John 10:27

P*art four continued:* If you thirst for righteousness, and yet are not satisfied, please consider: The least degree of grace is as sure of eternal life as the greatest. I do not speak this, that you should be content in any degree of grace, and the upright will not abuse it. Though the least degree of grace binds the bargain with God for eternal life, little grace does not honour God as much as a great deal. If you find your lack of righteousness to be your sickness, it makes your soul an object of his compassion, and not an object of God's wrath. Here is the difference between the remaining sin of a saint, and the corruptions in the ungodly. When your children are sick, you love them as well as when they are healthy. I appeal to any tender mother: do not your bowels yearn for your child when it is sick? So, as our unrighteousness remains, it is the sickness of our soul, and the bowels of God's compassions are towards his sick children as well as towards his strong children. Suppose you overhear your child, through the keyhole, who didn't know you were listening, crying and bemoaning himself—'Oh that I could please my father and mother more! How little I am able to do for them. Oh that I could obey them more. This would be the happiness of my life.' Would not your heart yearn toward such a child? God is a compassionate Father. Is not our compassion a drop of the infinite compassion of God? If you prayed to honour God more, in this your life would be happy. God knows, and will not cast off such a one. Suppose a sheep entangled in briars heard the shepherd's voice, but could not come, but was bleating and crying after the shepherd. When he found it, would not the shepherd pity the sheep and untangle it? So does Christ with his sheep that are striving, but are yet entangled in corruption.

Jeremiah Burroughs, *The Saints' Happiness*, pp. 128-130

And I am sure of this, that he who began a good work in you will bring it to completion at the day of Jesus Christ.

Philippians 1:6

Part four continued: If you are seeking grace, but cannot find that you have obtained it, for your encouragement, consider that the conquest of the will is a principal work of God on the soul! When the will is conquered, the great work is done. The will is the great hindrance. If your will desires to obey God, God accepts the will as if you were able to do the thing to the uttermost of your desire. Paul commends the Corinthians for the will to do, before they had the ability to do (*2 Cor.* 8:10). God is as much honoured in your will to do, as if you did the thing. This may be a great support to our souls if we find our wills submissive, though we lack the power to do. Further, know that the least degree of grace will increase and God will carry it on to perfection. When you long after this righteousness, and cannot do what you would, your desires are better than your abilities. Further, God may cause righteousness to appear in abasing and humbling you! Rather than giving you the power over your corruption, he keeps your heart sensible of its vanity, and discovers the excellency of his grace. God has not forsaken you. God's intentions are to humble you, not to leave you. God may have righteousness work upward in joy, in enlargements and in comfort, or work downward in self-abasement, soul-humbling, and spirit-dejecting. This humbling is working righteousness in the heart as much as joy and consolation! But take heed you are not deceiving yourselves, and that you do not actually have cold and lazy desires! One who says he desires grace, yet would have their lusts too, is deceived. If you say you desire righteousness, and yet take pleasure in unrighteousness, how can you say you thirst for righteousness? Though there is unrighteousness in the best, there is no taking pleasure in it!

Jeremiah Burroughs, *The Saints' Happiness*, pp. 130-133

By faith Noah, being warned by God concerning events as yet unseen, in reverent fear constructed an ark for the saving of his household.

Hebrews 11:7

Though it was a matter of great difficulty, and likely to be entertained with scoffs in the world, yet Noah prepared an ark. God must be obeyed whatever it costs us! Though duties cross our affections, and blast our reputation in the world, God must be obeyed. Noah was being tested, and in difficult cases we are also put to trial. We can't retract our duty if we have entirely given ourselves up, and all that is ours, to God. We are the Lord's (*Rom.* 14:7-8). We cannot say, 'this far I will obey, and no farther'. We cannot reserve a part of our will; God must be obeyed. Christ bids us to count the cost! Can you part with all for him? God is not a hard master; we have never lost anything by God. We were gainers when we were the greatest losers. Jesus did not fail to go to the cross and he freely offered himself—'I delight to do your will, O my God' (*Psa.* 40:8), and, 'shall I not drink the cup that the Father has given me?' (*John* 18:11). He was despitefully used by men, yet he did not repent of the bargain, and so we should never repent of our solemn pledges to God. Though Noah was certain of safety, yet he must use the means directed. If he didn't make the ark, he would share the punishment with the ungodly world! See also, the protection promised by Paul: 'except these abide … ye cannot be saved' (*Acts* 27:31, KJV). God has appointed the means as well as the result. This should put a check on license. We cannot be saved if we live as we desire. Assurance is no idle doctrine. Though we are under a sure covenant with God, we are to mind our duty! Elijah, who had foretold rain, yet prayed for it as earnestly as if the thing had been utterly uncertain and unlikely. We must use the means that God has instituted, in order to salvation, both with faith and obedience.

THOMAS MANTON, *By Faith*, pp. 369-371

And Simon answered, 'Master, we toiled all night and took nothing! But at your word I will let down the nets.'

Luke 5:5

It is a great part of the life of faith to live by faith in the use of means. As we use means, we can entrust ourselves to the mercy of God for blessing, edification, comfort, and grace. If we lack comfort a great while, we should try again in the means God has appointed. There is more grace in waiting upon God, though more comfort in receiving. Upon the bare command of God, we must keep up our endeavours, even if we have been discouraged by former experiences. So Peter (*Luke* 5:5). Lord, I have come again and again, and found no profit; yet I will come once more. Noah knew the ark was God's means, and waited in the ark many months until the rain ceased and the floods dried up. The ark is a type of Christ. The ark was the only means of salvation, and so is Jesus Christ (*Acts* 4:12). If men had built a tower, and gone up to the tops of mountains, and were giant-like men, they could not escape the flood. So all other things are but vain confidences; though you are strict and severe in life, and practise many duties, yet out of Christ these mean nothing. All outside the ark perished in the waters. Many saw the ark, but unless they were in it, they were not safe! You may hear of Christ, but if you are not in Christ, it will avail you nothing. There is salvation in no other. Money and large possessions did not help those outside the ark; 'Riches do not profit in the day of wrath' (*Prov.* 11:4). Those that were once in the ark were sure and safe and could not miscarry. So there is sure salvation in Christ. Once in Christ, salvation is forever. All the floods of calamity can never overwhelm you; they will be your safety, and not your ruin. The flood mounted the ark higher, and made it safe from the rocks. Floods rise to a great advantage. Both afflictions and blessings are faithful administrations.

Thomas Manton, *By Faith*, pp. 371-372

For Demas, in love with this present world, has deserted me and gone to Thessalonica.

2 Timothy 4:10

We abuse our souls. They are not made to close and embrace the world. A covetous man lowers himself. If we embrace Christ and the promises of salvation, we raise the soul in excellence, and it quiets and rests the soul. Faith enables the soul to be what it is made for. We may say to the soul concerning riches and honours, 'This is not your rest. You were not made to embrace and to cleave to these things. Our rest is in Christ and in the good things we have by him.' True faith delights in the things believed, and carries the soul with it. To the degree that we apprehend the goodness of a thing, so is our love for it, and our affections follow. If we do not embrace and cleave to it in the will and affections—you may say what you will—you don't truly believe. Deadness in the affections discovers atheism in the heart. How is it possible that a man should not be carried away in his affections to a good thing that he is persuaded of? And how is it possible that he should not loathe ill and destructive things? If he were persuaded that hell is such as it is, and that these courses lead to hell and destruction, he would not be affected with these courses as he is. To live as if we do not believe the excellency of things promised, or the terror of things threatened, shows we are not truly persuaded of them. A dead faith is no faith at all. Let us shame ourselves—'Lord, do I profess that I see Christ in heaven and see myself there? Where is my love and joy? Why does my heart run to other things? Lord, open my heart for your throne. Teach my heart to love you. Open my understanding to conceive holy things. Take off my love, my joy, and my delight from earthly things, and plant them where they should be, and enlarge them. Fill my heart with yourself as you have made it for yourself!'

Richard Sibbes, *Works*, VII:441-443

The aim of our charge is love that issues from a pure heart and a good conscience and a sincere faith.

1 Timothy 1:5

Is holiness your pursuit and business? If not, you fall short of sound conversion. Strait and narrow is the way that leads to life! Be exhorted, O man, to examine yourself. What does your conscience say? Does it accuse? Does it pierce you as you go? Does it tell you of a certain sin you are living in against your conscience? Does it tell you there is such and such a secret way of wickedness that you wish to pursue, or such and such a duty that you make no conscience of? Does your conscience carry you to your closet, and tell you how seldom prayer and reading are performed there? Does it carry you to your family, and show you the charges of God, and the souls of your children that are neglected there? Does your conscience lead you to your shop, your trade, and tell you of some iniquity there? Does it carry you to the public house, or private club, and blame you for the loose company you keep there, and the precious time which you misspend there—the talents which you waste there? Does it carry you into your secret chamber, and read there your condemnation? O conscience! do your duty. In the name of the living God, I command you, discharge your office! Lay hold upon this sinner, fall upon him, arrest him, apprehend him, and undeceive him. What? Will you flatter and soothe him while he lives in his sins? Awake, O conscience! What meanest thou, O sleeper? What? Have you no reproof in your mouth? What? Shall this soul die in his careless neglect of God and of eternity, while you altogether hold your peace? What? Shall he go on still in his trespasses, and yet have peace? Oh, rouse yourself, and do your work. Now let the preacher in your bosom speak. Cry aloud, and spare not. Lift up your voice like a trumpet. Let not the blood of his soul be required at your hands.

Joseph Alleine, *A Sure Guide to Heaven*, pp. 48-49

For what does it profit a man to gain the whole world and forfeit his soul?

Mark 8:36

It was a saying of a noble Roman when he was hasting with corn to a city in famine, and the mariners were loath to set sail in foul weather, 'It is necessary for us to sail—it is not necessary to live.' What is it that you count necessary? Is your bread necessary? Is your breath necessary? Then your conversion is much more necessary. Indeed, this is the one thing necessary! Your possessions are not necessary—you may sell all for the pearl of great price, and yet be a gainer by the purchase. Your life is not necessary—you may part with it for Christ, to infinite advantage. Your reputation is not necessary—you may be reproached for the name of Christ, and yet be happy. Yes, you may be much more happy in reproach than in good reputation. But your conversion is necessary—your salvation depends on it. Is it not needful in so important a matter to take special care? On this one point depends your making or marring to all eternity! Without conversion your very being is in vain! Is it not a pity you should be good for nothing, and an unprofitable burden of the earth?—a wart in the body of the universe? While unconverted, you cannot fulfil the purpose of your being. It was for the divine pleasure that you were created. Did not God make you for himself? Are you a man, and have you reason? Look how you came into being and why you exist. Look at God's workmanship in your body, and consider the noble faculties of your heaven-born soul. To what end? Did God rear this fabric for no other end than to please yourself and gratify your senses? Are you like the swallows, who gather a few sticks and mud, and build their nests, rear their young, and then away? *You are fearfully and wonderfully made!* Surely you were made for some more noble and exalted end! You must repent and be converted—without this you are to no purpose!

Joseph Alleine, *A Sure Guide to Heaven*, pp. 50-51

Put on the whole armour of God, that you may be able to stand against the schemes of the devil.

Ephesians 6:11

Satan designs to keep souls from holy duties. His first device is to present the world in such a dress as to ensnare the soul and win the affections. He represents the world in its beauty, and no sooner casts out his golden bait but we are ready to play with it, and to nibble at it. Ah! How many professors for a time follow hard after God, till the devil bewitch their souls with the world. They grow to have low thoughts of holy things, and become cold in their affections, and slight them, and at last turn their backs on them. Oh the time, the hearts and the duties this inordinate love of this wicked world eats up! When a thousand are destroyed by the world's frowns, ten thousand are destroyed by the world's smiles. The world sings to us, and sinks us. It kisses us, and betrays us, like Judas. It kisses us, and smites us under the fifth rib, like Joab. The honours, splendour, and all the glories of this world are but sweet poisons that will much endanger us if they do not eternally destroy us. Ah! The multitude of souls that have indulged these sweet baits and died forever. Remedy: Dwell upon—(1.) *The weakness and vanity of things here below.* The crown of gold cannot cure the headache, or the velvet slippers ease the gout. (2.) *The mutability of all things under the sun.* They are a shadow. No man can promise himself to be wealthy till night; one storm at sea, one coal of fire, one false friend may make you a beggar and a prisoner all at once. Oh do not let these uncertain things keep you from heavenly employments. (3.) *The great things of the world are a danger to the corruptions in the hearts of men.* A man's riches are a strong tower in his imagination (*Psa.* 30:6). They swell the heart with pride and make men neglect God, the rock of their salvation. They hinder the actings of faith and interrupt sweet communion with God!

Thomas Brooks, *Works*, 1:63-66

Though you have not seen him, you love him … and rejoice with joy that is inexpressible and filled with glory.

1 Peter 1:8

Remedy continued: (4.) *Consider that the joys of this world are mixed.* Our light is mixed with darkness, our joys with sorrow, our pleasures with pain, our honours with dishonour, and our riches with wants. Spiritual insight sees earthly joys as wine mixed with water, honey with gall, sugar with wormwood, and roses with thorns. Sorrow attends worldly joy, and danger attends worldly safety. Men's hopes are vain and their sorrows certain. (5.) *Get a better acquaintance with more blessed and glorious things.* Better and more durable things will trample upon all the beauty and glory of the world—'But as it is, they desire a better country, that is, a heavenly one. Therefore God is not ashamed to be called their God, for he has prepared for them a city' (*Heb.* 11:16). The main reason why men dote upon the world, and damn their souls to get the world, is because they are not acquainted with a greater glory. Ah that you would make it your business to mind more of the great things of eternity that will give you joy in life and peace in death. Minding the crown of righteousness we will receive in the day of Christ's appearing will lift up your souls above the beauty of this bewitching world. Assurance of a crown, sceptre, and royal robes breed in the soul a holy scorn of the poor things that the soul valued before. (6.) *Consider that true happiness cannot be found in the enjoyment of worldly goods.* True happiness is too glorious a thing. It does not lie in things a man may enjoy, and yet be miserable forever. Happiness lies not in those things that cannot comfort you on your deathbed. Honours, riches, and friends cannot comfort you, but faith in the blood of Christ, the witness of the Spirit, the love and favour of Christ, and reigning eternally with him can! A man may have enough of the world to sink him, but never enough to satisfy him!

Thomas Brooks, *Works*, 1:67-69

Now who is there to harm you if you are zealous for what is good?

1 Peter 3:13

A second device that Satan uses to draw the soul away from holy duties is to present the danger, losses, and sufferings that attend faithful service. By this device Satan keeps those who believe in Christ from confessing Christ (*John* 12:42). Oh, how we should help ourselves against this temptation. Remedy (1.) *Consider that all the troubles and afflictions you meet with in the way of righteousness shall never hurt or harm you!* Nobody is properly hurt but by himself and his own fault. Even the natural conscience honours the image of God stamped upon the nature of a godly man; so Nebuchadnezzar towards Daniel! The afflictions that attend men in the way of righteousness can never rob them of their treasure. They may rob them of some slight things, as the sword that is by their side, or the stick in their hand, or the flowers or ribbons that are in their hats. But the treasures of a saint are the presence and favour of God! The pardon of sin, the joy of the Spirit, the peace of conscience—these are given by Christ, and none can take them away. No affliction can strip a man of his heavenly jewels. His life is safe, his soul is safe, his grace is safe, his comfort is safe, and his crown is safe in the hand of Christ! (2.) *Remember that the saints that were shining lights on earth notwithstanding all the troubles that surrounded them, are now triumphing in heaven!* Nehemiah, Ezra, and Daniel were surrounded with dangers on the left hand and right, and yet, in the face of it all, they cleaved to God and his ways in the face of a world of very great discouragements. Though they were sore broken in the place of dragons, and covered with the shadow of death, their hearts did not turn back from his ways. Though Paul knew bonds and imprisonments, he held on in the work and service of the Lord. Why, then, should you degenerate from their worthy examples, which it is your duty and glory to follow?

Thomas Brooks, *Works*, 1:70-71

How shall we escape if we neglect such a great salvation?

Hebrews 2:3

Remedy continued: (3.) *Consider that the troubles and dangers that attend the performance of holy duties are temporal and momentary, but their neglect opens you to temporal, spiritual, and eternal dangers.* Heavenly service may lay you open to the frowns of men, but its neglect will lay you open to the frowns of God. You will suffer more by neglect of the heavenly duties that God commands, commends, and rewards, than you ever will by doing them! (4.) *God knows how to deliver from troubles by troubles, and from afflictions by afflictions, and from dangers by dangers.* God often delivers his people from greater trials by lesser. They may say, 'We had perished, if we had not perished. We had been undone, if we had not been undone. We had been in danger, if we had not been in danger.' We realize that God has so ordered the afflictions that, if they had not befallen us, it would have been worse with us. Oh the carnal security, pride, formality, dead-heartedness, lukewarmness and earthliness that God has cured us of by troubles and dangers we have met with along the way in the service of the Lord. He gives us a portion that makes us heartsick, but in order to make us perfectly well! (5.) *Solemnly consider that you will gain more in the service of God by walking in holy ways than you will lose even though you pass through trouble.* Oh, the joy, peace, comfort, and rest that saints meet with in the service of God! Oh, the sweet looks and words that gracious souls have from heaven. They will outweigh all the glory of this world, and richly recompense the soul for all its troubles. The saints may say under all their troubles, 'I have meat to eat and drink to drink that the world knows nothing about. I wouldn't exchange it for all the honours, riches, and dainties of this world.' Every penny of loss is a gain of a pound! We lose pins and find pearls. Momentary affliction has an eternal crown of glory!

Thomas Brooks, *Works,* 1:71-73

Looking to Jesus ... who for the joy that was set before him endured the cross.

Hebrews 12:2

A third device that Satan uses to draw the soul from holy duties is to present the difficulty of performing them. Satan says, 'It is too hard to pray as you should, and wait on God as you should, and walk with God as you should. You are better ten thousand times by neglecting them than meddling with them!' Remedy (1.) *Consider their necessity.* Though such duties are hard, they are essential to honour God, gain the victory over sin, strengthen weak graces, revive comfort, scatter fears, and raise your hopes! (2.) *Consider that the Lord Jesus will make your service easy to you, by the sweet discovery of himself to your soul!* God who is goodness itself, beauty itself, strength itself, glory itself, will sweeten your soul. Jacob's love for Rachel made his seven years' service seem but a few days because of his love for her. The Lord will give sweet assistance by his Spirit and grace so our service is a delight and not a burden. Ah, souls, while you are in the service of the Lord, you will find by experience that the God of heaven will prosper and support you, and strengthen and encourage you in the hardest service with cheerfulness and the choicest assistance. He will suit your strength to your work. (3.) *Consider the difficult things the Lord Jesus passed through for your eternal good.* What a sea of blood, of wrath, of sorrow and misery he passed through! Christ did not plead, 'This cross is too heavy to bear, this wrath too great, and this cup too bitter.' Resolutely and bravely he waded through all of it. He bravely bore the Father's wrath, our sin, the malice of Satan, and the rages of the world, and sweetly and triumphantly passed through all. (4.) *Though the work is hard, heaven will make amends for all!* One hour in heaven will pay for all. Look to the crown more than the cross, and more on glory than present misery.

Thomas Brooks, *Works*, 1:74-76

Fret not yourself because of evildoers; be not envious of wrongdoers. For they will soon fade like the grass and wither like the green herb.

Psalm 37:1-2

Men practically deny providence, abuse it, or condemn it when they envy. To be sad at the temporal good or gifts of another—counting him unworthy of them—casts a reflection upon the author of those gifts. It accuses providence of an unjust or unwise distribution. But God may do what he will with his own. If our eye is evil because God is good, we entrench upon his liberty, and deny him the disposal of his own goods as if God were but our steward, and we his lords. We are all prone to this temper. It is peculiarly the product of self-love that would control the conduct of God in distributing his goods only to whom we are pleased! It arises from a sense of our wants, but the language of it is that God is unjust in his providence to me, because he doesn't bestow on me the good that he gives to another. This sin is a companion to Adam and Eve's pride, which was the cause of their fall. They envied the happiness that God owned by himself. They wanted to be like him, they wanted to be as gods. Cain also denied God's providence when he envied his brother, because God accepted Abel's sacrifice over his. Jonah's passion rose from this pride, for fear he should be counted a false prophet; whereupon he envied God the glory of his mercy, and the poor Ninevites the advantage of it. Jonah desired God to conform the way of his providence to his pleasure and reputation. His pride made him more concerned about himself and his reputation, than about God's glory and honour in the providence of his mercy. Thus envy would direct God in what instruments he should employ. No craftsman would ever be directed by an ignorant person in what tools he should use in his work!

Stephen Charnock, *Works*, 1:48-49

For it is God who works in you, both to will and to work for his good pleasure.

Philippians 2:13

Impatience under cross providences is a denial and contempt of God's government, as if he were accountable to us for his dispensations. Must God alter his affairs according to our model? Do we get angry if he does not observe our rules and methods? It is a secret cursing of God when we see providence so cross that there seems to be no help for us either in heaven or earth. Take heed of fretting at God's management of things in the world. This is a secret swelling against him. Man is always like Adam—ambitious to become a god. This is (1.) *a wrong to the sovereignty of providence.* We usurp God's place and set ourselves on his throne. We invade his supremacy by desiring everything to be at our beck and call, and are displeased with him, because he does not put the reins of the world's government into our hands, as if we would command his will and become his sovereign. Shall the clay say to him that fashions it, 'What are you doing?' Do men summon God to the bar of their interest, and argue with him about his works, and pull the crown from off his head? It is (2.) *a wrong to the goodness of his providence.* It is a charging God with ill management. If patience honours God's righteousness, then impatience and murmuring charge him with unrighteousness! It is (3.) *a wrong to the wisdom of providence.* We degrade his omniscience and wisdom when we foolishly instruct him better in the management of the world, and direct him to a reformation of his methods. It is a secret boasting of some excellency in ourselves that we could govern better. Does the passenger direct the skilful pilot to steer the vessel according to his pleasure? Do we give our orders to God as though the counsels of infinite wisdom must roll about according to the conceits of our fancy?

Stephen Charnock, *Works*, 1:49-50

The sacrifices of God are a broken spirit; a broken and contrite heart, O God, you will not despise.

Psalm 51:17

Query: *'The Lord knows I know neither how to pray, or what to pray; what should I do?'* Poor heart! Do you see your misery? Has God revealed to you that you are by nature under the curse of the law? If so, I know you have grown most bitterly. I am persuaded that you can scarcely do anything, but prayer breaks out in your heart. Have not your groans gone up to heaven often? Is not your heart a witness to your tears? Does not your heart desire another world? *'When I go into secret, and intend to pour out my soul before God, I can scarce say anything at all!'* Ah! Sweet soul! It is not your words that God so much regards, as if you need to come with some eloquent oration. His eye is on the brokenness of your heart, and it is this that makes his heart to run over! David was so troubled at times that he could not speak (*Psa.* 77:3-4). It should comfort your heart if the anguish of your spirit keeps your words few. The Holy Spirit stirs up your heart in groans and sighs so much the more vehement when your mouth is hindered. Though your mouth is hindered, your spirit is not. If you would more fully express yourself before the Lord, first study your filthy estate, then the promises of God, and, finally, the heart of Christ. The heart of Christ can be seen, (1.) in his humble shedding of blood, and by (2.) the mercy he has extended to great sinners formerly. Plead your own vileness with grieving and earnest reasoning to apply Christ's blood! In your prayers, let the mercy he has extended to other great sinners, together with his rich promises of grace, be much upon your heart. Don't be content with mere words, or that God only considers them. Whether your words are few or many, let your heart go with them, and then you will seek him and find him, when you seek him with your whole heart (*Jer.* 29:13).

John Bunyan, *Works,* 1:634-635

But Jesus called them to him, saying, 'Let the children come to me, and do not hinder them, for to such belongs the kingdom of God.'

Luke 18:16

We ought to prompt one another to pray, but not make a form for others to follow. To exhort to pray is one thing, but to make stinted forms that may tie up the Spirit of God is another. Some may ask, '*If we do not use forms of prayer, how shall we teach our children to pray?*' My judgment is that men go the wrong way to teach their children to pray by teaching them a set group of words, which is very common to do. It seems better to me for people to tell their children what cursed creatures they are, and how they are under the wrath of God by reason of original and actual sin, and also to tell them the nature of God's wrath, and the duration of the misery—which, if they would conscientiously do, they would teach their children to pray sooner than they do. The way men learn to pray is by the conviction of sin, and this is the way to make our sweet babes pray also. But the other way, namely, to be busy in teaching children forms of prayer before they know anything else, is the next way to make them cursed hypocrites, and puff them up with pride. Teach your children therefore to know their wretched state and condition. Teach them of hellfire and their sins, of damnation and salvation, and how to escape the one and enjoy the other. This will make tears run down your sweet babes' eyes, and cause hearty groans to flow from their hearts. You can tell them to whom they should pray, and through whom they should pray. Tell them of God's promises and the grace he has formerly extended to sinners according to his word! Ah! Poor sweet babes, may the Lord open their eyes, and make them holy Christians (*Psa.* 34:11). The Spirit begets prayer when, in truth, they learn the gospel. The more you teach them this, the more their hearts will run out to God in prayer!

John Bunyan, *Works*, 1:635

Give us this day our daily bread.

Matthew 6:11

By bread is meant ordinary bread, or whatsoever is necessary for our subsistence in the world from day to day (see *Prov.* 30:8). We certainly pray for the good things of this life to be obtained in a lawful, regular manner, while not coveting that which is another's. There is a limitation in the petition in respect to time—'give us *this day* our daily bread!' Indeed, there is a great reason why we should pray for bread '*this day*'. Every day we stand in need of relief and supplies from God. Our needs and troubles grow up thick about us, and, unless God makes daily provisions for us, we would be overrun by them. Food nourishes us only for a day, and will not suffice for tomorrow. There is a continual fountain of needs springing up within us, and, therefore, we must have continual recourse unto God by prayer that he would daily satisfy the needs about us. By teaching us to pray for our temporal comforts *this day*, our Saviour tacitly intimates to us that we should be content with our daily allowance. It is enough to have our appointed food for the day. Tomorrow is in God's hands, and the care of it is his, and not ours! Therefore he bids us to take no thoughts for tomorrow—that is, no tormenting, distressing, and desponding thoughts (*Matt.* 6:34). In this we pray for life itself—that it might be prolonged while God has service for us in this world. It is a prayer for strength of body—the greatest of temporal blessings—and all the means to obtain this as directed by God's providence. It is a prayer for any conveniences and comforts of life to enable success in our lawful callings, and by them to increase our temporal enjoyments to his glory and our good. In it we beg a blessing from heaven upon all we enjoy, that it may indeed prove good and comfortable to us. Without God's blessing, all we possess may just prove to be a great heap of things with no comfort!

EZEKIEL HOPKINS, *Works*, 1:103-106

If you confess with your mouth that Jesus is Lord and believe in your heart that God raised him from the dead, you will be saved.

Romans 10:9

To excite fervency in praying for forgiveness, consider the multitude of your sins—God's book is full of them! God sets all our sins down in order in his debt book. Our crimes and heinous impieties; our presumptuous sins committed against light, knowledge, conscience, convictions, mercies, and judgments: how many thousands of these may we have been guilty of! God's patience has been long, but his justice will at last demand the debt. Indeed, we are apt to think that, because God is patient, he will never call us to account. But he will set our sins in order before our faces to our everlasting shame and confusion. The least of our debts makes us liable to be cast into the prison of hell, and to be condemned to eternal death and punishment. Beware that you do not entertain slight thoughts of sin. You can never pay or discharge the least of your debts forever by suffering hereafter. Oh what dreadful despair this will cause you when you have been in hell under insufferable torments millions of years, yet the payment value cannot satisfy the least of your sins. Your account is just as great as when you were cast into hell. Where shall we turn? What hope and relief can we find? There is abundant hope through the free mercy of our God! Christ has suffered the penalty for us. The pardoning grace of God is altogether free and undeserved. Christ was sent into the world to die an accursed death for our salvation. His satisfaction was sufficient, since he was infinite himself. He was able to bear the whole wrath of God in one bitter draught, and drink the whole cup of fury. And when God pardons, he no longer counts us as sinners, but as just! We are legally discharged. We are no longer malefactors, but just and righteous, as if we had never sinned!

Ezekiel Hopkins, *Works*, 1:109-117

In him we have redemption through his blood, the forgiveness of our trespasses, according to the riches of his grace.

Ephesians 1:7

Justification consists of remission and acceptance. Remission takes away our liableness to death, and acceptance gives us a title unto life. The righteousness and obedience of Christ is imputed to us, which gives us a right to heaven. It is not a bare negative righteousness that God intends in the pardon of our sin. It is not just the removal of the curse and wrath our sin deserves: it is the lifting us up to heaven, as well as plucking us out of hell. We have a right and title to a blessed and glorious inheritance. Our pardon comes from the passive obedience of Christ in his sufferings, and our right to heaven from his active obedience. In both we have a complete justification. The pardon of our sin in Scripture is set forth by very sweet and full expressions. It is called a blotting out of transgressions, as a creditor's marking through the debt book, and forgetting them (*Isa.* 43:25). It is called a covering of our sins (*Psa.* 32:1). Yea, it is a covering of God's face from them (*Psa.* 51:9). It is a casting them behind God's back, never to regard them again (*Isa.* 38:17). And lest we should suspect that he should turn again to behold them, it is called a casting of them into the bottom of the sea (*Mic.* 7:19), as we do with things we would have irrecoverably lost and gone. It is a scattering them as a thick cloud and a heavy mist (*Isa.* 44:22). When the vapours of the cloud are dissipated, there shall not remain the least spot to obstruct the shining of God's face and favour upon our souls. Yea, so perfect an abolition shall be made of all our iniquities, that if divine justice should enter into a strict search after them, they shall not be found (*Jer.* 50:20). God has heaped up expressions of his grace and mercy upon one another, with careful words, as it were, to assure us of the validity of our pardon. This gives us abounding consolations.

Ezekiel Hopkins, *Works*, 1:117-119

But when the fullness of time had come,
God sent forth his Son, born of woman,
born under the law.
Galatians 4:4

He who was the Ancient of Days became a helpless infant. He who was the light of the sun came into the world in the darkness of night. He who came that he might lay us in the bosom of the Father was himself laid in the manger of a stable. Though he was humbly welcomed on earth, heaven made abundant amends for all. A company of industrious shepherds, lying all night watching their sheep, suddenly found their own shepherd. Angels appear to tell of the birth of Christ, and bid them to search for him in a strange place; they will find the Lord of life and glory in an inn. It is a strange circumstance that holy angels would call the shameful debasement of the King of Heaven 'tidings of great joy', and make it their jubilee! The heavenly host left the glorious palace of heaven when their King lay here below, and with joyful acclamation cried, 'Glory to God in the highest!' Christ coming into the world brought glory to God. We might well wonder what should occasion such mighty expressions of joy in those blessed spirits. Is it a time of joy when the great God is introducing himself into our flesh, when he is abasing himself to dust and ashes, and when the infinite God is shrinking himself into a small worm? Is it a time of joy when the brightness of deity is now eclipsed in a frail body? Strange that they should make this day of heaven's humiliation their festival and day of thanksgiving! Well, angels rejoiced at the incarnation of the Saviour since it is the root and foundation of the salvation of sinners, and of our hope and happiness. There is joy in the presence of angels over one sinner that repents! (*Luke* 15:10). I might likewise add that the angels rejoiced at Christ's birth, because there is laid in it the great and wonderful design of God's glory.

EZEKIEL HOPKINS, *Works*, III:405-409

Suddenly ... a multitude of the heavenly host praising God and saying, 'Glory to God in the highest ...'

Luke 2:13-14

God's glory is of two sorts—essential and declarative. His *essential glory* is the infinite perfection of his own nature—wisdom, power, holiness and the like—that he is from all eternity, before ever there was a creature made to admire him. He was infinitely glorious in himself! The *declarative glory* is that visible splendour reflected from the essential glory that his creatures see. As we give glory to God, we do not contribute anything to his glory, or add jewels to his crown, but we admire his attributes as God expresses them. So here, the angels sang, 'Glory to God in the highest'—that is, let the earth behold with admiration and acknowledge the attributes of God that now shine forth in the incarnation of his Son. The abasing nativity of Jesus Christ is the highest advancement of God's glory. This is a strange riddle to human reason, which is prone to judge it a most preposterous course for God to raise his glory out of the humiliation and abasement, yea, out of the very ruin of his Son. What if God had thrown open heaven for all of the world to see his majestic throne with ten thousand flaming spirits ready to do his will: would not this be more expressive of his glory than to cloister deity up in clay? To expose him who was God to the miseries of wretched man, and to an ignoble and cursed death? The manger in which he lay, and the cross on which he hung, were not high places of any glorious appearance! Carnal reason may think this way, but the apostle, in speaking of the incarnation of Christ, calls it 'the mystery of godliness' (*1 Tim.* 3:16). It is a riddle, and a mysterious one: not only how it should be that the eternal and infinite God should unite himself in oneness of person with frail and despicable flesh, but why it should be done!

Ezekiel Hopkins, *Works*, III:409-410

We preach Christ crucified ... Christ the power of God and the wisdom of God.

1 Corinthians 1:23-24

Much glory abounds to God through the incarnation. In the birth of Christ, God glorified the riches of his infinite wisdom. This plan would never have entered into the heart of men or angels! Heaven, at this very day, stands astonished at it. Angels are continually looking into it and confess their understandings are infinitely too short to fathom it. Christ is called the wisdom of God (*1 Cor.* 1:24). He is the second person of the ever-blessed Trinity; he was with God, and is God himself. As Mediator, he was God-man united in one person. The salvation of man is a difficult case. Justice and mercy lay in their different claims for sinful man: justice pleads the law and the curse and is ready to drag man to execution; mercy interposes, and pleads God's other attributes. Call in an assembly of angels to debate the case, and, when all is said, there is no way to resolve the difference. It is beyond their reach how to satisfy justice in the punishment of sinners, and yet to gratify mercy in their pardon. The wonderful wisdom of God is seen; justice demands that man should die, and God says, 'My Son shall become man and die under the hands of justice. It will seize him, pursue him through all the plagues and curses which my law threatens, and there satisfy justice on my Son, the surety, and then my mercy shall forgive.' Think what a shout and applause heaven gave at the decision of this great controversy. Oh, God's infinite wisdom to contrive means to reconcile such different interests, and entwine his glory with them both! Oh, it is delightful for reason to lose itself in such a divine meditation. It is an unfathomable deep into which the soul may enter. We never find ourselves at such a ravishing ecstasy of loss, as when we trace out the contrivances and admirable ways chosen for our recovery!

EZEKIEL HOPKINS, *Works*, III:410-411

Joseph, son of David, do not fear to take Mary as your wife, for that which is conceived in her is from the Holy Spirit.

Matthew 1:20

The birth of Christ *glorified the almighty power of God*. The infinite power that spread abroad the heavens, and poised the earth in the midst of the air, joined heaven and earth together in the miraculous birth of Christ! He has made an inseparable union between them; he has caused heaven and earth to meet midway; he has raised earth to heaven, and lowered heaven to earth. It was the almighty power of God that united himself to human nature, to frail flesh. He put forth his power, only to make himself weak! Is it not almighty power that the infinite and inconceivable Godhead should unite to itself dust and ashes, and be so closely united that it should grow into one and the same person? The glory of God's power is hereby exceedingly lifted up! By the birth of Christ, God also *glorified the severity of his justice*. His Son must rather take flesh and die than his mercy remain unsatisfied. The justice of God was more fully satisfied in Christ than if it had seized upon the offenders themselves. Man is finite, and cannot bear the utmost severity of divine wrath. This the Son of God can and has done. The Son came triumphantly from under it all. The Father glorified the attributes of his justice more by sending the Son into the world to undergo the wrath due to sinners, than if he had taken particular vengeance on sinners, and sent away every soul of them to hell. No other sacrifice could avail to appease the divine justice but that of the Son of God (*Heb.* 9:14). Because the divine nature is not at all subject to grief, sorrow, or sufferings, it was necessary that the Mediator between God and men should be man as well as God. By this means, satisfaction is made unto justice in the same nature that sinned; man offended, so man was punished. The same nature that was shamefully foiled now gloriously overcomes!

Ezekiel Hopkins, *Works*, III:411-412

She will bear a son, and you shall call his name Jesus, for he will save his people from their sins.

Matthew 1:21

By the birth of Christ, *the truth and veracity of God are eminently glorified*, by fulfilling many promises and predictions that were made concerning the sending of Christ into the world. That primitive promise in Genesis 3, that the seed of the woman should bruise the serpent's head, which lay for many ages under types and figures, at the birth of Christ broke forth into accomplishment. All the prophecies and ceremonial types that contained the Saviour in embryo were in due time matured by the Holy Spirit, until the truth of God gave them all their expected issue in Christ's birth! (*Gal.* 4:4). Also, the birth of Christ *glorifies the infinite purity and holiness of God.* When God formed Adam, he drew upon him his own image. Holiness, the most illustrious part of his image, was impressed on Adam, that he might be a visible type of his infinite purity to all of the world. But sin despoiled mankind of that glory, and God was pleased to raise up a second Adam, who should be not only sinless, but impeccable, and to exhibit him unto the world as the most perfect representation of his own holiness. His birth must be miraculous, that it might be pure. His extraordinary conception preserved him from original sin, and the hypostatical union, together with the immeasurable unction of the Holy Spirit, from all actual sin. By imputation of sin, Christ was the greatest sinner in the world (*2 Cor.* 5:21), yet he had no sin either of nature or of practice in him!—'He committed no sin, neither was deceit found in his mouth' (*1 Pet.* 2:22). And this, that not only might he be to us an example of unspotted sanctity, but also that we might have a perfect idea of the infinite purity of God. I might finally add that the birth of Christ and the incarnation brought glory to God in *the display of infinite love and pity for fallen man!*

Ezekiel Hopkins, *Works*, III:412-413

Cast your burden on the LORD, and he will sustain you; he will never permit the righteous to be moved.

Psalm 55:22

When sad and afflictive providences befall you, set yourself to fulfil the design and goal of God in them. Seek to maintain spiritual joy and comfort in God under all (*Hab.* 3:17-18). There are two sorts of comfort—natural and spiritual. There are times to exercise both, and times when the former is suspended (*Psa.* 137:2). But there is no season when spiritual joy and comfort in God is unseasonable. Spiritual joy is nothing else but the cheerfulness of our heart in God, and the sense of our interest in him and in his promises. And it is sure that no providence can render this unseasonable to a Christian! Sad providences are but for a moment, while spiritual joys are eternal (*2 Cor.* 4:17)! Even at the lowest ebb, the saints have infinitely more cause to rejoice than to be cast down. There is more in one mercy to comfort them than in all their troubles to deject them. All their losses are but as the loss of a farthing to a prince. And why should they be sad as long as their God is with them in all their troubles? Can the soul be sad while God is with it? 'I will be with him in trouble' (*Psa.* 91:15) should bear you up in all burdens. Let them be cast down who have no one to turn to in troubles. Outward dispensations of sad providence cannot be interpreted as a sign of God's hatred or enmity: his heart is full of love while the face of providence is full of frowns! In all of these providences, God will do us good (*Rom.* 8:28). By these, God is but killing your lusts, weaning your hearts from a vain world, preventing temptations, and exciting desires after heaven. The change of our condition is so near! But a little while and all sorrows shall flee away, and you shall not suffer any more. God will wipe away all your tears (*Rev.* 7:17). You see, then, that there is no reason in sad providences to give up joy in God!

JOHN FLAVEL, *Works*, IV:428-429

For the sake of Christ, then, I am content with weaknesses, insults, hardships, persecutions, and calamities. For when I am weak, then I am strong.

2 Corinthians 12:10

We should be careful under sad providences. We should be careful to mortify inordinate affections to earthly things. Attention to these will make providences that deprive or cross us seem too heavy. Mortify your earthly affections, and you will lighten your affliction noticeably. Strong earthy affections make strong afflictions. Dwell much upon the Lord's near approach, and these things will seem but trifles to you. Exercise heavenly-mindedness, and keep your hearts upon things eternal. But alas! We find that sad providences often hinder our walk with God. In comfortable providences, how sensual, wanton, and worldly do our hearts grow, and, in sad ones, how lazy or distracted we are! Our hearts are narrow and do not know how to handle both earthly and heavenly matters without detriment to one. But a heavenly frame will enable us to keep on in an even and steady course with God whatever befalls us. Others have attained it, and why not we? Jehoshaphat was victorious in prosperity (*2 Chron.* 17:5-6), though prosperous providences are for the most part a dangerous state of the soul. David's life was full of cares and turmoil, but what a spiritual temper he had! The apostles were cast into great necessities as ever men were, yet how heavenly their spirits were amidst all! If it were not possible to maintain heavenly-mindedness in such a state and posture of affairs, God would not exercise any of his people with such providences. If our hearts were more heavenward, if we were more mortified to earthly things, and could keep our due distance from them, we would not hazard so sweet an enjoyment as our fellowship with God. Under all providences, maintain a contented heart in what the Lord allots you.

John Flavel, *Works*, iv:429-431

How long, O LORD? Will you forget me forever? How long will you hide your face from me?

Psalm 13:1

The Lord's people have the least reason of all men to be dissatisfied with any of God's providences, but are too frequently found in that temper. *Consider* your spiritual mercies and privileges, with which the Lord Jesus has invested you, when you want to complain! One of these mercies alone has enough in it to sweeten all your troubles in this world (*Eph.* 1:3). Oh, how could he who sees such an inheritance settled upon him in Christ, ever open his mouth to complain of his lot of providence! *Consider* your sins, and that will make you contented with your lot. We deserve eternal ruin from God! The merit of hell is in the least vain thought! Your corruptions deserve all the crosses and troubles that are upon you. After all the rods that have been upon you, do you not find a proud, vain, and earthly heart still? How many bitter potions are necessary to purge out this tough, malignant humour! *Consider* how near you are to the change of your condition. Have a little patience, and all will be as well with you as your heart desires. This world is the worst place you will ever be in. If a traveller spent all his money, it wouldn't trouble him much if he knew he was almost home. If there are no more candles in the house, it is of little concern if we are sure it is almost the break of day. If providence delays the performance of any mercy to you that you have long prayed for, don't be discouraged and grow weary of waiting upon God. It pleases the Lord oftentimes to try to exercise his people this way, and make them cry, 'How long, Lord, how long?' These delays are frequent, and when they befall us, we are too apt to interpret them as denials, and fall into a sinful despondency of mind. The Lord means to perform the mercies we desire, yet he will ordinarily exercise our patience to wait for them.

JOHN FLAVEL, *Works*, IV:432-433

At the beginning of your pleas for mercy a word went out, and I have come to tell it to you.

Daniel 9:23

In God's providence it is not always the same hour that the returns of our prayers are dispatched, and that for these reasons—(1.) *Because our desired time is not the proper season for us to receive our mercies.* The proper season for a mercy is a great circumstance that adds to the mercy's value. God does not judge as we do. We are all in a hurry, and would have it now! 'For the LORD is a God of justice; blessed are all those who wait for him' (*Isa.* 30:18). (2.) *Afflictive providences have not yet accomplished the design upon our hearts that they were sent for.* We are so earnest and impatient for a change of them, but until the design is accomplished, the rod must not be taken off! (3.) *The more prayer and searching of heart that comes between our wants and our supplies, and our afflictions and relief, the sweeter are our reliefs and supplies thereby made to us (Isa. 25:9).* This recompenses the delay, and pays us for all the expense of our patience. Even though there are such weighty reasons for the stop and delay of refreshing, comfortable providences, we cannot bear it, and our hands hang down and we faint (*Psa.* 69:3). For, alas, we judge by sense and appearance, and do not consider that God's heart may be towards us, while his hand of providence seems to be against us! If things continue at a slow rate for us, we think our prayers are lost, and our hopes have perished from the Lord. Much more, when things grow worse, and troubles increase, as usually they do just at the break of day—which will come to change our condition—we conclude that God is angry with our prayers. Note Gideon's reply (*Judg.* 6:13). This even staggered Moses' faith (*Exod.* 5:22-23). O what groundless jealousies and suspicions are found at such times in the hearts of his own children! (*Psa.* 77:7-9). This is our great evil!

JOHN FLAVEL, *Works*, IV:433-434

Therefore the LORD waits to be gracious to you, and therefore he exalts himself to show mercy to you.

Isaiah 30:18

To prevent the great evil of the suspicion of God's providence among his people, I will offer a few considerations in the case. (1.) *The delay of your mercies is really for your advantage.* Why is that? Delay is preparing your heart to receive mercy—that you may receive it with the greatest advantage of comfort. The foolish child would pluck the apple while it is green, but, when it is ripe, it drops of its own accord, and is more pleasant and wholesome. (2.) *It is a greater mercy to have a heart willing to entrust all to God, and to be at his disposal, than to enjoy presently the mercy we are most eager and impatient for.* In this, God pleases you; in your patience, you please God! A mercy may be given you as a fruit of common providence. But a patient temper of heart is given you as the fruit of special grace! As the glorifying of God is better than the contentment and pleasure of the creature, so this patient temper is better than receiving the mercy. (3.) *Expected mercies are never closer than when the hearts and hopes of God's people are lowest.* Thus it was with Israel in their deliverance from Egypt and Babylon. And so we have found it in our own personal concerns; when we look for increasing darkness, light arises. (4.) *Our unfitness for mercies is why they are delayed so long.* We put blocks in the way of mercies and are surprised that they do not hurry to us (*Isa.* 59:1-2). (5.) *Consider that the mercies you wait for are the fruits of pure grace.* You do not deserve them, and you cannot claim them upon any basis of desert. Therefore you have reason to wait for them with a patient and thankful frame. (6.) *Consider the millions who are cut off from all hope of mercy forever, with a fearful expectation of wrath.* This might have been your case therefore do not be impatient under expectations of mercy.

JOHN FLAVEL, *Works*, IV:434

Oh, the depth of the riches and wisdom and knowledge of God! How unsearchable are his judgments and how inscrutable his ways!

Romans 11:33

Do not pry too curiously into the secrets of providence, or suffer your shallow reason arrogantly to judge and censure its designs. There are hard texts in the works of God, as well as in the word of God. It is becoming for us to be reverent. Here the Scripture sets bounds to our curiosity, which no man can, or ought to, transgress. It is not for man to call God to account. His wisdom is called 'unsearchable', so the human mind may not weary and toil itself in vain, and not without the greatest danger, in searching out God. Man may easily get a strain by overreaching. Asaph so pried into the puzzling mystery of the afflictions of the righteous, and prosperity of the wicked, that it begat envy and despondency in him (*Psa.* 73). And this is all he got for summoning providence to the bar of reason. Holy Job was guilty of this evil (*Job* 42:3). There is nothing objectionable in the word or works of God to sound reason. But there are some things in both which are opposite to carnal reason, and beyond right reason. So our reason never shows itself more unreasonable than in summoning those things to its bar which transcend its sphere and capacity. Many are the mischiefs which ensue upon this practice. By this we are drawn into an unworthy suspicion and distrust of the faithfulness of God in the promises. This reasoning brings despondency of mind and faintness of heart under afflictive providences. Reason can discern no good fruit in them, and so our hands hang down in a sinful discouragement, saying, 'All these things are against us!' From this distrust of providence flows the temptation to deliver ourselves by sinful ways. Beware of leaning too much on your own reasoning. Nothing is more plausible, nothing more dangerous!

John Flavel, *Works*, iv:435-436

Bibliography

Alleine, Joseph—

A Sure Guide To Heaven, Edinburgh: Banner of Truth Trust, 1995

Baxter, Richard—

Practical Works, 2 vols., Ligonier: Soli Deo Gloria, 1990

Brooks, Thomas—

Works of Thomas Brooks, 6 vols., Edinburgh: Banner of Truth Trust, 2001

Bunyan, John—

Complete Works, 3 vols., Edinburgh: Banner of Truth Trust, 1991

The Pilgrim's Progress, Edinburgh: Banner of Truth Trust, 2009

Burroughs, Jeremiah—

The Saints' Happiness, Morgan: Soli Deo Gloria, 1996

Case, Thomas—

Select Works of Thomas Case, Ligonier: Soli Deo Gloria, 1993

Charnock, Stephen—

The Existence & Attributes of God, Minneapolis: Klock & Klock, 1977

Works of Stephen Charnock, 5 vols., Edinburgh: Banner of Truth Trust, 2010

Clarkson, David—

Works of David Clarkson, 3 vols., Edinburgh: Banner of Truth Trust, 1988

Bibliography

Edwards, Jonathan—

Selections from the Unpublished Writings of Jonathan Edwards, of America, Edinburgh: Ballantyne and Company, 1865

Flavel, John—

The Fountain of Life, New York: American Tract Society, 1820

Works of John Flavel, 6 vols., Edinburgh: Banner of Truth Trust, 1997

Gurnall, William—

The Christian in Complete Armour, Edinburgh: Banner of Truth Trust, 1989

Hopkins, Ezekiel—

Works of Ezekiel Hopkins, 3 vols., Morgan: Soli Deo Gloria, 1995-1997

Manton, Thomas—

By Faith, Edinburgh: Banner of Truth Trust, 2000

Works of Thomas Manton, vols. 1-3, Edinburgh: Banner of Truth Trust, 1993

Miscellaneous—

Puritan Sermons 1659–1689, 6 vols., Wheaton: Richard Owen Roberts, 1981

Owen, John—

Works of John Owen, 16 vols., Edinburgh: Banner of Truth Trust, 1987

Sibbes, Richard—

Works of Richard Sibbes, 7 vols., Edinburgh: Banner of Truth Trust, 2001

Swinnock, George—

Works of George Swinnock, 5 vols., Edinburgh: Banner of Truth Trust, 1992

Watson, Thomas—

The Beatitudes, Edinburgh: Banner of Truth Trust, 2000
The Lord's Prayer, Edinburgh: Banner of Truth Trust, 1999
The Ten Commandments, Edinburgh: Banner of Truth Trust, 2000

Watts, Isaac—

The Works of the Reverend and Learned Isaac Watts, vol. 1, London: J. Barfield, 1810

Author Index

Author Index

Author Index

Author Index

Author Index

Author Index

Author Index

Author Index

Author Index

Topical Index

Topical Index

Topical Index

Topical Index

Topical Index

Scripture Index

More titles from
The Banner of Truth Trust

Voices from the Past (volume one)

Edited by Richard Rushing

This is Richard Rushing's original compilation of daily devotional readings from his favourite Puritan authors. 'How thrilling it has been for me to read the Puritans on the glory and attributes of God, divine providence, fellowship with God, holiness of life and the mortification of indwelling sin, heavenly mindedness, prayer, evangelistic zeal, and trust in the Lord during times of affliction. At every turn these truths are eloquently taught, faithfully applied, and kindly offered as the subject of sweet spiritual meditation.'

ISBN 978 1 84871 048 1 | 428 pp. | clothbound

Also available as an ebook

The Puritans Day by Day

Compiled by H. J. Horn

Here in this unique selection from a wide range of reading, we have a noble army of memorable sayings. They have been drawn mainly out of the writings of the Puritans—men who excelled in their power of deep insight into both the word of God and the human heart, and who also had the rare gift of quaint and distinctive expression.

The Puritans Day by Day will be particularly helpful to young preachers, who would do well to keep this volume, with its careful ordering and its full indexes, close to hand. In days when minds are dull and spirits are weary, they will find it to be a rich source of mental and spiritual refreshment.

ISBN 978 1 84871 707 7 | 408 pp. | small clothbound

The Banner of Truth Trust originated in 1957 in London. The founders believed that much of the best literature of historic Christianity had been allowed to fall into oblivion and that, under God, its recovery could well lead not only to a strengthening of the church, but to true revival.

Inter-denominational in vision, this publishing work is now international, and our lists include a number of contemporary authors as well as classics from the past. The translation of these books into many languages is encouraged.

A monthly magazine, *The Banner of Truth,* is also published. More information about this and all our publications can be found on our website or supplied by either of the offices below.

THE BANNER OF TRUTH TRUST

3 Murrayfield Road
Edinburgh, EH12 6EL
UK

PO Box 621, Carlisle
Pennsylvania 17013,
USA

www.banneroftruth.org